Thinking about growth

STUDIES IN ECONOMIC HISTORY AND POLICY
THE UNITED STATES IN THE TWENTIETH CENTURY

Edited by
Louis Galambos and Robert Gallman

Other books in the series

Peter D. McClelland and Alan L. Magdovitz: *Crisis in the making: the political economy of New York State since 1945*

Hugh Rockoff: *Drastic measures: a history of wage and price controls in the United States*

William N. Parker: *Europe, America, and the wider world: essays on the economic history of Western capitalism*

Richard H. K. Vietor: *Energy policy in America since 1945: a study of business-government relations*

Christopher L. Tomlins: *The state and the unions: labor relations, law, and the organized labor movement in America, 1880–1960*

Leonard S. Reich: *The making of American industrial research: science and business at GE and Bell, 1876–1926*

Margaret B. W. Graham: *RCA and the VideoDisc: the business of research*

Michael A. Bernstein: *The Great Depression: delayed recovery and economic change in America, 1929–1939*

Michael J. Hogan: *The Marshall Plan: America, Britain, and the reconstruction of Western Europe, 1947–1952*

David A. Hounshell and John Kenly Smith, Jr.: *Science and corporate strategy: Du Pont R&D, 1902–1980*

Simon Kuznets; edited by Robert Gallman: *Economic development, the family, and income distribution: selected essays*

Thinking about growth

And other essays on economic growth and welfare

MOSES ABRAMOVITZ
Stanford University

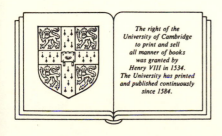

The right of the
University of Cambridge
to print and sell
all manner of books
was granted by
Henry VIII in 1534.
The University has printed
and published continuously
since 1584.

CAMBRIDGE UNIVERSITY PRESS
Cambridge
New York   Port Chester   Melbourne   Sydney

Published by the Press Syndicate of the University of Cambridge
The Pitt Building, Trumpington Street, Cambridge CB2 1RP
40 West 20th Street, New York, NY 10011, USA
10 Stamford Road, Oakleigh, Melbourne 3166, Australia

First published 1989
Reprinted 1990
First paperback edition 1991

Printed in the United States of America

Library of Congress Cataloging-in-Publication Data

Abramovitz, Moses.
Thinking about growth and other essays on economic growth and
welfare. (Studies in economic history and policy)
1. United States – Economic conditions.   2. Public
welfare – United States – History.   I. Title.
II. Series.
HC106.A33   1989   338.973   88-18902

British Library Cataloguing in Publication Data

Abramovitz, Moses
Thinking about growth: and other
essays on economic growth and
welfare. – (Studies in economic
history and policy; the United States
in the twentieth century).
1. Economic growth
I. Title II. Series
339.5

ISBN 0-521-33396-2 hardback
ISBN 0-521-40774-5 paperback

To Carrie, with love

Contents

vii

Editors' preface

Thinking About Growth brings together Moses Abramovitz's principal essays on long-term economic change, and introduces them with a new and previously unpublished piece, the fruit of over forty years of purposeful thought on the subject. Professor Abramovitz, a former president of the American Economic Association, is one of the world's most distinguished students of the process of economic growth.

The book begins with two essays on the nature of growth and the efforts of economists to understand and explain the phenomenon. The two constitute respectively the most recent and the earliest of Abramovitz's statements on these subjects, allowing the reader to see how far his views have been modified by the extraordinary events of the post–World War II period and by alterations in the intellectual apparatus deployed by economists. The volume then turns to the analysis of the proximate causes of long-term economic change, a subject on which the author has done pioneering work. Chapter 3, the first in this section, reproduces one of the most heavily cited articles ever written on the historical sources of economic growth in the United States.

One of Abramovitz's central concerns is with the factors responsible for periods of divergence and convergence in the levels of economic performance of modernizing countries. He pursues this subject in his analysis of the rise of American productive superiority in the first half of the twentieth century, and of the post–World War II efforts by Japan and the countries of Western Europe to emulate American successes.

American economic expansion in the nineteenth and early twentieth centuries proceeded in great surges and relapses. The essays in the third part of the volume are devoted to efforts to account for these long swings, with their recurring euphoric booms and great depressions, and to explain why they have disappeared in the second half of the twentieth century. The volume ends with a section devoted to the content and meaning of the experience of economic development. Once again, the book includes a very early expression of Abramovitz's views on this topic (Chapter 10), as well as a very recent one (Chapter 12).

These are important essays. They have influenced the course of work on economic growth and development, and they will repay much additional study. The editors are delighted that *Thinking About Growth* has now joined the series, Studies in Economic History and Policy: The United States in the Twentieth Century.

Preface

My interest in economic growth, like that of many other economists, began during World War II. I was involved first with efforts to plan the size of the U.S. war production program, and later with studies of German production capabilities.

How large could the U.S. program be? How much would the economy prove capable of producing if it could be stretched to its limits? The capacity of the U.S. economy had not been tested since 1929. Roosevelt's massive armaments programs were the result of a debate about the growth of U.S. capacity during the dozen years of the Depression. Economists took leading parts in the debate and differed widely. Richard Gilbert and Robert Nathan were among the economist–heroes of that bureaucratic and political struggle. In retrospect, I am convinced that the vision and calculations that backed a very large program were decisive factors in the war. Men and arms had to be deployed and terrible battles had to be fought; but once the huge armament contracts were awarded, it turned out that the capacity to execute them was there. The material advantage of the Allies over the Axis had been created.

Calculations of German production capabilities were far less successful. They rested at bottom on the assumption that the German economy had been fully mobilized when the war began. The high hopes that the British and U.S. governments placed in strategic bombing stemmed from this assumption. It was a mistake. In spite of increasing diversion of manpower to the armed forces and in spite of heavy bombardment, German armaments production continued to rise until nearly the end of the war. By that time, the mistake was apparent. Economists who had absorbed the later reports of the U.S. Strategic Bombing Survey were as a consequence less surprised than most people by the German postwar economic miracle. When the monetary obstacles to recovery were cleared away, not only German technology and skill but also a vast stock of capital remained.

Experiences such as these turned economists' thoughts to the long-term growth of national productive capabilities. Why had productivity in Europe lagged behind that in the United States for more than half a century? How had Japan, which had itself begun to emerge from a state of virtual feudalism only some seventy years before the war, gained the strength to challenge the United States? Questions such as these were reinforced by the determination in Europe not only to recover from the war but also to initiate a program of long-term growth. The U.S. interest in a strong Western Europe supported that determination. Furthermore, economic rivalry in long-term growth was part of the Cold War. Having supported the end of colonial regimes, people in the United States took an interest in the economic development of poor countries. Geopolitical calculation ran parallel with a generous impulse and both supported a strong U.S. program of aid to the Third World. The new interest of economists in economic growth arose from all these sources.

I had an early chance to join in this work when Bernard Haley asked me to prepare an article on the economics of growth for the American Economic Association *Survey of Contemporary Economics* (1952). This paper is included as the second essay of Part I of this volume. Its heavy emphasis on capital accumulation as a source of growth reflected an outlook common to the economic thought of the time. I could not let it stand alone, and the long essay "Thinking About Growth," with which this book opens, is my attempt to epitomize the new view that has emerged from the resurgence of growth studies in the postwar decades.

My own conception of the subject and, as it turned out, that of others changed with the paper "Resource and Output Trends in the United States Since 1870" (this volume, Chapter 3). I prepared the paper for an American Economic Association meeting on economic history. My modest assignment was to summarize U.S. economic development since the Civil War. In some desperation, I turned to the national product figures. Simon Kuznets had extended them back to 1870. John Kendrick, preparing his big book *Productivity Growth*, was calculating indexes of the joint input of capital and labor as well as indexes of national product per unit of input. I followed his practice. I did not regard it as a particularly radical device, but viewed it as another exercise in decomposition of a sort familiar in many other contexts. If real national product had risen between two dates, the increase could be attributed partly to an increase in factor inputs, assuming that product per unit of each input remained constant, and partly to an increase in output per unit of input. An index of the first would be given by the factor input quantities of each year multiplied by their base year earnings. What remained of national product increase would be a measure of the change in output per unit of input, that is, of the productivity of employed resources.

What could be simpler? The exciting thing was the lopsided result. In a decomposition of per capita output growth, it emerged that very little was attributable to the rise of employment per head of the population or even to capital per head. Productivity growth, the remainder, had been the apparent source of virtually the whole increase of per capita income for nearly a century. How could that be? To me it was crystal clear that the productivity increase was not solely a sort of costless advance of knowledge, an unintended but welcome spinoff of activities pursued for other purposes. The calculus was incomplete. It failed to account for costly investments in human capital or for economies of scale, which were a productivity bonus for larger output from every source. Longer schooling, research and development, the restructuring of occupations, and the relocation of population were large, but as yet unmeasured, elements of capital accumulation. This was a pointer for later work.*

In the 1950s, my research was supported by the National Bureau of Economic Research. The bureau's director, Arthur Burns, was impatient with my interest in long-term growth. He distrusted the data I used, and he pressed me to work on more solid materials and more immediately practical subjects, preferably on business cycles, which had been my early concern. I tried to straddle the issue by studying "long swings," the fluctuations that appeared in the statistical record when the influence of shorter business cycles themselves was removed.

It was a straddle for several reasons. In output series, the swings appeared in rates of growth rather than in levels of output, that is, in the same data with which growth studies proper were concerned. The duration of the swings, fifteen to twenty years, was intermediate in length between the shorter business cycles and the longer periods appropriate to secular growth. Like secular growth, output change over much of the long swings was attributable mainly to input and productivity growth – not, as in business cycles, to change in the intensity of use of employed resources. On the other hand the culminating episode of each swing was a major depression or period of

---

*My article was not the only work pointing in this direction, nor the first. My paper was quickly followed by those of Kendrick, on whose work my own depended, and of Robert Solow. There had been earlier, less-noticed, publications by Jacob Schmookler, Solomon Fabricant, and George Stigler. So far as I now know – no one in the United States seemed to know it then – ultimate priority belongs to Jan Tinbergen (1942).

prolonged stagnation. One phase of each swing did involve a large fluctuation of intensity of use.

I tried to bring the two elements together by viewing the long fluctuations in the growth rates of input and productivity as functions of change in intensity of use. And I speculated on the possibility that real and financial developments associated with long stretches of relatively stable growth made economies more vulnerable to serious depressions.

Included in Part III of this volume are two essays based on studies of long swings. The ideas they generated emerged again in later work on growth proper. I came to see rates of long-term growth as the outcome of two classes of causes, those that determined the potential for growth, and those that governed the rate of realization of potential. The conditions that support prolonged expansion or that impose sustained stagnation overlap with those that govern the realization of potential.

In the late fifties and early sixties, people became aware of the fact that the growth experience of the postwar period was strikingly different from anything known in prewar times. Europe and Japan were advancing at unprecedentedly rapid rates. U.S. productivity growth was as fast as ever before, perhaps faster, but it was much slower than that in Japan or Europe. The dominant position this country had enjoyed in the fifties was being lost. One unwelcome symptom was the disappearance of the "dollar shortage." The U.S. balance of payments had turned weak.

Observations such as these were a scholarly challenge; they were also a matter of public concern. In 1963 the Social Science Research Council asked Simon Kuznets to organize a series of comparative historical studies of economic growth in several European countries, in Japan, and in the United States. Because I was in Paris at the time and in a good position to make contact with European scholars, Kuznets asked me to join him in organizing the work.

Postwar growth may have been rapid, but the historical studies were not. A decade passed before much of the work was completed. Afterwards (1977), I prepared a summary paper for the International Economic Association. It has a longish title, "Rapid Growth Potential and Its Realization: The Experience of Capitalist Economies in the Postwar Period" (Chapter 6 in this volume). Here I tried to account for the most prominent features of the growth experience of the time. I saw these as the extraordinarily rapid rate of productivity advance among industrialized countries generally; the systematic gradation of the pace of growth among the leading countries from Japan at the top of the scale to the United States at the bottom; the unprecedentedly long, quarter-century duration of the expansion, about twice as long as the long-swing expansions of the past; and the concerted character of the boom, which was shared by all the industrialized countries and by much of the Third World as well.

Many elements of both potential and realization contributed to these developments. On the side of potential, the European and Japanese opportunity for fast growth by borrowing and adapting advanced technology was very strong. The technological gap between these countries and the United States had grown much larger between 1913 and 1950, when two great wars, the territorial, political, and financial disturbances that followed, and the Great Depression with the collapse of international trade had joined to inhibit their development. Meanwhile, their ability to exploit advanced technology, their levels of education, and their experience with large-scale industry and commerce had become stronger. All this made for rapid growth generally and accounted for the systematic differences among countries. The potential for a technological leap was greatest for the countries furthest behind the United States. Japan, among the "followers," advanced most rapidly, Britain most slowly, and other countries were spread between them in positions about inversely proportionate to their initial levels of productivity.

As to realization of potential, rapid progress was fostered and sustained by stable monetary conditions. These were established by U.S. policy and enforced by the Bretton Woods exchange rate system. It was supported further by the liberalization of international trade, which offered countries an easier route to adoption of the scale-dependent technologies pioneered by the United States, and by flexible conditions of labor supply. As industrial and commercial demands for labor vaulted, they were satisfied by large migrations from farms to cities. Farm productivity in Europe and Japan was rising rapidly, releasing workers for industrial and commercial employment. Immigrants from the poor farms of the Mediterranean countries flocked to western and northern Europe. At the same time, U.S. restrictions on immigration limited the drain from the rapidly growing side of the Atlantic to our own more slowly growing side. Both sides could more easily advance together, a marked departure from the older pattern of Atlantic community growth.

The opportunity to "catch up" was a central feature of the postwar growth boom. It constituted the potentiality on which the rapid pace of advance and the convergence of productivity levels among presently industrialized countries was based. This experience presents a host of questions. How far can the tendency to convergence by catching-up be extended? Does it apply also to countries in earlier stages of development? Did it also operate in the past? If so, did it work just as powerfully? If not, what inhibited its operation? What is involved in the catch-up process besides technological borrowing? Is the process self-limiting, weakening as technological gaps became smaller? Or are there also self-reinforcing elements in the process so that countries that are catching up may also move into the lead? I take up this range of questions in "Catching Up, Forging Ahead, and Falling Behind," the last essay in Part II of this book.

Economists' thoughts are almost entirely fixed on the causes of economic growth. Not for them to appraise its worth. The essays of Part I and Part II are in that tradition. Yet the worth of growth is not beyond question; and a powerful strain of opinion remains skeptical. Few may doubt the value of higher incomes in poor countries, but why should very rich countries press so hard to become still richer?

The classical economists, writing almost two centuries ago, had an answer. They thought that only by continuing to forge ahead could a country keep the Malthusian process at bay. A country in which the "state of the arts" had ceased to advance would find its high income dissipated to support a growing population. John Stuart Mill, who had begun to sense the possibilities of birth control, was not sure. Modern methods of contraception put the matter beyond dispute. It is now clear that rich countries can maintain high levels of average income without rapid growth. And it is clear also that growth itself has serious costs in its dislocation of established occupations, its disturbance to family relations and to modes and places of living, and its damage to the environment. On the other hand, the satisfactions of still higher incomes are less than certain. Is it so important to have more if we never cease to want still more?

Answers are proposed to these questions as well. There are international rivalries for power that carry fears of losing in a growth race. Our lives, it is true, may be disturbed by growth, but they are also disturbed, and very unpleasantly, when we fall behind. Even rich countries have some very poor people; it is easier to sustain and perhaps improve their situation and their capabilities out of the incremental income provided by growth than to face the political tensions of redistributing a stable income. People want both material goods and knowledge. The two desires depend on each other. Both the quest for economic growth and the income it has brought have been powerful supports in our quest for knowledge. What would the position be if we stopped pressing for economic growth? By how much would the search for knowledge be weakened? The satisfactions of still higher incomes may not be transparent, but happiness, say some, is not the true goal. Higher incomes mean wider horizons, a broader range of choice. We should not deny ourselves the possibilities of choice even if we do not know if we can use them well.

Are these answers fully satisfactory? There is a powerful strain of antigrowth opinion in this and in other rich countries. The questions have returned to plague me many times. I explore them in the series of essays in Part IV.

Part IV also contains one essay, "Growing Up in an Affluent Society," that touches these issues from a somewhat different angle. I prepared the paper for a White House Conference on Children and Youth held in 1960, and I tried to say something about adolescence in the United States in that time of sustained and confident growth. I tried to point out that our economic development meant more than greater comfort and even more than better health. It meant a longer period of economic dependence as years of schooling were extended. Yet it also meant that aspiring young professionals could, if they wished, have younger courtships and earlier marriages. At that time they did so wish. It meant the removal of many mothers from the household as women faced a world more open to education and career. And it also meant the return of fathers to the household as hours of work were progressively shortened. And more such – it was an optimistic essay, and it went wrong in some respects. It pointed out, correctly for the time, that more children were growing up in intact families simply because both parents were surviving long enough to see their children through adolescence. It failed to foresee the great increases of divorce rates and of illegitimate births, both of which have their connections with economic growth. There are other such failings. I thought the movement to the suburbs was bringing the children of different income classes closer together. I did not foresee the sharper differences that were arising in the cities, between the rich and the well-to-do, who could still afford city life, and the very poor, who could not escape it. Despite these failings, I think the article may be useful because it illustrates the variety of ways in which the social concomitants of economic growth impinge on our lives.

Preparing a collection of one's old essays makes one think of teachers, colleagues, and friends. I cannot name them all. Edward Mason, Douglass V. Brown, and Frank Taussig introduced me to economics. John Maurice Clark was my teacher when I was a graduate student. Arthur Burns and Simon Kuznets guided my early work and helped form my outlook on research. Milton Friedman was an early friend. We have tilted often and broken many a lance. I have enjoyed a long, happy, and fruitful collaboration and friendship with Paul David. Paul Baran and Emile Despres, too soon lost, were my close companions at Stanford. Tibor Scitovsky and Marvin Chodorow still are. Eli Ginzberg has been my closest friend for more than half a century. Willy-nilly, they have put their mark on these essays.

I have dedicated this book to my wife, the first I have so inscribed. I cannot any longer sustain the illusion that I shall one day write a book worthy of her.

Stanford, California   M.A.
November 1988

Part I

Growth and the economists

1

Thinking about growth

Economic growth is one of the oldest subjects in economics and one of the youngest. It was a principal concern of the *Wealth of Nations*, and it filled the thoughts of economists for the next three quarters of a century. As the Victorian Age wore on, however, growth lost its hold on the attention and imagination of the great body of academic economists. It was left to Marx and his followers, whose premature obsession with the demise of capitalism appealed to neither the political tastes nor the scientific bent of the discipline's exponents. And then, after the Second World War, following a hundred years of comparative neglect, there was a resurgence of interest and study that has been proceeding with vigor for the last four decades.

In the new effort, much that had been known a century and more ago had to be relearned. The new effort has had the benefit, however, of far better and more extensive historical and statistical materials and a more sophisticated theoretical framework. The accomplishments of the new research, however, have been modest, which is testimony both to the complexity of the subject and to the limitations of economics and of the other social sciences as well. Yet the study of growth is going on energetically. It is interesting, therefore, to ask what the newer work has added to the older and where the subject now stands.

This sketch of the erratic involvement of economists with economic growth, although it stretches over many pages, is still no more than a sketch. It is spare and unshaded, as a sketch must be. It deals mainly with the causes of economic growth, not its consequences. It looks at

I acknowledge with thanks the careful review and encouragement of colleagues who read early drafts of this paper. They include Eli Ginzberg, Charles Kindleberger, Richard Nelson, Nathan Rosenberg, Walt Rostow and the editors of this volume, Louis Galambos and Robert Gallman. I owe a special debt to Paul David's thorough and critical reading.

past work largely in terms of what it has contributed to our present understanding. It deals with growth only as this presents itself in advanced capitalist countries. It concentrates on the increase of productivity, the principal component of per capita output growth; and it sets aside the companion subject of population growth. It is concerned mainly with the overall productivity growth of nations; it neglects the structural change that growth requires, except as a country's capacity to accomplish such change limits its rate of aggregate growth. In all these ways, this sketch of the terrain is incomplete; even so, it serves a purpose, particularly if more complete and detailed maps are not at hand.

I. Growth and the older economists

Adam Smith was the father, not only of modern economics, but more particularly of the political economy of growth. The *Wealth of Nations* in its very title announces Smith's concern with the forces that govern the relative levels of prosperity among countries and that cause some to forge ahead and others to fall behind. His very first chapters are devoted to the advantages of the division of labor and its dependence on the scale of activity and the extent of the market. Smith saw that large-scale activity permitted a specialization and simplification of trades and tasks that raised the skills of workers, saved their time, and enabled clever artisans to devise labor-saving tools and devices; it enlarged the outlet for capital to embody the improved methods, and afforded businessmen a profitable and productive way to employ their savings. In Smith's view, therefore, the advance in productivity was an interactive process that ran from scale of market to the division of labor, thence to the enhancement of skills, the invention of new tools, and the accumulation of capital, finally feeding back to market scale. Smith saw the political institutions under which people lived as the main determinant to their ability to exploit the scale advantages made possible by trade and, therefore, to their ability to make full use of their talents and natural resources.

With few exceptions, Smith thought, the "policy of Europe" should be one of laissez-faire. But the *Wealth of Nations* also displays Smith's lively sense of the tendency of people to multiply their numbers and to press on the physical limits of a stationary supply of land. He thought a nation best off and most progressive when there was still a gap between its population and the maximum number its land could support. Growth tended to be rapid, therefore, when an increasing population and a growing aggregate income were expanding markets and opening the way to a still more intense division of labor.

Smith's theories were developed and refined in the decades after the appearance of his great book. Malthus's famous essay on population, taken together with Ricardo's treatment of diminishing returns in the use of land, sharpened the sense of conflict between population and resources. At the same time, there was a growing appreciation of the possibilities of progress based on the advance of knowledge. John Stuart Mill's *Principles of Political Economy* (1848) gave the economics of growth its definitive statement at the hands of the classical economists.

The organizing theme of Mill's treatise has a distinctly modern ring:

> We may say, then, . . . that the requisites of production are Labour, Capital, and Land. The increase of production, therefore, depends on the properties of these elements. It is a result of the increase either of the elements themselves, or of their productiveness. The law of the increase of production must be a consequence of the laws of these elements; the limits to the increase of production must be the limits, whatever they are, set by these laws. (*Principles*, Ashley edition, p. 156)

What are these laws? On labor, Mill is a Malthusian. Free of restraint, population multiplies rapidly so long as output per head exceeds some minimum standard. "The use [people] commonly choose to make of any advantageous change in their circumstances, is to take it out in the form which, by augmenting the population, deprives the succeeding generation of the benefit" (p. 161). But Mill is a reluctant and somewhat qualified Malthusian. Conceivably people can come to raise their minimum standard. "Every advance they make in education, civilization and social improvement, tends to raise this standard and there is no doubt that it is gradually, though slowly, rising in the advanced countries of Western Europe" (p. 161).

Mill noted that population growth rates in these progressive countries had been declining; yet he did not fully trust such hopeful signs. He feared the force of people's power of natural increase.

Capital too tends to increase under the impulse of its earning power. As with the earnings of labor, however, the profit rate must exceed a minimum standard. This threshold level is low where wealth is abundant and people's "effective desire for accumulation" is strong. It is high where business is risky and property insecure.

If labor were the only element in production, output would increase proportionately with population. But capital, since it is also an element in production, imposes a limit, unless it grows at the same rate as labor; but capital cannot long increase faster without swiftly driving the profit rate downward. And since land, which is by definition in fixed supply, is a third element, the increase of both capital and labor must decline and eventually come to a halt, even if they themselves increase in step with one another. They meet diminishing returns as they are employed together with a fixed amount of land; the return to capital is then driven down as rents increase at the expense of profit. The consequent decline in the rate of capital accumulation, together with the rise in the price of food, reduces the real income of workers. The rate of population growth is also reduced. There is, therefore, an inherent tendency for growth to cease:

It must always have been seen, more or less distinctly by political economists, that the increase of wealth is not boundless: that at the end of what they term the progressive state lies the stationary state, that all progress in wealth is but a postponement of this, and that each step in advance is an approach to it. (p. 746)

Unlike his great predecessors, however, Mill did not believe that the "progress of society must 'end in shallows and in miseries' " (p. 747). Malthus himself had recognized that the increase of population could be brought to a halt before incomes fell to the bare minimum required to support life. It might remain much higher if people came to insist on a higher standard of living. Mill argued that restraints on births were necessary even in progressive countries to prevent population from outstripping the increase of capital. The same restraints, however, might maintain a comfortable condition even in a stationary state, which then would hold out very favorable prospects for the intellectual and moral development of people (Book IV, Ch. VI).

Whether the stationary state that looms before nations is one of comfort or misery, however, loom it does: ". . . we are always on the verge of it, and . . . if we have not reached it long ago, it is because the goal itself flies before us" (p. 746).

The force that, in the last analysis, keeps the stationary state at bay is "improvement in the productive arts" – technological progress, we would say. Mill's discussion reduces the emphasis that Smith had placed on an extension of the market and division of labor. Mill viewed the economies of scale as affording only transitory relief until population becomes dense enough "to allow the principal benefits of combination of labor" (pp. 191–92). Thereafter, progress becomes a race:

Whether, at the present or any other time, the produce of industry proportionally to the labour employed, is increasing or diminishing . . . depends upon whether population is advancing faster than improvement, or improvement than population. (p. 191)

Mill's shift of emphasis reflects the seventy-five years that had passed between Smith, who wrote only on the eve of the Industrial Revolution, and the mid-nineteenth century, when powered machinery, the railroad, the steamship, and the electromagnetic telegraph had begun to create a sense of the further possibilities of technological progress.

Of the features which characterize this progressive economical movement of civilized nations, that which first excites attention, through its intimate connexion with the phenomena of Production, is the perpetual, and so far as human foresight can extend, the unlimited, growth of man's power over nature. (p. 696)

Mill's view of the matter is ample and spacious, and it has taken later economists some time to regain his sweeping view, if, indeed, they have.

Improvement must be understood . . . in a wide sense, including not only new industrial inventions, or an extended use of those already known, but improvements in institutions, education, opinions and human affairs generally, provided they tend, as almost all improvements do, to give new motives or new facilities to production. (p. 192)

Mill, like his predecessors, laid great stress on the institutional arrangements and public policies of national economies. He was particularly concerned with four matters: the security of property as a condition of saving and investment; the capacity of people for effective cooperation as a basis for the conduct of industry on a large scale; the proper principles of taxation – to make taxes as little arbitrary, burdensome, and distortional as possible – and finally, the proper extent and limits of the principle of laissez-faire.

As to the last, Mill felt torn. He maintained the common conviction of political economists from Hume and Smith forward that individuals should enjoy the greatest possible scope to engage in trade and to contract freely with one another. Yet he insisted that this principle was itself limited in extent and admitted of exceptions. He treated the subject at length; but in an essay on growth, four instances of desirable public activity or intervention stand out:

> The protection of those kinds of goods that belong to people in common but are used by all individually – the environment.
> The provision of goods or the support of services whose social utility exceeds their private – education and scientific research (besides lighthouses and buoys).
> The regulation of activities that can only be done by "delegated agency" – for example, by joint stock companies – and the regulation or public provision of services that are natural and practical monopolies – gas and water companies, railroads, canals.
> More generally, the provision of such facilities, important to the public interest, that private individuals might provide, but will not because, "in the particular circumstances of a given age or

nation," the public is either "too poor to command the necessary resources, or too little advanced in intelligence to appreciate the ends, or not sufficiently practiced in joint action to be capable of the means" (p. 978).

No one can read, or reread, Mill without feeling how far he and the other classical economists had anticipated contemporary work, how much we may learn from them, and also how much we had forgotten during the century-long hiatus when growth studies were neglected.

II. Growth and economics during the hiatus

One of the strong impressions one takes from Mill is his ambivalence about the balance of growth forces. He sensed that population growth was beginning to be limited, but he feared the strength of the human capacity and drive to multiply. He perceived the possibilities of human kind's growing mastery over nature and of the cumulative advance of the industrial arts, but he was unsure of their pace and continuity. The result was his vision of a race between population and improvement whose winner was uncertain.

This ambivalent attitude gradually disappeared as the last century wore on. In Britain, in the United States, and in a gradually widening sphere in Europe incomes rose from decade to decade. Power and machinery applied to industry increased productivity in agriculture as well as manufacturing. Applied to transportation, it opened new lands and brought food and raw materials cheaply to more populous countries. The population response became weaker while technological advance continued at a rapid pace. Even the dismal science learned to smile; it absorbed the century's wider faith in unbounded Progress.

Yet the place of growth in the studies and writings of economists did not expand. Quite the contrary! Perhaps because economic growth had become absorbed into a more general vision of human progress, it was no longer seen as a problem. Or perhaps it was displaced by other pressing concerns. Higher incomes, more widespread education, and the extension of suffrage – all concomitants of economic growth itself – made working people a stronger political force. Correspondingly, the claims of labor and, more generally, the question of income distribution became more urgent issues. Or perhaps economists were seduced by the logical coherence of the neoclassical theory of relative prices and resource allocation, which came to seem such a solid construction on its static foundations. The theory treated a nation's institutions, its population, and its technology, the central elements of the growth process, as autonomous data. They were viewed as the constraints and conditions to which prices and resource allocation adjusted. But the causes of their changes were not subjects for economists to investigate, and their implications were mainly neglected. Neoclassical theory, therefore, imposed boundaries on economics, at least on the science that economists had the ambition to build. It left growth outside its borders. Even the subject of scale, the division of labor and increasing returns – Adam Smith's basic insight – came to be viewed as just a problem for the theory of the equilibrium of relative prices. And Allyn Young had to write a famous essay (1928) to remind economists that it was something more, part of an interactive and cumulative process involving capital accumulation, productivity growth, rising incomes, and the extension of markets, an element in economic growth as well as a problem for static theory. Finally, whatever impulse there was to break out of the borders of static theory was absorbed by the troubles that engulfed the industrial world after 1914. Two great wars, the postwar hyperinflations, and the Great Depression provided a quarter-century of distractions for those economists who were minded to study something other than the conditions of general equilibrium.

To all this Joseph Schumpeter was an honorable and notable exception. His early classic, *The Theory of Economic Development* (1911), argued that in the absence of population growth and technological advance neither a positive interest rate nor net profit would persist. Profit is, indeed, the reward for the successful introduction of new methods and products. If economic activity followed an unceasing repetitive round, there would be no function for entrepreneurs and no occasion for profit. And interest would disappear as continued accumulation embodying an unchanging technology drove the marginal product of capital to zero.[1]

Schumpeter's arguments were intended first of all to enlarge the foundations of the neoclassical theory of factor prices. As a positive contribution to the economics of growth, they repeated and reinforced the older views about the tendency of gross profit (interest plus net profit) to a minimum and the dependence of net capital accumulation and the return to capital on the rate of improvement.

Schumpeter went further. He distinguished between "invention," or the advance of knowledge useful in production, and "innovation," which was the exploitation of such knowledge, the actual introduction of new products or new methods in commercial operations. The older economists had treated both as autonomous developments, but Schumpeter argued that innovation was an economic activity, the peculiar function of entrepreneurs. His view implied that market competition included rivalry in the introduction of new products and processes. Relative prices, therefore, were in flux, constantly disturbed by the same market competition that in the received theory was thought to establish their equilibrium.

Schumpeter taught that innovation was the central element in the economics of growth. As such, he stressed the requirements for successful innovation: open markets to permit the appearance of "new men" and "new firms," access to credit, and sufficiently stable macroeconomic conditions so that businessmen could gauge their markets and their prices and costs without an undue sense of risk. Schumpeter saw business cycles, particularly the longer waves of accelerated growth and retardation and the financial distortions they brought in their train, as part of the innovatory process. He was among the first to suggest that the uncertainties accompanying inflation and other financial disturbances could pose a lasting obstacle to innovation and productivity growth – a lesson for the contemporary scene and season. Schumpeter was widely admired for his brilliance and long neglected for his originality. His innovative theories were not easily accommodated within the dominant neoclassical model.

When interest in economic growth finally revived after World War II, economists studied Schumpeter again. They were attracted especially by the theses of his later work, *Capitalism, Socialism, and Democracy* (1942). Here he enlarged on his earlier ideas about the role of profits. He now argued that innovation rested not only on the lure of high but competitive profits; often it also conferred monopoly power and its concomitant monopoly profits. All these he viewed as necessary, therefore useful, inducements and rewards – an acceptable price for the benefits of innovation and growth. Moreover, these prizes were transient, being diluted and eventually eliminated by the imitative inroads and further innovations of rival entrepreneurs. Some degree of monopoly power, therefore, was a regular feature of a progressive economy – constantly limited, but also constantly renewed by the innovative activity of entrepreneurs.

Schumpeter now also abandoned the sharp distinction that his early writings had drawn between invention, the product of activities outside the economic system, and innovation, which was regarded as business investment of a bold and risky sort. Recognizing that large and long-lived corporations had displaced the individual entrepreneur, he suggested that both the search for new technology and its commercial exploitation had become "routine" aspects of business activity. Economists' present models of technological progress incorporate versions of the same ideas; but that revival of Schumpeterian economics remained for the future. While their attention was directed elsewhere, economists' views about economic growth remained unformed. Guided by neoclassical theory, they treated technological advance as independent of economic incentives and saw only capital accumulation as a source of productivity growth responsive to economic causes.

III. The postwar revival of interest in growth and the response of economics

That was how matters stood as World War II came to an end. Interest, however, quickly shifted. Growth became a primary goal of national policy and consequently an absorbing subject of study by economists. There were considerations of national security and rivalry, of the conquest of poverty, and of advances toward prosperity, and there were pressures for growth to achieve other urgent social objectives.

People, including politicians, realized that the outcome of the war had been determined by GNP. More than ever before, nations viewed their security and power as resting on an economic base. To ensure their independence and safety, they concluded they must grow; if ahead, stay ahead; if behind, catch up.

Europeans became aware that they had lost ground to the United States in levels of living not only during the war but since 1913 and even earlier. They correctly felt that their levels of scientific and general education, their experience with modern commerce, industry, and finance, and their political institutions should be able to support a much higher relative status.

Similarly, the newly independent countries, the former colonies, saw economic growth not only as the means of rising from poverty but as a necessary condition for consolidating their new political regimes.

On another level, the rivalry between the USSR and the United States made each country anxious to prove that its system was capable of producing ever higher material conditions and was therefore worthy of emulation, friendship, or even alliance.

Internal political forces also pressed for growth. The enlargement of the democratic suffrage in the industrialized countries, a stronger egalitarian sentiment, and people's heightened appreciation of the risks and costs of advanced capitalist life drove countries to develop systems of protection and benefit – the welfare state. It was quickly appreciated that it would be easier to pay for these systems from rising incomes than from redistributive taxes. The political tensions and social conflict inherent in redistribution would be mitigated by growth.

Economists responded to the challenges of new public problems and political interest by opening three large branches of research. One was the study of secular development in those countries that were already far advanced on the path of industrialization and were capable of operating at or near the frontiers of modern technology. Another was the study of development in poor countries still emerging from a preindustrial condition, the countries in which the basic institutions and capabilities for exploiting contemporary technology remained to be established. A third concerned the communist countries, where a new set of institutions based on the state ownership of resources and a system of central planning and control had been established. This essay deals with the first of these, growth in the presently industrialized countries whose economies depend mainly on private enterprise and market guidance.

The growth studies fell into two divisions. The first was principally historical and descriptive. Its aim and, indeed, its solid accomplishment was to establish the observable characteristics of growth on the basis of a wide survey of experience over long periods and across a considerable number of countries. Simon Kuznets's work is the great exemplar of such studies, although in some respects Colin Clark was his precursor.

Kuznets's great achievement was the foundation of the modern national product and national income accounts. He worked out their conceptual bases, made the early estimates for the United States, and extended the U.S. national product series back to 1870. He encouraged the compilation of long-term statistical data to supplement the national product figures and assembled many of them himself – population and other vital statistics, labor force, wealth, and many others. He stimulated and supported similar efforts in other countries. The empirical generalizations that he and his collaborators and followers established comprise many of the broad facts towards an explanation of which much analytical work is directed. A list of such generalizations, incomplete but illustrative, includes the following:

> The rise of aggregate and per capita growth rates associated with the onset of "modern economic growth."
>
> The demographic transitions from rising to declining rates of population growth in the course of industrialization.
>
> The gradual spread of modern growth from Britain to the United States, Europe, the countries of European settlement, and Japan.
>
> The secular acceleration of productivity growth; in particular the pronounced acceleration following World War II and the retardation of the last 15 years.
>
> The qualified tendency to convergence in the productivity growth rates and levels of industrialized countries.

The many structural changes associated with growth, notably the
shifts in output and employment from agriculture to manufacturing and then to the services and government and from rural to
urban location.

The rise of government as an economic agent in production, investment, and income distribution and as a regulator of private
activity.

The tendency towards retardation in the output and productivity
growth of particular commodities and industries, combined with
constant or even rising growth rates of the per capita output and
productivity of all industries combined; the associated shift in the
importance of industries from older to younger.

These and other empirical generalizations are the necessary framework within which efforts to understand historical changes and national differences in growth rates must proceed. Since theories of
economic growth must have implications consistent with these observations, they are the indispensable background for analytical work.
This analytical work is the second division of the subject, and it is the
concern of the rest of this paper.

IV. The proximate sources of growth

The descriptive efforts of Colin Clark, Simon Kuznets, and the other
pioneers in the measurement of national income and product and of
associated data on labor force and capital stock were not aimless excur-
sions into the statistical cosmos. They were guided by the conception
of a production function, which is to say by the idea that output is a
function of the inputs of labor, accumulated capital, and land and of
the productivity of these factor inputs. This idea had been part of the
outlook of the classical economists, and, as we have seen, it was the
organizing theme of Mill's *Principles*. The same fundamental notion
was taken over by the neoclassical economists and became a central
feature of their static models of price and income distribution. It was
therefore as natural for economists, when they returned to the study
of growth, as it had been for Mill himself to think that the "increase of
production . . . is a result of the increase of the [inputs] themselves,
or of their productiveness." But how much was due to the increase of
each of the inputs and how much to that of their productiveness? That
was an obvious first question. "Growth accounting" was the attempt
to answer it.

The discovery of the Residual

Calculations that decomposed the growth of output into the
contributions of labor input and labor productivity had been made

for many years.[2] They left open the question, how much of the rise of labor productivity was attributable to the increase of capital per worker. A series of studies published over just a few years returned a surprising answer and revealed a great gap in economists' understanding. The studies that first caught the attention and roused the interest of economists were by the present writer (1956), John Kendrick (1956, 1961) and Robert Solow (1957).[3]

The calculations proceeded from the assumption that the wages of labor and the returns to capital also represented the additional product from increments of these factor inputs. This assumption permitted the deduction that the growth rate of output could be decomposed into a portion contributed by "total factor input," which was the joint contribution of labor and capital (including land), and a portion contributed by "total factor productivity." The first was the sum of the growth rates of the factor inputs, each weighted by the share of its earnings in national income. The second was the difference between the growth rate of output and that of total factor input. Since it had long been known, however, that the growth of output per capita was due almost entirely to that of labor productivity, not to that of labor input per head, it was the decomposition of labor productivity growth that was the most interesting matter. But the same assumption, that earnings = marginal productivity, led to the conclusion that the growth rate of labor productivity could be resolved into a portion contributed by the growth rate of the capital–labor ratio weighted by capital's income share and a portion contributed by total factor productivity.

Although the several early investigators used somewhat different data and studied somewhat different periods, they reached identical qualitative conclusions. Only a small fraction of U.S. per capita growth over many decades could be attributed to total input growth per capita. Only a small fraction of labor productivity growth could be attributed to growth of capital per worker or per man hour. An overwhelmingly large fraction (approximately 90 percent) was due to the advance of total factor productivity, that is, to something whose contents were as yet unidentified and unmeasured.

Perhaps because Solow, whose paper (1957) best revealed the underlying theory of the calculations, called the unknown factor "technical change" and showed that, in his theoretical scheme, it corresponded to shifts in an aggregate production function, many economists at first came to speak of the unknown element as "technological progress." Still more, they tended to view the progress so represented as having its source in the advance of knowledge. None of the early growth accountants, however, viewed the matter in this light, and all explained carefully that the very large unmeasured component must include the contributions of many elements besides new knowledge. Of these the more important were the following:

1. Growth of "human capital" by investment of resources in longer schooling, on-the-job training, nutrition and health care, and research and development. The accumulation of human capital would tend to raise the effectiveness of labor hours, just as tangible capital would, and other matters, such as the age and sex composition of the labor force and the intensity of work, would also affect the productivity of labor.
2. Economies of scale. Since the division of labor is limited by the extent of the market, productivity gains become possible when aggregate output increases, even if the stock of knowledge itself remains unchanged. Productivity, therefore, may rise when output grows for whatever reason, not only technological progress proper, but also labor force growth or the accumulation of capital or the discovery of new resources.
3. Better resource allocation – that is, the shift of workers or capital of standard quality from employments in which their earnings and presumably their productivity are relatively low to others in which they are higher.

Errors and biases in the data must also be part of total factor productivity growth as this is actually measured, because its value in the accounts is no more than the difference between the measured growth rate of output and that of total factor input. Because of its unmeasured, heterogeneous content, the present writer characterized this difference as "some sort of measure of our ignorance about the causes of economic growth" (1956, p. 11). In the end, all this came to be well understood, and the mysterious element of total factor productivity growth was dubbed simply the *Residual*.

The development of growth accounting
The dominant importance of the inscrutable Residual was an irresistible challenge, and economists set themselves to reduce it by devising ways to measure its contents. Edward Denison's work is representative of growth accounts for the United States, but others, especially John Kendrick and Dale Jorgenson, have made impressive contributions. And there have been many similar studies by these and other scholars that provide accounts for European countries, Japan, Canada, and others.[4]

Table 1.1, drawn from Denison's latest publication (1985), illustrates the results. The column refers to the sources of growth of labor productivity, measured by national income per person employed, during the 31 years from 1948 to 1979. When Denison confines his

Table 1.1. *Sources of growth in labor productivity, Denison's estimates, 1948–79*

	Percentage points per year	Percent of total growth rate
1. National income per person employed	1.81	100
2. Hours per person	−0.41	−23
3. Capital stock per person[a]	0.43	24
4. Total factor input (lines 2 + 3)	0.02	1
5. Total factor productivity (= primitive residual) (line 1–4)	1.79	99
6. Labor quality	0.53[b]	29
a. Efficiency offset	0.05	3
b. Age–sex	−0.16	−9
c. Education	0.41	23
d. Other	0.22	12
7. Adjusted total factor input (lines 4 + 6)	0.55	30
8. Adjusted total factor productivity (line 1–7)	1.26	70
Resource allocation	0.24	13
Scale	0.31	17
Intensity of demand	−0.13	−7
Other	−0.08	−4
Knowledge and n.e.c. (final residual)[c]	0.92	51

[a]Includes land.
[b]Total does not equal sum of components because of rounding.
[c]n.e.c. = not elsewhere classified.
Source: Denison (1985), Table 8.3. Figures are weighted arithmetic averages of growth rates for 1948–73 and 1973–79.

concept of inputs to labor measured in natural units (labor hours) and to capital and land measured by their base-period cost, it appears that total factor input per worker hardly rose at all. The contribution of additional capital per worker was essentially offset by the decline in hours per worker. The growth of total factor productivity – I call it here the Primitive Residual – therefore accounts for virtually the entire growth of labor productivity. This result corresponds to those of the early studies.

Denison, however, did not stop there. He found ways to measure the contributions of those changes in the quality of work that cannot, at least in the first instance, be ascribed to technological progress but represent either greater effort, change in the demographic composition of the labor force, or longer schooling. His "efficiency offset" (to the reduction in hours) is an allowance, admittedly somewhat arbitrary, for the greater intensity, care, and accuracy of work that has probably accompanied the decline in hours. His allowances for the effects of changes in the demographic and educational composition of the work force are based on evidence of systematic and persistent differences in the earnings of workers classified by age, sex, and length of schooling. The contribution of longer schooling is an especially impressive figure.[5] It says that the rise in the educational level of the average worker added as much to the growth of output per worker as did the accumulation of machinery, structures, and other forms of ordinary capital.

If we follow Denison, the allowance for the rise in labor quality makes a big difference. Now three-tenths of the rise in output per person employed can be attributed to an increase in factor inputs, either more conventional capital per worker or more human capital (education) or greater intensity of work. But seven-tenths of the increase in output per worker is still left unexplained in "adjusted" total factor productivity.

Denison went on. He attempted measurements of the effects of changes in "intensity of demand" on the degree of utilization of employed labor and capital, in the "better allocation" of resources as labor and capital shifted from farming and petty trade to more productive occupations in industry and commerce, and in economies flowing from the enlargement of scale as national income and the size of close-knit metropolitan markets increased. The allowance for economies of scale is again a somewhat arbitrary figure, but the other two sources are calculations from relevant data. In the end, the Final Residual, although substantially reduced, is yet by far the most important source (51 percent) of labor productivity growth in the postwar period.[6] Because Denison judged that he had measured a very large part of the content of total factor productivity growth which does not arise from new applied knowledge and because his Final Residual proved to be nearly constant during the period of generally stable development from 1948 to 1973, he regarded it as a measure of growth due to the "advance of knowledge" incorporated into production.[7]

The aim of the growth accounts is to measure the importance of the proximate sources of growth. If these sources were completely identified and accurately measured, we should still want to understand the deeper causes of the process; we should want to know why schooling was extended as much as it was and why an extra year of schooling made the difference to output that it did; we should want to know why capital per worker grew just as fast or slow as it did, and why the incremental productivity of capital was just as high as it was. The accounts themselves, however, would take us a long way. They would tell us that observed changes in a country's productivity growth were due to certain proximate sources and not to others. They would tell us that the causes of differences between one country's growth rate and that of another had to be sought in certain directions but not in others.

So viewed, the development of growth accounting is a potentially important contribution. It remains subject to serious limitations to which I now turn; but the limitations themselves, as we have come to understand them, point the way to better understanding.

Limitations of the growth accounts

As with any set of measurements, the growth accounts are subject to error. The accuracy of some of the underlying data is in question. There are also problems about proper definitions and concepts. The most important is whether aggregate product should be measured net or gross of capital produced to offset capital depreciated or retired. The answer makes a small difference to the measured growth rate of the capital stock. It makes a very large difference to the weight attributed to the growth of capital input. The net basis is more appropriate in analyses of output growth as a source of economic welfare. Labor and capital, however, must be used to produce replacement capital, so the gross basis is more appropriate for measures of productivity. There are other questions. Should depreciation include obsolescence? Can earnings differentials be treated as unqualifiedly good measures of the effectiveness or "quality" of different classes of labor or capital? How should the income earned by the proprietors of unincorporated firms be divided between labor and capital in determining factor shares? There are problems of principle as well as accuracy of data embedded in these and similar questions.

A comparison between the accounts compiled by Denison and Dale Jorgenson appears in Table 1.2. It shows how vulnerable the figures are to differences in concept and modes of estimation. The figures in Table 1.2 are decompositions of total output growth, not of output per worker. I use them to make possible an easy comparison between Denison and Jorgenson because the latter does not provide a decomposition of labor productivity. An accounting of the growth of total output, instead of output per worker, does not in itself alter the growth rate of total factor productivity, but it adds the effect of the growth of the employed labor force both to total input growth and to that of output. So total factor productivity makes a smaller proportionate contribution to total output growth. A comparison of the Denison figures in Table 1.2 with those in Table 1.1 shows how this cuts the

Table 1.2. *Sources of growth in total national output, 1948–79: comparison of estimates by Edward Denison and Dale Jorgenson*

	Percentage points per year		Percent of total growth rate	
	Denison	Jorgenson	Denison	Jorgenson
1. Output[a]	3.49	3.42	100	100
2. Total labor hours	0.93	0.68	27	20
3. Labor quality	0.53	0.37	15	11
4. Capital stock[b]	0.77	1.15	22	34
5. Capital quality	–	0.40	–	12
6. Total labor input (lines 2 + 3)	1.46	1.05	42	31
7. Total capital input (lines 4 + 5)	0.77	1.56	22	46
8. Total factor input (lines 6 + 7)[c]	2.23	2.61	64	76
9. Total factor productivity (line 1–8)[c]	1.26	0.81	36	24

[a]Denison output is net national income; Jorgenson output is gross value added.
[b]Includes land.
[c]Sums of lines do not necessarily equal totals due to rounding.
Sources: Denison (1985), table 8.1. Figures are weighted arithmetic averages of growth rates for 1948–73 and 1973–79. Jorgenson, Gollop and Fraumeni (1987), table 9.5.

adjusted total factor productivity share in half – from 70 percent to 36 percent of output growth.

Jorgenson's estimate of adjusted total factor productivity growth, however, is a third less than Denison's. The major part of the difference arises because Denison measures output by net national income, Jorgenson by gross value added. For Denison, therefore, the share weight attached to the growth of capital is determined by capital's net earnings; for Jorgenson it is earnings gross of the allowance for capital consumption. Mainly for this reason, the weight Jorgenson attaches to capital accumulation is twice Denison's; and the weight he attaches to labor input is correspondingly smaller. Since capital is the faster-growing input, Jorgenson's total factor input makes a larger contribution to output growth than Denison's and leaves less to be attributed to total factor productivity. Jorgenson's capital input makes a larger contribution than Denison's for another reason. Corresponding to the growth of labor quality, Jorgenson estimates the growth of capital "quality." This is, in effect, the difference between the growth of the capital stock when its annual increments are measured by the estimated base-period cost of different asset classes and its growth when the different asset classes are combined by their annual "rental prices," that is, by what they must earn to make the investment worth while. On Jorgenson's gross output basis, rental prices must include depreciation, which is necessarily higher for short-lived than for long-lived assets. And since short-lived equipment was growing faster than long-lived structures in the postwar period, capital "quality" rises and, in Jorgenson's figures, raises the contribution of his total capital input growth to 1.56 percent a year, which is 36 percent larger than the contribution of capital stock proper and twice as large as capital's contribution according to Denison.[8]

The upshot is that whereas the early growth accounts centered attention on total factor productivity and presented capital accumulation as a much less important source of output growth, the picture is very different according to Jorgenson. His account elevates capital input to the premier position, more important even than labor input and well-nigh twice as important as adjusted total factor productivity. Although Jorgenson does not estimate the "advance of knowledge" itself, that is, Denison's final residual, that would necessarily be still less important in his view.

Differences of concept and method such as those that separate Jorgenson and Denison are not, however, the most serious problems of the growth accounts. The conceptual bases of both these accounts are clearly identified. One can use the figures that fit the purpose – the net national income basis, for example, in studies directed to the growth of economic welfare, the gross product basis to analyze the advance of productivity. Other problems, to which I now turn, are less easily resolved or evaded.

Arbitrary or uncertain estimates

If growth accounting could do no more than generate the huge and undefined Residuals of the primitive early tables, it would be of little value. The Residuals in the later accounts are much smaller, and the effort to decompose "total factor productivity" has taught us much about the statistics we use, about the conceptual problems of measuring the unmeasured parts of human capital accumulation, and about the services of both human and conventional capital. Making and using the accounts has forced economists to think rigorously about the theoretical bases of the production-function approach to an understanding of growth.

On the surface, there has been progress. The advance of knowledge, the final residual, in the Denison account (1948–79) is but half the original primitive residual. The same is true of adjusted productivity in the Jorgenson account. But are the measurements that lead to the reduction reliable? The sad fact is that they are not. They include arbitrary or uncertain estimates.[9] I use the justly admired Denison account to illustrate the problem.

1. Denison's account includes an allowance for an inverse association between average hours of work and the intensity of effort and care displayed by workers. He reasonably supposes that when average hours decline from very high levels, intensity rises by more than when they decline from lower levels. He proposes a formula to describe the association. But there is little evidence to support it. The proper offset may have been much less or more than his estimate.

2. Denison estimates the contribution of longer schooling as the difference between the growth rate of labor input in natural units (hours worked) and the growth rate of a weighted sum of hours in which hours worked by members of the work force, cross-classified by age, sex, and years of schooling, are weighted by factors proportionate to their average pay. Do the differences in earnings of workers classified by number of school years represent the effect of schooling on pay? They do not, because people who have remained in school for more years are, on the whole, more intelligent, energetic, persistent, and ambitious than those who left school early. They have, on the average, better-educated parents, who are more well-to-do and are better-connected than the parents of less-schooled people. The more highly educated students, on average, have had a better start at home, a better start in their careers, and more help along the way. Denison makes an allowance for these correlates of longer schooling; but the evidence to support the size of the allowance is problematic.

In extreme form, the problem raised by the correlates of education becomes the "screening model" of the role of schooling (Berg 1970). In this model employers use school records, certificates, and diplomas to identify workers with the sorts of personal characteristics (intelligence, energy, etc.) they desire for different kinds of jobs. They pay more to workers with longer schooling because the supply of people with the personal characteristics associated with longer schooling is limited. When the average level of schooling rises, so the screening model alleges, this does little or nothing to raise the capabilities of workers. It means only that employers must raise the schooling standard they associate with given levels of personal talent. Is the present-day secretary with two or four years of college training a better secretary than the high school graduate of fifty years ago? Carried to the limit, the screening model is absurd. The literacy, numeracy, and communication skills acquired in school, to say nothing of technical and scientific training, all count. The screening model, however, serves to remind us how hard it is to measure how much they do count.

There is a still larger problem. In the growth accounts, the value of a year's schooling is its worth to individual employers. But education has a wider significance. It raises the tolerance of consumers for novel products. It makes workers and their families more willing and able to accept the shifts of place and community that growth requires, from country to city and from region to region. It affects the operations of government and, in a democracy, influences its goals. Education, in short, is one of the governors of the social climate of economic activity. The growth accounts, as they now stand, catch none of these diffuse but important effects of education.

3. When the volume of a country's total output expands, there is an additional bonus. The larger output extends the market and opens the way to all the advantages of the division of labor. These advantages are also obtained when advances in transportation and communications and the removal of political barriers make it possible to trade over longer distances and across national boundaries. And markets are also enlarged when people come together in large cities and metropolitan areas.

The contribution of the economies of scale is one source of total factor productivity growth, and Denison proposes a measure for it. The basis for his measure, however, is uncertain. There are few studies of scale economies at a national level. Moreover, it is unlikely that there is a uniform association between scale of market and productivity growth. The productivity bonus from growth of scale is presumably larger in sparsely settled than in densely settled countries. The source of the enlargement of the market also makes a difference. Technological progress raises per capita incomes as well as aggregate output. Population increase may raise aggregate output with little or no change in per capita incomes. The accompanying changes in the composition of demand and output will not be the same; so the scale of effects will differ. And population growth increases congestion in densely settled countries. So does metropolitan concentration, which brings with it a host of other problems. None of these complexities in the measurement of scale effects has yet been seriously tackled.[10]

Denison's estimate of the three sources just discussed were 43 percent of his growth of labor productivity in the postwar period and 84 percent as large as his Final Residual ("knowledge, etc."). Allowing for errors in other, perhaps better-measured, elements leaves one with a disturbing sense of the uncertainty that surrounds the growth accounts and, more particularly, our understanding of how much we may have gained from work, capital, and knowledge.

The uncertainties associated with the Denison estimates attach as well to those of the other accountants. They face the same problems

Denison does when they make measurements of the same elements, and of course the problems remain when they do not.

Interaction among the sources

The most serious weakness of the growth accounts lies still deeper. The aim of the accounts is modest but definite. It is to measure the proximate sources of the rise of output and so to tell us where we must look if we are to find its more basic causes. Whatever the underlying causes may be, growth accounting asserts that they act through the sources identified in the accounts with a force that the accounts measure. Growth accounting in effect holds that if the measured contribution of capital accumulation was 2.0 percentage points per annum, aggregate output growth would have been 1.0 percentage point slower if capital accumulation had been only half as fast as it was. If the apparent contribution of the "advance of knowledge" was 1.0 percentage point per annum, aggregate output growth would have been just 1.0 percentage point slower if there had been no progress in technology at all. Growth accounting, therefore, holds that the sources it measures act independently of one another so that each makes its own contribution. There are good reasons, however, to question that claim. The growth sources feed from one another. The most important interactions are those between technological progress and the accumulation of tangible capital and between technological progress and the build-up of human capital through education and training.[11]

Technology and tangible capital. Causation runs in both directions. It runs from capital accumulation to technical progress in part because some new knowledge is incorporated into production only when newly designed capital equipment is actually emplaced in producing establishments. How much the exploitation of new knowledge depends upon the installation of newly designed equipment is not known. Some progress certainly takes the form of improvement in managerial routines, in the flow of work, and in the motivation of workers. Some requires but minor modifications in existing equipment. But the experience of most observers suggests that much progress is embodied in new capital. When that is the case, a speedup in the rate of growth of the capital stock also permits new knowledge to be incorporated into production at a faster pace. Otherwise stated, the average age of the capital stock falls and both labor and capital become capable of operating at a level closer to the frontier of knowledge itself.[12]

How important for the exploitation of new technology are the observed differences in rates of capital accumulation? If new capital is always invested in the economically most advanced forms, the effect depends, first, on the pace of advance of knowledge and on the age of the existing stock. Together these two factors determine the size of the technological leap that can occur when new capital replaces, or is added to, old. It depends, second, on the degree of speedup or slowdown in the rate of capital accumulation, because that controls the change that occurs in the average age of the capital stock between two intervals of time. Close calculations by Edward Denison suggest that changes in the pace of capital accumulation could not have made much difference in the pace of technological progress in the United States in the postwar period.[13] The rate of advance of knowledge was not fast enough and the changes in the average age of the stock were not large enough to make much difference.

Those findings, however, cannot be extended to other countries in other circumstances. For the United States, it was reasonable to assume that investments by and large embodied the most advanced knowledge of the time when they were made. There the technological leap that could be made by replacing old by new equipment was governed by the pace of advance in knowledge over a period represented by the age of the capital that is retired. For many other countries, however, investments have not always embodied the most advanced practice of the times they were made. Inadequate markets, managements inexperienced in large-scale business, scarcity of capital, poor engineering guidance, and sheer lack of information combined to make their old capital stocks technologically obsolete even for their age. That was the case with much capital in Europe and Japan when the postwar years began. If conditions then come to support investment in new equipment that represents best practice, much larger technological leaps can be made than the chronological age of existing capital might suggest. Then a rapid rate of capital accumulation can push technology forward substantially faster than slower accumulation. The rapid growth rates in Europe and Japan for twenty-five years after the war were, in some part, based on the combined effects of an initial capital stock that was technologically obsolete even for its age, a new capability for making effective use of best-practice technology, *and* speedy embodiment through rapid capital accumulation.[14]

New capital is needed not only to exploit the advance of practical knowledge but also to take advantage of the economies of scale in larger or more specialized firms as the enlargement of markets makes such change profitable. Furthermore, the changes of output composition and location that accompany the growth of aggregate output also demand new capital. So in these ways, too, the pace of technological progress actually incorporated into production depends on the rate at which new capital can be laid down.

The rate of capital accumulation not only influences the pace at which the advancing knowledge frontier can be exploited, it is also part of the process of acquiring new knowledge. Costs of production fall as experience with novel capital equipment accumulates. And still further, the incentive to conduct research and to develop and produce new products depends on the market for them. When the new products are capital goods, the size of the market is governed by the level of investment. I return to these matters in the next section.

The support that capital accumulation gives to technological progress is matched by the support that technological progress lends to both the growth of capital and the contribution that capital can make to output. The simplest and most important reason is that the prospective earnings of investment depend on the ability of new capital to increase the efficiency of production and to permit better products to be offered to consumers. This is to say, both the volume of new investment and what a unit of capital can contribute to output growth depends on technological progress. The profitability of new investment and therefore its volume also depend on the possibility of using it to shift output to the industries and locations that new technology and the demand it supports require. Since capital has been increasing so much faster than labor, one might have supposed that the returns to capital would have dropped continuously, slowing down the rate of accumulation and reducing the contribution of each new increment to output and labor productivity. That indeed was the expectation and fear of the classical economists. But they did not appreciate how continuing technical progress would permit each year's new investment to take more effective forms. In the experience of the presently industrialized countries, moreover, technological progress has, on the whole, been "capital-using." It has tended to increase the demand for capital compared with that for labor. The return to capital and the pace of capital accumulation have therefore been further supported, and the contribution of capital accumulation to output growth has been sustained.[15]

Technology and education. Interactions of a similar sort make it hard to separate the contributions of technological progress from the accumulation of the human capital. I illustrate the connection by considering the human capital that takes the form of education, which has so prominent a place in the growth accounting tables.

The level of education in a country, provided its content is modern, manifestly supports the pace at which an economy can exploit the possibilities of technical advance. All forms of education count – scientific, technical, and other forms of professional training, as well as simple reading, writing, and arithmetic. Scientific and technical training count for progress at the frontier. And they apply as well when it comes to acquiring and exploiting methods and products already in use elsewhere. Firms striving to "borrow" technology must have the technical competence to recognize it, to appraise its value, and to adapt it to their own conditions and requirements. Other forms of professional education count, too, because the introduction of new methods and products or their transfer to new places involves the organization of new firms or the reorganization or relocation of old ones, the design of new facilities, training of workers, and the solution of many problems of marketing and materials supply. The cost of exploiting and developing new or borrowed technology, therefore, depends on the availability of legal, administrative, managerial, and marketing, as well as engineering, skills. It is dependent on the capabilities of workers of all types to learn new jobs and routines and to respond to opportunities in new places, and also on the willingness of consumers to accept new products and to adapt their patterns of living to the opportunities they open up. Schooling enhances all these capabilities and thus the rate of technological progress itself.[16]

Finally, there is the influence that runs from technology to education. The pace and character of technological progress affects both the rate of rise of education and the contribution of advances in schooling to output growth. In the past, it has supported them strongly; so it may be said that technological progress supports output growth not only directly but also through its influence on the growth rate and, with a lag, the level of education.

The process by which this occurs runs from technological advance to the earnings premiums that reward workers who have more years of schooling more generously than those with fewer. Firms value workers with technical and general education in part because they contribute to their ability to conduct research, to evaluate and adapt the innovations of others, and to learn new functions and routines. And these qualities are more important in a progressive than in a stagnant economy (Nelson and Phelps 1966).

Earnings premiums enter the process in two ways. First, they determine the financial returns to the costly investment that students and their families make when they undertake to extend their education. They act, therefore, to govern the personal decisions that underlie the length of schooling. They are also a powerful influence on public support for the extension of schooling. They influence voters with children because government support for education reduces the costs that students or their families must meet. They sway voters generally because their vision of the social benefits of education rests partly on their perception of how much the earning power of the working population will rise if young people have longer schooling. In all these ways the size of the earnings premiums associated with schooling help to govern the growth rate of the level of education.

Secondly, the growth accounts treat the premiums themselves as measures of the marginal productivity of increments to the length of education. They tell us how much an additional year in school adds to a worker's productivity and, therefore, how much the growth of schooling contributes to output growth.

In the United States, for which our estimates are strongest (or least weak) it appears that the earnings profile of workers classified by level of education remained approximately constant from the early years of the present century until about 1970. This presents a challenging question. How did it happen that the earnings premiums on schooling – the marginal productivity of education – should have remained stable over so many years when the proportions of people with high school, college, and graduate education were rising so rapidly?[17]

In the face of a large increase in the relative supply of more educated workers, one might suppose that the earnings differentials associated with longer schooling would have declined decisively. They did not. They remained high enough to encourage a rapid extension of the length of education and to translate the rapid rise of education into a large contribution to output growth.

The solution of the conundrum lies, again, in technological progress. This acted to increase the demand for workers with longer education in three ways. First, it contributed to a larger rise in income which in turn led to a shift in the composition of consumer wants. Demand turned away from the products of agriculture, where workers typically have little schooling, and toward the production of services and government, including health care services and education itself, in which workers typically need longer schooling. Second, technical progress took a form that caused labor savings to be concentrated in those occupations in which the schooling of workers is typically short. These are the blue-collar occupations in farming, manufacturing, mining, and construction. The technology that produced those gains, moreover, demanded an expansion of employment in managerial, technical, and administrative jobs, in the professions and services auxiliary to blue-collar work, and in communications, distribution, and finance – all occupations in which levels of education are relatively high. And, third, it changed the nature of jobs generally in ways that made schooling more valuable. Concurrently there was a change in the content of education that made it more useful to business and practical pursuits.

The upshot of this extended argument is that growth accounting yields results that have a serious limitation. The accounts purport to measure the independent contributions of the growth sources they identify. But the sources are, in fact, not independent of each other. The accumulation of tangible capital, the expansion of human capital in the form of schooling, and the advance of technology interact. They support one another and make joint rather than separate contributions. The contribution of any one of these sources, as this is measured in the accounts, may be too small because it does not give adequate weight to its effect in generating the contributions of the others. Or it may be too large because it makes no allowance for the effect of the others in supporting its own. The sound instinct that technological progress lies at the core of modern economic growth rests at bottom, not only on its own independent action, such as it is, but also on the support it lends to the accumulation of both tangible and human capital and to the support that they in turn lend to it.

V. The search for deeper causes: technological effort as investment

That the advance of knowledge lies at the core of the modern growth process is more than an inference from the growth accounts. It is a perception enforced by well over a century of common experience. Economists have therefore applied themselves to learning more about the ways that practical knowledge is gained and exploited. A new outlook has developed and spread. It is not yet well defined. In what follows I sketch what I see as its three main features:

> Science, technology, and business are distinct, but no longer separate realms. They are closely intertwined, and at some points have fused.
>
> The new knowledge applied to production, in its discovery, in its initial exploitation, and in its spread, is the product and yield of costly and risky investment. With some qualification for the work of academic scientists, such investment responds to incentives and constraints that are, in every general sense, the same as those that control all other investment decisions.
>
> The strength and effectiveness of the technological efforts of business are, in part, controlled by conditions peculiar to individual firms, industries, and technologies. In part, however, they are governed by conditions that are national in scope. These serve to differentiate the growth experience of one country from another

and the experience of each country in one era from its experience in another.

I take up the first two features in the present section and reserve the third for the next section.

Science, technology, and business

When economists' attention was focused on matters other than growth, they sometimes spoke as if new knowledge proceeded in a linear progression from pure to applied science, thence to potentially useful inventions, and finally to the exploitation of such inventions in industry and commerce. Engineers were prone to express themselves in a similar way. That, however, was not a seriously held belief among economists. It was simply another way of saying that, for purposes of understanding relative prices, a satisfactory model could treat the state of the arts as a datum, the outcome of a process that was independent of that by which the relative prices of goods are determined. When economic growth and technological progress itself became the subject of serious study, such primitive views were quickly abandoned.

That our knowledge about how to make things and to transport them does not derive from a prior knowledge of scientific laws alone is obvious on the face of the matter. Most, perhaps almost all, of the practical knowledge embodied in the methods of settled agriculture, and even in the advances of the first century following the Industrial Revolution, had become common practice long before the scientific principles on which they rested had been discovered.

Many advances in processes of production and in the tools and materials that they employ are the fruits of experience with their production and consumption. The contemporary and generalized form of this elementary but fundamental fact is contained in the principles of learning-by-doing and learning-by-using. Broadly conceived, these principles can be seen to incorporate many common and plausible ideas about the process of learning that are well supported by the history of technology. Engineers, businessmen, and workers themselves learn to make things more easily and quickly as they study, dissect, and experiment with the production process and the business in which they are engaged. When problems emerge in the conduct of production, engineers and scientists are impelled to find the physical or chemical bases of the trouble, to learn more about the scientific elements of the materials and processes, and to discover solutions. If proper materials are unavailable or costly, they look for substitutes. If alternative materials are plentiful, they are driven to find ways to use them. The commercial and financial sides of business influence the trade-offs that engineers must make between cost and quality. In the same way, firms learn by experience to adapt their products better to the needs of their customers, to the uses to which they are put, and to the conditions under which they must operate.[18] Indeed when a technological innovation is first introduced, more particularly an important new product, its potential range of application to its most valuable and extensive uses remains to be discovered; and the adaptation of the product by redesign and by the development and provision of ancillary and supplementary devices and services is best viewed as a response to experience in use.

Kenneth Arrow, who introduced "learning by doing" to the lexicon of economics, based his thesis on a generalization common among psychologists: "Learning is the product of experience." He drew a second generalization from the many classic learning experiments, that "learning associated with repetition of essentially the same problems is subject to sharply diminishing returns." (Arrow 1962b, p. 155). Arrow argued that the tendency to diminishing returns to experience was offset by the environmental changes that experience itself generates. In effect, he suggested that experience leads to the improved design of capital goods and, therefore, that each successive vintage of capital provides a new set of problems and a new field for exploration and improvement. He therefore proposed that productivity growth is a function of the growth rate of cumulative gross investment, which served as his embodiment of experience. This carried the implication that productivity growth would be constant, other things being equal, if the growth rate of cumulative investment were stable. However, Paul David (1975, Chaps. 2 and 3), in a variant of the argument, contended that experience cumulates with time as well as with the volume of investment.

Arrow's and David's hypotheses may be regarded as generalizations of the early and important empirical studies by Simon Kuznets (1930) and Arthur F. Burns (1934). They had found that the growth rates of output of particular commodities and industries were almost invariably subject to retardation. To this Burns added that there was no evidence of retardation in measures of aggregate output growth. The central, though not the sole, element in their explanations of specific commodity retardation, was the same: The early exploration of a new technology yields relatively rich returns in productivity growth and cost reduction. But as production proceeds and experience cumulates, it becomes progressively harder to achieve equally significant improvements. Barring an occasional dramatic breakthrough, productivity growth slows down and the pace of market expansion falls. Burns and

Kuznets found their explanations of stable aggregate output and productivity growth in the emergence of distinctly new products and industries, founded on novel technologies, whose still untapped potentialities furnished fresh fields for exploration and improvement in the course of production, investment, and growing familiarity. Their emphasis on the emergence of new products and industries as a source of renewed vigor proved to be consistent with evidence. Their hypothesis implies, and it is true, that the industrial composition of output is subject to steady alteration. As total output and the level of productivity rise, relatively new products and industries displace the older.

The feedback from industrial and commercial experience to technology is manifestly one source, and likely an important source of new knowledge. It proceeds by multiple channels. It is closely linked to the deliberate and systematic efforts of business firms to discover better things to make and better ways to make them. Indeed, experience by itself does not, as a general rule, directly yield solutions to production or product-line problems immediately applicable in manufacturing and commerce. It is normally one element in the corporate process of research, development, and commercial exploitation that is now the standard method by which the more important changes in applied technology occur. This process itself involves a many-faceted interchange between the research, manufacturing, and commercial arms of firms, and this interchange expresses in a practical way the interdependence of technological advance and business operations (Kline and Rosenberg 1986).

The feedback from business and the market to the advance of knowledge does not stop with the direct effects of industrial experience on methods of production, design of products, and provision of ancillary services. It goes on by still other paths to the development of basic sciences itself and so, by indirection, to far-reaching extensions of fundamental knowledge on which applied scientists and engineers can build.

The influence that business experience and business motives exert on science proceeds, first of all, from the fact that the technology of production and the character of products are, in many spheres, now closely tied to the scientific principles of which they are discernibly applications. Scientific research, therefore, has the potential of making great contributions to people's health and satisfaction and of yielding large financial gains. Thus it is easy to understand that the deployment of scientific talent and laboratory resources should be strongly influenced by the practical prospects so opened. There are several channels of influence.

A major channel is again the experience of industry itself, the problems that arise in production or from the scarcity of materials or from the difficulty of designing reliable, durable, and cheap products. Numerous and significant examples testify to the response of scientific effort and advance to a challenge posed by industry (Rosenberg 1982, Chap. 7). Moreover, when science has met the immediate challenge, it often happens that the principles that offer a solution have much wider application than to the problems for which they were originally intended.

Because technology has drawn closer to science itself, technological advance is now typically sought by methods closely akin to those of scientific research. True, the motivations of the scientists who work in corporate and university laboratories are very different. The former seek advancement by guarding their firms' proprietary interests in their discoveries. The latter seek fame by the earliest and widest diffusion of new results (Dasgupta and David 1987). But the modes of work and even the intellectual products of the two groups have come closer together. Their members are often the graduates of the same university courses. Professors are commonly drawn into commercial research as consultants, and corporate scientists sometimes return to join university faculties. More often they return for short periods of study and research. In a limited way, business firms, seeking early access to the discoveries of university laboratories and to their talented students, have begun to give financial support to academic research. Increasingly, therefore, as the technology of industry has become more explicitly based on scientific principles, the problems and interests of industry have also come to shape the direction and content of academic science.

The conviction that the advance of knowledge applied to production is a process intimately involved with economic activity itself is supported by numerous empirical studies. These are especially persuasive in connection with the diffusion of innovation, and they run to the conclusion that the spread of new methods and products is a response to economic factors, to calculations of profit as influenced by the size of markets and firms (Griliches 1957; David 1975, 1986b). Jacob Schmookler, however, went further and argued that not only the application of inventions but also the pattern of inventive activity itself was governed by the size of the market for its products (Schmookler 1966).

Schmookler's studies aimed to explain the forces that governed the changing rate of invention in an industry over time and the differences in the rate of invention among industries at a given time. He chose patents as his units of invention and found a strong association between patents in the capital equipment of an industry and the industry's level of investment. Schmookler rationalized the association by arguing that, as the proportion of income spent on different classes of goods changes in the course of economic growth, the yield to inventive activity also changes and the direction of inventive activity changes accordingly. In this argument, the level of investment stands as a proxy for the yield to investment activity, which is itself governed by the changing size of the industry's market. Although the technological characteristics of inventions, whether mechanical, chemical, electrical, or biological, will depend on the current state of science, the classes of commodities or services to which inventions are directed are determined by the relative strength of their markets. When Schmookler's results appeared to be confirmed by other studies (Myers and Marquis 1969; Langrish et al. 1972), his views gained wide acceptance. Indeed, the primitive idea that the state of the industrial arts was the outcome of a wholly autonomous process running from science through technology to business appeared to be reversed. It now seemed that the evolution of market demand "called forth" useful new technology by inducing scientists and engineers to bend their efforts to whatever objectives market demand made most profitable.

Read literally, this second position was no more sustainable than the first. For one thing, the relation between the market and invention cuts two ways. A large market increases the potential yield of an invention, and it does appear that demand-side factors regularly trigger inventive effort. Nevertheless, successful inventive efforts also serve to expand markets. One must therefore look at the association between the direction of invention and that of market sales as a cumulative process.

That demand matters is inherent in the fact that business R and D, and its relations to the universities and basic science, is a process now fully incorporated into normal, profit-seeking business life. It does not follow that only demand matters in determining the direction of inventive effort, to say nothing of its results. As Nathan Rosenberg has contended, the twentieth century advances in medical science and in the chemical and biological elements of modern agricultural technology would all have met urgent needs and enjoyed vast markets long ago. That such advances did not appear in response to the latent demands for antibiotics, chemical fertilizers, pesticides, and high-yielding strains of drought-resistant, and insect-resistant crops reflects the inherent complexity of the branches of science on which they depend. Inventive activity could not be directed earlier to such subjects because, before the development of chemical and biological sciences, the difficulty of generating useful inventions made such efforts unprofitable, however wide the potential market.[19]

One is left with a conception of the relations between economic forces and the advance of practical knowledge, which is an amalgam of the two extreme positions. The progress of technology, which is the major source of productivity growth, is itself strongly swayed by the business activity that it stimulates. Its pace and its industrial direction are influenced by the pace of production and investment in the various branches of the economy. It responds to the incentives provided by the potential demand for its fruits, and it is constrained by the difficulties and risks of technological investment and its commercial exploitation. It is driven by the potential competition that rivals may offer, and it is aided and guided by the experience gained in the course of production and use.

The feedback from the economy to the advance of knowledge does not stop at the level of technology but extends to science itself. Technological effort and progress respond to the deployment of resources subject to business decision. The potential response, however, is not uniform in all directions. It is stronger in some, weaker in others, depending on the existing state of science and technology and on the complexities of nature that at times impede further progress. Where the potential response is weak, the costs of progress may be forbiddingly high, and a great market potential will not call forth expenditures or effort, to say nothing of advance itself. We must therefore recognize the existence and importance of "latent knowledge," a state of affairs that is in some degree determined by the cumulative progress of science and its own internal logic. The constraints so imposed can act to retard technological progress and productivity growth more at some times than at others and more in some directions than in others. And, depending on countries' patterns of consumption and on their industrial structure, therefore, it may favor advance in some countries more than in others.

Technological investment from the standpoint of firms and industries

1. The relations between business activity and technological progress imply that, as business firms look at matters, technical advance is the result of investment. The dependence of capital accumulation on technological advance is here reversed. Technological progress is dependent on investment. That is manifestly true when a firm's product lines and production methods lie at the frontier of what is both known and economically efficient. Then further advance requires a costly expenditure of funds in a search for products better adapted to the needs of actual or potential customers or for methods of production that promise lower costs. The search is spurred by

hopes of larger profit from expanding markets or greater efficiency in production or by fears of smaller profits if rivals catch up or move ahead. To maintain or improve their markets and profitability, research and development activities have become routine and, in large firms, are normally carried on in separate departments devoted to the search for commercially profitable knowledge.

The costs of such departments and those costs of manufacturing and commercial departments that are involved in the work of application and development, together with the work of testing, breaking in, and training staff, constitute investment expenditure that is qualitatively identical with investment expenditure in general. Costs are accepted in one period in the expectation of revenues to be obtained in a series of later periods.

Investment in the search for and application of new knowledge, however, has its own special characteristics. The costs of search are highly uncertain. Indeed, it is often not known in advance whether any commercially useful result will be obtained. Since other firms are engaged in similar searches, or may soon be engaged, the potential market promised by technological advance is not likely to be enjoyed alone. Over a period of time, longer or shorter, such markets will in any event have to be shared with imitative, if not innovative, rivals. The profits of new knowledge are therefore subject to commercial obsolescence and decay whose rapidity cannot be predicted in advance. The danger of obsolescence and loss of market spurs the effort to make still further advances, but the danger of very rapid obsolescence discourages the effort by diluting its prospective returns. Investment in knowledge, therefore, carries peculiar and heavy risks, which may discourage private investment unduly (Arrow 1962a), and it has other special characteristics that create problems for public policy to which I shall return.

2. In the older literature, a sharp distinction was made between innovation and imitation. The first required an expensive effort to acquire and apply new knowledge and subjected firms to the uncertainties and risks just described. The second, however, required only choices among products and techniques already in use, and, apart from the expense of choosing, imitation could proceed immediately to production and sale. The distinction was vastly overdrawn. Technology – even that which has in some form been developed and commercially exploited – is not a public good to be freely and easily adopted by all comers. In many instances, though not in all, prospective users must maintain a degree of professional competence simply to be aware of existing alternative possibilities and to appraise them. Next, the innovative knowledge is generally the well-guarded property of

the innovating firm. It may be patented property demanding a license fee for use. But even a license, if it can be obtained, is not a transfer of the innovator's know-how, which is the knowledge that is not obtainable from patent disclosure and not even from the blueprints and instructions that may accompany a license. Much of it lies in the experience of engineers and management to be acquired partly by transfer of personnel, but largely by an investment in study, testing, and production in the acquiring firm itself. R and D that breaks new paths doubtless eases the way for firms that follow. Yet followers as well as leaders must engage in technological investment programs.[20] The programs of followers resemble those of leaders all the more because both are mixtures in some degree of the search for the new as well as the acquisition and adaptation of the old. And all firms are constrained by their own prior history and experience. This has caused them to focus their efforts and has therefore left them, to some extent, restricted in the directions in which they are able to conduct research effectively and in their ability to exploit the results gained by others. Here we have another, but less clearly beneficial, aspect of the dependence of learning on experience. Experience lends an impulse to technological effort, but it may also circumscribe the area of search, to the neglect of alternative lines of advance (David 1975, Chap. 1).

3. The fact that technical advance rests on technological investment helps us understand some of the observable patterns of expenditure on research and development. In particular, one can see why such investment is associated with the scale of firms' general business activities. There are scale factors that affect both the cost and the yield of technological search.

On the side of cost, the effectiveness of technological effort in many fields has become scale-dependent. Supported by venture capital, the lone inventor or the pair of inventive partners still have an important place. In many spheres, however, large and very expensive facilities and the cooperation of many specialists or even specialized departments is needed. Such large-scale efforts can be carried on only by large firms or by the government. There has been a tendency, therefore, for R and D to become concentrated in large firms and this tendency has become stronger as technology has become more complicated and more closely entwined with its scientific base.

On the side of yield, the revenues from innovation depend on the possibilities of maintaining the advantages of an early start, that is, of developing a large market for a new or cheaper product and of holding it for a long time in the face of the imitative efforts and investments of rivals (Nelson 1987; Pavitt 1987). The nature of the knowledge itself and the laws of property in knowledge affect the speed with which rivals can acquire and exploit the new technology. But the ability of an innovative firm to develop and hold a market also depends on the prior possession of a large market position that confers on it public trust, access to channels of distribution, servicing capability, and in some instances the ability to provide ancillary products or services that complement the innovative product itself and make it more valuable to potential users. Scale, therefore, confers advantages, not only in production and distribution, but also in the conduct of R and D and in the protection and exploration of its fruits. The acquisition and protection of market share has, therefore, come to be a critical consideration in the competitive strategies of firms in technologically progressive industries.[21] And when lone inventors or small firms invent, they must often sell their inventions to larger firms to develop and exploit.

When an industry consists of many firms who use essentially the same production process, the industry itself is not normally the source of its own productivity advances. An upstream supplier enjoys two advantages. The supplier can know as much or more about the processes and products of the downstream users as any user firm itself, which suggests another factor governing the focus of research. And the supplier can enjoy a far larger market for its novel products than any single user firm unless, indeed, the latter enters the supply business itself (Nelson 1987). In farming, therefore, R and D is generally carried on by much larger firms in the industries that supply farming with materials or capital goods – that is, by firms in the chemicals industry who make fertilizers, pesticides, and fungicides or by manufacturers of farm machinery. Here the government also plays a large role in a search for better strains of seed and for more efficient methods of farm management. Such considerations run across the whole spectrum of industry, commerce, and finance and influence the way in which investment for knowledge is undertaken by the producers of commodities and services themselves, by the firms who supply materials and capital goods, or by governmental agencies.[22]

The paramount consideration in the location of technological investment is presumably the presence of latent, commercially applicable knowledge. This is hard to confirm persuasively because the existence of latent knowledge is revealed only by its discovery and that occurs only when some effort has been made to uncover it. Early successes, however, have convinced businessmen in chemicals and pharmaceuticals, electronics, computer software, and aerospace that research on the borders between science and technology, as well as in the relevant technologies of production, will explore rich, still untapped fields of knowledge, and a great share of all research expenditure therefore takes place in those industries.

The demonstrable presence of technological opportunities acts to

create a competitive environment that incites technological investment. It offers new firms a chance to carve out lucrative markets to the
peril of old firms. And it impels existing firms to make large investments in new products and process research and its application in an
effort to enlarge or, at least, to protect the markets they have. The
threat posed by the obsolescence of existing products and methods
leaves them little choice. In a less technologically competitive atmosphere, established firms may well prefer to extend the market life of
existing commitments to products, tools, methods, and distribution
channels, and they would correspondingly limit their investment in
research, retooling, retraining, and market development. But the
threat posed by the possible advance of rivals prods firms generally to
increase their efforts and to accept the costs and risks of keeping up
and moving ahead. Technological progress is then speeded by both
the more intense effort and the experience it yields.

The relation between opportunity and effort is another example of
the many feedbacks that the process of technological advance presents. Opportunity impels investment and supports the technological
rivalry that drives technological effort to high levels. The opportunity
that search and innovation offer, however, are not a datum known in
advance. It is, as said, a nebulous quantity that is revealed only by
investment itself. It is therefore a condition influenced by the complex
of factors that governs the state of competition in an industry. The
structure of markets and industries and the attitudes of their leaders
may act to restrain rivalry. Where the firms in the industry have
settled into established market niches, the possibilities of technological advance may be neglected, and only the intrusion of new rivals, if
and when it occurs, may rouse older firms from their somnolent state
and inject new vigor into the search for improvement.[23]

4. All investment, indeed all productive activity of whatever sort,
has a social marginal product that may be different from its private
marginal product. When investment is directed to knowledge, however, there is reason to think that the social product may exceed the
private by a large margin. That is because knowledge cannot be forever kept in the exclusive possession of its discoverer. Sooner or later,
in the same or modified form, the new knowledge comes to be known
to others, who exploit it and take a share of its product and profits.
The public has an interest in the full and diffused exploitation and use
of knowledge. But the private return on, and therefore the private
incentive to invest in, the search for better products and processes is
confined to that part of a discovery's potential yield that its finder can
appropriate and hold. In general, therefore, there is a stronger social
interest in technological investment than private individuals and

firms can have. Subject to important limitations, empirical studies suggest that the private return to *successful* innovations (N.B.: *not* to the total technological investment of firms) is higher than that to investment in general, which is consistent with the heavy risk that technical investment involves. But they also suggest that the *social* rate of return to innovation may be much higher.[24]

5. The fact that technological progress, whether by way of innovation or imitation, involves technological investment in general implies that the conditions that support and encourage investment also support technical advance. These conditions include those that apply to investment generally and those that are specific to investment in knowledge.

One may well believe, therefore, that technological investment, like other investment, is encouraged by macroeconomic conditions, including fiscal and monetary policies, that support intensive use of existing capital, high current profits, and easy access to finance at low cost. Given high levels of capital use, such investment will also be supported by a strong propensity to save, which helps keep long-term interest rates low. A fiscal policy consistent with budgetary surplus at high levels of employment is part of a strong propensity to save. Technological investment is also supported by a highly developed and efficient system of financial intermediation and more particularly by specialized financial facilities that can appraise, accept, and spread the risks of supplying venture capital. Tax provisions that favor investment in technology work in the same direction, and such subsidies are justified to the extent that the social benefit of technological investment exceeds its private return.

A plentiful supply of scientific and technical personnel serves to reduce the costs of research and development and, therefore, to raise the rate of return to technical effort. An adaptable labor force, relatively ready to accept new routines of work, train for new occupations, and move to new locations, helps to reduce the costs of exploiting innovations and to increase their yields. All these purposes are served by education at various levels from primary schooling to advanced scientific training. Again, the excess of the social benefit over private return of technical effort joins many other reasons that justify public support for a broad general education and for the development of strong scientific capabilities.

The social interest in technological investment is furthered by a well-devised system of property rights in new knowledge. Here there is need to balance the potential private rewards of innovation, which are the incentive for private investment, against the social interest in spreading knowledge and encouraging its widespread and rapid commercial application. The first element calls for protecting the private investor in an exclusive right to exploit the new knowledge he has gained. The second calls for limiting that exclusive privilege to permit diffusion and to support the competitive investments of rivals. Our patent system and our limited legal protection against the theft of trade secrets are attempts to achieve a proper balance; but the workings of our system under contemporary conditions needs study and appraisal.

Finally, there is need for direct government subsidy of, or participation in, both basic and applied research. That is because there are areas of the search for knowledge where the outcome is valuable – sometimes very valuable – but the prospective private returns are small. That is the case when the costs and risks are great or the time frame is very long, or when the possibilities of commercial application are diffuse and hard to define, or when the results, so far as they can be seen, would be hard to appropriate privately. Much scientific work falls in this category, because even the most exotic and detached fields of study support a generalized capability for scientific investigation that may one day make possible further progress in the material conditions of life. In the absence of support from governments or philanthropic foundations, scientific investigations would exist almost entirely as the joint product, along with their teaching duties, of university scientists. Moreover, industrial laboratories, with their commitments to the more direct application and proprietary exploitation of research, compete for the services of scientists. When the commercial potentialities of investigation appear to be very rich, science may suffer an undue drain of talent to industry, with costs to the training of the next generation of both technologists and scientists and with loss of potential scientific knowledge from which future technology might spring. There is therefore a nice balance to be preserved between support for science and that for the technological investments of private business.[25]

The argument of this section runs to the conclusion that investment in research and its commercial exploitation tends to be too low unless subsidized or otherwise supported by the public or unless supplemented by government research. The conclusion needs qualification. If the fruits of invention are protected by patents or secrecy for significant intervals, competitors are driven to invent around the protected innovation while denied the use of what might be the best technique. If the rewards of science go to the investigator who establishes priority, many will work independently for the same prize. The result may be duplication of effort and possibly duplication under unfavorable conditions. There is a danger of over- rather than underinvestment.

Yet, in the uncertainty that obscures early effort to explore new fields, it would be quite unwise to concentrate all effort on a single approach to a still cloudy goal. It would be wrong to suppress competitive effort, but the private incentives that produce it qualify the need to spur research by subsidy (Dasgupta and Stiglitz 1980a, 1980b; Dasgupta and David 1987).

In addition, although the general argument justifies subsidy, this is not to say that existing levels of support are too low. There are massive government expenditures in all industrial countries to support education at all levels, which is an indirect subsidy for science, technology, and innovative investment. In the United States and most other industrialized countries, there are direct subsidies for scientific investigation and a variety of supports for industrial research. And governments themselves engage in research and promote the diffusion of its fruits.

With government support for education and research in the background, the institutions of the industrialized countries of the West have proven to be an effective support for technological progress.[26] They have rested on the solid integration of technical skills with the commercial departments of industry and on close relations between industrial and academic research. Given the relatively open competition of industrial firms within and across national boundaries, the system of patent laws and property in knowledge has worked much as intended.

Although effective, the institutional system manifestly suffers from defects that make it less than ideal. It balances the private protection of inventions against the social interest in their widespread use in ways that we do not yet sufficiently understand. It is moving towards novel arrangements between business and universities that raise difficult questions about the balance of open science with proprietary technology. There is persistent debate about the volume of government support for research, about its instrumentalities, and about its allocation between education at its various levels and more direct aid to academic and commercial R and D. So the processes by which knowledge is produced, spread, and exploited need continuing hard study.

VI. The search for deeper causes: national and historical determinants

Simon Kuznets proposed that the proper unit of study of economic growth is the nation. He had in mind the fact that a large proportion of economic activity takes the form of exchange within national boundaries and that "strategic decisions" bearing on growth are taken by national governments and apply to activity within their own jurisdictions. There are other powerful considerations that support Kuznets's view, and some are suggested below.

The broad facts about national rates of productivity growth in the modern era that call for explanation are these:

1. The notable difference between the very slow rate of advance that preceded the Industrial Revolution and the more rapid pace characteristic of industrialized nations since that time.
2. The secular shifts in the average pace of advance by the industrialized countries of the "West" since 1870, when data for a considerable number of countries became available. The major shifts are the acceleration of labor productivity growth from about 1.6 or 1.7 percent per annum in the eight decades from 1870 to 1950 to about 4.5 percent in the quarter-century after World War II and the subsequent retardation to a rate of about 2.5 percent.[27]
3. The strikingly different record of the United States, marked by a moderate acceleration from about 2 percent from 1870 to 1913 to about 2.4 percent during the six decades from 1913 to 1973 and the relapse since that time to about 1.2 percent.[28] The United States, therefore, enjoyed no great postwar acceleration; but unlike most other industrialized countries, its subsequent slowdown has brought its rate of advance well below its prewar rate.
4. A tendency in cross-country comparisons among industrialized countries for productivity growth rates to vary inversely with relative levels of productivity and, therefore, for national productivity levels to converge. The strength of this tendency varied over time. It operated somewhat weakly before the postwar era, very strongly from 1950 to 1973, and more weakly since.[29]
5. The tendency to convergence was not uniform across countries. There were many shifts in ranks and the notable transfer of leadership from the UK to the United States near the turn of the century, followed by the great decline in the standing of the UK.
6. The tendency to convergence did not, for a long time, include a uniform general tendency for other industrialized countries to catch up to the United States. Although the productivity levels of other industrial countries were converging among themselves, the United States pulled further and further ahead of the average of other countries from 1870 to 1913. But there has been a strong general tendency to catch up to the United States since World War II.

The earlier discussion of the relations between technological advance and business investment had a particular bearing on differences among firms and industries in their technical efforts and results. These factors also underlie intertemporal and international differences in productivity growth. Insofar as a country's firms or industries display general differences from those of other countries or other times in respect to the factors governing investment in technological search or in the yield of investment, we have a clue to differences in productivity growth rates among countries and over time. To move from interfirm and interindustry differences to those that separate nations and periods, however, requires some further consideration. One must find a place, moreover, for factors other than the characteristics of firms and industries that bear on international differences and intertemporal changes in growth rates. It is convenient to employ a somewhat different framework of discussion than we have used so far. One structure that helps depict the broad outlines of the subject and that also displays its difficulties is to classify its parts under two headings:

> The *potential* for productivity growth; and
> The factors governing the *realization* of potential.

Potential

Potential has to do with the opportunity that exists during a period to raise productivity. In principle, one should consider every source of productivity growth. To retain the focus needed in a single essay, I take up only technological advance itself. The interdependence among sources, nevertheless, emerges because other elements of productivity growth appear either as conditions influencing the potential for technical progress or as factors governing the pace of realization of potential.

The potential for technological progress differs among countries, according to the degree to which their industries, or at least some firms in their industries, already employ the best practice that the current state of knowledge in the engineering sciences and in management permits. During the period of largely unchallenged U.S. technological leadership in the fifties and sixties, it could well be said: "it seems unlikely that in the US economy . . . the rate at which advances [in knowledge] were incorporated [into practice] departed much from the worldwide rate of new advance" (Denison and Chung 1976, p. 79). For such a country and in such conditions, the potential for progress is controlled by the scientific, engineering, and administrative possibilities that limit the pace at which effort devoted to search can further extend the frontiers of practical knowledge. This is the factor referred to earlier as "latent knowledge." This implies that countries whose industries stand generally at the forefront of technological practice may sometimes enjoy periods of rapid advance because the states of science, technology, and administration make the next steps easy and far-reaching. And they may sometimes suffer periods of slow growth when the path of advance is difficult.

Countries whose firms and industries are not up to worldwide best practice are in a different position. Subject to other considerations, they too enjoy an opportunity to make investments in capital that embodies the currently emerging technological frontier; but because, by contrast with the firms of a technological leader, their existing capital was technologically obsolete even when it was first built, the technological advance open to them is larger. They have a chance to close a technological gap inherited from the past. The chance to borrow existing technology added to that of searching at the frontier for new knowledge means that, for equal investment in R and D, the productivity rewards of followers will be greater than that of leaders. Other things being equal, the lower the productivity level at which a country works at any given time, the larger the leap it can make.

This difference between the technological potentials of leaders and followers is the central idea behind the "catch-up hypothesis" that accounts for the tendency of productivity levels in industrialized countries to converge.[30] And an enlarged technological potential based on a larger gap between existing and best practice, together with other factors, helps account for the postwar acceleration of productivity growth in the industrialized countries of the West.[31] The arguments just put forward are, however, unduly simple, even simple-minded. They skip over very important qualifications. There is more, and less, to the potential for productivity growth than is contained in the notions of latent knowledge and technological gap.

One consideration is that knowledge does not advance equally fast on every front. New technologies are not neutral in the demands they make for land, other natural resources, tangible capital, and human skills. Nor are they neutral in their dependence on large-scale operations for efficient exploitation. We need to know much more about the biases of technological advance in different times than we do. The U.S. spurt into productivity leadership in the last third of the nineteenth century and its ability to hold and even increase that lead during more than a hundred years thereafter appear to have been based on a congruence between the resource endowments and scale of the U.S. economy and the most fruitful directions of technological advance in the past century. The potentials of latent knowledge lay in the directions of unskilled labor-saving and resource- and capital-using methods and scale-intensive technology. Relative shortage of unskilled labor, plentiful supplies of resources and capital, and a large market tolerant of uniformity were U.S. economic characteristics.[32] At the same time, insofar as technological progress stemmed more from the United States than other countries, the best-practice techniques were given forms well-adapted to U.S. needs. Other countries were then able to borrow U.S. technology more or less easily depending on how closely their own resource endowments and the size of their markets resembled those of the United States. Countries with very different resource characteristics would have had an especially challenging task to adapt U.S. practice to their own conditions and would have had to develop foreign markets to supplement their own much smaller scale.

Now that the technological leadership in important industries is passing to other countries, it will be for the United States to face similar problems in adapting technologies pioneered elsewhere to its own different circumstances. At the same time there is no reason to suppose that the directions imposed by latent knowledge on the character of technological advance are now and will be in the future what they were in the past. They may distribute the relative advantages of progress to different countries in a different pattern.

There are more important restrictions, however, on a country's ability to exploit the potential of science and best-practice technology than are imposed by its natural endowment and market size. These are the limits set by what others and I call *social capability*.[33] The elements of social capability have a bearing both on the use that a country can make of advanced technology and also on its capacity to acquire it in the first place. I regard a country's ability to make use of technology as one constituent of its potential for productivity growth, so I consider it here. I take up its capacity to acquire new technology in connection with the factors governing the rate of realization of potential.

I identify social capability in part with the technical competence of a country's people and suggest that, at least among Western countries, this may be indicated by levels of general education and by the share of the population with training in technical subjects. Complicated and delicate machinery cannot be used to good advantage if managers lack technical knowledge or if workers lack some acquaintance with rudimentary mathematics.

If advanced technology demands operation on a large scale, it will not be used effectively if managers have little experience with the organization and administration of large firms. Large-scale production, moreover, works well only in conjunction with a variety of ancillary services – merchandising and distribution, finance, law, accounting, statistics, personnel administration. These services may be organized within producing firms or they may be sought outside, but the specialized personnel and experience are needed in one way or another. Financial services include those devoted to the mobilization of capital, which is a function of the development of a country's banking system and capital market; these in turn depend on the experience of people with investment in financial assets. In short, technology applied to production demands an overlay of business services, commerce, and finance. This is part of the message conveyed by the Clark–Kuznets observations about the connection between growth and the composition of output and employment.

The effective use of advanced technology also demands an extensive and expensive infrastructure of capital devoted to power, transportation, and communication. In the past at any rate, it has required the assemblage of people in large cities and therefore the organization of the government services that make urban life possible.

The elements of social capability constrain a country in its choice of technology. But technological opportunity also presses for relief from the social constraints.[34] Inadequate levels of education are raised; experience with large-scale business is gained as it is attempted; ancillary services respond to demand; governmental institutions are modified. Such changes, however, occur only with the lapse of time. Some move only with the succession of generations. It takes many years to raise the general level of education of the labor force by as much as that of its new entrants. Change is retarded also by the resistance of vested interests, and by the customary relations among firms and between workers and employers. As this resistance is overcome and their social capability rises, countries can exploit their technological potential more fully.[35]

In these respects, the United States had a fortunate beginning. Its domestic economy had grown up free of the traditional restrictions imposed by guilds, local ordinances, and mercantilist barriers on trade and occupation. The Puritan taste and tradition that spread from the Northeast to the West gave an early impetus to education in these regions. The country's republican and democratic institutions made wealth the dominant mark of distinction and directed talent to business. In all these ways, European countries were at a disadvantage and their social capabilities developed more slowly. These considerations have a bearing on the surge of the United States to technological leadership and on its ability to maintain a productivity lead for so many decades even over the socially and politically advanced countries across the Atlantic. The institutional constraints imposed by the past lend force also to Mancur Olson's suggestion that it required defeat in war, that is in World War II, and the accompanying political convulsions to clear the way in Europe and Japan for new men, firms, modes of operation, and state policies better fitted to the technological potential of the time (Olson 1982).[36]

If the only elements of potential were the latent knowledge beyond current best practice and the technological gap between followers and leaders, there would be a clear tendency for the productivity growth rates of followers to be higher than those of leaders; but the former would tend to slow down as their productivity levels converged on those further ahead. If, however, the process of catching up itself causes social capabilities to rise, the expected convergence may be erratic. Some countries may then advance faster than their initial levels of productivity would suggest. The self-limiting character of the catch-up process becomes problematic, and initially laggard countries may not only overtake but surpass an earlier leader.

One may summarize the position with respect to potential as follows. Insofar as the potential for productivity growth depends on technological opportunity it is governed by latent knowledge and by the gaps between existing and newly emerging best practice. Taken by themselves, their larger gaps give follower countries a relatively strong potential. They tend to enjoy relatively rapid productivity growth rates in a catch-up process that is self-limiting as nations' productivity levels converge. The technological opportunities of different nations, however, vary according to the congruence between their resource endowments and market scales on the one side and the characteristics of technology on the other. They differ also because of the varied limitations of nations' social capabilities. The opportunity for rapid growth afforded by technological backwardness may be offset by social backwardness. Social capability, however, responds in time to technological opportunity and changes also for other reasons, and this puts in question the self-limiting aspect of the catch-up process.

Realization

The potentiality determined by latent knowledge, technological backwardness, and the congruence between technology, resource endowment, and market scale may be regarded as governing a country's rate of advance in the very long run. This implies, of course, that the elements of social capability adapt to economic opportunity over long periods of time. The pace at which a country's potentiality is actually realized, however, depends on still other conditions.

A first and obvious matter has to do with the conditions that govern the rates of investment in the search for new technology and for the acquisition and adaptation of old techniques still not fully exploited – and with the yields of such efforts. Earlier discussion bears on this subject, and I now take up its implications for international differences and for changes over time. There are considerations that concern the efforts of both private and public sectors within countries and that affect the diffusion of knowledge within and between nations.

The capability of private and public agencies alike to engage in technological investment at any time is largely an inheritance from the past. This is so for the supplies of scientific, engineering, and technical personnel. Their numbers cannot be increased rapidly but are determined by past decisions regarding support for higher education and the nature and emphasis of university curricula and by past incentives that directed young people into scientific and technical courses. At a still more remote level, they depend on facilities for general education and on the family and social influences that join in preparing students for such training.

Education developed rapidly in the United States during the last century, first at the elementary level and, in the second half of the century, at advanced levels. In a democratic country where wealth was the principal mark of distinction, it responded readily to a sense that education could be the foundation for both individual and national prosperity.

In the same vein, there was an early beginning of university research directed towards agricultural and industrial technology. This, indeed, was the declared mission of the land grant universities, which were intended to be institutions of higher learning especially concerned with the agricultural and mechanical arts. Schools of engineering and of agriculture, which supported research laboratories in these subjects, flourished for decades in the United States on a scale unknown in Europe. During the same period, industrial research laboratories began to be established and to multiply. There were 139 such laboratories founded before 1900 (Rosenberg 1985; Mowery 1981).

America's early lead in organized efforts to apply scientific knowledge and methods to technical problems was given a great impulse by the scale of the U.S. market and the associated development of very large firms. Large-scale operations put a great premium on uniformity of materials and on exact knowledge and control of their characteristics. The large-scale distribution of foods demanded reliable methods of preservation and therefore more exact knowledge of the chemistry of decomposition. The concentration of slaughtering and meatpacking in a small number of very large firms enormously increased the mass of waste materials and drove the industry to transform them into useful by-products. These were possibilities that were opened by scale but depended on systematic analysis to determine the exact chemical composition of the wastes. They serve to illustrate the general character of the process.

By contrast with the United States, the expansion of secondary and higher education in Europe on the whole took place more slowly. With certain notable exceptions in Germany, so did the provision of university and business laboratories directed to applied science and industrial technology. The result was that the United States gained an early advantage in industrial research[37] that it was able to keep for a long time and that contributed to that country's long-sustained lead in overall productivity. The size of the U.S. lead in provision for education and in industrial research was being slowly reduced all through the present century, and it was cut still more speedily in the years after World War II.

Apart from the channels and volume of support, there is the question of the orientation of scientific studies. During much of the nineteenth and early twentieth centuries, European scientists appeared to lead in theoretical work and fundamental science, whereas the United States seemed to be especially effective in using basic knowledge to advance technology. Since the 1930s and still more since World War II, to the accompaniment of a great expansion of public support, U.S. scientists – and more generally scientists working in the United States – have assumed the leading role in pure science without, however, abandoning their older cultivation of applied science. And it is now the Japanese of whom it is said that, although they are not leaders in pure science, they are especially capable in the technological exploitation of scientific knowledge. All this, however, is almost certainly in the course of change. As the postwar convergence of average productivity levels proceeded, Japan and the various countries of Western Europe assumed the technological lead in certain branches of technology. These will presumably become more numerous. Japan and Europe, moreover, are now able to devote larger resources to scientific research, and it is altogether likely that they will come to share widely in the leadership of science which the United States enjoyed in the years following World War II. It would then be natural if a certain degree of transitory specialization should emerge and if particular countries should, for varying periods, prove to be the leading centers of training and research in specific branches of science.

National differences in effort and achievement in pure science, however, have not in themselves been an important source of national differences in technological progress – at least not hitherto. The ethos and practice of science has ensured that knowledge, wherever it has been gained, has been promptly and widely disseminated and open to those capable of using it.[38] What has counted for individual countries has been their capability, technical and commercial, for exploiting the advances of science. What has counted for the industrial world as a whole has been the worldwide volume of such work, which has been much larger in the postwar period than ever before, and the interaction between scientific effort and practical needs, which has been more intense than ever before. Both changes contributed to the rapid pace of postwar productivity growth and, doubtless, are continuing to support the advance of technology.

Government support for research, of course, is not confined to research in universities; nor is it confined to the support of basic science. It extends to the search for more direct and immediate technological applications and involves a variety of instruments ranging across government laboratories, the organization and partial support of corporate research consortia, and research contracts with business corporations.

In the United States, much more than elsewhere outside the USSR, government support is skewed towards research for military purposes. Indeed, government expenditure for military research in the United States is disproportionate even to the large share of national product that goes for defense itself. The net effect of this disproportionate allocation is probably a reduction of support for work of civilian significance. The loss, however, may be smaller than it seems, because the proceeds of defense research contracts serve to some extent to support general university activities, because there is some civilian fallout from military research, and because the perceived urgency of research for military purposes has served to make the total volume of government support larger than it otherwise would be.

I recite these fairly well-known matters to reinforce a general point: The pace at which nations can exploit either latent scientific knowledge or technological gaps depends on a variety of institutional considerations, and among these are the established practices that govern the relations of government, universities, and business in the conduct of scientific work.

To complete this discussion of the facilities that govern the pace of technological search and its effectiveness, I add some remarks about factors that bear on the diffusion of knowledge both within and among countries. In the course of the postwar period, there was a great proliferation of technical and professional associations and publications. The channels for national, and still more for international, trade and investment were enlarged, and the increased flows of goods and capital, accompanied by faster and cheaper movements of people and messages, carried technical as well as commercial information from region to region and country to country. Whereas foreign investment before World War I had more largely taken the form of investment in securities, direct investment became more important after World War II. The foreign activities of leading U.S. corporations involving joint ventures, multinational corporate operations, and extensive cross-national agreements for technology transfer became a notable feature of postwar business. In all these ways, the pace at which working knowledge moved from place to place in a practical and effective way was speeded up. This helped to raise the rate at which the technological potential of the postwar period was realized and contributed to the progress made in Europe and Japan in catching up to the United States.

Furthermore, beyond the facilities and practices that are more or less directly connected with technological investment, there are the factors that control the speed with which the economies of nations can adjust to the structural changes required by productivity growth. The enlargement of total output and of per capita incomes does not, needless to say, take the form of a proportionate expansion of each component of consumption and production. The composition of consumption tends to shift away from the relatively unprocessed products of agriculture, at first towards the more highly processed products of manufactures and then towards services. The nature of technological progress, including specialization and division of labor, is such as to save labor in the fabrication of goods themselves but at the cost of a great expansion of the auxiliary services of administration, finance, transport, communications, distribution, and many other ancillary functions. The urbanization of production and population required by modern technology and organization demands an expansion of governmental services, first at a local level, but later in national governments. The human capital requirements of modern technology imply a continuing expansion of the resources devoted to education and adult training. In many spheres of industry and commerce, technological advance demands an increase in the scale of operations of firms and industries and comparable enlargement of markets. In other spheres, technology permits operations on a smaller scale. Consumption trends and technology itself, therefore, combine in a demand for radical changes in the sectoral structure of production, in its geographical distribution, in the occupational composition of the work force, and in the organization of industry and commerce.

The pace at which technological potential can be exploited depends on the speed with which the structural changes implied by productivity growth can be carried through. What conditions control that speed? Here, again, we know much less than we need to. However, there are reasons for thinking that relatively favorable conditions existed in the United States from the beginnings of industrialization and that in the postwar period they became much more favorable in Europe and Japan than they had been before World War II and to an even greater extent more favorable than before World War I.

In the United States, the occupational and geographical mobility of the labor force was supported by rapid population growth, which made the new classes of workers each year large compared with the classes of older, settled workers. The annual arrival of great numbers of immigrants added a special increment of relatively unattached workers. The westward expansion of the country prevented the growth of firm regional roots. The rapid movement from the Atlantic to the Pacific made for more homogeneous styles of life throughout the country than was the case in Europe. And these same conditions also helped form this nation's great domestic markets, which in turn made it easier to accommodate the technologies demanding large-scale production.

After World War II, structural mobility was supported in both Europe and Japan by large reserves of labor on the farms, reserves made still larger in the postwar years by rapid advances in labor productivity. By contrast with conditions before World War I, the redundant European farm populations were denied the chance to come to the United States. They moved to fill the domestic needs for urban employment in their own countries. Eager for growth, moreover, the West European and North European countries opened their borders to immigration from the Mediterranean, which was added to that into West Germany from East Germany and the territories lost to Poland. In all these countries, and still more in the United States, the entry of women into the labor force was another source from which jobs of new sorts in new places could be filled. And the liberalization of international trade together with the creation of the Common Market and of the European Free Trade Association eased the way to large-scale production even for firms in the smaller countries.

When the attempted pace of growth involves changes greater than the mobility of a country's labor force and population can absorb, bottlenecks develop, the skill standards of jobs are diluted, wages rise faster than productivity, and product prices rise. Inflationary tendencies unsettle business and finance, and the balance of international payments weakens. The resulting disjunction between the demand for monetary growth to support inflation and the supply of money that the international position of a country can support imposes a period of recession or retardation. But when and where conditions of mobility are favorable, rapid growth can be sustained for longer periods. Thus the conditions of resource mobility help to govern the pace at which technological change can be realized and they contribute to the uneven path that growth normally takes.[39]

Finally, there are the macroeconomic conditions that govern business investment decisions in general. These may be especially important for the risky, long-term decisions that control expenditures for research and the much larger expenditures needed to bring the results of research into actual production. These conditions involve a wide variety of matters. They include the fiscal and monetary institutions and policies of national governments and also the institutions and policies that influence international economic stability. The liquidity position and, more generally, the asset–liability structure of business is important. So are the activities of governments in providing the infrastructure of communications, transportation, and power on which the investments of private business can be built. Finally, there is the impact of extraordinary events, of which wars and their aftermaths and OPEC oil shocks are dramatic examples.

From the viewpoint of growth history, the essential point is that favorable or unfavorable macroeconomic conjunctures can persist over several decades – long enough, therefore, to make a difference to that long-term experience of nations with which economic growth is concerned. It is apparent, for example, that the years from 1914 to 1945 or 1950 saw a generally disastrous conjuncture of macroeconomic conditions that depressed investment and productivity growth rates for over three decades. By contrast, the next quarter-century enjoyed a most favorable conjuncture of institutions, policies, and circumstances, which gave way again to the much less favorable conditions that have ruled during the last fifteen years and that still persist.

The discussion of the elements of productivity potential and realization can take us some distance towards an understanding of certain leading features of the growth experience of the industrialized countries. The wars and the disturbed state of politics, finance, and business from 1914 until after the end of World War II produced a hiatus in European and Japanese growth relative to that of the United States. It left these countries at the end of World War II with greatly enlarged technological gaps. Because their social capabilities were strong and had continued to rise, however, their potential for productivity growth was especially powerful when the postwar period began. And that, together with the great improvement in conditions supporting the realization of potential, were the bases for the postwar growth boom, for the strong convergence of the productivity levels of these countries, and for their rise relative to the United States. Finally, a deterioration of the conditions supporting realization (the breakdown of postwar international monetary arrangements, the oil shocks, the unusual combination of inflation and recession, and the retreat from free trade) and a weaker potential, reflecting the presumptive narrowing of technological gaps, were contributors to the general productivity slowdown of the last dozen or more years.[40]

This outline of the elements of potential and realization, although quite broad and general in its range of application, is still limited in certain ways. It suggests that social capability rises in a linear fashion, becoming steadily more able to cope with the opportunities presented by technological potential. That is not necessarily so. Countries' physical, organizational, and doctrinal adaptations to the opportunities and requirements of older technological paths may limit their ability to exploit newer directions of technological progress. Considerations of this sort may have restricted British growth after 1870. Similar ideas are being revived now to account for the marked retardation in U.S. growth in recent years. U.S. firms were pioneers in the techniques of mass production, and the huge U.S. corporations were successful adaptations to the opportunities of scale-intensive technological progress. When superlarge conglomerate corporations appeared, they were regarded by many as effective ways to economize scarce talents in management and in the mobilization and allocation of finance. U.S. managerial doctrine absorbed these ideas and they have guided managerial practice. Now that technology appears to permit cheap production of more varied lines of goods more closely fashioned to meet the tastes and needs of smaller groups of industrial and commercial users, as well as ultimate consumers, observers question whether the immense U.S. corporation and its established managerial doctrine are effective instruments for exploiting the newer possibilities. If this is a difficulty, how serious is it, and how long will it take U.S. organization and practice to change?

The complexity of such questions appears as soon as one considers the fact that not every U.S. company is superlarge; nor are all Japanese or European firms much smaller than U.S. firms. And, of course, every firm, large or small, satisfies a large portion of its needs by purchases from others rather than by internal supply. Contemporary theory views the size, organization, and policy of firms as determined by the relative costs of supply from internal and external sources. In the evolutionary test imposed by market competition, the responsiveness of external suppliers to the needs of a purchasing firm is weighed against the cost of obtaining equal responsiveness from the firm's own staff. The outcome depends on the peculiarities of a given firm's own operations, which may limit the ability of a supplier to satisfy that firm's special needs, and also on the economies of scale and scope, the costs of communication and decision within the firm, and the difficulties of eliciting dedicated effort directed to its purposes, rather than to the possibly divergent interests of individual employees (Matthews 1986; Williamson 1985).

Technical innovations, such as computers, presumably propel industrial organization in different countries in the same direction. In contrast, a national ethos that controls people's honesty and sense of interpersonal obligation may produce national differences in company size and in their styles of organization and operation. Empirical work that may reveal how these considerations may share responsibility for change over time and for differences among countries has not yet gone very far. The theory itself does not yet incorporate the financial influences that may impede or facilitate institutional reorganization, a question urgently raised by the recent wave of mergers, takeovers, divestitures and so forth, in the United States. Reorganization in the direction of an increased capability for the effective exploitation of technological potential may, indeed, be in progress. How consistently it is moving and how fast relative to some undefined model of efficient organization is still a mystery.

VII. Longer thoughts about long-term growth

Considerations bearing on the size and organization of firms do not bring into view the full range of issues raised by the nature and evolution of economic institutions. There are more extensive, but also perhaps more elusive, questions to consider. Some passages from Simon Kuznets provide a start.

The epochal innovation that distinguishes the modern economic epoch is the extended application of science to problems of economic production. (1966, p. 9)
The application of science meant a proper climate of human opinion in which both the pursuit and use of science could be fostered; and thus when we say that the modern epoch is distinguished by the application of science to problems of economic production and human welfare, we imply that it is distinguished by a climate of human opinion, by some dominant views on the relation of man to the universe that fosters science and its application. (Ibid., p. 12)
The broad views associated with the modern economic epoch can be suggested by three terms: secularism, egalitarianism, and nationalism. (Ibid., p. 12)

Kuznets took secularism to mean "concentration on life on earth, with a scale of priorities that assigns a high rank to economic attainment." This stands in contrast with a view that earthly life is but a brief prelude to an otherworldly eternity. Secularism "makes man paramount and life on earth his main concern" (Ibid., p. 13).

He viewed egalitarianism as the denial of inborn differences among human beings except as they reveal themselves in activities regarded as valuable by others. Egalitarianism, therefore, recognizes no mythological, hereditary, or religious distinctions among people, but it tolerates and justifies large and unequal rewards if they are thought to be received by the economically efficient and used by their recipients "as capable stewards for society as a whole." Egalitarianism, as Kuznets saw it, protects individuals in the free pursuit of their highest economic potential and sanctions rewards proportionate to their productivity. It caused a "shift in the bases of social prestige and political power" and induced "a much larger flow of talent and energy into economic rather than other pursuits" (Ibid., p. 14).

Kuznets saw nationalism as a severe constraint on egalitarianism because it accords equal treatment only to those accepted as members of the national community. But it was also the foundation of the nation-state, an effective unit of power capable of taking and executing strategic decisions and providing services supportive of growth.

In Kuznets's argument, science-based technology and the three broad views needed for its successful cultivation and exploitation appear as distinctive features of the modern economic epoch. As such, they serve, in his view, to distinguish that epoch, for those countries that have entered it, from earlier epochs. So regarded, they are an important conception. However, it is a very generalized conception. It refers to an outlook on life and the world that may need to be accepted in some sufficient degree by all societies that aspire to modern growth. As we shall see, however, there are exceptions even to that minimal requirement. And even where it is met, it is an outlook that people in different societies may entertain in many degrees and in many variants. Notions about what constitutes the good life, the expectations and aspirations proper to different social classes, the bases of distinctions among them, and the standards of decent behavior were hardly the same in, say, Britain, the United States, and Japan when each entered the process of modern economic growth.

Moreover, even if we suppose that Kuznets's "broad views" are characteristic in some adequate degree of people in all countries that experience modern growth, yet it is apparent that this generalized outlook is embodied in political institutions and forms of economic organization that differ sharply among industrialized countries. The differences spread across countries in a wide range, from those that organize activity largely through private enterprises connected by trade in free markets, to the highly centralized, hierarchical systems of planning and command, as in the USSR.

Finally, neither the broad views that people hold about the ends of life, about the rights and obligations of people, and about the relations among classes, nor the political and economic institutions in which these views are embodied are grand constants. They evolve in the course of economic growth in response to influences generated by growth itself, as well as in response to other influences. I can do little more than indicate the directions in which these difficult and subtle issues take us. I do this, first, in the course of brief comments on the class divisions, personal aims, and standards of conduct in the United States, Britain, and Japan.

Classes, goals, and standards of behavior

To Europeans of the early and middle nineteenth century, the United States appeared to be a historical exception. It differed from Europe in respect to all three of Kuznets's broad views. It was more intensely secular in Kuznets's sense of being concentrated on earthly life and assigning a high priority to economic attainment. Because land was plentiful and cheap, ordinary people could aspire to a decent competence. Because the country was growing in population and trade, so were productivity and average incomes; so people could aspire to still greater prosperity. The Puritan strain in religion interposed no obstacle to the pursuit of wealth, and an intense egalitarian ethos lent powerful social support. The older European class distinctions based on birth and class had hardly survived the New World's wider dispersion of property and economic opportunity. People judged each other more largely on merit and, lacking other marks of merit, wealth had become the main badge of distinction and of class. Because the paths of wealth were relatively open, class lines were easily crossed; so the pursuit of social distinction joined more commonplace influences to heighten the priority assigned to economic attainment.

The U.S. nationalism of the nineteenth century also had its peculiarities. With the adoption of the Constitution and the subsequent growth of wealth, the United States became an effective nation-state, well able to make the strategic decisions that were among the foundations of its development. The singularity of U.S. nationalism was that it did not deny the benefits of residence and citizenship to foreigners. New arrivals faced difficulties of language and of adaptation to new ways and a new environment. These, however, were usually surmounted in the space of a generation or two, and the United States of the nineteenth and early twentieth centuries was a successful experiment in the assimilation of many nationalities and cultures. The country therefore benefited from growth in numbers of people through immigration and from the variety of talents that immigrants brought.

In such an egalitarian society, relations among people were founded on agreement and contract to a degree less qualified than elsewhere by custom and ancient usage. At the same time, the conditions of a relatively stable rural and small-town society combined with religious sanctions to enforce the faithful observance of agreement. To give less than full pay or full measure, to do less than an honest day's work, were even more matters of local shame than of legal default.

Fluidity of class lines softened class hostility and eased the relations between employers and employed. The individualistic presumption that relations among people should be matters of personal agreement weakened any feeling of governmental obligation of support of the poor and kept public regulation of economic activity within narrow limits. The goal of increased income, however, fostered an early concern for schooling, and a sense that the common interest in education exceeded the private encouraged support for schools from public funds. The U.S. system of public education was founded early and expanded relatively quickly.

The monstrous aberration in U.S. egalitarianism was black slavery and the persistence of discrimination that followed legal emancipation. Racial barriers and disabilities endure to this day and, besides other evils, deny to economic life the full talents of considerable portions of the population.

Britain, by constrast with the United States, entered its era of modern growth with a more substantial inheritance of caste and class. This separated the nobility and gentry from peasants and workers. Between these two classes, a middle class of businessmen and professionals had established themselves. Class lines were not rigid boundaries; they could be crossed with the help of wealth. However, Britain was less egalitarian than the United States, and wealth alone counted for less. Distinctions based on birth, education, and occupation persisted, and they had persistent effects.

One such effect is in the relations between workers and employers, which was, and still is, afflicted with a degree of hostility strange to most Americans. The employment contract in the United States shares some of the overtones of other commercial transactions. Many workers who take a job see that one day they may be on the other side of such a contract. In the past, that was often so. In Britain, however, employment is an enduring relation between people of different class. They feel their interests to be in opposition and workers, conscious of class, disdain to change sides; they prefer to stand and fight. Industrial conflict is therefore endemic, and the sense of permanence in worker status has the effect of inhibiting innovations that threaten jobs or even a shift of functions and occupations.

A second effect of the persistence of class distinction in the UK was the drain of talent from business, more particularly from manufacturing and trade. Members of the middle class were ambitious that their sons might be gentlemen, and that meant a proper occupation. So a manufacturer's son, if he was clever enough, was pointed to the law or, still better, to the civil service or, if not quite so clever, to the City or perhaps to the army.

Education, however, came first, and a proper education was one fit for a gentleman. In England, that meant, until comparatively recently, a classical education. It was imparted, following preparatory classes, first in public schools, whose students were the children of gentlemen or of aspiring gentlemen. And it was continued in the ancient universities which were hardly less class-bound.

All this gave the education of the British, more particularly the English, elite a peculiar, premodern bias, both in its subject matter and in the class divisions it helped to perpetuate. Class feeling also left its mark on British mass education. The upper class who controlled British politics in the nineteenth century were slow to be persuaded that mass education was needed and that state support was justified. The Church of England resisted state schools that would be nondenominational. Moreover, when a state system was at last established, British working-class feeling gave less than ardent support for its extension. Many workers resisted the view that schooling, at any rate schooling beyond the elementary grades, would be an advantage to their own class-bound children. The net result was that, although Britain had been the leader in nineteenth century industrialization, the school system expanded more slowly there than in the United States and more slowly also than in some continental countries (for example, Prussia) that were comparative latecomers to modern growth.[41] There is at least a strong suspicion that the biased character and slow growth of British education made some contribution to the relative decline of British productivity growth during the present century.

Kuznets's trilogy of secularism, egalitarianism, and nationalism is again a convenient way of describing the outlook and attitudes of the Japanese. In these respects Japan has been and is very different from the United States and Britain; and the differences help us see why Japan was able to accomplish her immensely rapid transformation from a backward, feudal society to a modern industrial power.

As regards secularism, the interest of Japanese people in the things of this life and the importance attached to economic success were and are very high, certainly comparable with the feelings of Americans. There was, however, this difference. From the beginning of Japan's modern era, the private interest in economic attainment was accompanied and, indeed, spurred and led by a powerful political interest. When Japan abandoned its older feudal regime, the imperial circles and lower samurai who were the driving force behind reform saw economic modernization as essential for the maintenance of national independence and power. A potent political motive, therefore, was a central element in Japanese secularism. That Japanese modernization was a state-planned and state-controlled enterprise was a consequence of this difference in the Japanese outlook (Norman 1940; Ohkawa and Rosovsky 1973, Chap. 1). To this there were added other great differences in the spheres of egalitarianism and nationalism.

Kuznets's egalitarianism, as we have seen, has the function of establishing merit, more particularly merit in productive activity, as the basis of material reward and social prestige. It opens the way to talent and sanctions rewards for its accomplishments, therefore providing an incentive for its exercise. The feudal Japan, from which modern Japan began to emerge little over a century ago, was not egalitarian in this sense. It assigned people roles in which each had a proper station clearly marked out by sex, age, and membership in a feudal caste – noble, warrior, peasant, artisan, tradesman. People's proper stations defined their rights and their strict obligations. The fundamental unit was the immediate family within which authority and obligations were defined by sex and age. Families and their members owed duty and obedience to their feudal superiors in a line stretching upward to shogun and Emperor. The obligation defined by station demanded the strict fulfillment of duties, failing which the shame and guilt that attached to the person and family were intense, and punishment, whether inflicted by authority or by oneself, was severe. Although caste lines were not utterly rigid (a rich merchant might ally his family with the lower samurai), the scope for exercise of talent outside one's normal sphere was restricted.[42]

The reforms following the Meiji restoration went some distance to inject an element of Western egalitarianism into Japanese society. The legal privileges and restrictions of the several castes, which controlled occupation, dress, and consumption, were abolished. The larger-scale firms that very gradually replaced the family farms and shops of premodern Japan enlarged the scope for talent. But much of the older feeling of proper station, and of the reciprocal obligations so defined, remained. In some ways they were extended. The loyalties and obligations that ruled within families proved to be transferable to the relations of employers and employed and to the relations among the larger assemblages of people in the huge firms of a modern economy. They seem to lie behind the loyalty that many observers say that Japanese workers and managers bear to their firms. They act as sanctions for the faithful execution of tasks and the single-minded attachment of executives and workers to the success of their companies (Benedict 1946;1974; Abegglen and Stalk 1985, Chap. 8).

A sense of hierarchy and of deference to those whose proper station is higher is also characteristic of Japan in the political sphere. Following the abolition of the feudal castes, the older sense of obligation and submission to authority was transferred directly to the Emperor and to the bureaucracy, who were his appointed officers. There was therefore an effective concentration of authority in the state. It enabled the group around the Emperor to carry through a series of social and economic reforms that were not widely popular. It enabled the state to establish the basic modern industries (and to transfer them to the private ownership of a restricted group), to arrange for the cooperation of foreign experts and for the technical and business training of Japanese both at home and abroad, to reform mass education, and to found modern universities. The special position of the Emperor and his bureaucracy, resting as it did on the Japanese sense of hierarchy and duty, satisfied one of the functions of nationalism as Kuznets saw it. It made the state, in superlative degree, an effective agent of economic modernization (Norman 1940).

The other characteristic of Kuznets's nationalism, its exclusive aspect, was also present in Japan in an intense degree. The Japanese were and are an ethnically homogeneous society. The sense of both kinship and exclusivity was doubtless reinforced by the centuries of isolation that preceded the Meiji restoration. In Kuznets's view nationalism works to restrict the significance of egalitarianism by limiting access to the benefits of economic opportunity to members of the nation. In this respect, the United States, a nation of immigrants, has been a generally open society. Britain, with a stronger sense of national identity, was still able to accept a long regime of freedom in the movements of people, goods, and capital. Japan's position, however, was extreme. Its intense nationalism was a natural and powerful support for development based on formal and informal protectionist policies and on the virtually exclusive participation of its own citizens. The counterpart of this nationalistic policy of development was the power of the state to make the decisions required for modernization and to enlist the cooperation of its population.

These comments on the outlook and climate of opinion that govern relations among people, between employers and employed, between people and the state, and between one national community and others are enough to suggest their importance. They influence technological progress and growth through their bearing on the scope for the use of talent and the direction it takes, on the spread and content of education, on the costs of innovation and structural change, and doubtless on much more. They also suggest that no single variant or combination of attitudes is consistent with growth. The differences between the United States, Britain, and Japan tell us that there are complexities and subtleties in the content and meaning of secularism, egalitarianism, and nationalism. These have promoted or hindered growth in each country, but the differences in social climate that we can connect with Kuznets's trilogy are not to be measured along some uniform scale. Attitudes and values have many dimensions and work along multiple axes. Egalitarianism, in the Kuznets sense, means scope for talent; together with secularism, it means energy and talent directed to economic achievement. But hierarchical authority and deference to superior station, which may appear to be the antithesis of egalitarianism, may support cooperative activity and the power of the state to make and carry through strategic decisions. Together with secularism and bolstered by nationalism, it may also mean energy directed to modernization and growth.

Besides attesting to the importance of social climate and to its complications, these remarks also testify to our ignorance about it. For lack of a theory of social climate and its consequences, economists have not known how to study the subject. And for lack of interest in the problem of growth, except perhaps as it concerns the less developed countries,[43] the other social sciences have also neglected it. When economists construct models of growth, they have been implicitly based on the assumption that social climate is a constant. In comparisons over time, it is assumed not to change; in comparisons among countries, it is assumed to be the same. When such an assumption is too implausible to maintain, as it would be in comparisons between industrialized and underdeveloped countries, studies keep the two sets of countries in different boxes, as this paper itself has done. So there are separate branches of growth studies, one for industrialized countries, another for less-developed countries.

From laissez-faire to the mixed economy

Our pronounced ignorance about the content of climates of opinion and how they operate to promote or thwart technological progress and growth is compounded by the fact that individual attitudes and social outlooks change in the course of growth itself. The secular and egalitarian outlook that, in various degrees, characterized the countries of Western Europe and North America in the middle nineteenth century had a dominantly individualistic coloration. It made families and their members responsible for their own fortunes and left governments with comparatively few responsibilities and functions. For these countries, but not for Japan, the transformation that matters is that from the relatively individualistic outlook and relatively laissez-faire policies of the nineteenth century to the mixed economies and welfare states of the present time. It is a change that is itself best viewed as part of technological development and modern economic growth as they proceeded in the Western political and cultural context. The change arises from people's latent desires, revealed by higher levels of income or aroused by the education and technology on which income growth itself was based; from the structural changes that are implied by growth, the costs and conflicts of the process, and the new organizations of population, production, and family life needed to sustain advanced levels of technology; from the inherent instability of growing economies organized mainly by private enterprise; and from the generally democratic or, as Kuznets said, the egalitarian, character of Western political systems. Economists and other observers and critics emphasize different aspects of these background causes, but all are involved.

1. The rise of income has released or aroused demands that impart a new content to the secularism and egalitarianism on which Kuznets contended that modern economic growth rests. Secularism continues to mean a "concentration on life on earth," but its scale of priorities no longer assigns the same "high rank to economic attainment" – not if that is identified simply with productivity, that is, the measured outputs of marketed goods and services and the time and effort spent in producing them. Rather, our concerns have come to emphasize other interests that are not included in measured productivity and that must be pursued in one way or another through the agency and activity of government.

One such concern is safety. The science that has given us novel and wonderfully serviceable products has also made us aware that products, materials, and occupations may carry dangers, immediate or remote. Unable, however, to make reliable judgments themselves about specific products or jobs, people press strongly for government regulation of both consumer products and services and of conditions of work.

The rise of income has also revealed a latent demand for protection against the most compelling incidents and hazards of life, for care in sickness and for maintenance in old age. This desire is all the stronger because the advance of technology has enlarged the scope of what medical care offers and because the extension of life has increased the span of years in retirement. These enlarged demands do not imply a diversion of resources to unmeasured output, except insofar as improvements in the effectiveness of medical care is a particular dramatic example of the qualitative improvement that national product fails to measure. But the demands have been the occasion for using the government as the tax-paid provider of at least a portion of health care, as the organizer and provider of health insurance and old-age pensions, and as the redistributor of their costs. Moreover, although the reliance on government in this sphere stems from a number of causes, one is the weakening of the family itself, an important matter to which I will return. This has called for an alternative source of protection in time of trouble and for another way of redistributing the costs of sickness and age between generations.

Next, the rise of incomes, and of the education on which it is partly based, has increased our concern for the environment in which we all live, and it has enabled us to support that concern with funds. This is only partly a matter of our enlarged demand for safety already noticed. It is also a demand for beauty, solitude, recreation, adventure, and solidarity with other living species. The protection of these scarce attributes of nature involves a diversion of resources to unmeasured output; and since the depradations of extended use are the external effects of individual consumption and production, the government becomes our natural protective agent. The concerns that John Stuart Mill voiced so many years ago and the role for government that he sketched became at last a matter of practical politics.[44]

Egalitarianism too has come to mean something different from what Kuznets saw in the outlook underlying modern economic growth. Kuznets thought of it as equal freedom to use one's abilities and to follow one's bent in the pursuit of personal fulfillment – careers open to the talents, with rewards according to one's production. He saw the rise of average income as a source of ease that made the concomitant income inequality tolerable. Matters appear to have taken a different course. In the ease created by higher incomes, the need to tolerate inequalities in order to support the inducement to work, save, and venture came to seem less urgent. The result was our governmental systems of redistributive income transfers, intended not only to add to the capabilities of the less well endowed, but also to increase their incomes directly.

2. The predilection for safety, security, and equality has a wide and compelling field for exercise in the structural changes required by growth and in its inherently unstable character.

Growth based on technological progress means large, often rapid, shifts in the distribution of employment among industries and occupations. It means migration of people from one locality or region to another, from country to country, from countryside to city, and from city to suburb – and back again. The shifts occur partly by attraction, as growing employment openings induce people to change jobs and homes. But they also occur by compulsion, when changes in demand, labor-saving techniques, cheaper sources of supply, or novel products bankrupt or shrink old firms or farms and close down old jobs. The adjustments can sometimes be made slowly and without great pain as young people take up new jobs in new places while jobs in old industries and localities shrink by attrition. But not infrequently the shifts are more rapid and drastic. Then the generalized rewards of growth are paid for by costs imposed on a minority who must pack up and move, abandon old skills, homes, and connections, and try in mid-career to rebuild a damaged life.

Growth, therefore, means cost, conflict, and resistance. Translated to the political sphere, these are a temptation to protectionism, and for a long time this has been a governmental response to the costs of structural change. It still is. Gradually, however, governments began to experiment, not always successfully, with more constructive alternatives, the elements of an "active" labor-market policy. These have gradually built up from employment exchanges and unemployment insurance to programs for retraining, grants to aid relocation, and subsidized work programs.

Insofar as growth involved urbanization, it called forth the first large expansion in the role of government – that is, the expansion of municipal government to provide the services that make possible large concentrations of people. And insofar as modern economic growth separated people from the land and required intergenerational shifts in occupation and location, it weakened the family's capacity to carry out its traditional functions of rearing children, caring for the sick, and maintaining the old, and it impelled governments to provide public substitutes for these services.

3. The inherent instability of economic activity and employment in private enterprise economies in the course of growth has consequences similar to those of structural change. It imposes severe burdens on the victims of business contractions. Its irregularity and unpredictability make it hard for individuals themselves to provide against the risk, whereas the moral hazard involved makes private insurance impracticably expensive. Publicly provided unemployment compensation, therefore, has become a universal feature of Western economies. And when it appeared that governments might be able, by monetary and fiscal policies, to take practical steps to stabilize business, these functions were also assumed. How much has been

accomplished by fiscal and monetary management remains in dispute. It seems clear enough, however, that the very growth in the size of government has had the welcome by-product of making a considerable share of all employment and income less vulnerable to fluctuations in market demand. The system of transfer payments, adopted for other reasons, has similarly reduced the cyclical vulnerability of income flows. And the regulation of securities markets, the insurance of bank deposits, and the standby resources of central banks have rendered financial markets and institutions less susceptible to the panics and crises that were among the most potent sources of past depressions.

4. Governments striving for national growth are driven to assume investment functions, as well as some current service functions, that private enterprise cannot or is not impelled to take on. They were again foreseen and defined nearly 150 years ago by J. S. Mill, himself a great defender of limited government. Their hallmarks are huge size, distant and uncertain returns, externalities that promise larger social than private products, the involvement of governmental authority (e.g., eminent domain), and the creation of natural monopolies. Transport, communications, and water supply systems, education and research, and the public provision of statistical and other information are common and well-understood examples. There are questions about methods – whether regulated private power companies are more efficient instruments than publicly owned enterprises, or whether education vouchers should be used to permit families to make financially unbiased choices between public and private schools. The functions themselves, however, are not in serious dispute.

5. The spirit of individualism that supported the relatively unregulated economies of the nineteenth century with their limited role for government was the outlook of those restricted classes in whom the political power of the time was concentrated. It was less objectionable to people generally because such a large proportion of them still lived on the land in accustomed ways, because the costs associated with industrial occupations in a growing economy were still not widespread, and because the egalitarianism spawned by the French Revolution was still a novel force. All these conditions changed as technological development proceeded and incomes rose. In particular, the new egalitarian spirit, joined with an appreciation of the possibilities and requirements of technologically driven growth, made for an expansion of education. The movement to universal suffrage and the diffusion of political power followed. They formed the political base on which the elements of economic welfare that are not measured by per capita income and that are pursued through government could be built.

This statement, though true enough as far as it goes, is insufficient. It does not deal with the limitations of the political democracy of the West as a means of representing the desires and interests of people at large. There are two problems.

The first is that our system of representative government is an effective but still a very imperfect instrument for expressing the general interest. The reason is well known. It is the political activism and, therefore, power of minorities, who stand to gain from legislation in their special interest. This is matched by the corresponding passivity and political weakness of the generality of people, who are not stirred to resist the diffused and therefore relatively small costs that particular governmental actions impose on individuals. The result is that the various goals that government has been led to pursue, whether justifiable in some general sense or not, tend strongly to be pursued in a biased fashion and often by inappropriate methods. The bias is in favor of the limited groups who, in each case, stand to benefit; the bias is against the general population who, in almost all cases, bear the cost.

In the minds of some critics, this political flaw stands as virtually the sole stimulus or source of the rise of government. In their view, the distortions to which it leads are great enough to make state intervention in general a negative force. Laissez-faire with all its tolerance for market failures would be better, they contend, than the governmental failures that are the unavoidable concomitants of government action. And even those critics who concede that government action in some spheres, by some methods, and in some degree is desirable are clear about the direction that reform should now take. They would reduce the scope of government generally and drastically.

There is a second flaw. We often have only vague ideas about the needs to be met, what government can do to satisfy them, and the costs of trying to do so. Governmental action, therefore, has the character of a series of expensive experiments. Costly mistakes are inevitable, their lessons are hard to learn, and, when learned, are politically difficult to correct.

One is left, therefore, with a sense of great change in the social climate underlying technological progress and economic growth, and of great change in the economic institutions that the new social climate has tolerated and supported. The developed countries of the West now enter a new phase of modern economic growth with new views of what our societies should try to do and of what in the changed circumstances created by past growth, individual effort, and market-organized exchange can do. The much larger role that has been assigned to governments represents our attempts to pursue aspects of economic welfare that are, in one degree or another, beyond the competence of free-market action. They are functions that respond to needs that have been created by growth, or that people have become more sensitive to with the increase of incomes and the expansion of education, or that the diffusion of political power has permitted people to transform from an individual to a collective responsibility. They respond to desires or values that have no counterpart in the goods that form part of the measured national product, which means that measures of future growth, if they remain restricted to the national product accounts so far employed, will not reflect them.

Most, but not all, of the welfare goals now sought through government fall under these headings. They cover the attempts by education and income transfer to make a closer approach to equality of opportunity and income. They include the legislation and regulation that seeks to ensure the safety of consumers and workers and the protection of the common environment. They embrace the provision of capital in the form of infrastructure, education, and the advance of knowledge. They also cover the public assumption of a portion of the costs of growth in the form of compensation for losses suffered due to the obsolescence of jobs, skills, and financial capital and of localities themselves. And they include the new public responsibility for the care of children, the sick, and the old. They include, therefore, the obligations that used to be borne within families but that families are now less able to bear, or that, in view of the alternative afforded by government, they are less willing to bear. One should add, with reference to the care of the aged, that this is also a responsibility that, in view of the alternative afforded by government, older people are less willing to see borne by their families.

All this represents the positive side of the new social outlook and its institutionalization. The new functions assumed by government, however, obviously have their costs in the taxation, transfers, and regulation that alter the rewards, costs, and risks of work, saving, and investment in their many shapes and forms. These have not been successfully measured and presumably there is no common rule that applies to all countries and circumstances.[45] There remains a presumption, however, that they act to inhibit work, saving, investment, and enterprise and that the welfare goals we seek through government must be paid for by some slowdown of measured output growth itself.

This, however, is a tentative judgment and an incomplete one, and it must be qualified carefully. The judgment has to do with the effects of taxation that is raised to support income transfers and to the effects of regulation to promote safety and environmental protection. It is not a judgment about the net effects of taxation to support investments in human and physical capital that have the aim and effect of increasing our productive capabilities. It is a judgment, moreover, that neglects the contribution of transfers to the increase of output itself. Because the growth of output involves the obsolescence of industries and localities, there is a conflict between the interests of those whose jobs, skills, capital, and homes are threatened by change and the interests of the community at large, whose incomes are raised. The various developments that have brought women out of the home and the very movement of people in the course of economic growth have placed strains on the family and limited its ability to carry out its traditional functions. Conflict and resistance are, therefore, part of the growth process. And the transfer system, the public health care system, and other elements of government activity are the means by which we resolve conflicts or moderate the resistance that otherwise would operate to inhibit growth.

The considerations that qualify a judgment about the costs of the new roles assigned to government are matched by very practical considerations that qualify a judgment about its benefits. The private sector, guided by markets, can do more than it is generally thought it can do. And government agencies, without market guidance and exempt from market pressure, can do less. Faulty knowledge leads to faulty decisions about the functions of government, and the same is true about the methods that public agencies use to carry out the functions they are given. Moreover, our decisions about the scope and methods of government action, of what to try to do and how to try to do it, are distorted by the interest-group biases that are inherent in the democratic process. The welfare benefits we seek through government are reduced by faulty knowledge and political distortion.[46]

What lessons does this discussion teach? The sources of economic growth spring at bottom from a social climate, the outlook that expresses people's views about the relation, as Kuznets put it, between "man and the universe" and between one person and another. Kuznets thought that the outlook that supports modern economic growth could be epitomized in his triad – secularism, egalitarianism, and nationalism. It is easy to see, however, that these views have taken different forms in the countries that have entered the modern growth process. Indeed, they do not stretch far enough to capture the full spectrum of attitudes consistent with the advance and application of science. It is hard to see Japanese growth as the expression of an egalitarian spirit, but the Confucian ideals of hierarchy and obligation on which Japanese society is founded proved to be an effective alternative. The social climates characteristic of nations, moreover, are not stationary matters. The secularism and egalitarianism on which modern economic growth in Europe and North America was based have themselves changed in the course of the past century, very largely in response to conditions that growth itself has created.

The social climate of a time and place shape the political and economic institutions that are among the underlying determinants of technological progress and economic growth. Secularism and egalitarianism in their nineteenth century forms were consistent with the generally individualistic spirit of that century's economic and political policy. A change in the content and character of that outlook and the diffusion of political power that growth has brought have given us the mixed economies and welfare states of the contemporary West. They are a far cry from the unequivocal laissez-faire for which modern-day libertarians claim Adam Smith's authority. Yet they are not alien to the spirit of John Stuart Mill, the great individualist who was Smith's mid-nineteenth century exponent. The Western welfare state in its present form is still a relatively new regime. Its content, scope, and mode of operation remain in flux. After some experience with excesses of government, one now sees a notable revival of a more individualistic outlook. Yet the boundaries and methods of the mixed economy are not likely to change much unless our social outlook and the distribution of political power undergo a more radical alteration than is now in sight.

It is clear enough that the new regime expresses a great change in the character of the society in which people choose to live and of the economic satisfactions they seek. One can see that to some degree their goals have been met. We know little as yet about how much the new regime has already cost, and may in the future cost, in terms of the growth of measured national product, that is, of the older welfare goal that has not been abandoned. As befits a mixed economy, we can see that the new institutions and policies have mixed effects. To learn more about the effects of the new political regime, as well as about the effects of the evolving institutions through which the private sector operates, must be an important task of growth studies today.

Notes

1. Neoclassical economists resisted these contentions. They appealed to time-preference, a psychological trait, to defend the persistence of positive interest in a stationary state. They argued that there are an infinitude of possibilities to substitute capital for labor even where technology – the state of practical knowledge – is unchanging. If capital accumulates faster than population, the marginal productivity of capital would decline, but it would do so very very slowly. All this remains in contention. History provides no test.

2. The U.S. Bureau of Labor Statistics made many such estimates, and a notable series of studies were made in the National Bureau of Economic Research beginning in the later twenties and continuing in the thirties and forties.

3. Theirs were not, however, the earliest work of this sort. Priority belongs to Jan Tinbergen (1942), followed by George Stigler (1947), Jacob Schmookler (1952) and Solomon Fabricant (1954).

4. Representative publications are Denison (1974, 1985), Kendrick (1961, 1973) and Jorgenson, Gollop and Fraumeni (1987).

5. "Other" sources of changes in labor quality consist mainly of an allowance to offset the fact that when workers shifted from farming or from self-employment or small family businesses to wage and salary work in nonfarm occupations, their hours of work declined. Denison judged, however, that the effective work done per year was not reduced by such shifts.

6. It is perhaps a noteworthy matter, however, that in measures over a still longer period, from 1929 to 1981, which includes the Great Depression and World War II, Denison's estimate of adjusted total factor productivity growth was a distinctly less important source of the advance of labor productivity (52 percent) than it was in the postwar years themselves. And his Final Residual, the putative "advance of knowledge" accounted for only 22 percent of labor productivity growth.

7. To be quite accurate, the Final Residual also includes the effect of minor sources unmeasured and not classified under other rubrics in his account, as well as errors in the measured elements.

8. The relatively high depreciation rate on fast growing equipment is the main reason for the large contribution of Jorgenson's capital quality. Actually, however, his breakdown of investment reflects not only capital by durability, but also by industry and legal form of organization; correspondingly his rental prices also reflect sectoral differences in net rates of return and taxes, besides depreciation.

9. Compare the discussion in Chapter 4, below.

10. Denison's own discussion of the measurement of the scale effect is sophisticated and subtle (Denison 1974, pp. 71–6). In particular, he recognizes that the effect is likely to become weaker as the scale of output expands, so long as the state of technology is unchanging, and the benefits may be offset by problems of coordination and congestion. But he holds, sensibly enough, that the advance of knowledge opens new opportunities to use resources in more intense and specialized ways and so renews the potential benefits of enlarged scale. Needless to say, however, neither he nor anyone else can yet say how strong these opposing tendencies are.

11. Richard R. Nelson (1964) provides an illuminating discussion, and I make use of it.

12. Robert Solow (1962) devised the basic model. See also Nelson (1964).

13. Edward Denison (1964; 1967, pp. 144–50).

14. See Chapters 6 and 7 in this book.

15. In principle, the growth accounts, which neglect these considerations, are proceeding on the assumption that the elasticity of substitution of capital for labor is just unity and that technological progress is neutral. Repeated studies, however, suggest that the elasticity of capital-labor substitution is less than unity. In the absence of capital-using technological progress, capital's income share and the contribution of given rates of accumulation to output growth would be driven down as the capital stock rises relative to labor. In a different formulation, we depend on technical progress to augment the labor power of workers and so to prevent the ratio of capital to *effective* labor input from rising even as the quantity of capital increases relative to the number of workers.

During much of the nineteenth century, the impact of technological progress on the demand for capital in the United States more than offset the effect of the growth in its supply relative to labor. Capital's share in national product increased. In the present century, the capital-using character of technology has been weaker. Still, the gross earnings share of capital has not retreated much, and the rate of growth of capital's contribution to productivity growth has remained large (Abramovitz and David 1973).

16. One should be aware of an important, if technical, point. The connection traced in the text runs from the *level* of education to the pace of technological progress incorporated into production. The growth accounts, however, recognize, not the level, but rather the growth rate of the education level as a proximate source of output growth. In the framework of the accounts, the level of education itself is one of those underlying causes of increase in output with which the growth accounts do not pretend to deal. Strictly speaking that is true; and the distinction between the level and growth rate of education is clear when growth is measured over relatively short intervals of years. Over short intervals the growth that occurs does not affect the level substantially. When, however, we are concerned with the long periods that are the proper sphere of growth studies, differences in growth rates of schooling can have a significant affect on the level itself. And then it operates to influence the contemporaneous pace of technical progress.

17. One striking indication of this change is the figures for school enrollment. Between 1900 and 1960, the percentage ratio of students enrolled in secondary school to those in elementary school rose from 4.3 to 29.6; that for students in institutions of higher learning to those in elementary school rose from 1.4 to 9.9. Between 1910 and 1960, the average number of school years completed by men 25 years of age and more rose by nearly 50 percent.

18. Stephen J. Kline and Nathan Rosenberg provide a vivid and detailed exposition of the interdependence of technological advance and business experience.

19. Rosenberg (1974). See also David C. Mowery and Rosenberg, in Rosenberg (1982, Chap. 10); Nelson (1979); and Nelson, Peck, and Kalachek (1969, Chap. 2). Nelson, like Rosenberg, argues that knowledge relating to certain technologies is stronger than that to others, that strong knowledge reduces the cost and increases the potential yield of inventive effort, and that differences in background knowledge help explain differences among industries in research effort. He goes on, however, to relate such variation to the differential capacity of firms to translate the benefits of invention into private returns, a matter to which I turn in later pages.

20. Edwin Mansfield studied the costs of imitations and the times required to carry them out for 48 products in four industries. He found that, on average, the ratio of imitation cost to innovation cost was about 0.65, and ratio of imitation to innovation time was about 0.70. For about half the products, however, the cost ratio was either less than 0.4 or more than 0.9; and for about half the products again, the time ratio was either less than 0.4 or *greater than 1.0*. The cost ratio was 1.0 or higher for some one-seventh of the products. Imitation evidently is a costly procedure (Mansfield, Schwartz, and Wagner 1981; Mansfield 1986).

21. A special and important aspect of the relations between scale, innovation, and technological competition arises in the case of a technical system subject to "network externalities." These stem from the system's dependence on the technical compatibility of all its elements and on its capacity to yield larger benefits to each user as the scale of its use increases. The leading contemporary examples of such systems are the increasingly common computer hardware–software systems, local-area computer networks, electronic mail systems, cellular telephone networks, and many others. These, however, are only the latest in a series of great developments with similar characteristics: the railway, telegraph, telephone, radio, and still others.

The technical interrelatedness of such systems makes the profits of each component supplier depend on its compatibility with all the others. The system-scale aspect means that the system's utility to consumers, and therefore the demand for its product, increase with the number of its users. The second aspect presses each rival system sponsor to seek the cumulative returns of increasing market share by aggressive competition. The first means that the apparent success of any system drives component suppliers to design to the technical standards of the successful system – which enhances the cumulative benefits of market share, and the competition to achieve it, still more. The cumulative pressures of this dual competitive drive is towards de facto industry monopoly, or at least substantial industrial concentration, and towards universal adoption of the technical standards of the successful system. The first tendency raises obvious problems of market power. And the second raises problems as well, if it occurs either prematurely (that is, before the merits of possible alternatives have been explored) or mistakenly (that is, if the successful system's drive for customers triumphs over a technically superior alternative system). See Kindleberger (1983); David (1986b); and Arthur (1987).

22. Keith Pavitt (1985) has written a compact explanation of the location of R and D activity and its determinants. And Nelson (1988) has an especially useful discussion.

23. Technological rivalry and its interactive relation to industrial competition and technological investment and advance is a relatively new subject. Burton H. Klein (1977) and Nelson and Sidney Winter (1982) have made influential contributions, and my statement reflects the views they have developed at length.

24. Edwin Mansfield et al. (1971). In studies of a wide range of innovations, Mansfield and his associates found that the median private rate of return was 25 percent, whereas the median social rate was 56 percent. This applies, however, only to successful innovations. A truly representative sample might yield different results.

25. Dasgupta and David (1987) discuss this whole range of issues in an illuminating and subtle argument. See also Pavitt (1987).

26. My expression here is an adaptation of both the title and theme of Richard Nelson's essay, "Institutions Supporting Technical Change in Industry", *op. cit.*, 1988.

27. These are average rates of gross domestic product per hour for 16 industrialized countries as presented by Angus Maddison (1982, Table 5.3).

28. The Maddison figure for GDP per man-hour for 1973–84, comparable with his figures for 1870–1973, is just 1.0 percent (Maddison 1987, Table 1). The BLS growth rate for the productivity of all persons in the private business sector rises very little from 1984 to 1986.

29. The facts regarding convergence and an extended discussion are presented in "Catching Up, Forging Ahead, and Falling Behind," Chapter 7, in this volume. I am making no statement about a more general tendency to convergence. The evidence I cite refers to the presently industrialized countries and suffers from a certain sample selection bias, as my own paper just cited states. Indeed, the evidence suggests that the tendency may not extend much beyond the group of presently industrialized countries, although its precise range is still unclear (Baumol 1986, Baumol and Wolff forthcoming). My own paper below proposes an explanation for this limitation. On the matter of sample selection bias in the Baumol paper and my own (this volume, Chapter 7) see J. Bradford DeLong (forthcoming).

30. The growth potential of laggard countries may be strong for reasons other than the chance to replace obsolete capital with best-practice equipment. There is also a chance to adopt advanced management practice. Next, the rate of capital accumulation, including human capital accumulation, is supported by the high returns on using more advanced techniques. Finally, the expansion of manufacturing and distribution permits workers to transfer from low productivity jobs in farming or from self-employment in petty trade to higher-productivity wage and salary work in industry, commerce, and finance. See Chapter 7 in this volume.

31. Chapters 6 and 7 in this volume present an extended argument and evidence in support of these views.

32. The general question of the congruence between the directions of nineteenth century technological advance and American resources and market scale is also taken up in Chapter 7. My argument is based on Rosenberg, "Why in America" (1981), and Abramovitz and David (1973). See also Chandler (1977). A succession of authors have argued that, by comparison with Britain and continental Europe, not only were U.S. consumers tolerant of uniformity, but also their consumption habits were malleable. U.S. producers were relatively free to design products to make them suitable for low-cost, mass-production methods. The initiative in product design lay more largely in the hands of the producer. This not only made consumer goods industries more open to the economies of scale; it also conduced to uniformity of product and large-scale production in the capital goods industries. See Samuel Hollander (1965); Tibor Scitovsky (1960) and Nathan Rosenberg (1970).

33. The term itself was first proposed by Kazushi Ohkawa and Henry Rosovsky (1973, Chap. 9) in the course of a discussion of institutional development in Japan. Simon Kuznets (1968, Chap. 13) takes up the same subject in its bearing on the "relevance" of the existing stock of unexploited technology to less-advanced countries. Thorstein Veblen (1915) and Alexander Gerschenkron (1952) are both devoted to what I here call "social capability" in relation to "catching up."

34. There is indeed, a line of theoretical speculation that holds that institutional change not only consistently favors efficiency and increasing incomes and wealth but even that institutional adaptation occurs speedily (Posner 1977). Neither contention seems valid, and R.C.O. Matthews (1986) cites numerous instances of state action that operate to frustrate efficiency and growth, of which protectionist measures of every sort are the most familiar. Countries that succeed in industrializing, however, do respond positively to the demands of modern technology, and there may be a general tendency towards such response, if only in the very long run.

35. Veblen was an early exponent of the idea that institutions constrain countries in their exploitation of new technology, but that they adapt to technological opportunities and requirements (1915). Also see Ohkawa (1979). Douglas North (1981) presents a complex, systematic, and somewhat abstract general theory of institutional adaptation and makes some preliminary attempt to illustrate its historical application.

36. Wars and their aftermaths, however, are not uniformly favorable to an advance of social capability. The territorial, political and financial convulsions following World War I were on a scale commensurate with those after World War II, but they did not set off a comparable European growth boom. Indeed, the European response on that occasion was quite unfavorable to growth. Protectionism, not a common market, was then the answer to territorial change. Cartels more than innovation and competition were the instrument for industrial reorganization and the elimination of "excess" capacity. Trade unions became more powerful than they had been both in the market and in politics. The lessons learned from the failures of post-World War I policies were one reason why policies after World War II were more conducive to growth.

37. This was not a lead universally present in all fields of technology. Germany was a pioneer in chemicals and in electrical power production methods and made notable advances in the ferrous metals industry.

38. As already noted, there are recent developments that qualify this condition. Universities have begun to accept industrial, as well as government (defense), support that, in some cases, imposes restrictions on the early publication of results. And both

universities and their scientists have increasingly sought patents to control the commercial applications of their discoveries. This in turn has restricted the prompt dissemination of scientific findings.

39. On all these matters bearing on labor supply and the control of inflation, see Chapter 6 in this volume. See also Kindleberger (1967) and Ohkawa and Henry (1973), Chaps. 2 and 5.

40. Chapter 6 in this volume treats these matters at greater length.

41. "Not long after Queen Victoria came to the throne, Prussia was spending 600,000 pounds annually on public education. England in the same year . . . voted 30,000 pounds for education – and 70,000 pounds for building royal stables. That spirit still lingered up to the late sixties" (Garvin 1932, Vol. 1, p. 89).

In the United States, 72 percent of children aged 5 to 17 were enrolled in schools in 1880 (almost all in elementary schools). The British ratio (in government-supported schools) reached 69 percent in 1950. In that year two-thirds of U.S. children between 15 and 18 were enrolled in government-supported secondary schools; the British ratio barely exceeded ten percent (Abramovitz and Eliasberg, 1957, p. 15 and Table 14).

42. See Ruth Benedict (1974, first published 1946). Of course, the United States was far from being free of sex and age discrimination. Yet the restricted roles imposed on women were not so rigidly fixed as in Japan. As to age, there were marked differences. The Japanese revere age and accord it, not only respect, but rights of leadership in family, business, and public life. Old age in the United States imposes disabilities, which opens leading positions earlier to younger people. Which outlook is more functional is not entirely clear, and it may be that each works well in its own setting.

43. One prominent exception is the study by Alex Inkeles and David H. Smith (1974).

44. See above, p. 7. Here, at any rate, was one subject connected with economic growth to which the neoclassical writers attended. The externalities of production and consumption became a staple of the welfare theory of standard economics (Pigon 1932).

45. The effects of an incremental tax burden equal to one percent of net national product are not likely to be the same in a country where the level of taxation exceeds 50 percent of total income as in another where it is no more than 30 percent. Allowing for levels of taxation, effects are likely to differ among countries according to their states of tax morale, general respect for law, and the severity of law enforcement. The forms taken by taxation count as well. And similar considerations apply to the effects of transfers and regulatory measures.

46. Our troubles with the political process stem in part from our own impatience with it. We invest only reluctantly in the expensive task of recruiting and supporting a talented and devoted civil service. We find it hard to tolerate in government the costs of learning by experiment and failure that we find natural in the private sector. We have a penchant for illusory programs if they promise quick and easy solutions to complex and stubborn problems. Since in government as in the private sphere, learning is based on investment and experience, the present partial recoil from government carries the danger of reducing still more our limited capability for communal action.

References

Abegglen, James C., and George Stalk, Jr. *Kaisha, The Japanese Corporation*. New York: Basic Books, 1985.

Abramovitz, Moses. "Resource and Output Trends in the United States Since 1870." *Am. Econ. Rev., Papers and Proceedings* (May, 1956):5–23.

Abramovitz, Moses, and Paul A. David. "Economic Growth in America." *De Economist* 121 (No. 3, 1973):251–72.

Abramovitz, Moses, and Vera Eliasberg. *The Growth of Public Employment in Great Britain.* Princeton: Princeton University Press for the National Bureau of Economic Research, 1957.

Arrow, Kenneth J. "Economic Welfare and the Allocation of Resources for Invention." In *The Rate and Direction of Inventive Activity: Economic and Social Factors,* pp. 609–25. A Conference of the Universities National Bureau Committee for Economic Research and the Committee on Economic Growth of the Social Science Research Council. Princeton, N.J.: Princeton University Press, 1962a.

Arrow, Kenneth J. "The Economic Implications of Learning by Doing." *Rev. Econ. Studies* 29 (June, 1962):155–73.

Arthur, W. Brian. "Competing Technologies: An Overview." In *Technical Change and Economic Theory,* edited by G. Dosi, C. Freeman, R. Nelson, et al. International Federation of Institutes of Advanced Study, March, 1987.

Baumol, William. "Productivity Growth, Convergence and Welfare." Am. Econ. Rev. 76 (December, 1986):1072–85.

Baumol, William, and E. N. Wolff. "Is International Productivity Convergence Illusory"? Forthcoming.

Benedict, Ruth. *The Chrysanthemum and the Sword,* first published 1946. Paperback edition, New York and Scarborough, Ontario: New American Library, 1974.

Berg, Ivor. *Education and Jobs: The Great Training Robbery.* New York: Praeger, 1970.

Burns, Arthur F. *Production Trends in the United States Since 1870.* New York: National Bureau of Economic Research, 1934.

Chandler, Alfred. *The Visible Hand: The Managerial Revolution in American Business.* Cambridge, Mass.: Harvard University Press, 1977.

Dasgupta, Partha, and Paul A. David. "Information Disclosure and the Economics of Science and Technology." In *Arrow and the Ascent of Modern Economic Theory,* edited by George R. Feiwel. New York: New York University Press, 1987.

Dasgupta, Partha and Joseph Stiglitz. "Industrial Structure and the Nature of Innovative Activity," *Economic Journal* 90 (1980a):266–93.

"Uncertainty, Industrial Structure and the Speed of R and D," *Bell Journal of Economics* 11 (1980b):1–28.

David, Paul A. *Technical Choice, Innovation and Economic Growth.* New York: Cambridge University Press, 1975.

"Narrow Windows, Blind Giants and Angry Orphans." In *The Dynamics of Systems Rivalries and the Dilemmas of Technological Policy"* (1986a). Center for Economic Policy Research, Stanford University, March 1986.

"Technology Diffusion, Public Policy and Industrial Competiveness" (1986b). In Landau and Rosenberg (1986), p. 373–92.

DeLong, J. Bradford. "Have Productivity Levels Converged? A Note on William Baumol's 'Productivity Growth, Convergence and Welfare.' " *Am. Econ. Rev.,* forthcoming.

Denison, Edward F. "The Unimportance of the Embodied Question." *Am. Econ. Rev.* 54 (No. 2, Pt. 1, March, 1964):90–4.

Accounting for United States Economic Growth, 1929–1969. Washington, D.C.: The Brookings Institution, 1974.

Trends in American Economic Growth, 1929–1982. Washington, D.C.: The Brookings Institution, 1985.

Denison, Edward F., assisted by Jean-Pierre Pouillier. *Why Growth Rates Differ: Postwar*

Experience in Nine Western Countries. Washington, D.C.: The Brookings Institution, 1967.

Denison, Edward F., and William K. Chung. *How Japan's Economy Grew So Fast*. Washington, D.C.: The Brookings Institution, 1976.

Fabricant, Solomon. *Economic Progress and Economic Change*. National Bureau of Economic Research, Thirty-fourth Annual Report, May 1954, Part One.

Garvin, J. L. *The Life of Joseph Chamberlain*, vol. 1. London: Macmillan, 1932.

Gerschenkron, Alexander. "Economic Backwardness in Historical Perspective." In *The Progress of Underdeveloped Areas*, edited by Bert F. Hosilitz. Chicago: Chicago University Press, 1952.

Griliches, Zvi. "Hybrid Corn: An Exploration in the Economics of Technical Change." *Econometrica*, October, 1957.

Hollander, Samuel. *The Sources of Increased Efficiency*. Cambridge, Mass.: MIT Press, 1965.

Inkeles, Alex, and David H. Smith. *Becoming Modern: Individual Change in Six Developing Countries*. Cambridge, Mass.: Harvard University Press, 1974.

Jorgenson, Dale W., Frank M. Gollop and Barbara M. Fraumeni. *Productivity and U.S. Economic Growth*. Cambridge, Mass.: Harvard University Press, 1987.

Kendrick, John W. *Productivity Trends: Capital and Labor*. National Bureau of Economic Research Occasional Paper No. 53. Ann Arbor, Mich.: University Microfilms, 1956.

Productivity Trends in the United States. Princeton: Princeton University Press for the National Bureau of Economic Research, 1961.

Postwar Productivity Trends in the United States, 1948–1969. New York: National Bureau of Economic Research, 1973.

Kindleberger, Charles F. *Europe's Postwar Growth: The Role of Labor Supply*. Cambridge, Mass.: Harvard University Press, 1967.

"Standards as Public, Collective and Private Goods." *Kyklos* 36 (Fasc. 3, 1983):377–96.

Klein, Burton H. *Dynamic Economics*. Cambridge, Mass.: Harvard University Press, 1977.

Kline, Stephen J., and Nathan Rosenberg. "An Overview of Innovation." In Landau and Rosenberg (1986), pp. 275–305.

Kuznets, Simon. *Secular Movements in Production and Prices*. Boston and New York: Houghton Mifflin Co., 1930.

Modern Economic Growth: Rate, Structure and Spread. New Haven and London: Yale University Press, 1966.

"Notes on Japan's Economic Growth." In *Economic Growth: The Japanese Experience Since the Maiji Era*. Homewood, Ill.: Richard D. Irwin, 1968.

Landau, Ralph, and Nathan Rosenberg, eds. *The Positive Sum Strategy*. Washington, D.C.: National Academy Press, 1986.

Langrish, J., M. Gibbons, W. G. Evans, and F. R. Jevons. *Wealth from Knowledge*. New York: Halstead/John Wiley, 1972.

Maddison, Angus. *Phases of Capitalist Development*. Oxford: Oxford University Press, 1982.

"Growth and Slowdown in Advanced Capitalist Economies." *Jour. Econ. Lit.* 25 (No. 2, June 1987):649–98.

Mansfield, Edwin. "Microeconomics of Technological Innovation." In Landau and Rosenberg (1986), p. 313.

Mansfield, Edwin, J. Rapoport, J. Schee, S. Wagner, and M. Hamburger. *Research and Innovation in a Modern Corporation*. New York: W. W. Norton, 1971.

Mansfield, Edwin, M. Schwartz, and S. Wagner. "Imitation Costs and Patents: An Empirical Study." *Econ Jour.*, 1981.

Matthews, R.C.O. "The Economics of Institutions and the Sources of Growth." *Econ. Jour.* 96 (December, 1986):903–18.

Mill, John Stuart. *Principles of Political Economy*, edited by Sir W. J. Ashley (1848). London: Longmans, Green and Co., 1929.

Mowery, David. *The Emergence and Growth of Industrial Research in American Manufacturing, 1888–1945*. Stanford University, Ph.D. dissertation, 1981.

Mowery, David C., and Nathan Rosenberg. "The Influence of Market Demand Upon Innovation: A critical review of some recent empirical studies." In N. Rosenberg, *Inside the Black Box: Technology and Economics*, ch. 10. Cambridge: Cambridge University Press, 1982.

Myers, S., and D. G. Marquis. *Successful Industrial Innovation*. Washington, D.C.: National Science Foundation, 1969.

Nelson, Richard R. "Aggregate Production Functions and Medium-Range Growth Projections." *Am. Econ. Rev.* 54 (No. 5, September, 1964):575–606.

  "R and D, Knowledge, and Externalities: An approach to the puzzle of disparate productivity growth rates among manufacturing industries." In *Natural Resources*, edited by Christopher Bliss and M. Boserup. *Proceedings of the Fifth World Congress of the International Economic Association*, vol. 3, pp. 146–61. New York: St. Martin's Press, 1980.

  "Institutions Supporting Technical Change in the United States." In *Technical Change and Economic Theory*, edited by Giovanni Dosi, Christopher Freeman, Richard Nelson, Gerald Silverberg, and Luc Soete. Irvington, NY.: Columbia University Press, 1988.

Nelson, Richard R., M. J. Peck, and E. D. Kalachek. *Technology, Economic Growth and Public Policy*. Washington, D.C.: The Brookings Institution, 1969.

Nelson, Richard R., and Edmund Phelps. "Investment in Humans, Technological Diffusion and Economic Growth." *Am. Econ. Rev.* 56 (No. 2, May, 1966):69–75.

Nelson, Richard R., and Sidney G. Winter. *An Evolutionary Theory of Economic Change*. Cambridge, Mass., and London: Harvard University Press, 1982.

Norman, E. Herbert. *Japan's Emergence as a Modern State*. New York: Institute of Pacific Relations, 1940.

North, Douglass C. *Structure and Change in Economic History*. New York and London: W. W. Norton, 1981.

Ohkawa, Kazushi. "Comment." In *Economic Growth and Resources*, edited by Edmond Malinvaud. Proceedings of the Fifth World Congress of the International Economic Association, vol. 1, pp. 31–34. London: Macmillan, 1979.

Ohkawa, Kazushi, and Henry Rosovsky. *Japanese Economic Growth*. Stanford, Cal.: Stanford University Press; and London: Oxford University Press, 1973.

Olson, Mancur. *The Rise and Fall of Nations: Economic Growth, Stagflation and Social Rigidities*. New Haven, Conn.: Yale University Press, 1982.

Pavitt, Keith L. R. "Technology Transfer Among the Industrially Advanced Countries." In *International Technology Transfer*, edited by Nathan Rosenberg and Claudio Frischtak, pp. 3–23. New York: Praeger, 1985.

Pavitt, Keith L. R. "On the Nature of Technology." Social Science Policy Research Unit, University of Sussex, 23 June, 1987.

Pigou, A. C. *The Economics of Welfare*. 4th ed. London: Macmillan, 1932.

Posner, R. A. *Economic Analysis of Law*. 2nd ed. Boston: Little, Brown, 1977.

Rosenberg, Nathan. "Economic Development and the Transfer of Technology: Some historical perspectives." *Technology and Culture* (October, 1970):558–63.

"Science, Invention and Economic Growth." *Econ. Jour.* 84 (No. 333, March, 1974):90–108.

"Why in America?" In *Yankee Enterprise: The Rise of the American System of Manufactures*, edited by Otto Mayr and Robert Post. Washington, D.C., 1981.

"Learning by Using." In *Inside the Black Box: Technology and Economics*, Chapter 6. New York: Cambridge University Press, 1982.

"Commercial Exploitation of Science by American Industry." In *The Uneasy Alliance: Managing the Productivity–Technology Dilemma*, edited by Kim Clark et al. Boston: Harvard Business School Press, 1985.

Schmookler, Jacob. *Invention and Economic Growth*. Cambridge, Mass.: Harvard University Press, 1966.

"The changing efficiency of the American economy, 1869–1938." *Rev. Econ. Statistics* 34 (1952):214–31.

Schumpeter, Joseph A. *The Theory of Economic Development* (1911). Translated by Redvers Opie. Cambridge, Mass.: Harvard University Press, 1934. Paperback edition, New York: Oxford University Press, 1961.

Capitalism, Socialism and Democracy. New York: Harper and Bros., 1942. 3rd ed. Harper and Row, 1950.

Scitovsky, Tibor. "International Trade and Economic Integration as a Means of Overcoming the Disadvantages of a Small Nation." In *Economic Consequences of the Size of Nations*, edited by E. A. G. Robinson. St. Martins Press, 1960.

Solow, Robert. "Technical change and the aggregate production function." *Rev. Econ. Statistics* (August, 1957):312–320.

"Technical Progress, Capital Formation, and Economic Growth." *Am. Econ. Rev. Papers and Proceedings* 52 (No. 2, May, 1962).

Stigler, George S. *Trends in Output and Employment*. New York: National Bureau of Economic Research, 1947.

Tinbergen, Jan. "Zur Theorie der langfristigen Wirtschaftsentwicklung." *Weltwirtschaftliches Archiv*, 55, (No. 3, 1942).

U.S. Department of Labor, Bureau of Labor Statistics. "Trends in Multifactor Productivity, 1948–81." Bulletin 2178, September 1983. Washington, D.C.: Author.

Veblen, Thorstein. *Imperial Germany and the Industrial Revolution*. New York: Kelley, (1915), 1964.

Williamson, Oliver E. *The Economic Institutions of Capitalism*. New York: The Free Press, 1985.

Young, Allyn A. "Increasing Returns and Economic Progress." *Econ. Jour.* 38 (No. 152, December 1928):527–40.

2

Economics of growth

Unlike most of the topics treated in this and in the first volume of the *Survey*,* the problem of economic growth lacks any organized and generally known body of doctrine whose recent development might furnish the subject of this essay. In spite of a continuing interest which began very early, the question has remained on the periphery of economics. But having said so much one must add that some individuals and schools of the nineteenth and the early twentieth centuries gave some aspects of the problem close attention. Adam Smith, Ricardo, and J. S. Mill analyzed the effects of different kinds of progress on the distribution of incomes and speculated about the emergence of a stationary state. The German historians, the American institutionalists, and Marx and his followers studied the appearance and possible decline of capitalist institutions. Weber, Tawney, Veblen, Mitchell and, more recently, Schumpeter explained the development of the mental attitudes that fostered the growth of science and its application to industry. The theory of capital and saving, as developed by the classical and neoclassical economists, has obvious relevance to a theory of long-term economic change, and so has all the work on population theory and the long-run supply curve of labor. Orthodox economics has also furnished us with theories of diminishing and increasing returns that clearly have their place in any general explanation of economic growth. Meanwhile, economic history generally, and statistical work on secular trends in particular, has furnished some of the information so badly needed. Yet it is clear that these various strands of work are not yet organized into a useful hypothesis providing a consistent explanation of the different rates of growth characterizing given economies in different periods, different contem-

*Reprinted by permission from *A Survey of Contemporary Economics*, ed. by Bernard F. Haley, published for the American Economic Association. Homewood, Ill.: Richard D. Irwin, Inc., 1952, pp. 132–78.

80

poraneous economies with similar institutional framework, or economies with different institutions at the same or different times. Nor
have we gone far in developing detailed models of the process of
growth.

Modern work on the economics of growth has been fragmentary. It
deals with many varied questions. The studies have often been undertaken under the stimulus of other interests and, while their general
relevance to economic growth is clear, their precise significance has
not been developed. Keynesian stagnation theory is an example. It is
designed to explain chronic unemployment. Presumably the forces it
studies are significant for long-term growth, but their connection with
secular trends in output is not immediately apparent. Other work
concerns changes in the forms or patterns of economic life that accompany growth, but again the role that these changing patterns play in
furthering or retarding the pace of economic advance is not clear. A
good example is the hypothesis advanced by Colin Clark and others
about the changing industrial composition of employment which accompanies economic development.

These characteristics of contemporary studies raise a serious problem for this essay. To attempt to deal with current literature as one
finds it would imply a review of numerous studies each of which
bears – often in obscure fashion – only on some special aspect of the
problem. Space would prohibit any comprehensive treatment of so
many heterogeneous topics and, at the same time, the general outlines of the theory of growth would not be developed. To meet this
difficulty, the present writer has tried to work on a different plan,
namely, to define the boundaries and describe the general content of
the economics of growth and to notice current work as it bears on the
development of this outline. This plan has required rather more extensive attention to older literature and rather less attention to current
work than the purpose of this volume would normally make desirable. But the theory of growth is an underdeveloped area in economics. It is more important to map the chief features of the country than
to concentrate on detailed descriptions of many small quandrants
which together would cover but a fraction of the terrain.

Even within this general plan, however, satisfactory treatment of
the entire subject proved impossible within the space available. In
consequence, the essay has been divided into three parts. Part I presents an extremely condensed description of the general content of the
economics of growth with occasional references to relevant literature.
Part II presents a fairly full treatment of one aspect of the subject,
namely, capital formation and its relation to economic growth. Part III
contains some brief remarks about problems of research.

I. The scope and content of the economics of growth

A. Character of growth theory

The theory of economic growth has to do with the pace of sustained change in the output of economic communities measured in the aggregate, or per head of the population, or per member of the labor force, the particular variant depending on the problem in view.[1] The crucial aspects of this definition are its references to output and to sustained or long-term change. Our interest in economic growth stems from, and is relevant to, our interest in long-term changes in economic welfare. But the two subjects are not equivalent.[2]

Theories of economic growth can be constructed at various levels, all of which are useful, but which become increasingly significant the more complex and far-reaching the set of factors brought under active study. This can be illustrated if we begin with the conventional statement that the level of output at any given time is determined by the supply of resources (labor, "land," capital), the state of the arts, the organization of markets, the legal framework of economic life, and the psychological attributes of the population. Call these the *immediate determinants* of output. We can then distinguish the following levels of analysis:

Level 1. Assume that all except some one of the immediate determinants remain unchanged and examine the effects on output of some specified secular changes in the variable factor.

Level 2. Assume that two or more of the determinants are subject to secular changes of specified kinds and examine the effects on output, the other factors being assumed constant.[3] This can be varied and extended up to the point at which all determinants are assumed to change in ways specified by assumption.

Level 3. Treat the immediate determinants as variables whose movements are to be explained rather than assumed. The immediate determinants, usually treated as data by economists, now become true dependent variables, and the investigation necessarily reaches into regions normally assigned to other disciplines, particularly the other social sciences.

Level 4. Theories on the first two levels are unsatisfactory to explain the observed growth of economic communities because they do not deal with the causes of the immediate determinants. The third level is unsatisfactory because it does not deal with the significance of changes in these factors. The fourth level is necessarily a combination of the first three and brings us to the point at which we obtain theories of observed changes in output at a satisfactory level of understanding.

Hypotheses at this level would presumably be able to explain observed differences in rates of growth among communities and also
differences in the growth of a single community over time. These
theories can also be more or less general. They may limit themselves
to explaining differences between countries which differ markedly in
only one particular, say those between "old" and "new" countries
which may be distinguished chiefly by the ratios of land and capital
per head of the population. Or the theories may go further and try to
explain more complex cases, say differences between "progressive"
and "backward" areas which differ partly in terms of factor supply
and partly in terms of institutional and social organization.[4] Or conceivably the theories might be completely general and try to grapple
with observed differences among all countries. It goes without saying
that the fewer the respects in which the communities resemble each
other, the more difficult the task.

B. Central questions in the theory of growth

While work on the economics of growth can be usefully done
on all the levels suggested above, the content of the problem can be
envisaged most easily by centering attention initially on the factors
identified above as the immediate determinants of the level of output.
The theory of growth is then a matter of explaining long-term changes
in these factors, on the one side, and the influence of such changes
upon output on the other.[5]

1. *The supplies of the factors.* The explanation of changes in factor
supply is usually treated in connection with their long-term supply
schedules. So far as concerns labor, the determinants are extremely
complex. They include both the causes of population growth and the
causes of change in the proportion of the population included in the
labor force. The latter turns on numerous factors, including the age
composition of the population, the level of income, the degree of
urbanization and the character of family organization in its bearing on
family responsibility for the young, the aged, and the infirm. Labor
force is also influenced by social attitudes toward work by women,
children, and miniority groups, by educational requirements, standards, and opportunities, and by various kinds of government intervention, including the regulation of hours and working conditions,
taxation, and social security arrangements. Finally, there is the large
subject of union organization.[6]

Changes in the supply of land are often supposed to be nonexistent by definition; apparent changes are attributed to some form of
human action – to invention and increase of knowledge generally, to
enterprise, or to changes in the composition of demand – and are,

therefore, classified under capital accumulation (or consumption). Even in this restricted view, however, there are real changes in the land supply of a community to be taken into account. These may result from governmental acts like conquest, seizure, or purchase or from regulations reserving land for conservation or opening a public domain to exploitation. There may also be changes in the supply of privately held land put to productive use. These may occur if there are changes in the value schemes of land owners with respect to the use of their land for commercial *versus* noncommericial use. There may be changes in the distribution of land among social classes as a result of land reform laws or otherwise, and this may affect land use significantly. Finally, land use may be affected by taxation or by government regulation.

More broadly conceived, the effective supply of land is no mere matter of area, but a value compounded of fertility, mineral content, climate, topography, and all the factors influencing accessibility. It is, therefore, highly sensitive to technological progress which affects the economic significance of all these qualities. It is a matter of choice whether the effects of technology on the supply of land are treated as an aspect of technological progress or of changing land supply. In either event, the theoretical work which grapples with the question is the recently developed dynamic location theory. Starting from the static theory of location, with its analysis of the influence of transport costs, the newer work goes on to consider the effect of technological change of specified kinds upon the spatial distribution of new activity and the spatial redistribution of old. The upshot is a body of ideas which helps to make clear the contribution of natural resources and location to the relative rates of progress of economic communities. A good example is the work of W. H. Dean, Jr.[7] who extends the older theory of location to explain a tendency observed during the last two centuries for centers of economic activity to shift from surplus food areas to places rich in sources of power and industrial raw materials.

The forces affecting the supply of capital is the subject of the bulk of the present essay, and the scope of the subject is indicated in Part II.

As to the influence of changes in factor supply on economic growth, this raises two questions. The first is the process by which changes in supply are transformed into changes in the quantities of the factors actually employed. Traditional economic theory reduced this to a matter of suitable changes in relative prices which were assumed to bring into employment as much of each factor as was satisfied by the marginal rate of real return it could produce. Keynesian theory, however, has argued that the process may be frustrated indefinitely either by price rigidities, by adverse expectations, or by inability of workers to affect their real wage rates.[8] More recent writings have revealed the theoretical adequacy of relative price changes to produce full employment, but have stressed the probable sluggishness of the process.[9] Keynesian and post-Keynesian writing has, therefore, tended to favor mild price inflation as a condition facilitating the absorption of additional factor supplies. Realistic studies of the process of factor absorption are still lacking.

The second question concerns the effects of changes in the quantities of the factors actually employed. This is nothing but the hoary subject of the laws of return. Nothing need be said about it here, so far as the theory of the subject is concerned, but it is to be noted that empirical work has not begun and that more is needed.[10]

2. *Psychological and other qualitative attributes of the population.* In part, these attributes have already been raised implicitly under other headings, for example, under the determinants of labor supply. In general, they are involved in and underlie almost every economic relation. More directly than do other topics in this outline, they indicate the extent to which an understanding of economic growth rests on research outside the usual fields of economic investigation. The range of topics may be suggested by illustration.

First, the effective supply of labor is a matter not only of the numbers but also of the productivity of the labor force so far as that turns on the qualities of the workers themselves. And productivity depends on strength and health,[11] and on the social valuation assigned to income, work, and reliability. It is raised by a tradition of familiarity with mechanical operations and by habituation to cooperative activity.[12] Changes in productivity affect the growth of output directly and, by influencing its level, also help determine the volume of surplus income and, therefore, the rate of capital formation.

A second set of social-psychological traits governs the pace at which new techniques are adopted and exploited. These are the traits of mobility, adaptability, and tolerance for change. They have often been associated with environmental factors controlling exposure to new experiences like access to the sea, with recent historical experience like the influence of the frontier in new countries or of a heterogeneous population built up by immigration,[13] and with more strictly cultural factors in which religion often figures prominently.[14]

The acceptability of the new is a question of the psychic traits of the population at large. The introduction of the new, however, depends heavily on the efforts of a few who must possess a more active disposition. Enterprise, or leadership, directed to industry, seems to be the key phrase. Its sources are explored at some length in Part II.

Besides the traits that underlie a community's effectiveness as producer, and as innovator and exploiter of change, its traits as a consuming group affect growth in numerous ways. There is first the degree of its tolerance for standardized consumption in its bearing on the economics of scale and the scope for the use of capital equipment. From the same point of view, there is the relation between changes in income levels and the kind of goods demanded. Engel's Law and similar correlations between income per capita and the composition of demand connect with our problem at this point. Next, there is the fact that leisure is a form of consumption (as well as a condition for the enjoyment of goods), and the demand for leisure affects production in the most direct fashion. Again, emulation and competition in consumption influence the demand for income and, therefore, the effort devoted to production and the risks that people will accept in industry. Consumption, further, may be a type that develops the strength, skills, and efficiency of a people, or it may be dissipative and deteriorating in its effects. Finally, there is consumption as the opponent of saving.

3. *Industrial, commercial and financial organization.* Forms of organization affect growth in at least three important ways: through their influence on investment and improvement, on saving, and on finance. As to investment and improvement, there is, first, the scale and internal organization of firms which may favor or discourage the selection of enterprising leaders,[15] which may or may not provide them with scope and staff aid appropriate to their talents, and which may facilitate or hamper the efficient exercise of initiative at all levels.[16] There is, secondly, the question of market organization, the relation between monopoly power and the incentives to invest capital and to introduce new methods and products. Thirdly, there is the extent and character of labor organization in its bearing on capital formation and innovation.[17]

Organization influences saving and, therefore, capital formation through the influence of monopoly power on the distribution of income between wage earners and profit makers.[18] It also makes itself felt because of the importance of retained earnings as a source of savings when business is organized in large corporations.[19] Organization, finally, affects the types of assets available to potential savers and, therefore, the incentive to save. The essential thing, in this connection, is that the variety of modern business and financial organizations produces many kinds of assets in the form of securities the ownership of which, in different degrees, involves little or no supervision, limits risk, provides liquidity, satisfies other needs of savers besides safety and return (for example, insurance, annuities), and still furnishes a significant yield.

Between opportunities to invest and the supply of saving lie the functions of the financial sector. Upon the efficiency and variety of financial organization depends the cheapness with which business is able to raise capital and the rate of real return actually obtainable by savers. It, therefore, plays a vital role in capital formation in ways further developed in Part II.

4. *The legal and political framework of economic life.* This is itself a huge subject and it would be impossible within a page or two to catalogue the many ways in which it probably bears on growth, let alone to discuss its bearing. The topics mentioned below can only be illustrative.

    a. The laws of property and contract: The essential questions here are: What may a man do with his property; what must he do by virtue of his property? What may others do to his property? In what activities may he engage? What agreements may he make? What claims can be enforced, and to what extent? With specific reference to the factors determining growth, this heading covers such matters as: (1) laws affecting the establishment and exploitation of monopolies; (2) laws controlling land development: zoning, exploitation and conservation of minerals and forests, water rights; (3) debts and bankruptcy.

    b. Economic associations: the permitted areas of operation, powers, privileges and limitations of corporations, banks, labor unions, co-operatives, securities exchanges, investment trusts, etc.

    c. Indirect regulation of specific activities: the use of taxes, tariffs, subsidies, fees, etc. to discourage certain activities and to encourage others.

    d. Indirect regulation of general economic activity: the use of taxes and the laws of inheritance to control the distribution of income and wealth.

    e. Direct provision of economic facilities by public action: it is well known that private action will not exploit opportunities to increase output in certain classes of cases, or at least will not exploit such opportunities fully. The principal cases are those in which most or all of the benefits yielded by investment are difficult to appropriate and sell privately (e.g. flood control, education), those in which universal or nearly universal use is required if benefit is to be obtained (e.g. many public health facilities and controls), and those in which initial cost is heavy and returns long deferred and uncertain (e.g. railroads, harbor and power developments). These investment opportunities are among the most important open to a community; and its progress, therefore, depends on the extent to which it provides for such exploitations by direct public action.

5. *Discovery and exploitation of knowledge.* While it is clear enough in a general way how technical improvement leads to increases in output, and while we may be confident that, directly and indirectly, a very large share, if not the bulk, of the increase in output is to be

attributed to advances in knowledge, measurement of the relation between changes in the stock of knowledge and the pace of economic growth has so far proved impossible. The chief difficulty is that no useful measures of the stock of knowledge or its changes have yet been contrived. And while interesting new attempts to measure production functions and their changes are now in progress, these have yet to come to fruition.[20] These difficulties of measurement will certainly hinder the process of increasing our understanding not only of the effects of technological advance on growth, but also of the factors making for an increase in knowledge and its economic application.

The general subject of technological change in its bearing on output growth requires study on at least two main levels: the discovery of knowledge, and its exploitation. The latter stages of the process of discovery interlace closely with the early stages of the process of commercial exploitation. This was less true some decades ago when the independent inventor still flourished and engineering was still in its infancy as a profession. But with the development of the industrial research departments of corporations, and of industry- and government-sponsored research, almost all engineering work and a considerable portion of applied scientific work is undertaken only in conjunction with the deliberate entrepreneurial decision that some new product or process can, in fact, be developed and that the various business problems involved – finance, labor, distribution – can also be satisfactorily overcome.[21]

The difficulties of commercial exploitation are at their height when a product is utterly new. This is Schumpeter's problem of innovation. After its first introduction there ensues a process of diffusion in which the new product or process is substituted for the old with increasing facility as experience is gained and knowledge of the new art becomes widespread. But there is presumably no sharp break. Innovation, however bold and pathbreaking, draws on some past experience, and there is no investment utterly devoid of novel elements. So enterprise, as well as routine calculation of differential advantages, is involved at all levels, though in different degree.

We are interested in the influences that determine the pace of all these processes, the advance of fundamental knowledge, the translation of fundamental knowledge into commercial applications, and the diffusion of such applications.[22] The factors involved include cultural characteristics like the influence of rationality as a thought pattern, the status of science as an occupation, the place of material progress as a social and individual goal, the importance of pecuniary standards, especially in their bearing on the size, quality, and vigor of the entrepreneurial class, the mobility of the population among occupations and places, and its tolerance for novel methods and products.

Organizational and institutional arrangements form a second group of causes. These include the quantity and kind of government support for education, especially scientific education, and for research; the legal protections afforded to the interests of inventors through patent systems and otherwise; and the effects of taxes as incentives and disincentives to investment in the discovery and application of technology. They also include the organization and size of firms and the character of competition insofar as these affect the funds devoted by private firms to research and development and the incentives to introduce and exploit new methods and products. Union controls are still another instutional factor of importance.

Finally, the outcome is influenced by more narrowly economic causes. The size of the market is important since it limits the field of application of a discovery. The abundance of saving and the cheapness of finance, particularly for new firms, influence the pace of exploitation and, therefore, the pressure that is brought to bear on established firms to be technically progressive. The character and quantity of resources affects the relative economy of capital-using, land-using, and labor-using methods and, therefore, the direction if not the pace of technical advance. And the amount of such capital and its degree of obsolescence clearly influence the profitability of exploiting new goods and ways of making them.

This list of factors is only illustrative of the range of questions that are raised. It seems plausible to think that cultural factors will be most significant at the level of fundamental discovery and that the more narrowly economic causes become increasingly dominant as we approach the level of routine exploitation. But much more research will be needed before it will be possible to develop a trustworthy list of conditioning factors, to say nothing of assigning them proper weights at the various stages of the process of scientific discovery and application.

It is obvious that the various topics identified above as involved in the economics of growth are interrelated in a most complex fashion, which is only inadequately suggested by the discussion itself. But further illustration of the extent and importance of the interconnectedness of the several parts of the subject is furnished by Part II of the present paper, which deals with capital formation in its bearing on economic growth.

C. Mechanism and patterns of growth

A serious limitation of the discussion above is that it directs attention to the basic determinants of growth, but it leaves in the background or neglects entirely many portions of the subject concerned with the mechanism through which the basic factors operate and with the economic forms that growth takes. Again, there is space only to mention a very few topics.

1. *Business fluctuations and economic growth.* Many scholars, notably Schumpeter,[23] have contended that business fluctuations with several distinctive periods are a necessary concomitant of growth. Their argument stresses either the effects of the uneven action of growth factors or the tendency of capitalist economies to magnify and transform slight changes in rates of growth into substantial expansions and contractions of activity. In addition to further confirmation of these ideas, there remains questions about the price in terms of growth which these fluctuations exact and about the probable influence of economic stabilization upon growth.

2. *Growth in aggregate production and the changing composition of output.* This reveals itself in many ways. Colin Clark has emphasized the tendency for employment to shift from "primary" to "secondary" to "tertiary" industries as an economy grows.[24] Arthur F. Burns has established a marked tendency toward retardation in the growth of individual industries while progress in total output is unabated.[25] Composition of output must be changing. Folke Hilgerdt found that the character of the goods sold in foreign trade by advanced countries tended to exhibit increasing refinement and elaboration as they and their trading partners advanced.[26] In part, these pehnomena are to be attributed to the well-known tendency for the composition of consumer demand to shift as per capita income rises.[27] In part they are presumably connected with the introduction of new products and processes and their competition with the old. As for the influence of these changes in output structure on rates of growth, this connects on one side with the significance of technological improvement, for such improvement is hardly conceivable without economies in the use of some old materials, combined with more widespread consumption of other old materials and with the introduction of some new ones. From another point of view, the changing patterns bear on incentives to effort and investment. If the composition of output could not change, or if new products were not introduced, the desire for additional consumption and income and, therefore, the stimulus to economic activity would be weaker.

3. *Trends in saving-income ratios in their relation to growth.* The *a priori* expectation that the proportion of aggregate income saved would tend to increase as per capita incomes rose has been belied by observation. Relative constancy or decline in the ratio of saving to income seems to be the long-run rule for the few countries for which data are available. This tendency and the possible circumstances back of it will be further discussed.[28] It is clear that any such circumstances as tend

to stimulate consumption affect the need for income and, therefore, the incentives to work, save and invest. The trend of consumption also influences opportunities for investment and bears on the argument that as communities become richer they tend to stagnate because of a surfeit of saving.

These and similar relations are clearly part and parcel of the mechanism of economic growth conceived of as a process of cumulative change. They are relations which would hardly be discovered in the absence of deliberate observation, and our understanding of the determinants of growth will surely be extended by further study along these lines. Moreover, the multiplication and verification of such relations probably furnish the most fruitful opportunities for empirical work on growth in the immediate future.

II. Capital formation as a cause of economic growth

This part is an attempt to suggest the scope and present state of the theory of economic growth by more intensive treatment of a single growth factor, capital formation. It is probably safe to say that only the discovery and exploitation of new knowledge rivals capital formation as a cause of economic progress. The two factors are indeed closely related. Knowledge is often characterized as the most important element in the community's stock of capital. And, insofar as new applied knowledge results from the deliberate devotion of resources to its discovery and use, the stock of knowledge is increased by a process identical with that which produces an increase in the stock of material equipment. Conversely, the actual exploitation of new knowledge virtually always involves some gross innvestment and, it seems probable, usually requires some net addition to the stock of capital. To some, this has justified a virtual merger of the two factors. In this essay, however, we distinguish them by making capital formation refer only to quantitative changes in the stock of instruments of production. We discuss the subject under four heads. The first three are considered from the point of view of their bearing on the level of capital formation at a given time. They are: first, saving; second, the productivity of capital; and third, the functions of finance. The fourth topic is the progress of capital formation over time.

The treatment of these subjects is limited to the conditions of countries in which governmental direction of activity is not the dominant feature of economic organization. It is especially relevant, therefore, to capitalistic economies at higher or lower levels of development, but not to Soviet Russia or to other countries in which major sectors of economic life have been subjected to control by governmental decision.

A. The role of saving

1. *The influence of saving on capital formation.* In the neoclassical view, an increase in the supply of saving stimulates capital accumulation by causing the rate of interest to fall. Full employment being the rule, moreover, the willingness to save leads to an effective release of scarce resources without which the production of capital goods could not take place. It follows that capital formation at any given time varies directly with the ability and willingness to save. An increase in thrift was taken to be a universally reliable prescription for progress.

The nub of this argument is the idea that consuming and investing are exhaustive alternative uses of income. The nub of the modern view is the Keynesian idea that there is a third way to dispose of income, namely, hoarding (or adding to cash balances, or increasing liquidity). But if hoarding is a third means of disposing of income, it is no longer clear that an increase in the supply of saving will be beneficial to investment. If funds are diverted from consumption, they may be hoarded rather than invested. And conversely, since, in Keynes' view, there may be chronic unemployment, the resources exist for raising the level of capital formation without trenching further on consumption.

The logic of Keynes' view has been ably exposed by J. R. Hicks.[29] The demand for money to be hoarded (Keynes' "speculative demand") varies with the rate of interest. There is a high range of interest rates in which the speculative demand is zero. The returns from assets are too attractive to be foregone, particularly since interest rates are likely to be lower in the future. In this range, more thrift, the traditional prescription for progress, is appropriate. This is Hicks' Classical Case.

Next comes an intermediate range of interest rates in which the quantity of money people desire to hoard varies inversely with the rate of interest. If the willingness to save increases, consumption and income decline, and the released funds press for absorption in speculative balances. Hence interest rates decline and investment increases. But this rise in capital formation may be dearly bought. If speculative demand is elastic, or if the demand for new capital equipment is inelastic with respect to interest rates, the drop in income required to produce a unit rise of investment may be large. If thrift does not weaken the inducement to invest, it is still a prescription for growth, but it is costly medicine.

Finally, there is a minimum level of interest rates at which the speculative demand for money becomes indefinitely elastic. The yield of securities is too low to attract additional purchasers. More saving is wasteful or worse. It causes income to fall, but it leaves interest rates and, therefore, investment unaffected. This is Hicks' Keynesian Case.[30]

It might seem, then, that on Keynesian reasoning, thrift is beneficial to growth over the presumably wide range of situations in which rates of interest stand above the minimum. But this was not Keynes' view, for the reduction in interest rates that an increased propensity to save effects is purchased only at the expense of a reduction in income. And a reduction in income weakens the inducement to invest, a connection neglected above. If we recognize it, then lower interest rates obtained by greater thrift may not promote capital formation.[31] In Keynes' judgment they would not. So the practical conclusions from the Keynesian argument are that saving promotes capital formation in conditions of full employment or, short of full employment, when the net speculative demand for money is zero. In other conditions, saving is probably, but not necessarily, a depressant to investment.[32]

Like so much of Keynes' work, this hypothesis is plausible for the short run and in the context of business cycles. It is less clearly applicable in the construction of a theory of secular growth. In the short run, thrift reduces money and real income and may (in Keynes' judgment, probably will) reduce investment. If prices are flexible in the long run, however, as seems plausible, the eventual result should be the attainment of full employment combined with a high propensity to save – a combination that obviously yields larger real saving than full employment based on high consumption.[33]

This reasoning indicates that Keynes may be wrong, but it does not make the traditional view right. Business cycles are short-run events, but one succeeds another; they are always with us. So the question is whether a community that saves and invests a great deal at the peak of cyclical prosperity is in greater danger of being thrown into depression than an economy whose prosperities are based more largely on consumption demand. And if so, does the average investment performance of an economy with a high propensity to save tend to be worse than that of an economy with a low propensity to save? Are the same answers appropriate for the nineteenth century as in contemporary conditions? For industrial and agricultural economies? Keynesian theory has helped to clarify the role of saving, but neither Keynesian nor traditional economics has yet grappled successfully with the question of the long-term significance of thrift in an environment of business fluctuation.

2. *The determinants of the supply of saving.* Whatever the precise sig-

nificance of the supply of saving, it obviously has an important part to play in capital formation, and we should understand the factors that control it. But our understanding is still lamentably deficient.

Our most secure theory concerns the relation between income and saving. Marshall's dictum was that saving per capita varies directly with per capita income: not, however, with total income, but with the "excess of income over necessary expenses."[34] From this the easy inference was drawn that, as per capita income increases, savings rise more than proportionately. This proposition was long accepted for its *a priori* plausibility. But serious doubt was cast on it by the publication of S. S. Kuznets' estimates for the United States since 1869.[35] In spite of an enormous rise in *per capita* income, the ratio of saving to net national income has remained virtually constant.[36] Less reliable figures of similar import for Canada and Sweden were published by Modigliani.[37]

The reasons for this breakdown of theoretical expectations are still far from clear. Arthur Smithies has advanced the view that the savings function has been dropping secularly as a result of the trend toward urbanization and more equal distribution of income.[38] Smithies and Modigliani[39] have argued that increments to income are absorbed by expenditures on new types of products. Duesenberry[40] has contended that these factors are inadequate to account for the failure of the saving-income ratio to rise and has argued that an individual's propensity to consume is heavily influenced by a disposition toward competitive emulation. His saving-income ratio is, therefore, related primarily to his *rank* in the income scale rather than to the absolute level of his income. If the relative inequality of income remains stable, Duesenberry's theory is consistent with the facts about the trend of the saving-income ratio. But other explanations are possible, and some independent test of the importance of emulative drives is still necessary.[41]

Another widely accepted inference from the supposed dependence of saving on excess income is the idea that the saving-income ratio tends to rise as the distribution of income becomes more unequal. This proposition is still untested by comparisons among countries or over time. It is based on the plausible assumption that "necessary expenses" do not rise as fast as individual income. And as between income classes, this seems to be true. One of the clearest results of studies of the disposition of income by members of different income groups is that the proportion devoted to saving increases as one moves from lower to higher income classes. What is doubtful for the community as a whole over time is clearly sound as among the members of a community at a given time.[42]

At least it is true for the United States and for such highly developed countries as have produced the necessary statistics. Would it be true for all South American countries? Would it have been true for Russia, Poland and the Balkans under their old regimes? It may be true for the United States because our population is relatively homogeneous as between income classes, the members of which share a common set of values and aspirations and differ mostly in their incomes. It may not be true if the highest income groups are composed of a nobility and squirearchy inheriting a noncommercial scheme of values which emphasizes the virtues of lavish hospitality, display, and extravagance, while thrift resides in a less wealthy business and professional class.

Considerations of this sort presumably gave rise to the view shared by the early nineteenth-century classicists and Marx, that the almost exclusive source of savings was profits. The workers had no excess income. The landowning gentry lacked a bent toward thrift. But the profit-making commercial classes had both. This heterogeneity in values and aspirations may also explain the alleged paucity of savings in many backward areas in which the richer classes are supposed to lack a bourgeois appreciation of the satisfactions of accumulation and live instead with lordly magnificence and openhandedness.[43]

Within economically advanced communities, the importance of the distribution of income between profits and other types of income is presumably considerable, as is indicated by the figures cited in the note below.[44] Indeed, these figures probably underrate the importance of profits, for they neglect the large elements of salaries, wages, fees, and bonuses directly or indirectly attributable to profits. More of our income, particularly the income of the classes which do the bulk of our saving, has its origin in profit than is named profit. But our thinking is also colored, in this instance in a contrary sense, by an unduly restricted view of the forms of savings. Expenditure on education and on the betterment of health and skill is also a form of saving – indeed, a very important part. And in these ways, a considerable portion of the apparent consumption of the professional and working classes goes to improve the productive equipment of many communities.

The contribution of profits to saving has a twofold basis. When distributed they go largely to the rich, so they augment saving by aggravating income inequality. In addition, however, a large proportion of profits are retained by corporations and so wholly saved.[45] Indeed, the savings of corporations may well be understated if it is true, as many suspect, that depreciation allowances are normally more than adequate to maintain the productive equipment of industry.[46] How important the corporate organization of business may be in accounting for differences in savings among countries and over time is yet to be established.

Other facets of our organizational outfit, though presumably significant, make contributions that are still unmeasured. A large volume of saving takes the form of insurance policy purchases. Another large quantity is used to purchase the securities of corporations, investment trusts, and governments. How much smaller would our savings be if these attractive kinds of assets did not exist?

Finally, even if we could allow for differences in per capita income and in the organizational structures of communities, there are still the basic problems of accounting for the level of per capita saving and for residual international and intertemporal differences. This is the aspect of the matter of which economists usually wash their hands by saying that the amount of saving that people are willing to do depends on their thriftiness, a form of words used to mark the traditional borders of economics. Of course, the border has sometimes been violated in speculative fashion, particularly by the older economists. Marshall, for example, wrote:

> Thus, the causes which control the accumulation of wealth differ widely in different countries and in different ages. They are not quite the same among any two races, and perhaps not even among any two social classes in the same race. They depend much on social and religious sanctions; and it is remarkable how, when the binding force of custom has been in any degree loosened, differences in personal character will cause neighbors brought up under like conditions to differ from one another more widely and more frequently in their habits of extravagance or thrift than in any other respect.[47]

Insecurity of every kind, he added, is a most powerful hindrance to the development of habits of thrift and foresight. Family affection is the chief positive motive for accumulation. But it operates most strongly within a milieu in which an increase in wealth lifts a man and his family up the social ladder.[48]

Marshall's is a good example of the level of analysis and study to which the subject has been carried. With insignificant differences, simular remarks will be found in the writings of his contemporaries and predecessors. And among modern economists the question has been the subject of increasing neglect. The motives and conditions identified presumably are something less than established. They certainly do not exhaust the subject. And, insofar as they operate, what we really want to know is what sort of cultural and psychological forces create the required social and religious sanctions, provide the security, make wealth the hallmark of distinction, and establish family affection as the most respectable of passions. We are, in fact, pushed beyond the limits of economics as that subject has so far developed, and it is no wonder that we find the theory in a rudimentary state.[49]

B. The productivity of capital and the level of capital formation

If we interpret the productivity of capital to mean the net yield of additions to the capital stock, the relation between productivity and capital formation is obvious, at least qualitatively. But to do justice to the problem, we must distinguish between what may be called *potential* (or perhaps, *ideal*) productivity and *effective* productivity. The yield under perfect competition is, perhaps, a sufficient characterization of potential productivity. It is the yield that an investor would expect if he had perfect knowledge of the present state of markets and of technical opportunities, could penetrate the future with clairvoyance, had no power to influence prices, and operated in a market in which private and social products were equivalent. Effective productivity is the yield on which potential investors will actually count, having regard to their limited knowledge of techniques and markets, present and future, their anticipations of financial rewards and dangers, and their ability, real or fancied, to control the future state of the market. Moreover, insofar as we credit potential productivity with influence over the inducement to invest, we are implicitly saying that investment will be made whenever and wherever there is an opportunity for monetary gain. When we move from potential product to effective product, however, we must depreciate the prospect of monetary gain according to the relative valuation that investors place on potential gains compared with risk, work, worry, and the strenuous life in general. Finally, we must take into account the fact that there are many opportunities to increase the productivity of society by investments which, either by their own nature, or because of institutional arrangments, or because of government action, do not have a private yield equal to their real worth. For these reasons, this section is divided into: (1) the determinants of potential productivity, and (2) the difference between potential and effective productivity.

1. *The determinants of potential productivity.* This is the area in which orthodox theory is most at home. Its starting point is the older static theory of income distribution. This theory makes the marginal productivity of the various factors depend on their relative supply. And since the canons of economy for individual firms demand that the factors be combined in such fashion that increasing use of any one brings smaller incremental products, a law of diminishing returns to changes in factor proportions is embedded in the theory. Although explicit

treatment is hard to find, it is this static analysis of distribution which seems to have determined the orthodox view of the determinants of capital productivity in its bearing on the level of capital formation. We may state this view as follows: Given the structure of demand for final goods and the "state of the arts," the marginal productivity of capital will be high or low depending on the proportions of the factors. The greater the supplies of labor and natural resources, the higher the productivity of capital. The greater the volume of capital already accumulated, the lower the productivity of capital. Given the supply schedule of saving (unless it be completely inelastic), the volume of current capital formation will be greater, the higher the marginal productivity of capital. It will, therefore, vary directly with supplies of labor and other natural resources and inversely with the stock of existing capital.

An increase in the supply of a factor, however, brings an increase in aggregate output in addition to a change in factor proportions. And with an increase in scale of output there are increases in efficiency due to improvements in the organization of industry. That is to say, there are increasing returns associated with scale of output and, therefore, with the change in factor supply to which an increase in output is due. If we admit the importance of increasing returns in problems of secular growth,[50] we should have to amend the traditional conclusions to read: Capital formation will vary directly with supplies of labor and other natural resources, and *either* inversely *or* directly with the stock of existing capital depending on the relative strength of the forces making for diminishing returns – which depend on changes in factor proportions – and for increasing returns – which depend on changes in the scale of output.

Failure to take due account of the force of increasing returns – to say nothing of factors outside the range of the discussion of potential productivity – has often led to careless thinking. One implication of the influence of scale on returns is that *a priori* there is no clear and definite reason to think that the potential productivity of capital will begin to drop when the ratio of capital to other resources increases. The demand price for capital will not necessarily be relatively high in a "new" country. Another implication is that there is no convincing reason to believe, *a priori*, that capital will flow from countries with high to countries with low ratios of capital to other resources. There is, no doubt, a tendency of that sort, but how strong is it, and how many exceptions would be found if one looked? Even at the level of potential (as distinct from effective) productivity, there is more to the problem than the capital-labor and capital-land ratios which traditional theory stressed.[51]

In recent theoretical work at the level of potential productivity, the most important development is probably Keynes' analysis of the schedule of the marginal efficiency (or productivity) of new capital.[52] From the viewpoint of economic growth, chief interest attaches to his emphasis on the cost of producing new capital equipment. In the older writings, the marginal rate of return over cost was conceived to vary with the level of investment because the marginal product of capital declined as its volume increased. Keynes emphasized a second cause for variation in the rate of return with the level of investment, namely that the cost of capital goods at any given time tends to be higher, the greater the volume of durable goods production.[53]

The practical importance of Keynes' treatment for questions of growth is simply stated. In a closed economy, the rapidity with which marginal productivity of capital declines as investment increases must depend on the ease with which capital goods production can be expanded. It must depend, therefore, on the size of a country's capital goods industry and on the number of workers who are appropriately trained and located. Keynes' view leads to the simple and obvious but important conclusion that the level of capital formation that a country can attain at any given time depends significantly on the size of the capital goods industry it has already built. It also implies that, if a backward country wishes quickly to attain a high rate of progress, what is necessary is not simply capital formation, but capital formation directed to the capital goods industries. The policy of Soviet Russia exhibits this principle in practice.

Strictly speaking, this analysis is limited to closed economies. Capital goods, however, can be bought as well as built, and in this way the capital goods industry of the world becomes available to a country. But now another limitation operates. To import more capital goods requires an expansion of exports, and this expansion will be limited at any given time by increasing costs of production which reflect the existing capacity of the export industries and by declining marginal revenues which reflect the existing demand for a country's products. In order for a country that imports capital goods to have a high rate of investment, it must have a large export industry. And to move from a low to a high rate of capital formation quickly it must concentrate on the expansion of its exports. It can escape this limitation only by restricting imports of consumer goods or by borrowing. So the need to borrow may reflect not simply a scarcity of internal sources of saving. It may also reflect a small capacity to produce capital goods at home and a small export industry.

2. *The difference between potential and effective productivity.* Resources, labor, existing capital and potentially usable knowledge define, in

some sense, a set of opportunities. By themselves, however, they clearly do not determine when those opportunities will be seized or the rate at which they will be exploited. This becomes perfectly evident when we ask ourselves why the level of capital formation was greater in Britain than in France in the nineteenth century, greater in Germany than in France after 1870, and greater in Western Europe than in Russia before the Russian Revolution. The factors analyzed by traditional capital theory, therefore, provide only a partial catalogue of the incentives to invest. We may express this by saying that traditional theory provides no explanation for the gap between the potential and the effective productivity of capital.

The factors that determine how successfully that gap is leaped may be conveniently arranged under three headings. There is, first, a group of subjective attributes which together we can call *enterprise*. They control the energy with which investment opportunities are sought and exploited. Next, there are organizational, institutional, and legal arrangements which qualify the opportunities investors face. They create what are below called *institutional disparities* between potential and effective productivity. Finally, there are opportunities to raise income by investment which exist for the community but not for individuals. This subject is treated under the heading, *private versus social productivity*.

a. Enterprise. As stated above, the capital theorist's data, labor supply, resources, and the rest do not define that ordered array of identified assets, each clearly labeled with its appropriate rate of return, which the conceptual device of a "schedule of the marginal productivity of capital" suggests. What it does define is a largely unexplored and unevaluated set of possibilities for useful investment of unimaginable magnitude and complexity. Hence, the effective incentives to investment do not depend on the usual data alone. They also depend on the vigor, intelligence, and open-mindedness with which the universe of unknown opportunities is searched and combed and on the willingness of potential investors to accept the work, worry, risk, and general sacrifice of ease which accompanies the establishment of a new, enlarged, changed, or relocated production unit. This constellation of qualities, combining energy in search of economic improvement, tolerance for novelty and uncertainty, and courage in the face of risk, is the group of attributes which together constitute the substance of enterprise.

The role of enterprise has been slighted by traditional theory because of the theory's generally static character which leads easily to assumptions about perfect knowledge, absence of risk, and rational calculation of profit.[54] The classic treatment of the problem is, of course, Joseph

Schumpeter's.[55] Space does not permit adequate development of his views, but his position may be sufficiently characterized by the statement that the marginal productivity of capital depends on enterprise to such a degree that in its absence the incremental yield of capital would fall to zero. The reason is that all important productive applications of capital involve innovation, that is, some act of search and discovery, some new departure in business life, some conquest of the active or passive resistance offered by labor, finance, or the market to new products or ways of working. Some act of enterprise is, therefore, involved; and in the absence of these special talents of leadership, it would be found that the remaining opportunities within the horizon of routine management are scant. The marginal productivity of capital would vanish.

The implication of this view is that labor supply, resources, existing capital, and the state of the arts only create a potentiality for capital productivity, while it is enterprise which performs the miracle of transforming potential into effective productivity.[56] A substantial part of the explanation of differences in the level of investment between developed and undeveloped countries, among advanced economies, and between different stages in the progress of any single country, is to be found in the size, energy, and scope of operations of the entrepreneurial or business class.

The question of the conditions controlling the vigor of enterprise is, therefore, sharply raised. On this, the leading treatments exhibit a remarkable similarity in basic theme. Whether we read Marshall's appendix on "The Growth of Free Industry and Enterprise,"[57] Karl Marx' *Capital*, Thorstein Veblen's *Theory of Business Enterprise*,[58] Schumpeter's *Capitalism, Socialism and Democracy*, or Wesley C. Mitchell's essay on "The Role of Money in Economic History,"[59] we find, with differences in emphasis and explicitness, the same central idea: that the vigor of economic enterprise or leadership under capitalism depends on the degree to which pecuniary values and pecuniary institutions have come to dominate the culture of a country.

The main expression of pecuniary culture in the limiting case is the elevation of money wealth and money income to pre-eminence among the overt goals in life. The important thing is that, from the viewpoint of motivation, real assets and consumables, in bulk, if not in composition, are valued not for themselves but for their monetary equivalent. All things are thought of as exchangeable and saleable, and therefore as convertible into money, the universal solvent. The money measure of goods becomes the *real* expression of their value. Goods are money, and, from the viewpoint of capitalist motivation, it is from this equivalence that they derive their worth.[60]

Now it will readily be seen that the more completely the culture of a community is saturated with such a scheme of values, the greater will be the energy with which economic advantage is pursued and the more thoroughly and uncompromisingly will opportunities to use income to get more income be sought and exploited. The substantial needs of men for material goods are by no means insatiable, and, particularly among the richer elements in the community upon whom the function of enterprise devolves, would hardly justify and elicit the work, danger, and general woe, the sacrifice of leisure, sport, travel, and family (to name only the more obvious losses) which the effort to increase income entails. There is no specific instinct for capital accumulation, but there is in humans a powerful stream of moldable energy; and it is in the particular cultures in which prime value is attached to money that this stream becomes harnessed to the process of accumulation and that the drive for income becomes (more or less) insatiable.

In such cultures, all the avenues along which human energy may seek release – sex, distinction, power, security – are opened, or at least substantially smoothed and eased, by the possession of a relatively large income and stock of capital. The crucial phrase is, of course, "relatively large." Social distinction turns on relative income status. Political power may be wielded indirectly or obtained directly by the possession and use of money. Beauty may be purchased, and respectability and admiration achieved, by it. Indeed, to such an extent do all the facets of life reflect its influence that, at last, no specific visualization of its substantial uses is necessary. The desirability of accumulation comes to be taken for granted, an end – the end – in itself; to engage in the pursuit of money becomes a virtue (and, therefore, beyond price) and to shrink from the costs of the chase a mark of the sloth, the fool, the eccentric, or the rebel. Thus the energy and ability which, in some societies, are directed toward religion, politics, art, or war are, in the developed capitalist milieu, channeled into business.[61]

All this is, of course, hypothesis of a particularly vague kind. The very words employed have no standard connotation in the context of the subject. It goes without saying that the force and range of application of the theory are still to be established. It poses problems of investigation most of which lie outside the normal borders of economics and will certainly resist measurement in the foreseeable future. If, blinking these difficulties, we now pass to the question of the factors controlling the origins and development of a pecuniary culture, we again enter territory which is as fascinating to visit as it is stony to cultivate. What economists know about such matters they owe to the studies and speculations of the economic historians and the students of economic institutions. From the work of Marx, Sombart, Weber, Pirenne, Veblen, Commons, Clark, their colleagues and successors, we can piece together a more or less common set of ideas. Five more or less independent but still closely related factors appear to have been of importance in the emergence of the pecuniary culture of the West. Their significance can be expressed categorically, if inadequately, in the following propositions:

First, the growth of modern science and technology, by its achievements in transport, geographical exploration, and powered machinery, broke the local subsistence economies, encouraged production for the market and, therefore, for money, and supported the emergence of those strong national governments which were needed for the security of trade and investment.

Second, an increased supply of money, itself an offshoot of exploration and improvements in methods of extraction, placed in relatively few hands a mass of purchasing power which, in numberless ways, strained the capacity of local sources of supply, led to dramatic price rises and, therefore, greatly stimulated the movement of goods from distant areas. Profits anticipated in meeting those demands spurred emerging enterprises to organize production on commerical lines, and the profits realized furnished the saving and finance required.

Third, the institutions of private property and of economic organization based on free contract and exchange developed and spread with the material inducements which free commerce and industry could offer and with the growing influence of the business class. These institutions, in turn, widened the scope of business operations, increased the political and social power of business, and so made the pursuit of wealth and income both more rewarding and more respectable.

Fourth, more purely ideational factors encouraged the deliberate, disciplined, and rational pursuit of material progress which is the hallmark of the commercial mentality. These factors are variously taken to be of the character of religious beliefs (Weber, Tawney) or of a defensive reaction to insecurity on the part of minority groups (Sombart) or of release from the inhibitions of convention, personal relations, and vested interests which is afforded when communities are organized in new countries or when new techniques are introduced in old countries (Veblen, F. J. Turner and his followers).

Fifth, the growth of political freedom and democracy, itself a reflection of the growing power of commercial groups, made for social mobility and added the rewards of social and political distinction to economic success.

The general conclusion suggested by this survey of the factors controlling the vigor of enterprise is that a vast deal of emphasis must be placed on forces that, in the ordinary conception of the bounds of economics, would have to be classed as political, psychological, or sociological. On these matters, a fund of vague ideas has formed the background of the thinking of economists. This vagueness is regrettable, but from it we can draw one solid proposition. That is that the foundation of an adequate theory of capital formation does, in fact, involve grappling with a complex sociological tangle which can hardly be unraveled with the aid of such concepts and hypotheses as economics now furnishes.[62]

b. Institutional disparities between potential and effective private productivity. The range of issues arising under this head and the next brings us back to topics more familiar to economists, and we merely touch on them to recall the problems involved. There is a gap between the potential and effective productivity of capital, viewed as an investment stimulus, partly because of the subjective factors already discussed, but partly also because institutional arrangements or the very nature of the assets prevent the private appropriation of part or all of the gain.

With regard to disparities of institutional origin, one large topic concerns forms and rates of taxation and subsidy in all their variants. Government regulation of business of every kind is a topic that is relevant here. Another has to do with the distribution of property and legal provisions surrounding property. In certain poorer countries, for example, the nub of the investment problem is to be found in the concentration of wealth, particularly land, in the hands of a noncommercial upper class combined with the poverty, insecurity of tenure, and ignorance of their tenants.

Still another problem concerns the kind and extent of monopoly controls over markets. The general feeling tone of orthodox economics is that competitive market structures are favorable, and monopolistic market structures inimical, to capital formation. But there has been little analysis in aggregate terms. What there is proceeds on extremely restrictive assumptions.[63] At less abstract levels, the correlation between market structure and competitive behavior breaks down.[64] Moreover, even the general contention that monopoly power and its exercise are normally unfavorable to investment has recently been challenged by J. M. Clark[65] and Schumpeter.[66] To grapple with these questions in a realistic way evidently will require empirical work of a more penetrating sort than we have yet seen.

The facets of the problem just mentioned are, of course, only examples of the kind of questions involved. These and many more deserve further investigation for their bearing on the long-term growth and capital.

c. Private versus social productivity. Organization, institutions, and laws effect the degree to which real productivity can be converted into private gain. But there are many types of investment, part or all of the gains from which cannot, by their nature, be appropriated and sold to furnish the reward for enterprise. If such investments are to be made, and certainly if full advantage of such opportunities is to be taken, they must be exploited by some public agency. Such agency may, of course, act directly, or indirectly by means of grants or subsidies of one kind or another.

Situations requiring social investment have been identified in Part I, Section B, 4, e. At this place, it is possible only to draw attention to one salient point. As regards an explanation of variant rates of progress, the problem is to understand why the social and political milieu in some countries and at some times lends itself to vigorous communal action, and in other places and times does not. Study of this question will lead us again to considerations of conflicts of political and economic interests and to more subtle problems connected with the intensity of group life and with the value structures of societies.[67]

C. The role of finance

Finance is the process whereby funds from whatever source are placed at the disposal of investors. It involves two chief classes of activities: financial mediation, that is, the transfer of funds from savers to investors; and credit creation, that is, the provision of credits to investors in excess of planned saving.

1. *Financial mediation.* In the perfect market of traditional pure theory, there is no place for financial mediation. The available savings flow smoothly and costlessly to the most productive investment opportunities. The net yield of assets to savers equals the effective marginal productivity of new capital. The distinction between saver and investor essentially disappears.

In reality, however, active investment is a function confined to a special class of businessmen who command relatively good, though far from perfect, technical and market information and have the temperament to act on their knowledge. And the provision of capital traditionally takes the form of a loan contract in which the lender (saver) substitutes a risk on the general credit of the borrower (investor) for a risk on the outcome of the investment itself. Under these circumstances a spread – call it the *financial spread* – develops between the effective marginal productivity of capital, which is what borrowers can afford to pay, and the net yield of loans in the eyes of savers, which is the reward of lenders.

The size of the financial spread depends partly on the economic and social environment within which borrowing and lending proceed, and partly on the efficiency with which the capital market and its agencies are organized and operate. So far as the environment is concerned, the size of the spread turns on such matters as the level of commercial honesty, the character of the laws protecting creditors and the vigor with which they are enforced, the extent to which the habit of security buying has spread among the public, the level of development of general commercial information, the public's attitude toward risk, and the safety of the investments for which finance is actually demanded.

The size of the spread also depends heavily on the efficiency of the financial organization of a country. Indeed, in its broadest aspects, a country's financial organization may be considered a device for reducing the size of the financial spread. If it works well, the cost of financing to investor-borrowers will be low while the net return to saver-lenders will be high. Investment and saving and, therefore, the volume of capital formation will tend to be large. But if it works poorly, capital formation will be discouraged.

The many ways in which financial organization helps – through the creation of liquidity, through brokerage, by providing information, by converting the securities offered by investors into forms more acceptable to savers – is too long a story for this space. But it should be noted that, besides the banks, brokers, investment houses, and other agencies of the credit and securities markets, the corporate organization of business is an important part of the organization of finance. It is not too much to say that without the invention and public acceptance of the limited liability share and the development of efficient securities exchanges, the extensive financing of large-scale firms and, therefore, the effective use of modern technology would have proved impossible. Apart from that, however, corporations, by their size and method of organization, create a divergence of interest and power between controllers and nominal owners which has encouraged the development of self-financing. Corporations desirous of financing new investment can do so by withholding net earnings which their nominal owners might be loath to permit if they had any effective choice. Perhaps of comparable importance, the fund of such automatically financed investment is swelled by conservative methods of depreciation accounting which produces large amounts of net saving that never officially appear as such.

All these agencies, institutions, and devices can be interpreted as ways and means of reducing the financial spread, that is, of increasing the net yield of securities in the eyes of savers and, therefore, increasing the supply of saving and of bringing finance to business at low cost. Now it goes without saying that the width of the spread varies from country to country and that for given countries it has changed in the course of the development of capitalist institutions. It remains for historical study to establish how wide the spread is and has been in various countries and thus to provide a measure of the contribution that financial law, institutions, and agencies have made over time and in some places to the accumulation of capital. Meanwhile, it is safe to say that the financial spread was, say 150 years ago, everywhere very wide and constituted a most serious block to saving and investment. It is also clear that it is still very wide today in many countries with undeveloped capitalist institutions and that one of the most pressing needs of backward economic communities is to promote financial integrity, establish effective and cheap protection for the rights of creditors, and create the financial institutions through which the savings of the community can be efficiently channeled into the hands of active investors.

2. *Credit creation and the role of commercial banks.* In recent years, attention has shifted from the role of financial mediation and come to be focused on the significance of the aggregate supply of money and, therefore, on credit creation through commercial banks. The older view of this matter was that in the long run the quantity of money, provided it is constant, affects only the price level, but not the level of saving or investment.[68] The reason is that the supply of productive factors, including saving, was held to be determined by the real returns they could obtain. An expansion of the money supply may push interest rates below their equilibrium levels and so temporarily stimulate investment. The benefit, however, cannot last. For in the face of lower interest rates, the real supply of saving would increase only if real output and income increased. But since real wage rates must fall as output rises, output cannot for long remain above its initial level. The real supply of saving must, therefore, tend to decline. To maintain low nominal interest rates and so to stimulate investment means that the banks have to assume an ever-larger share of the burden of financing new investment. In the end, this must lead to credit restrictions and higher interest rates. Contraction ensues. What money creation by banks causes, therefore, is an unsound cyclical spurt of investment, the real gains from which will be swallowed up in an ensuing crash and depression.[69]

The general tenor of recent, that is Keynesian, theory is that the quantity of money counts even if it is constant.[70] There are two conditions required to reach this conclusion. The first is that the demand for additional hoards of cash should not be infinitely great and, therefore, that interest rates lie above their conventional minima.[71] The other is that more labor and other productive factors be available even though the real rewards of factors decline when output rises. Given these conditions, an increase in the quantity of money will reduce interest rates, stimulate investment, and so raise output. And the increased income thus generated will bring out a greater real supply of saving in spite of lower real interest rates.[72]

The supply conditions which make these results possible are concomitants of unemployment which is involuntary in the Keynesian sense. But can involuntary unemployment persist for periods long enough to be significant for economic growth? In a stable economic environment presumably not – for, in the long run, it is plausible to think that the supply of productive factors is based on real returns and, again in the long run, wages and prices are probably flexible enough to reflect the real supply prices of factors. Private enterprise economies, however, are not stable. There may be some tendency for full employment conditions to be established, but there is also an effective tendency for business cycles to recur and for technological improvements to be introduced. Unemployment due to these causes may not be an aspect of economic equilibrium, but it is a typical condition.

One question, then, is whether in an environment which typically includes some involuntary unemployment, the quantity of money makes a difference to the level of investment, even if money supply is constant. The answer would seem to turn on whether prices, in the long run, fully reflect differences in the quantity of money in spite of recurrent unemployment. If they do, the real value of the money supply would not, in the end, be altered by changes in its nominal size. Hence the rate of interest and the level of investment would be unaffected. But it is not at all clear that prices and the quantity of money are so closely tied.

Moreover, even if such a long-run tie between prices and money be admitted, it does not follow that a secularly *increasing* supply of money cannot stimulate investment over long periods. The traditional argument is that such a process involves "forced" saving which can only be maintained by an ever-increasing supply of money which it is not practicable to provide. Such secular increases of money supply have, however, occurred in the past, and it would be sheer speculation to insist that savers and workers come to anticipate the upward trend of prices and to make contracts only at prices which take price-level movements into account.[73] The fact is that neither on the level of theoretical analysis nor of history has the influence of money supply on investment been established for a cyclically disturbed environment.

D. The progress of capital formation

The history of economic thought exhibits a marked cyclical swing between periods when hopes of cumulative progress were dominant and periods living under the shadow of the fear of stagnation.

Adam Smith's *Wealth of Nations* asserted a theory of steady progress. The increasing division of labor, he argued, makes for larger output and larger capital stock. From this flow higher incomes and so a larger population. This in turn means a wider market, still greater division of labor, a spur to invention, and so still more rapid capital formation.

Ricardo and John Stuart Mill turned their eyes away from the possibilities of increasing returns. Their stress was on diminishing returns attributable to the pressure of population and capital on a limited supply of land. For a time the increased income of the saving classes tends to speed the process of capital formation by raising the current supply of saving. Moreover, invention and improvement are forces working to raise the productivity of capital. But in the end, the tendency to diminishing returns to capital applied to scarce land would be controlling. Profit rates would fall to that practical minimum at which they no longer afforded either a source of saving or a sufficient risk premium and reward for investment. Saving and investment would both cease and a stationary state supervene. Stagnation at full employment was the destination of economic development.[74]

The neoclassical writers, deriving their outlook from Marshall, beheld a fairer future. For them, the Malthusian ghost was already laid. Now it was capital pressing on a limited supply of land and of labor as well. But to even the score, there was a stronger faith in the possibilities of invention and improvement in widening the field for capital. This faith was partly founded on the demonstrated progress of science and on a conception of science as a process of cumulative advance without limit. And, partly, it was founded on an intuition of the possibilities of increasing returns, a process whereby capital accumulation, by increasing income, broadened the market, and so created ever larger opportunities for the application of capital. In essence, their theory marked a return to Adam Smith.[75] F. H. Knight has pronounced the verdict of this school on the specter of stagnation:

It rests on the questionable assumption that accumulation could proceed without opening up new demand by occasioning invention and discovery, and in any case is reasonably supposable only as a vague limit at the end of an indefinitely long course of development. During this process any prediction of given conditions tends to become fanciful. The reasonable prediction is that over long periods changes tending to raise the rate of return will more or less predominate during some intervals and changes of the opposite kind in other intervals.[76]

The relative optimism of this outlook was nourished by a century and a half of rapid growth and capital accumulation. But for many, perhaps most, economists it was not proof against the shock of the depressed thirties. The virtual cessation of advance which marked that decade, its very low levels of investment, its persistent unemployment, its disappointing recovery, made a contemporary impression which caused theorists to search for an explanation, not merely in *ad hoc* circumstances, but in some deeper-rooted change in the basic conditions of economic life. The result is the modern theory of stagnation. We may fairly call it Hansen's Theory.[77]

The primary objective of this theory is to assert the existence of a tendency toward chronic and growing unemployment and to offer an explanation for it. The full implications of the theory are, therefore, beyond the scope of the present paper.[78] One of its main props, however, is the idea that net investment tends to decline, after a point, in developed capitalist economies. It is this proposition which is of particular interest here.

The outlook of Hansen's theory is dominated once more by the assumption of diminishing returns. At a given level of technical knowledge, the yield of increments to capital stock tends to sink as its quantity increases relative to labor supply and resources. Increasing returns may be characteristic of the early stages of a country's development, but the economies of Western Europe and the United States of America are mature. At a given level of technical knowledge, therefore, the current inducement to net investment will fall unless population growth and the discovery and development of resources keep pace with capital formation. Moreover, if we may assume that investment outlets generated by past developments have been fully exploited, the marginal productivity of capital will rise or fall together with the level of population growth, resource discovery, and technical progress.

Of these three stimuli, it is argued that population growth and resource discovery are clearly declining in strength. The third factor, technical progress, may indeed be proceeding with undiminished vigor, but it cannot be expected to offset the enfeeblement of the first two. One reason is that with the accumulation of wealth, innovation turns in a capital-saving direction. When capital equipment was scant, few opportunities existed for reducing costs by saving capital. But as the mass of equipment increases, more and more improvements have the effect of economizing capital. A second reason is that the composition of demand changes, as per capita income rises, in the direction of greater emphasis on services compared with commodities. And services, supposedly, are less heavily capitalized. Thus the stream of innovations must be increasing if the level of investment is to remain even level. It must increase still more rapidly to offset the effects on investment of retarded growth of population and resources.[79]

If we accept these views about the time trends in the three dynamic factors, it is argued that we must infer an actual decline in capital formation. For even though the supply of saving rises with per capita income, this will not stimulate investment. The elasticity of the schedule of the marginal efficiency of capital with respect to interest rates is very low, and the response of interest rates to an increase in the supply of saving is extremely limited. This, of course, assumes that the inducement to invest is already deficient compared with saving. At this point, indeed, increases in saving are worse than useless, for they generate declines in income which cause further deterioration in the expected yield of investments.

So far as it is concerned with the demand for additional capital, Hansen's theory represents a departure from the neoclassical view in that it expresses a more limited faith in the possibilities of opening new outlets for capital through the advance of knowledge. Briefly stated, the basis for this change in view is found in calculations – admittedly only suggestive – which "point unmistakably to the conclusion that the opening of new territory and the growth of population were together responsible for a very large fraction – possibly somewhere near one-half – of the total volume of new capital formation in the nineteenth century."[80] With these important outlets for investment rapidly narrowing down, it seems too sanguine to think that technical progress can speed up sufficiently to close the gap, particularly in view of the growing tendency for invention and consumption to take a capital-saving direction.

The argument is attractive, but it is not difficult to enter a plausible rebuttal. The experience of the 1940's has made the outlook for population growth far less gloomy than it appeared to Hansen in the late thirties and early forties.[81] The same decade has belied predictions, at least so far as the United States is concerned, that the population appears to be approaching stabilization in geographical distribution.[82] Again, very large portions of the world, even outside the sphere of communist control, remain unsettled or only partly settled. And, while climate and location interpose obstacles to development, science is steadily reducing these barriers. Even within the settled areas, the discovery and creation of resources proceeds at a rapid pace – witness, among other things, the rapid advances in agricultural productivity. Meanwhile, there are signs that the pace of advance of pure science is accelerating and that deliberate devotion of resources to technological exploration is becoming more and more extensive. That much technical progress will be capital saving may be taken for granted. But such innovations need not be alternative to capital-using innovations; they may also be additional. And services are becoming increasingly capitalized. Is it clear, for example, that a dollar spent on education or medical care requires less capital in buildings, equipment, and personnel training than a dollar spent on a representative commodity?

A second differentiating mark of Hansen's theory is its implicit assumption that capital yields diminishing returns, at least in advanced economies. Perhaps it does; but are we at all sure that, on balance, an increase in the scale of the market in the United States does not still permit economies more sizeable than the diseconomies it causes through pressure on resources and otherwise? If it does, the inducement to invest can feed on itself, at least so far as secular trends go, with capital formation limited by the supply of saving and the size of the capital goods industries.[83] It seems right to conclude that, so far as the barebones of Hansen's theory are concerned, it is plausible but far from completely persuasive. Its detailed contentions and implications need more careful examination than they have yet received. In particular, those drawn to the subject might do well to regard the phase of assertion and counterassertion as closed and a phase of empirical study as the need of the times.

In the terminology used in earlier portions of this essay, the basic elements in Hansen's theory are time trends in the determinants of *potential* productivity. They bear particular comparison, therefore, with the neoclassical theory which depends on the very same elements. Hansen's theory has, however, been both supported and attacked in the light of considerations relevant to the difference between potential and effective productivity. Briefly stated, the argument is that the development of capitalism has also raised a series of barriers to the exploitation of potential productivity. These barriers are identified as business monopoly,[84] labor unions, government intervention in economic life by taxation, regulation and direct participation, and hindrances to foreign investment.

These barriers between the potential and effective productivity of capital are regarded by Hansen and his adherents as developments strengthening their main case.[85] By others, however, they are considered as a full-fledged alternative explanation for such evidence of declining investment opportunity as has appeared.[86] The nub of the issue is the question whether the substantial elimination of the special barriers, to the extent that they are judged to be removable, would also eliminate the tendency to declining investment opportunity. Hansen and his adherents, while welcoming policies designed to reduce obstacles to investment, believe such policies would not be sufficient. His critics believe they would.

The gap between potential and effective productivity was also used by Schumpeter to accommodate a systematic theory of the progress of capital formation which is basically antagonistic to Hansen's theory and, in the main, also at variance with the views of Hansen's opponents outlined above.[87] His view is a logical extension of his general theory about capital formation. For it turns neither on some autonomous change in the taste for saving, nor on an independent decline in opportunities for investment, but on the metamorphosis through which the entrepreneurial function passes as capitalism develops. This is, of course, utterly consistent, for Schumpeter saw both saving and investment opportunity as the creations of enterprise.

As capitalism develops, the vigor of enterprise begins to decline. In part this is due to the emergence of a political and social environment which is hostile to business, which reduces its rewards, and limits the scope of its activities. The appearance of this hostile milieu stems from the fact that the position of the business class, both its status in society and its power in politics, is progressively undermined. As firms grow in size and experience, the entrepreneurial function tends to become routinized, an affair for salaried employees; so the businessman gradually loses his chief moral title to social leadership. Next, with the spread of pecuniary values and commercial habits of thought, the bourgeois class loses its main political supporter, the old aristocracy, whose romantic sway is inconsistent with the spirit of calculation. The growth of big business also destroys another important political ally, the small tradesman and artisan. And finally, the rational and critical attitude fostered by capitalism nurtures an intelligentsia whose questions do not stop at the "credentials of kings and popes." It goes on to dissect private property and the system of bourgeois virtues themselves. It rationalizes dissatisfaction with existing institutions and ruling classes and so provides the necessary intellectual leadership for anticapitalist forces. The result, as stated, is the gradual appearance of political and social conditions unfavorable to business activity, taxing its gains, regulating its movements, and limiting its scope.

Quite as important as these environmental changes, however, is the transformation which occurs in the nature of capitalist motivation. The same rational spirit which is responsible for the material triumphs of business also leads businessmen to a critical analysis of their own goal. This was the creation of a great personal fortune in order to found and support a family and home. But the income statement of the proceeds and costs of home and family, as modern businessmen compute it, shows a psychic deficit. And as these institutions cease to be the centers and goals of bourgeois life, the driving force of enterprise begins to disappear.

For Schumpeter, all this meant a gradual reduction in the pace of capital formation – at least under capitalism. This may not become visible, the effects of random causes and special circumstances being what they are, for many years. But it constitutes a persistent force that will be controlling in the end. It does not mean breakdown or chronic unemployment necessarily, for the saving motive will weaken with the investment drive. But, with the passing of the function of the individual entrepreneur, it does mean the socialization of economic activity.

All these theories admittedly are of limited application at best. They are hypotheses intended to illuminate the latter stages of the economic and sociological processes of industrialization, but not its beginnings or its life course. They are, moreover, restricted to capitalistic economies and so do not apply to countries in which capital formation is determined or heavily influenced by the decisions of central authority. If we restrict the application of Hansen's theory, for example, to countries in which population growth is markedly retarded and which already enjoy relatively high per capita incomes, it may be said to be relevant to perhaps 20 per cent of the world's population.[88] Even within this limited sphere, however, there are doubts about the applicability of the theories as interpretations of observable events, as distinct from predicted future events. For it is not clear which, if any, advanced capitalist countries have as yet given evidence of a persistent decline in the level of capital formation.

Insofar as such evidence may be found, moreover, there is doubt about the relative validity of the rival theories now in vogue and, it must be added, about their fitness compared with other theories that may be or have been propounded. Modern theoretical literature, for example, puts little stress on certain older ideas that have often been advanced to explain the laggard pace of British and French advance in recent decades. It has been plausibly contended, for example, that these countries are now suffering a penalty for their early lead in the industrial race. Their older equipment, the specialized experience of their population and their geographical layout make it more difficult for them than for their newer rivals to take full advantage of modern techniques. And their older industries now feel the competition of more recently equipped competitors.[89] If this line of argument has validity, it implies that any observed retardation in the pace of capital formation may be but temporary and that the turn of the old countries will come again as time presents opportunities for renewing old equipment and gradually loosens the industrial and geographical ties of their people.

Finally, all this bears only on the question of maturity and its concomitants. With so much of the world undeveloped, and with so many of the relatively advanced countries in the full tide of capital accumulation, the theory of the progress of capital formation needs filling out. What is the path by which a country passes from its precapitalistic doldrums into a state of industrial animation? Is there not a cumulation of investment opportunities and of the means of exploiting them in these earlier stages? If so, what are the specific developments by which the process of capital formation gathers strength? What obstacles must be surmounted and what adjustments must an economy make in the training and allocation of its labor force, in the composition of its output, in its domestic and foreign trade? Is the nature of these adjustments very similar from case to case, or does it differ widely depending, say, on a country's physical endowment and location? We now have an uncertain and incomplete gerontology of capital formation. A paedology and a theory of maturation are utterly lacking.

III. Problems of research

The foregoing survey of the scope and content of the economics of growth serves to illustrate its far-reaching character. It is, in fact, to be regarded as one of the major branches of economics, coordinate with the economics of resource allocation and income distribution and the economics of short-term, or cyclical, fluctuations. As such, there are few, if any, facets of economic life and, therefore, few, if any, subjects in economics that are foreign to it. This, then, may be said to be the first of the difficulties which the study of growth poses. It is extremely many-sided and will call for the cooperation of specialists in all the major branches of economics.

These various branches are relevant from a special point of view, namely, in their bearing on long-term change. And that means that the causes, or factors, which become relevant are not merely the relatively objective, relatively easily definable, variables with which economics has usually dealt, but others far less familiar. We shall be involved not only with numbers of workers, machines, acres, tons, or square yards of commodities, and the like; we shall also need to consider less easily grasped attributes like mobility, industry, enterprise, thriftiness, knowledge, and skill and their diffusion. The first problems that this raises are those of sheer definition, observation, and measurement. These problems have seldom been faced in the past, because so long as our interests lay in short-run questions, these less tangible factors could be taken to be constant and so neglected. From the viewpoint of long-term problems, however, they are variables of first-rate importance.

To understand the causes and processes of economic growth, moreover, it will not be enough to relate these and similar growth factors to output change. We shall also want to understand and explain the movements of these immediate determinants. And such explanations will involve investigations which, in almost every instance, lie outside the normal boundaries of economics. The location of those boundaries hitherto has been fixed by the reach of money income as an explanation of behavior. Economics, in fact, if not in intention, has been the science which studied the implications of changes in pecuniary advantage. But population growth, changes in industrial and financial organization, technological progress and its diffusion, the changing vigor of enterprise, differences in industrial and geographical mobility – none of these can be adequately, or probably to any considerable extent, understood in terms of pecuniary advantage. The economics of growth is, therefore, the field of work in which the dependence of economics upon its sister social sciences appears in a supreme degree.

The study of economic growth also presents in aggravated form that universal problem of economics and of social science, the distillation of dependable uniformities from a process of cumulative change. A dependable law implies some stable system of structural characteristics (tastes, propensities, motives, physical obstacles, organization, law, etc.) which cause a set of recognizable tendencies to emerge in the relations among variables. Social structure, however, is notoriously in flux, so that in practice it is some sort of relative stability on which we must depend – relative usually to the period of time that is relevant. But the longer the period, the less likely are we to find the degree of stability we need. No one can say ahead of time how grave an obstacle this will be, but it will certainly be far more serious than in studies of short-term fluctuations in which it has already proved disturbing. Long-term growth presumably constitutes a process of cumulative rather than repetitive change to a greater degree than other economic phenomena.

The study of economic growth, therefore, stands closer to history than do other economic subjects. Not only will study of the past, even the distant past, furnish us the bulk of the necessary data, but it seems unlikely that, for the foreseeable future, the economics of growth can be much more than economic history rationalized here and there to a limited degree as uniformities in the process of development are established. The sweeping visions of Marx, Sombart, Weber, and others will, no doubt, color and direct our thoughts and work, but the generalizations we trust will be less profound and of narrower application.

These doubts and fears are no more than natural. The work of finding uniformities in the variety of historical change and national difference has hardly begun. Economists so far have preferred the easier job of discovering the necessary implications of arbitrarily chosen premises. The study of the political, psychological, and sociological foundations of economic life has been even more neglected. Economists have preferred to cultivate a science of pecuniary advantage. The study of economic growth will not permit them to indulge these proclivities. The insights which traditional theory can furnish will, of course, have to be worked to the limit. But we may expect that limit to be reached sooner in studies of secular change than elsewhere. If the economics of growth attains the rank it ought to have in our subject, we should expect to see history, geography, psychology, and sociology take a prominent place in the training of economists in the future. Experience suggests that we cannot be sanguine about the strength of these allies. But more than ever, our problems seem to lie within their domains, and a closer federation is in order.

Notes

1. Compare the discussions by Simon Kuznets, J. J. Spengler, E. M. Hoover and J. L. Fisher and by J. M. Clark in *Problems in the Study of Economic Growth*. Nat. Bur. Econ. Res. (New York, July 1949; mimeographed).

2. See the contribution by Clark cited above.

3. This represents the level of analysis attempted by B. F. Kierstead, *The Theory of Economic Change* (Toronto, 1948).

4. See P. A. Baran, "On the Political Economy of Backwardness," *Man. School Econ. Soc. Stud.*, Jan. 1952, XX, 66–84.

5. The reader should compare the present outline with somewhat similar, though more condensed, lists of factors influencing the level of output prepared by J. J. Spengler, "Theories of Socio-Economic Growth," *Problems in the Study of Economic Growth*, p. 53; *idem*, "Economic Factors in the Development of Densely Populated Areas," *Proc.*

Am. Phil. Soc., Feb. 1951, XCV, 21–25; *idem*, "The Population Obstacle to Economic Betterment," *Am. Econ. Rev., Proc.*, May 1951, XLI, 344–46.

6. Apart from population problems, the leading recent references of a general sort on the long-term supply of labor are: P. H. Douglas, *Theory of Wages* (New York, 1934), Pt. 3; C. D. Long, *Labor Force, Income and Employment* (New York, forthcoming). A highly interesting and important study of the influence of cultural values and social organization upon the size and capabilities of the labor force is W. E. Moore, *Industrialization and Labor* (Ithaca and New York, 1951). See also, Pei-Kang Chang, *Agriculture and Industrialization* (Cambridge, Mass., 1949), Ch. 2, 5.

7. *The Theory of Geographic Location of Economic Activities* (Ann Arbor, 1938).

8. J. M. Keynes, *The General Theory of Employment Interest and Money* (New York, 1936), Ch. 19; Oscar Lange, *Price Flexibility and Employment* (Bloomfield, 1944).

9. A. C. Pigou, "The Classical Stationary State," *Econ. Jour.*, Dec. 1943, LIII, 343–51; *idem*, "Economic Progress in a Stable Environment," *Economica*, Aug. 1947, XIV, 180–90; Don Patinkin, "Price Flexibility and Full Employment," *Am. Econ. Rev.*, Sept. 1948, XXXVIII, 543–64; Franco Modigliani, "Liquidity Preference and the Theory of Interest and Money," *Econometrica*, Jan. 1944, XII, 45–88. The last three of these four articles are also in *Reading in Monetary Theory*, F. A. Lutz and L. W. Mints, ed. (Philadelphia, 1951), pp. 186–283.

10. Cf. Douglas, *op. cit.*, Pt. 2; Colin Clark, *The Conditions of Economic Progress* (London, 2nd ed., 1951), Ch. 11; also a considerable amount of periodical literature developing and criticizing the work of Douglas and Clark. In addition, there is the important development of input-output analysis proceeding under the leadership of W. W. Leontief.

11. Spengler estimates that the potential productivity of the population of underdeveloped countries would rise some 20–30 per cent if the age composition and state of health of their peoples could be "Westernized." Cf. "The Population Obstacle to Economic Betterment," *loc. cit.*, p. 344.

12. Cf. Moore, *op. cit.*, pp. 44–47.

13. Cf. H. B. Parkes, *The American Experience* (New York, 1947).

14. Cf. R. B. Perry, *Characteristically American* (New York, 1949).

15. Cf. J. A. Schumpeter, "The Instability of Capitalism," *Econ. Jour.*, Sept. 1928, XXVIII, 361–86.

16. Cf. C. A. Barnard, *The Functions of the Executive* (Cambridge, Mass., 1938); A. D. H. Kaplan, "The Influence of Size of Firms on the Functioning of the Economy," *Am. Econ. Rev., Proc.*, May 1950, XL, 74–84.

17. A representative modern reference is L. G. Reynolds, *Labor Economics and Labor Relations* (New York, 1944), Ch. 10.

18. See Michael Kalecki, *Essays in the Theory of Economic Fluctuations* (London, 1939), pp. 13–41. This is merely a matter of definition. Under perfect competition, profits would tend to disappear. It leaves open the question of what determines monopoly power and how it is exercised under different conditions and to what extent union organization can be a counterweight. See William Fellner, *Competition Among the Few* (New York, 1949).

19. See S. S. Kuznets, *National Income and Its Composition* (New York, 1941), Ch. 4.

20. See the series of papers submitted to the Conference on Quantitative Description of Technological Change sponsored by the Social Science Research Council, April 6–8, 1951, mimeographed. Also Anne P. Gross, "Textile Production Funcitons, Equipment Requirements, and Technological Change," *Econometrica*, July 1950, XVIII, 305–06; Boris Stern, "Mechanical Changes in the Cotton-Textile Industry, 1910–36," *Mo. Lab. Rev.*, Aug. 1937, XLV, 316–41.

21. W. R. Maclaurin, "The Process of Technological Innovation: The Launching of a New Scientific Industry," *Am. Econ. Rev.*, Mar. 1950, XL, 90–112; *idem, Invention and Innovation in the Radio Industry* (New York, 1949).

22. There is, of course, much good material on the first introduction of mechanical devices and other technical advances. Cf. A. P. Usher, *History of Mechanical Inventions* (New York, 1929). But the antecedent process, as well as the factors determining the pace of diffusion remain mysterious. Cf. Yale Brozen, "Invention, Innovation, and Diffusion," paper submitted to the Conference on Quantitative Description of Technological Change, *op. cit.* Brozen, Maclaurin, *op. cit.*, and Gilfillan all emphasize the long lag, often amounting to a century or more, between an advance in fundamental knowledge and successful commercial application based on it. The meaning of these lags is not clear since our most ancient knowledge is still being applied in new inventions. But their examples emphasize both the need to clarify the factors that account for the pace with which knowledge is gained and turned to practical use, as well as the conundrums of measurement which are involved. See S. C. Gilfillan, *Sociology of Invention* (Chicago, 1935), and *idem*, "The Lag between Invention and Application, with Emphasis on Prediction of Technical Change," submitted to Conference cited above.

23. *Business Cycles* (New York, 1939). See also D. McC. Wright, *Economics of Disturbance* (New York, 1947), the literature centering about the work of Harrod and Domar (cited note 78), and among earlier writings, D. H. Robertson, *Banking Policy and the Price Level* (London, 1926), and J. M. Clark, *Strategic Factors in Business Cycles* (New York, 1934).

24. *Op. cit.*, Ch. 9.

25. *Production Trends in the United States since 1870* (New York, 1934).

26. *Industrialization and World Trade* (Geneva, 1945); also Henry Frankel, "The Industrialization of Agricultural Countries," *Econ. Jour.*, June–Sept. 1943, LIII, 188–201.

27. Colin Clark, *op. cit.*, Ch. 8; National Resources Committee, *Consumer Expenditures in the United States* (Washington, 1939).

28. *Infra*, pp. 94–97.

29. "Mr. Keynes and the 'Classics'; A Suggested Interpretation," *Econometrica*, Apr. 1937, V, 147–59; also in *Readings in the Theory of Income Distribution*. William Fellner and B. F. Haley, ed. (Philadelphia. 1946), pp. 461–76. Cf. Keynes, *op. cit.*, Ch. 15.

30. This seems a somewhat misleading identification. Keynes based his argument as much on the costliness of thrift in the intermediate range as on its utter wastefulness when interest rates are at rock bottom.

31. The connection has been well developed by Oscar Lange, "The Rate of Interest and the Optimum Propensity to Consume," *Economica*, Feb 1938, V, 12–32; also in *Readings in Business Cycle Theory*, Gottfried Haberler, ed. (Philadelphia, 1944).

32. Keynes, *op. cit.*, Ch. 24. Also A. P. Lerner, *The Economics of Employment* (New York, 1951), Ch. 17.

33. Cf. Patinkin, *op. cit.*, Modigliani, *op. cit.*

34. *Principles of Economics* (London, 1890; 8th ed., 1920), p. 229.

35. *National Product since 1869* (New York, 1946), Pt. 2.

36. Kuznets, indeed, presents evidence that the savings ratio for individuals has tended to fall. See his "Proportion of Capital Formation to National Product," *Am. Econ. Rev., Proc.*, May 1952, XLII, 519–24.

37. "Fluctuations in the Saving-Income Ratio: A Problem in Forecasting," Conference on Research in Income and Wealth, *Studies in Income and Wealth*, Vol. XI (New York, 1949), pp. 371–440.

38. "Forecasting Postwar Demand," *Econometrica*, Jan. 1945, XIII, 1–14.

39. "Fluctuations in the Saving-Income Ratio," *loc. cit.*, pp. 384–85.

40. James Duesenberry, *Income, Saving and the Theory of Consumer Behavior* (Cambridge, Mass., 1949). Very similar equations consolidating the trend and cyclical relations between income and saving were independently developed by Modigliani and Duesenberry.

41. Cf. Kuznets' interesting suggestions in his "Proportions of Capital Formation to National Product," *loc. cit.*

42. O. L. Altman, *Savings, Investment and National Income*, Temp. Nat. Econ. Com. Monograph 37 (Washington, 1941), p. 18.

43. Baran, *op. cit.*

44. Making use of information about the distribution of dividends by income classes, Martin Taitel was able to estimate the amount of savings from corporate dividends in the United States for a number of years between 1920 and 1937. See *Profits, Productive Activities and New Investment*. TNEC Monograph 12. If we add to his data estimates of net savings by business firms, we have an approximation of total savings from profits. The order of magnitude of the results is suggested by the figures for one year. In 1925, total profits were about 10 per cent of national income; savings from profits were 41 per cent of total savings. Question arises, of course, about the stability of such a figure over the full course of a business cycle during which profits typically fluctuate far more violently than other sources of income. Cf. the article by the present writer, "Savings and Investment: Profits *vs.* Prosperity?" *Am. Econ. Rev.* Suppl., June 1942, XXXII, 53–88.

45. S. P. Dobrovolsky, *Corporate Income Retention, 1915–43* (New York, 1951), Ch. 3. Also Kuznets, *National Income and Its Composition*. Ch. 4.

46. At the present time, the reverse may be true. The recent rapid price rises may have made depreciation allowances based on historical cost inadequate.

47. *Principles of Economics* (8th ed.; London: Macmillan & Co., Ltd., 1920), p. 225.

48. *Ibid.*, p. 228.

49. It can safely be said that modern economics has paid almost no serious attention to this last-mentioned portion of the subject. Among recent developments, the most hopeful are the experiments being carried out by George Katona and others at the Survey Research Center of the University of Michigan and partly reported in George Katona, *Psychological Analysis of Economic Behavior* (New York, 1951).

50. The classic modern statement is by A. A. Young, "Increasing Returns and Economic Progress," *Econ. Jour.*, Dec. 1928, XXXVIII, 527–42. See also, P. N. Rosenstein-Rodan, "Problems of Industrialization of Eastern and South-Eastern Europe," *ibid.*, June–Sept. 1943, LIII, 202–11.

51. Moreover, the two factors held constant by traditional theory, the composition of demand and the state of the arts, represent important neglected areas. The productivity of capital depends on the kinds of goods to be produced, and these vary among countries and over time in a way probably related to a country's state of development. The relevance of the question may be illustrated by the fact that recent discussion has often stressed that the growing importance of services tends to reduce the inducement to invest. Cf. A. H. Hansen *Fiscal Policy and Business Cycles* (New York, 1941), p. 357.

As to the effect of variations in the state of the arts, this too has still to be given thorough analysis. The beginnings of some necessary classification and study may be found in the various distinctions between "capital-using" and "capital-saving" inventions and in accompanying discussion. See A. C. Pigou, *Economics of Welfare* (London, 1920; 4th ed., 1932), Pt. 4, Ch. 4; J. R. Hicks, *Theory of Wages* (London, 1932), Ch. 6; R. G. Hawtrey, *Capital and Employment* (London, 1937), Ch. 3; Hansen, *op. cit.*, p. 356.

52. *Op. cit.*, p. 135. Also, A. P. Lerner, *Economics of Control* (New York, 1946), Ch. 25.

53. This relation was, of course, not unknown. It figures prominently in business-cycle literature. But it was not clearly recognized in general economic theory.

54. But this is not to say that the role of enterprise was overlooked entirely. By looseness in theoretical formulation, or by adding notes on applied economics to the pure theory, neoclassical economics did develop a body of ideas. Marshall's *Principles* abounds in suggestions about the importance of a vigorous business class. But in the central structure of Marshall's work, variations in enterprise are not treated as one of the factors affecting the productivity of capital. And later writers, intent on rigorous formulation of static theory, paid it even less attention.

55. *Theorie der wirtschaftlichen Entwicklung* (Leipzig, 1911), translation by Redvers Opie, *The Theory of Economic Development* (Cambridge, Mass., 1934); *Business Cycles;* and *Capitalism, Socialism and Democracy* (New York, 1942; 3rd ed., 1950), Pt. 2.

56. Schumpeter's position is, indeed, more radical. For he attributes much of the growth of basic knowledge, all of saving, and much of population growth to the activities of the entrepreneur. Cf. *Business Cycles*, Ch. 3.

57. *Principles*, App. A. Cf. also his *Industry and Trade* (London, 1919; 3rd ed. 1920), Pt. 1.

58. New York, 1904.

59. *The Tasks of Economic History*, Dec. 1944 (Suppl. to the *Jour. Econ. Hist.*, Vol. IV), pp. 61–67.

60. In this view the classical distinction between real and money economics is effectively reversed. To the classicists, the important things were pleasures and pains; commodities and services were the sources of pleasure and pain; and money was the means by which commodities are procured and services remunerated. Thus money-making is the way we get goods. All this, of course, is as it should be. But from the viewpoint of capitalist motivation, we do not make money to get goods. We make goods in order to get money.

61. Cf. Marshall, *Industry and Trade*, p. 156. Current investigations of underdeveloped areas have produced no more universal finding than that the process of investment is frustrated, not by any lack of potential opportunity for gain, and not by any lack of surplus saveable income, but rather by the lack of a vigorous business class intent on searching out and exploiting local opportunities. The energies of leading elements in such countries are instead diverted to political and social activity, sport, display, and travel. And the normal desire of a businessman is to convert himself, or his children, into members of the dominant group expending energy and income in nonproductive channels. Cf. United Nations Group of Experts, *Measures for the Economic Development of Under-Developed Countries* (New York, 1951), Ch. 3; Report to the President of the United States by the Economic Survey Mission to the Philippines (Washington, 1950); J. H. Adler, *The Under-Developed Areas: Their Industrialization*, Yale Inst. Internat. Studies, Memo. 31, Mar. 1949, pp. 20–22 and Summary.

For analysis of similar factors in a "developed" country, see D. S. Landes, "French Entrepreneurship and Growth in the Nineteenth Century," *Jour. Econ. Hist.*, May 1947, IX, 45–61; and the chapter by John Sawyer in *Modern France*, E. M. Earle, ed. (Princeton, 1951).

62. There has, indeed, been a marked resurgence of interest in the cultural and political bases of entrepreneurial activity. The economic historians have once again been in the van, but with more conscious attention than was true a generation ago to the implications of their work for economic theory at large and, more particularly, for the theory of economic growth. See the series of papers published since 1941 in *The Tasks of Economic History*, annual supplement to the *Jour. Econ. Hist.* Also the more recent publications of the Research Center in Enterpreneurial History: *Change and the Entrepreneur* (Cambridge, Mass., 1949); and *Explorations in Entrepreneurial History*, the journal of the Center, commencing in 1949.

63. Cf. Joan Robinson, *Economics of Imperfect Competition* (London, 1932), Bk. 10.

64. Cf. J. M. Clark, *Economics of Overhead Costs* (Chicago, 1923), Ch. 20, 21; K. W. Rothschild, "Price Theory and Oligopoly," *Econ. Jour.*, Sept. 1947, LVII, 299–320; Fellner, *op. cit.*, and the present writer's "Monopolistic Selling in a Changing Economy," *Quart. Jour. Econ.*, Feb. 1938, LII, 191–214.

65. "Towards a Concept of Workable Competition," *Am. Econ. Rev.*, June 1940, XXX, 241–56.

66. *Capitalism, Socialism and Democracy*, Ch. 7. Schumpeter did not deny the existence of those monopolistic influences which led traditional theory to an unfavorable view of monopoly. But he thought the traditional view failed to appreciate other forces which make monopoly part of the engine of progress. It is, at bottom, a quantitative matter in an area where measurement has, so far, proved impracticable. So the question for him became one of "ideology," as Mason has said. See E. S. Mason, "Schumpeter on Monopoly and the Large Firm," *Rev. Econ. Stat.*, May 1951, XXXIII, 139–44. For a rebuttal of Schumpeter's argument from the traditional side, see G. H. Hildebrand, "Monopolization and the Decline of Investment Opportunity," *Am. Econ. Rev.*, Sept. 1943, XXXIII, 591–601. For a defense, see R. V. Clemence and F. S. Doody, *The Schumpeterian System* (Cambridge, Mass., 1950), pp. 61–63.

67. Cf. R. R. Nathan, O. O. Gass, and Daniel Creamer, *Palestine: Problem and Promise* (Washington, 1946) which provides an analysis of a dominantly capitalistic society in which intensely held and widely shared ideals and goals support a comprehensive program of public development. The capacity of Americans for group action in the face of their supposedly individualistic cast of mind had puzzled many. Ralph Barton Perry (*op. cit.*) is of the opinion that theirs is "a *collective* individualism – not the isolation of one human being, but the intercourse and cooperation of many." (P. 9.) "American self-reliance is a plural, collective, self-reliance. . . . The appropriate term is not 'organism' but 'organization.' " (P. 19.) The question for us is: Why did American conditions produce this cast of mind?

68. Cf. Marshall's testimony before the Royal Commission on the Depression of Trade and Industry (1886) and before the Gold and Silver Commission (1887–88), *Official Papers by Alfred Marshall* (London, 1926). See also the summary of the traditional view by J. R. Hicks in "Mr. Keynes and the 'Classics,' " *loc. cit.*

69. For these reasons, neoclassical theorists thought that financial agencies, including banks, were beneficial chiefly in their role as financial intermediaries. This, of course, is still the view of that substantial body of opinion which supports the substitution of some variant of a 100 per cent reserve system for fractional reserve banking. But the chief motive of this group is economic stabilization rather than economic growth. Cf. Henry Simons, *A Positive Program for Laissez-Faire*, Public Policy Pamphlet 15 (Chicago, 1934); *idem*, "Rules vs. Authorities in Monetary Policy," *Jour. Pol. Econ.*, Feb. 1936, XLIV, 1–30; Irving Fisher, *100% Money* (New York, 1935); Milton Friedman, "A Monetary and Fiscal Framework for Economic Stability," *Am. Econ. Rev.*, June 1948, XXXVIII, 245–64.

70. *General Theory*, Ch. 15.

71. See pp. 92–93.

72. The essentials of Keynes' argument are well brought out by Modigliani, "Liquidity Preference and the Theory of Interest and Money," *loc. cit.* Other leading articles bearing on the problem may be found in the three volumes published for the American Economic Association, *Readings in Business Cycle Theory, Readings in the Theory of Income Distribution*, and *Readings in Monetary Theory*.

73. An expanding money supply, of course, need not involve rising prices. If productivity is increasing, it may simply mean that prices tend to stand at a high level relative to costs. But both costs and prices may be stable or falling.

74. Marx's views were equally stagnationist. But since he was an early scoffer at Say's Law, he saw a secular decline of investment demand as a cause of aggravated crisis and depression. His views, therefore, are markedly similar to the theories of stagnation dominant today. Cf. Joan Robinson, *An Essay on Marxian Economics* (London, 1942), Ch. 5; Maurice Dobb, *Political Economy and Capitalism* (London, 1937); P. M. Sweezy, *Theory of Capitalist Development* (New York, 1942), Ch. 6, 12.

75. Young, *op. cit.*

76. "Capital and Interest," *Encyclopedia Brittanica*, 1946, IV, 779–801; also in *Readings in the Theory of Income Distribution*, pp. 384–417. Cf. A. C. Pigou, "Economic Progress in a Stable Environment," *loc. cit.*

77. Although some of the ideas were foreshadowed by Keynes, the theory was given its leading expression by A. H. Hansen in "Economic Progress and Declining Population Growth," *Am. Econ. Rev.*, Mar. 1939, XXIX, 1–15; also in *Readings in Business Cycle Theory*, pp. 366–84; *idem, Fiscal Policy and Business Cycles; idem,* "Some Notes on Terborgh's 'The Bogey of Economic Maturity,' " *Rev. Econ. Stat.*, Feb. 1946, XXVIII, 13–17. Literature based on similar ideas is voluminous. See the bibliography in *Readings in Business Cycle Theory*, pp. 483–84. Reliable systematic exposition is provided in Benjamin Higgins, "Concepts and Criteria of Secular Stagnation," in *Income, Employment and Public Policy: Essays in Honor of Alvin H. Hansen* (New York, 1948), pp. 82–107, and *idem,* "The Theory of Increasing Under-Employment," *Econ. Jour.*, June 1950, LX, 255–74.

78. For the same reason, we neglect the theories of R. F. Harrod, "An Essay in Dynamic Theory," *ibid.*, Apr. 1939, XLIX, 14–33, and *idem, Towards a Dynamic Economics* (London, 1948); and E. D. Domar, "Capital Expansion, Rate of Growth and Employment," *Econometrica.* Apr. 1946, XIV, 137–47; *idem,* "Expansion and Employment," *Am. Econ. Rev*, Mar. 1947, XXXVII, 34–55. These theories, though often referred to as theories of growth, are, properly speaking, theories of the requirements of steady growth at full employment. They make no assertions with respect to the likely development of capital formation over time.

79. A third reason is stressed by Michael Kalecki, *Studies in Economic Dynamics* (London, 1943), pp. 89–92. Innovation stimulates new investment, but it causes the liquidation of old capital in competing uses.

80. Hansen, "Economic Progress and Declining Population Growth," *loc. cit.*, p. 9.

81. J. S. Davis, *The Population Upsurge in the United States*, Food Research Inst., War-Peace Pamphlets, No. 12 (Stanford, 1949).

82. *Ibid.*, p. 21.

83. Along the same lines, we must take note of the opinion of at least a portion of neoclassical thought about the character of the returns to capital. Witness H. C. Simons, who asserts that: "in the sense of potential 'social yield' or of marginal efficiency under free-market conditions, investment opportunities are and have been nearly limitless. Holding fast to Cassel notions, I believe that the productivity curve for new capital is extremely flat; that investment, proceeding at the maximum rate consistent with high thrift, would have little effect for the significant future, even failing large accretions of innovations, on yields in this sense." "Hansen on Fiscal Policy," *Jour. Pol. Econ.*, Apr. 1942, L. 170, Cf. F. H. Knight, "Diminishing Returns from Investment," *ibid.*, Mar. 1944, LII, 26–47. For contrary views, see Keynes, *op. cit.*, pp. 374–77, and D. McC. Wright, "Prof. Knight on Limits to the Use of Capital," *Quart. Jour. Econ.*, May 1944, LVIII, 331–58.

84. Hildebrand, *op. cit.*; E. D. Domar, "Investment, Losses, and Monopolies," in *Income, Employment, and Public Policy*, Ch. 2.

85. Cf. Domar, "Investment, Losses, and Monopolies," *loc. cit.*; Higgins, *op. cit.*

86. E.g., H. C. Simons, *op. cit.*; H. S. Ellis, "Monetary Policy and Investment," *Am.*

Econ. Rev., Proc., Mar. 1040, XXX, 27–38; S. H. Slichter, "The Conditions of Expansion," *Am. Econ. Rev.*, Mar. 1942, XXXII, 1–21.

87. *Capitalism, Socialism and Democracy*, Ch. 10–14.

88. J. J. Spengler, "The Population Obstacle to Economic Betterment," *loc. cit.*, pp. 343–54.

89. Thorstein Veblen, *Imperial Germany and the Industrial Revolution* (New York, 1915), pp. 128–33. See also Rutledge Vining (Testimony before the Interstate Commerce Commission, Dockets No. 29885–6, pp. 47–53), who applies the same ideas to the experience of New England compared with other regions in the United States. Chang employs similar arguments in comparing the pace of advance of a number of leading industrial countries. *Op. cit.*, pp. 111–12.

Part II

Studies in long-term growth

3

Resource and output trends in the United States since 1870

Introduction

This paper is a very brief treatment of three questions relating to the history of our economic growth since the Civil War: (1) How large has been the net increase of aggregate output per capita, and to what extent has this increase been obtained as a result of greater labor or capital input on the one hand and of a rise in productivity on the other? (2) Is there evidence of retardation, or conceivably acceleration, in the growth of per capita output? (3) Have there been fluctuations in the rate of growth of output, apart from the short-term fluctuations of business cycles, and, if so, what is the significance of these swings?

The answers to these three questions, to the extent that they can be given, represent, of course, only a tiny fraction of the historical experience relevant to the problems of growth. Even so, anyone acquainted with their complexity will realize that no one of them, much less all three, can be treated satisfactorily in a short space. I shall have to pronounce upon them somewhat arbitrarily. My ability to deal with them at all is a reflection of one of the more important, though one of

Reprinted by permission from *American Economic Review*, vol. 46, no. 2 (May 1956), 5–23.

I should like to thank Professor Simon Kuznets and Mr. J. W. Kendrick who made available to me certain unpublished estimates of national product, productivity, capital stock, and hours of work. Their contributions are further described in the notes to Table 1. I am grateful to Richard A. Easterlin, Solomon Fabricant, J. W. Kendrick, and G. H. Moore for their critical review of the manuscript and to Mrs. Charlotte Boschan for assisting in its preparation.

This paper was approved for publication as a report of the National Bureau of Economic Research by the Director of Research and the Board of Directors of the National Bureau, in accordance with the resolution of the Board governing National Bureau reports (see the 35th Annual Report of the National Bureau of Economic Research, May, 1955). It is reprinted as No. 52 in the National Bureau's series of "Occasional Papers."

the less obvious, of the many aspects of our growing wealth, namely, the accumulation of historical statistics in this country during the last generation.

For the most part, the figures which I present or which underlie my qualitative statements are taken directly from tables of estimates of national product, labor force, productivity, and the like compiled by others. In a few cases I have ventured to compute ratios or extend the tables forward or backward by combining estimates. But no original estimates depending on the compilation or reworking of primary data are included.

The period since 1870 has an important unifying characteristic in that throughout these eighty years the economy has been growing in response to the complex of cumulative forces which we generally call industrialization. It is quite clear, however, that 1870 was not the beginning of the process of industrialization in this country. The proportion of gainful workers in agriculture fell from 71 per cent in 1820 to 64 per cent in 1850. It fell another 10 percentage points by 1870. Steam transport by water and rail was already common when the period begins. The proportion of the gainfully employed engaged in manufacturing and construction rose from 12 to 21 per cent between 1820 and 1870. Real per capita output rose significantly during the 1850's. It was set back by the Civil War, but aggregate output wellnigh doubled from 1850 to 1870.[1] The data before 1870 – and still more before 1850 – are highly dubious, but it seems clear that the period since 1870 does not include the entire era of industrialization and rapid income rise in this country. We are, in an important sense, dealing with a period arbitrarily delimited by the availability of fairly reliable comprehensive figures.

It may be of some use if I try to state at the very beginning the three main conclusions of my paper. First, between the decade 1869–78 and the decade 1944–53, net national product per capita in constant prices approximately quadrupled, while population more than tripled. The source of the great increase in net product per head was not mainly an increase in labor input per head, not even an increase in capital per head, as these resource elements are conventionally conceived and measured. Its source must be sought principally in the complex of little understood forces which caused productivity, that is, output per unit of utilized resources, to rise.

Second, it is not clear that there has been any significant trend in the rates of growth of total output and of output per head. It is true that national product estimates, on their face, suggest some decline in the rates of growth – somewhat more clearly for total output; somewhat less clearly for output per capita. It is doubtful, however, whether the data can be accepted with confidence for this purpose and still more doubtful whether the apparent retardation in growth, such as it is, represents the effect of persistent forces. Insofar as one can observe a decline in the rate of growth, its source is not in the productivity of resources, which has continued to grow at a steady, perhaps an accelerating pace. Its source has been a decline in the rate of growth of labor input per head and of capital input per head.

Third, the rate of growth of output has not been even. In addition to ordinary business cycles, the rate of growth has risen and fallen since 1870 in long waves of approximately twenty years' duration. Preliminary study suggests that these waves represent, in the main, surges in productivity or resource supply rather than in the proportion of our resources employed. An adequate understanding both of the history of our growth and of our prospects during the next generation depends on our ability to determine whether these surges and relapses are to some significant degree truly recurrent or wholly fortuitous.

The average rate of growth, 1869–1953

My first problem has to do with the over-all expansion of our economy since 1870. My principal criterion of growth is net national product per capita in 1929 prices, and since I use Kuznets' data, I follow him in measuring the increase by comparing average product and related data for labor, capital, and so on, for the decade 1869–78 with that for the decade 1944–53.[2] Comparisons based on such decade averages eliminate most but, of course, not all the effects of business cycles, which might otherwise serve to distort somewhat our impressions of the long-term rate of growth. They do not protect our measures from the effects of fluctuations longer in duration than business cycles, the so-called "secular swings," which I shall discuss later. It would be better to calculate rates of growth from properly derived trend values. But in measures for a period as long as eighty years, when growth was so rapid, the distortion resulting from secular swings will not prevent us from seeing the broad outlines of the picture, and I judged it unnecessary to calculate statistical trend lines for this purpose.

1. Net national product in the decade 1944–53 stood about thirteen times as high as it had in 1869–78 (Table 3.1). This increase implies an average rate of growth of 3.5 per cent per annum. Population, however, more than tripled in the same period. Net product per capita, therefore, approximately quadrupled, implying an average rate of growth of 1.9 per cent per annum.

Table 3.1. *Measures of U.S. economic growth, 1869–78 to 1944–53*

		Relatives for 1944–53 (1869–78 = 100)
(1)	Net national product	1,325
(2)	Population	334
(3)	Net national product per capita	397
(4)	Labor force	423 (393)
(5)	Ratio: labor force to population	127 (118)
(6)	Employment	427 (396)
(7)	Ratio: employment to population	128 (119)
(8)	Standard hours	73
(9)	Man-hours	312 (290)
(10)	Man-hours per capita	94 (87)
(11)	Capital	993
(12)	Capital per capita	297
(13)	Index of total input of resources	381 (361)
(14)	Index of input per capita	114 (108)
(15)	Net national product per employed worker	310 (334)
(16)	Net national product per man-hour	426 (458)
(17)	Net national product per capital unit	134
(18)	Index of net national product per unit of total input	348 (367)

Note: Figures in parentheses exclude armed forces.

All the figures in this table, unless otherwise noted, were drawn from series of averages for overlapping decades running 1869–78, 1874–83, etc.

The units of the data from which the relatives were calculated are shown in the notes to each line.

Line:
(1) Newly revised estimates by Simon Kuznets (now published in *Capital in The American Economy*, see note 2 of this chapter [billions of dollars in 1929 prices]).
(2) *Ibid.*, App. E. Decade averages computed from annual data underlying five-year moving averages.
(3) Line (1) ÷ line (2) (1929 dollars per person).
(4) See line (2).
(5) Line (4) ÷ line (2) (per cent).
(6) Line (4) less estimated unemployment (millions) as follows:
1869–78 to 1884–93: from J. Schmookler, "The Changing Efficiency of the American Economy, 1869–1938," *Review of Economics and Statistics*, August, 1952, Table 3, col. (2).
1889–98 to 1939–48: by applying unemployment percentage from Kuznets, "Long-Term Changes," (see reference in note 1), Table 10, col. (1) to his estimates of the civilian labor force and adding armed forces. From 1889–1918, the labor force figures were first divided into agricultural and nonagricultural segments. The unemployment percentages, which for those years represent only nonagricultural unemployment, were applied to the latter only.
1944–53: By applying ratio of civilian employment to civilian labor force as esti-

mated by Census (*Survey of Current Business*, 1955 Biennial Edition, p. 56) to Kuznets' estimate of civilian labor force and adding armed forces.

(7) Line (6) ÷ line (2) (per cent).

(8) *1869–78 to 1939–48:* from Kuznets, *op. cit.*, Table 7, col. (1). *1944–53:* extrapolated on the basis of the movement of estimates kindly supplied to the author by J. W. Kendrick. (Hours per week.)

(9) Line (6) × line (8) (millions of man-hours per week).

(10) Line (9) ÷ line (2) (weekly hours per capita).

(11) *1874–83 to 1939–48:* Kuznets, *op. cit.*, Table 11, col. (3). Single figures are provided once each decade, 1879 to 1939, for years running 1879, 1889, etc. In addition there are figures for 1934 and 1944. The data are assumed to represent averages for decades whose central points they approximate (1879 for 1874–83, etc.). Overlapping decades interpolated where necessary by straight line arithmetic interpolation from both preceding and succeeding observations. The two results were then averaged.

1869–78: Extrapolated from 1874–83 by movement of estimates by Schmookler, *op. cit.*, Table 5, col. (3).

1944–53: Extrapolated from 1939–48 on basis of estimates kindly supplied by J. W. Kendrick (billions of dollars in 1929 prices).

(12) Line (11) ÷ line (2) (dollars per person).

(13) Weighted index of relatives (1919–28 = 100), combining man-hours × 3 and capital × 1. Weights represent the relative values of service incomes and property incomes respectively as estimated by J. W. Kendrick for 1929 and supplied to author. Kendrick's relative weights were more precisely, 72:28.

(14) Weighted index of relatives (1919–28 = 100), combining man-hours per capita and capital per capita with weights as in line (13).

(15) Line (1) ÷line (6) (dollars per employed in 1929 prices).

(16) Line (1) ÷ line (9) (dollars per man-hour).

(17) Line (1) ÷ line (11) (cents per dollar of capital).

(18) Index of NNP ÷ index of total input of resources (1919–28 = 100).

These calculated rates of increase are only rough approximations of the figures we are really after. Long-term estimates of national products are inevitably marred by statistical weaknesses, biases, and uncertainties of conception. (Cf. Kuznets, "Long-Term Changes," pages 33–47). We must accept the fact that even the most comprehensive and consistent measures of our rate of expansion must be treated with a great deal of reserve.

2. The quadrupling – more or less – of net national product per capita resulted in part from an increase in the input of resources per capita and in part from a rise in their productivity, that is, the output per unit, of representative units of resources. However, the shares of these two elements, insofar as they can be separated, were very different. The input of resources per head of the population appears to have increased relatively little while the productivity of resources increased a great deal. How does this arise?

The input of resources is usually conceived to consist of labor services, including salaried management, and property or capital services, to which is attached the contributions of entrepreneurship made in connection with the investment of capital in industry. If we measure labor services in man-hours, as is usually done, we find that labor input per capita declined slightly between the seventies and the present. This resulted from the counteraction of two trends. The labor force ratio, that is, the ratio of labor force to population, grew about 25 per cent as a result of changes in the age composition of the population, because of the shift of people from farms to cities, and because the great increase in the participation of women in work offset the withdrawal of young people to school and of elderly men to earlier retirement. On the other hand, the reduction in working hours more than counterbalanced the increase in the labor force ratio.[3]

The physical volume of capital, of course, increased much more rapidly than population. An estimate of total capital, which takes account of land, structures, producers' durable equipment, inventories and net foreign claims, increased to nearly ten times its size seventy-five years ago. Capital per head of the population approximately tripled.[4]

What has been the increase in the input of all resources per capita? Suppose we combine our indexes of labor input per capita and of capital supply per capita with weights proportionate to the base period incomes going to labor and property, respectively. If we may equate productivity with earnings, we obtain a combined index of resources which has a particular meaning. It tells us how net national product per capita would have grown had the productivity of resources remained constant at base period levels while only the supplies of resources per head increased. Such an index, based on the twenties, rises only some 14 per cent between the seventies and the last decade. To account for the quadrupling of net national product per capita, the productivity of a representative unit of all resources must have increased some 250 per cent. This seems to imply that almost the entire increase in net product per capita is associated with the rise in productivity. This result may arise in some part from our choice of a base period. We chose a fairly recent base period, 1919–28, close to the valuation base of the national produce estimates, 1929. Since the relative importance of service and property incomes remains fairly stable over the entire period (cf. Kuznets, "Long-Term Changes," pages 135–137), and since capital increased far more rapidly than labor, the price of a unit of capital service must have fallen over time compared with that of a unit of labor. The choice of a fairly recent year as a base for our relatives in effect means weighting each unit of capital by a relatively low price.

Experiment, however, indicates that choice of base is of minor importance for the question at hand. If we shift the base of the index of resources to 1869–78, the increase of total input between 1869–78 and 1944–53 becomes 44 per cent. If we compare this with the rise of net national product per capita in 1929 prices, the indicated rise in productivity is still much greater, 175 per cent. This calculation, however, overstates the importance of the shift in base. If we shift the base for our resource index to 1869–78, we should also value national product in the prices of that decade. This would, in all likelihood, make the trend of national product steeper and so indicate a greater increase in productivity than the 175 per cent mentioned above. (See Kuznets, "Long-Term Changes," pages 44–47.)

3. This result is surprising in the lopsided importance which it appears to give to productivity increase, and it should be, in a sense, sobering, if not discouraging, to students of economic growth. Since we know little about the causes of productivity increase, the indicated importance of this element may be taken to be some sort of measure of our ignorance about the causes of economic growth in the United States and some sort of indication of where we need to concentrate our attention. Since it will do little good to provide a catalogue of the possible causes of the rise in efficiency, I shall merely add two notes which have to do with a proper understanding of calculations which resolve the growth of output into the growth of resources and productivity, respectively. They will, I hope, also take some of the edge off my conclusion and serve to put the importance of factor input in somewhat better perspective.

First, although input of resources per capita has not increased much, this does not mean that the increase of resources has not contributed significantly to the rise in output per head. Total input of labor and capital has increased a great deal. Population more than tripled. The nearly constant number of man-hours per capita, therefore, meant a tripling of total man-hours. The tripling of capital per head meant a more than ninefold increase in total capital. The quadrupling of net national product per capita meant a twelvefold rise of total national product. But "the division of labor is limited by the extent of the market." If there is anything to the notion that when raw materials are plentiful resources and output will be connected according to a law of increasing returns to scale, then the great expansion of total resources must have contributed substantially to the increase in productivity.

Second, our calculations of resource inputs are based on usual definitions of labor supply and capital. These conventional methods of measuring resource inputs are faulty and, in the case of this country during the last seventy-five years, probably understate the increase in factor input. We therefore tend to overstate the rise in productivity.

On the side of labor, it is clear that the reduction in the importance of teenagers and old men in the labor force has concentrated employment in the age groups whose output per man is relatively high. It also seems likely that with the urbanization and commercialization of work there has been an increase in the intensity of labor. These changes may perhaps be offset by the augmented importance of women in the labor force. It seems possible, however, that a properly weighted index of man-hour input would have increased significantly over the period even if we leave out of account such matters as improvements in skill and managerial capacity which reflect training and other capital investment. (Cf. Kuznets, "Long-Term Changes," page 77.)

On the side of capital, there is a chronic underestimate of investment and accumulated stock because, for purposes of measurement, we identify capital formation with the net increase of land, structures, durable equipment, commodity stocks, and foreign claims. But underlying this conventional definition of investment is a more fundamental concept which is broader, namely, any use of resources which helps increase our output in future periods. And if we attempt to broaden the operational definition, then a number of additional categories of expenditures would have to be included, principally those for health, education and training,[5] and research. These are fairly obvious because one is conscious both of an income motivation and an income effect. But there are other classes of expenditures where motives are mixed or disguised but which have at least the incidental effect of increasing productivity, namely, expenditures for food, clothing, and some recreation. The fact is that, in a thoroughly commercialized economy, disposing of a large surplus above its requirements for minimum consumption, very few expenditures are wholly without the aim and effect of increasing income. If this is so, effective capital formation, broadly conceived, must be sought in certain types of consumption and governmental expenditures as well as in conventional net investment.

The point of these two comments is simply that the relation between the contributions of resource expansion and of productivity growth is more complicated than our conventional measures can reveal. Two morals may be drawn. First, the long-term expansion of the labor supply must be restudied so as to provide a measure of the value of its changing composition as well as its changing size. And the expansion of the capital stock must be restudied to take account of a broader conception of accumulated resources. It may well be that we shall find it inconvenient to merge these additional categories of accumulation with conventional capital. But whatever our terminology, we have to pay close attention to all the ways our society uses its resources to increase its future product.

When all due allowance for the concealed increase in resource expansion has been made, however, there will remain a huge area to be explained as an increase in productivity. Our capital stock of knowledge concerning the organization and technique of production has grown at a phenomenal pace. A portion of this increase – presumably an increasing proportion – is due to an investment of resources in research, education, and the like. This part we may possibly be able to attribute accurately to the input of these resources insofar as we learn to trace the connection between such investment in knowledge and its marginal social contribution, as distinct from those small parts of its value which can be privately appropriated. Beyond this, however, lies the gradual growth of applied knowledge which is, no doubt, the result of human activity, but not of that kind of activity involving costly choice which we think of as economic input. To identify the causes which explain not only the rate at which our opportunities to raise efficiency increase but also the pace at which we take advantage of those opportunities will, no doubt, remain the central problem in both the history and theory of our economic growth. The chief excuse for attempts to separate the measurable contributions of resources from those of productivity is to pose this problem as clearly as possible.

The trend of the rate of growth

From these measures of the net expansion of output and resources since the Civil War, I turn next to the often asked question: has our rate of growth been slowing up. The retardation of growth in Great Britain and in other leading industrial countries and our own experience in the thirties have made the possibility of retardation a source of widespread anxiety.

Unfortunately, the information now available does not permit us to make a secure answer. The sources of error and bias in national product estimates – already noticed in connection with the measures of expansion – apply with aggravated force when we try to compare rates of growth at different times. We can often guess the direction in which national product estimates are biased, but in most cases we do not now know whether a particular bias affected the figures more strongly in one decade than another. It is clear, for example, that our inability to take consistent account of household production makes the rate of growth of national product too high during a period in which household production was giving way to commercial production. It is probable also that the rate of transfer from home to business changed over time. But did the transfer proceed more rapidly in the last quarter of the nineteenth century than in the second quarter of the twentieth, and by how much? This is the question relevant to changes in the rate of growth. We cannot answer it with any confidence. It is certain, therefore, that any statements about a long-term tendency in the rate of growth of national product must be treated with the greatest reserve unless the drift is so large and so persistent that no likely combination of biases and errors could account for it. In my judgment, the drift of the figures is not so clear. It is, nevertheless, worth while to review them, partly to check the bases for much current interpretation and speculation and partly because it is interesting to try to allocate the apparent changes in output growth to inputs and productivity.

Taking the figures as they stand, they give some indication of a slowing down in the rate of growth over the course of the eighty-odd years since 1870. To see this, one has to take account not only of the ordinary business cycles, which generally run their course well within a decade, but also of the longer fluctuations which appear in the rate of growth of output. I shall have something more to say about these fluctuations in the next section. A smoothing of the data to eliminate both types of fluctuations suggests that total net product rose more rapidly during the last quarter of the nineteenth century than it did during the second quarter of the twentieth century. The apparent decline in the rate of growth of product per capita is less pronounced.[6] (See Figure 3.1.)

Whatever the showing of the figures, however, it is not at all clear that they are accurate enough for the purpose or, if accurate, that they represent the work of persistent forces in the economy. The very high rate of growth in the last quarter of the nineteenth century reflects an exceptionally high rate of increase during the late seventies and early eighties. If we neglect this apparently remarkable decade and take into account the possibilities of error and bias, the rates of growth afford no significant indication of retardation until we reach the depression of the thirties.[7] The early figures of rapid growth are the least secure portions of the estimates. If valid, they may reflect a temporary surge of output.[8]

On the other hand, the low rate of growth in the second quarter of the present century is entirely a reflection of the Great Depression. The rates of expansion since 1934 are as high as in any earlier period other than the (possibly exceptional) period in the late seventies and early eighties. They would look still higher on the basis of the Commerce figures than they do on the basis of the Kuznets estimates.

Whether there has been a significant degree of persistent retardation in the growth of national product per capita would, therefore, seem to turn on the answers to two questions presently unanswerable. Do the various biases and weaknesses in the estimates make for an appearance of acceleration or retardation? Did the surge of the early years and the deep depression of the latter years represent fortuitous or persistent forces?

Whatever the answer to these important questions of history, it is possible to reach some conclusion with regard to the sources of the apparent retardation. Whatever tendency there may have been for growth of net product per capita to decline is traceable very largely, if not entirely, to a decline in the rate of growth of resources used per head of the population. Until the last two decades, which were years of accelerated growth both of input and output per capita, all the elements of resource input had grown less rapidly or declined more rapidly in later decades than in earlier. The ratio of labor force to population, which increased fairly steadily from 1870 until around 1910, thereafter fell, or grew very little, until the decade of the forties. With the exception of these recent years, hours of work fell at a more rapid rate during the 1900's than during the late 1800's. As a result, man-hours per head rose at a declining rate until the turn of the century and then fell at an increasing pace until the mid-thirties. One may add that the diversion of labor force to military purposes increased over time. So the decline in the rate of growth of civilian man-hours per head was even more pronounced than in that of total man-hours. In the thirties, of course, great unemployment was an aggravating element. The growth of capital per head, as conventionally measured, slowed down drastically. It rose at a constantly slower rate until the end of the twenties, and then declined during the depression. In spite of rapid growth during the last fifteen years, capital per head in the late forties was only a little more plentiful than in the twenties. Until relatively recent years, therefore, every major element of resources made for retardation in the growth of net product per capita. The combined index of resources per capita rose at a declining rate until the early 1900's and then fell at an increasing rate until the middle thirties.

It was these changes in the growth of resources per head which account for most, if not all, the retardation in the growth of net product per capita recorded in the estimates. Productivity per man-hour, on the other hand, has been rising at a fairly constant rate since the eighties, and this trend has dominated the movement of the produc-

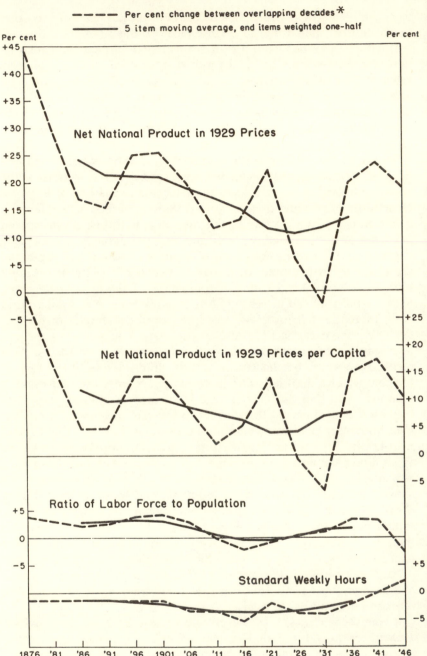

*Values are percentage rates of change since preceding overlapping decade, plotted at decade centers.

Figure 3.1. Trends in growth rates, 1869–1953.

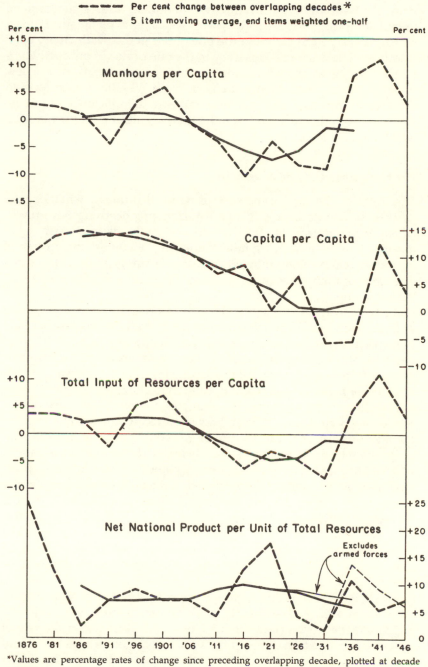

Figure 3.1 (continued). Trends in growth rates, 1869–1953. *Sources:* see notes to Table 3.1.

tivity of all resources. The productivity of capital, taken alone, seemed to be falling until about World War I. It has been rising since, a fact which has helped to maintain the rate of rise in the productivity of all resources. The essential constancy in the rate of rise of productivity is perhaps the most significant single fact which emerges from a review of our economic record since the Civil War.[9] Whether this reflects an essentially unweakened capacity to increase the efficiency of our resources in the future is perhaps the most significant single question which requires an answer.

Fluctuations in the rate of growth

The trend of the rate of increase of national product, whether constant or slowly declining, is a generalization concerning our growth which abstracts from its fluctuations and pretends to describe only its persistent or underlying movement. But, of course, the growth of output in reality is anything but steady. It rarely runs in the same direction for many months and almost never for even two months at the same rate.

We have learned to think of these alterations of the rate of growth as in part accidental and in part systematic. Aside from seasonal fluctuations, the systematic movement principally identified in the past has been the short-term business cycle either in its minor or major variant. If, however, to reveal the secular trend in output we calculate moving averages for periods long enough to eliminate business cycles (nine-year moving averages, for example), the resulting curve of output for the period since 1870 still reveals striking fluctuations – not in the level of output but in its rate of growth. The curve mounts relatively steeply for a time and then exhibits retardation in a pattern which has repeated itself roughly every twenty years. The same observations may be made if one calculates rates of increase in decade averages of output for overlapping decades (see Figure 3.1). (Cf. Kuznets, "Long-Term Changes," pages 48–57.) The possibility, therefore, arises that there is a significant cycle in the secular trend of output – meaning by this, movements which persist over a period longer than a business cycle – with an approximate duration of twenty years.[10]

In relatively recent times, the hypothesis of a twenty-year growth cycle starts with Kuznets' early work on secular trends in which he suggested the existence of fluctuations of this duration in the rate of growth of production of many individual commodities, in the rate of rise of many prices, and in several other types of time series. (*Secular Trends in Production and Prices*, Houghton Mifflin, 1930, Chapter IV.)

The hypothesis was then taken up by Arthur F. Burns in his *Production Trends in the United States Since 1870* (National Bureau of Economic Research, 1934, Chapter V), in which he showed not only that twenty-year growth cycles were characteristic of the output of many commodities but also that the cycle was general in the sense that the growth cycles of different commodities tended to concur in time and that they also appeared in indexes of aggregate industrial production. Burns also found his secular swings in nonagricultural prices, in shares traded, in business failures, and in patents issued. Finally Kuznets in later work has shown that the same swings appear in his long-term estimates of gross and net national product ("Long-Term Changes," pages 48–57), in labor productivity, in population and immigration (with a lag), and in residential construction (with a longer lag).[11] Unpublished work by Kuznets and Dorothy S. Thomas carries the subject further, particularly as regards population change, internal migration, construction, and certain financial series. Still others suggest the presence of a similar cycle in foreign countries.[12] Both Kuznets and Burns considered their work only exploratory and neither was persuaded that the evidence so far accumulated established the existence of significant recurrence of movement, that is, of true cycles.

Kuznets finds three complete swings in the rate of growth in the period since 1870 and one incomplete swing – a rise beginning 1932 and (tentatively) reaching its peak in 1945.[13] The variation in the rate of growth between the expansion and contraction phases of the growth cycles is large compared with the average rate of growth itself. For example, in the period 1873–1926, that is, before the huge fluctuations associated with the Great Depression and World War II, the over-all average rate of rise of GNP per worker was about 20 per cent per decade. But the average rate of growth in upswing periods was about five times as rapid as in the downswing periods. The average difference between the rate of growth in the upswing periods and that in the downswing periods was as large as the average rate of growth itself.[14] If we add the last long swing, which covers the Great Depression and the upswing of the forties, the size of the average fluctuation becomes very much greater than the average rate of growth.

The significance of these long swings is not yet established. At least two possibilities are present which would rob the observed fluctuations of most of their meaning. It may be that what we observe are only accidental variations in the severity or duration of ordinary business cycles, which assume the appearance of long swings when their effects are stretched out and smoothed by moving averages or some similar device. And even if it is true that the swings reflect forces which operate over periods longer than business cycles, it may still be true that these forces are predominantly irregular and haphazard.

These negative possibilities cannot now be dismissed. Indeed the influence upon the swings so far experienced in this country of substantial irregular forces was patent and undeniable. Thus it seems reasonable to attribute some significant responsibility for the swing beginning around 1873 to the recovery from the Civil War, for the swing beginning around 1912 and continuing through the twenties to World War I, and for the swing beginning in 1932 and continuing into the forties to World War II. It would be impossible to try to review the considerable body of relevant evidence in the short space available to me. For purposes of this discussion, I can simply record my conviction that there is sufficient evidence to make the long-swing hypothesis worthy of closer investigation.[15]

If supported by further study, the long-swing hypothesis promises to make a serious contribution to our understanding of economic change. I shall cite three reasons:

First, if it be true that the long swings reflect, in significant degree, the operation of systematic responses to either regular or irregular stimuli, then study of our past growth will best be organized in periods corresponding to the long swings. And a proper understanding of these waves of growth will presuppose an ability to separate the unique from the recurrent forces at work in each period.

Second, the long swings appear to represent fluctuations in productivity growth and in the increase of manpower and capital to a greater degree than business cycles whose most prominent characteristic is that they are fluctuations in the intensity with which resources are employed. (Before the Great Depression, quinquennial changes in the level of employment were not well correlated with the long swings in the rate of growth of output, nor were the magnitude of the changes in employment percentages comparable in size with those in output. Cf. Kuznets, "Long-Term Changes," Tables 3 and 10. These facts also bear on the question of the independence of the longer swings from business cycles. It is not yet clear, however, that the unemployment figures are sufficiently accurate for the purpose, and the conclusion needs to be checked by further study.) Unless it turns out that fluctuations in the growth of productivity or of resource supply are themselves chiefly governed by business cycle movements, we must anticipate fluctuations in the rate of growth of output even if we succeed in maintaining employment at high levels. Since past fluctuations in the rate of growth were wide relative to its long-term average, projections of output looking forward a decade or two – such as are often made –

would need to take into account the current phase of the long swing. This presupposes a capacity to define the recurrent features of long swings – something we cannot do today.

Finally, our past experience with long swings shows that every upswing in the rate of growth has terminated in the depression of great severity. This may, as Burns has tentatively suggested (see note 15, p. 147), be connected with a tendency for growth to become increasingly unbalanced as the upswing proceeds, presumably leading to a decline of investment in the overexpanded industries. Or a mere slowing down of the rate of growth of output for any reason may lead to a reduction of investment, as one variant of the Harrod-Domar theory suggests. In either case, there is reason to expect that whenever our rate of progress begins to slow down markedly, forces will also be present making for serious depression. Such depressions will not necessarily be experienced in view of the role government may play in counteracting them. But certainly the wisdom and energy of the government will be put to a severe test. The experience with long swings suggests that our liability to severe depression may be a normal part of a swing in the rate of growth, which may itself be due, in part to recurrent causes. If these could be identified and better understood, our ability to prepare for, and to meet, the emergency of depression would undoubtedly be enhanced.

Notes

1. These are W. I. King's figures (*The Wealth and Income of the People of the United States*, Macmillan, 1915, Table XXIII), as deflated by Simon Kuznets ("Long-Term Changes in the National Income of the United States of America since 1870" – hereinafter called "Long-Term Changes" – published in *Income and Wealth of the United States*, edited by Simon Kuznets, Cambridge, Bowes and Bowes, 1952, p. 240.)

2. Professor Kuznets has very kindly permitted me to use his newly revised estimates extended to 1953. These are, as yet, unpublished, but very similar figures are published in "Long-Term Changes." The broad concepts on which the data are based and the methods of estimate are described in that volume, pp. 29–34. The latter have been altered in certain details in ways which Professor Kuznets will describe in a later publication. (See *Capital in the American Economy: Its Formation and Financing*, Princeton University Press /or National Bureau of Economic Research, 1961, Appendixes A–C.)

3. Cf. C. D. Long, *The Labor Force under Changing Employment and Income* (National Bureau of Economic Research; 1958), Chap. XI. While there may have been some difference in the percentage of unemployment between the 1870's and the 1950's, the great decline of working time per member of the labor force was due to a reduction in hours of work. The change in working hours recorded in our table is based on a series appearing in Kuznet's "Long-Term Changes" extended an extra decade on the basis of Kendrick's figures. But other estimates make the long-term decline somewhat less or more. For comparison, the following alternatives are of interest:

	Base period	Given year or period	Index of average hours in given year (base = 100)
(1) Kuznets, Standard Hours	1869–78	1944–53	73
(2) Dewhurst and Fichlander, Actual Hours	1870–80	1950	62
(3) Barger, Actual Hours in Commodity Production	1869–79	1949	83
(4) Barger, Actual Hours in Distribution	1869–79	1949	66
(5) Kuznets, Standard Hours	1894–1903	1944–53	79
(6) Kendrick, Actual Hours	1899	1953	83

Sources:

Line (1) – "Long-Term Changes," Table 7. Figures extended from 1939–48 to 1944–53 on the basis of estimates kindly supplied by J. W. Kendrick

Line (2) – Dewhurst and Associates, *America's Needs and Resources, A New Survey* (Twentieth Century Fund, 1955), Appendix 20-4.

Line (3) – *Distribution's Place in the American Economy since 1869*, Table 5.

Line (4) – Same as line (3).

Line (5) – Same as line (1).

Line (6) – Supplied by J. W. Kendrick.

4. Estimates of capital wealth are extremely rough and must be treated with great reserve. While there is no doubt that capital increased much faster than population, we may well doubt whether the relative increase was just that suggested by the figures. Our figures are based on the table presented by Kuznets for the years 1879–1944 ("Long-Term Changes," Table 11). See notes to Table 3.1. These figures may be compared with R. W. Goldsmith's estimates ("Derivation of a Perpetual Inventory of National Wealth since 1896," *Studies in Income and Wealth*, Vol. 14, National Bureau of Economic Research, p. 18.

	Relatives for 1944		
	Goldsmith (1900 = 100) (1)	Kuznets (1899 = 100) (2)	Ratio (2) ÷ (1)
Land	133	208	1.56
Reproducible wealth*	271	344	1.27
Total	216	284	1.31

*Structures, producers' durable equipment, inventories and net foreign claims.

Neither Godlsmith's figures nor Kuznets' are free of serious difficulties due to weaknesses in the statistical sources of capital data and to problems of valuation and deflation. (See Kuznets, *op. cit.*, pp. 79–80, and Goldsmith, *op. cit., passim*, and following comments by Kuznets.) It is possible that the true increase of capital lies outside the range suggested by both sets of figures. Our figures make no allowance for changes in the service hours of capital comparable with that for labor. There is no statistical basis for such an adjustment. The decline in labor hours is not a reliable indication since capital is often operated on multiple shifts or even continuously. It is not clear whether such practices have grown or declined.

5. A properly constructed index of labor input which gave due weight to the higher productivity of more highly educated or trained workers and to differences in vigor would be an alternative way to try to take these inputs into account.

6. Kuznets' original estimates of net national product, which appear in the form of decade averages of annual data for overlapping decades, may be taken to eliminate most of the effects of ordinary business cycles. The same may be said of the rates of change between the overlapping decade averages (essentially rates of change per quinquennium). If we then take five-item moving averages of these rates of change (end items weighted one-half), we average experience for a twenty-year period, which is probably long enough to eliminate most of the effects of the longer fluctuations in the rates of growth. Both the quinquennial rates of change and the moving averages are shown in Figure 3.1.

7. Compare Arthur F. Burn's conclusions for the period 1870–1930 based upon his study of physical output indexes. While he is highly skeptical about any conclusion which might be reached on the basis of the data available to him, he ventured to write: ". . . if there has been any decline in the rate of growth in the total physical production of this country, its extent has probably been slight, and it is even mildly probable that the rate of growth may have increased somewhat." (Cf. *Production Trends in the U.S. Since 1870*, page 279.) Since the retardation in the growth of the physical volume of production was almost certainly less than that in population, Burns felt it was still less probable that the growth of per capita output had been drifting downward.

8. There is, indeed, some evidence that rates of growth were lower in the immediately preceding decades. After a discussion of W. I. King's older estimates for the period 1850–80, Professor Kuznets comments: ". . . the only safe comparison one can draw is that per capita real income did show some increase from 1850 to 1880, perhaps as much as 50 per cent or more, perhaps as little as 20 per cent or less." This contrasts with Professor Kuznets' own estimate that per capita real income rose some 50 per cent in the single decade interval 1869–78 to 1879–88. Cf. Kuznets, "Long-Term Changes," p. 240.

9. It is a "fact" heavily qualified by all the errors and biases in the national product figures and in the estimates of labor input and capital. Moreover, it measures both labor input and capital in a fashion which neglects some increase in labor input due to change in the age composition of the labor force and probably in the intensity of work. It also neglects the fact that a substantial volume of resources has been devoted to the improvement of intangible capital: technology, labor skills, health, and organization. The rate of accumulation of such intangible capital may be increasing. It is a "fact" which is somewhat bolstered by the showing of other over-all measures of productivity. These measures, to which I refer below, are not based on data which are wholly independent of those on which I rely, but they involve some degree of independence and they are each calculated on a somewhat different plan: (1) John W. Kendrick's estimate of "national output per unit of labor and capital combined," 1899–1953, shows no retardation in growth. Its rate of growth since 1919 is somewhat greater than it was in the two earlier decades. (National Bureau of Economic Research, *35th Annual Report*, May, 1955, page 45.) (2) The Twentieth Century Fund estimate of "real private national income per private manhour," 1850–1952, has a trend which suggests a mild degree of

acceleration. (Dewhurst and Assocates, *op. cit.*, pp. 39–42.) (3) Jacob Schmookler's estimate of gross national product per combined unit of labor and capital, 1869–1938, shows no tendency to retardation in growth after the first decade. (*Op. cit.*, Table 9.) (4) Harold Barger's estimates of productivity per man-hour in commodity production (agriculture, mining, and manufacturing) and distribution, 1869–1949, show either a steady rate of growth or else acceleration, whether taken individually or in combination. Since Barger's estimates are based on indexes of the physical volume of production in the four industrial branches, his figures are more nearly independent of our own than are the other alternatives. Barger's figures take no account of productivity in the service industries other than distribution. It is possible that a productivity index for the remainder of the service trades, if one could be devised, would change the picture. (*Distribution's Place in the American Economy since 1869*, National Bureau of Economic Research, 1955, pp. 37–41.)

   10. Although my discussion is restricted to the twenty-year cycle, I do not mean to suggest that the secular trend of output may not be subject to other significant types of fluctuations. If it is, however, their period is too long to be distinguished clearly from the underlying trend in a review covering some seventy to eighty years.

   11. Simon Kuznets and Ernest Rubin, *Immigration and the Foreign Born* (National Bureau of Economic Research, "Occasional Paper 46," 1954), pp. 30–34. The findings of this paper are, to some extent, similar to those of Brinley Thomas.

   12. See Walter Hoffman, *British Industry, 1700–1950* (Oxford: Blackwell, 1955; a translation of the German original published 1940), Part C. Brinley Thomas (*Migration and Economic Growth*, Cambridge, 1954, especially Chaps. VII and VIII) argues that there were twenty-year cycles in the United States (and, to some extent, Canada and Australia) connected by immigration and capital movements to inverted cycles in Great Britain, Sweden, and perhaps Germany. B. Weber and S. J. Handfield-Jones ("Variations in the Rate of Economic Growth in the U.S.A., 1869–1938," *Oxford Economic Papers*, June, 1954, pp. 101–131) attempt to connect the long waves in Kuznets' figures for national product with successive waves of innovation in the application of steam power to industry and transport (1870–82), in the further extension of steam and steel and in the development of new resources (1894–1907), and in electricity, industrial chemicals, and the internal combustion engine (1919–29).

   13. The suggested chronology runs as follows:

Trough	Peak
1873	1884
1892	1903
1912	1926
1932	1945

The dates were determined by observing a graph of a nine-year moving average of GNP per worker in 1929 prices and locating the points at which the slope became significantly steeper and flatter. The first and last dates are set only tentatively until the data can be extended far enough backwards and forwards to confirm the position of the inflection point. This chronology was presented in an unpublished memorandum, "Swings in the Rate of Secular Growth," prepared for the Capital Requirements Study of the National Bureau (March, 1952). A similar chronology based on the movement of rates of change of net national product in 1929 prices between overlapping decades appears in "Long-Term Changes," p. 55. An earlier chronology, based on the consensus of many commodity production series, but containing an extra cycle in the decade 1910–20, was presented by A. F. Burns, *op. cit.*, p. 196. Since but few examples have as yet been traced in the American data, neither the average duration of the alleged cycle nor its variability can be considered established.

14. These are geometric means weighted by the duration of phases. The data are from Kuznets' memorandum, "Swings in the Rate of Secular Growth."

15. Merely to indicate that this position has some tangible basis, one may cite the following:

A. In support of the proposition that the long swings are more than merely an illusory reflection of business cycles: (1) The persistence of long swings in figures arranged to show average levels in identified business cycles (Kuznets, "Swings in the Rate of Secular Growth"). (2) The persistence of long swings in figures for business cycle peaks alone, which thus partially eliminate the effects of long and deep depressions (*ibid.*). (3) The existence of long swings in British data which, at least for 1870–1914, appear to fluctuate inversely to the swings in this country, whereas the normal business cycle relation is positive (B. Thomas, *op. cit.*, Chap. VII). (4) The fact that the period required for the exploitation of major innovations or new territory is certainly longer than the five or six years associated with even major business expansions. This does not account for the twelve or thirteen year long-swing expansions or for twenty-year cycles, but it argues for the presence of unsteady expansive stimuli which carry over from one business cycle to another.

B. In support of the view that the long swings exhibit at least some regular features, in addition to the impact of many irregular circumstances, confident assertion is prevented by lack of study and by the fact that U.S. production data in fair quantity now reach back only to 1860 and, therefore, reveal only three and one-half long swings. Subject to these limitations, there are clear hints of regularities which suggest the presence of an internal structure with some stability. I refer only to certain prominent observations in published sources: (1) Burns's finding that during periods of long-swing expansion, the rates of growth of production of different commodities become increasingly different and that this dispersion of the rates of growth declines in long-swing contractions (*Production Trends*, pp. 242–247). (2) Burns's finding that each period of long-swing expansion is followed by a business cycle depression of great severity, a finding which he tentatively connects with the increasing dispersion in the rate of expansion of individual industries during the upswing (*ibid.*, pp. 247–253). (3) Kuznets' and Rubin's finding ("Immigration and the Foreign Born") confirming B. Thomas' finding (*op. cit.*, Chaps. VII and VIII) concerning the lagged response of immigration to the rate of growth of output, and Kuznets' finding that the rate of increase of population showed a lagged response to economic growth ("Long-Term Changes," p. 55). (4) The common finding (cf. Kuznets and Rubin, *op. cit.*) that there is a lagged response of construction to population growth.

4

Economic growth in the United States:
a review article

Few things have been more common in recent economics literature and in political pronouncements than expressions of dissatisfaction with the pace of U.S. economic growth, accompanied by ringing demands that we "can and must" speed the pace of our development. And, of course, few things have been less common than objective analyses of the grounds for dissatisfaction or coherent and comprehensive programs for accelerating our growth. This is the gap that Edward Denison's book* attempts to fill. His work is, in fact, a notable contribution to a vexed and difficult subject. In astonishingly brief compass, Denison presents a picture of past trends in output growth and in the development of the various sources to which the growth of productive capacity can be traced, a projection of the probable future flows from these sources, and a measured evaluation of the possible steps that might be taken to make the flows still larger. Moreover, in grappling with these complicated and still largely unexplored issues, he has achieved a quite remarkable combination of technical finesse and depth with clear and almost deceptively simple exposition. The book is, therefore, a minor miracle of lucidity and persuasiveness which calls for the most serious study by economists while it engages the attention of a much wider audience.

It would perhaps be too much to say that, with the appearance of Denison's book, the whole subject of U.S. economic growth has been decisively clarified, that we now know where we have come from,

*A review of E. F. Denison, *The Sources of Economic Growth in the United States and the Alternatives Before Us*. Supplementary Paper No. 13. New York: Committee for Economic Development, 1962.

Reprinted by permission from *American Economic Review*, vol. 52, no. 4 (September 1962), 762–82.

The author gratefully acknowledges the help of his colleague Paul David, whose suggestions made it possible to clarify a number of points of substance and exposition.

where we are going, and what we can reasonably try to do about it. Unfortunately, our statistical records do not permit some issues regarding past trends to be resolved. Crucial questions regarding the sources of growth are settled in Denison's book by the author's *ex cathedra* pronouncements rather than by reference to those empirically tested production functions on which the author would prefer to rely but towards which economists are only now beginning to grope. Unavoidably built on shaky foundations, Denison's judgments about future trends and about policy issues, though models of caution and restraint, are necessarily of uncertain value. Nevertheless, Denison's book does more than any other to bring our knowledge – inadequate as it is – to bear on the amazingly wide range of issues involved. It is, at the very least, a beautifully ordered program for research and a reasonable, indeed an indispensable, basis for discussions of policy.

While Denison's work challenges attention and comment in its sections dealing with the trend of past growth and in those which attempt projections of the future, the core of the book, as its title suggests, consists in its analysis of the "sources" of past growth and in its discussion of the various measures we might now take to make the flow from these sources more rapid in the future. It seems best, therefore, to confine this review chiefly to these two subjects.

The sources of growth in the United States

The growth Denison seeks to explain is growth in *capacity* to produce or, as he sometimes calls it, *potential production*. The production with which he is concerned is *measured* output, that is, the output whose value is aggregated to form the net or gross national product. The *sources* of growth are changes in those elements into which output can be immediately resolved, that is, inputs of factors of production and factor productivity, changes in the latter being further attributed to the advance of knowledge, scale effects, and gains or losses from reductions or enlargements of market restraints, lags in application of knowledge, and similar causes.

Denison's approach represents an expression of the method of analysis introduced by Jacob Schmookler [8] and by various students at the National Bureau of Economic Research and given its most complete and systematic statement in John W. Kendrick's recently published work [4].[1] The novelty and contribution of Denison's analysis is best brought out by comparison with that of Kendrick and his colleagues. In simplest form, these writers distinguished two broad categories of inputs: labor services measured in employed man-hours; and services of capital stock, including land, measured as the real net stock available after depreciation. The two categories of inputs were combined into an index of total input of resources, weighting each category by its base-period earnings. The essential meaning of the index of total factor input is that it shows how national product would have grown had earnings per unit of each unit remained at its base period level with changes only in the quantities of the inputs. If these index numbers are now divided into corresponding index numbers for national product, one obtains an index of output per unit of input, sometimes called an index of productivity.

Denison did not follow Kendrick in one further step: Kendrick's labor input is a weighted aggregate built up from the man-hours utilized by 13 separate major segments of the economy and by industry groupings within 5 such segments, the weights being average hourly earnings; and his input of capital is likewise a weighted aggregate of net capital stock available in some 5 major segments and 20 manufacturing industry groups, the weights being average capital compensation (or nonlabor income) per unit. The net effect of this weighting scheme is that input increases if *either* the physical quantity of labor or capital used in any sector grows *or* if the proportion of labor or capital used in sectors with relatively high returns becomes larger. The rationale for the use of such weighted indexes of inputs is that interindustry differences in average earnings are thought to represent differences in the quantity of actual input or contribution to output associated with a nominal unit of labor or capital reflecting ultimately differences in the quality of such units (cf. Kendrick [4], p. 33). This is clearly a moot point with which Denison takes issue.

Indexes of input and productivity obtained by this procedure can be given precise significance only to the degree that several far-reaching assumptions are valid. First, units of inputs in each class distinguished must be of uniform quality and their relative rates of remuneration in the base period proportionate to their marginal productivities. Next the quality of resources in each class should remain unchanged over time and relative marginal productivities should not alter because the relative quantities of the factors vary or because shifts in the production function are not neutral.[2] To the extent that these conditions of constancy do not obtain, the index of "productivity" derived will reflect the effects of changes in the quality or relative quantities of factors of production. Even so the index of productivity will only represent the effect of "costless" advances in applied technology, managerial efficiency, and industrial organization ("cost" – the employment of scarce resources with alternative uses – is, after all, the touchstone of an "input") when, in addition, we can neglect the undifferentiated consequences of other factors: the so-called "unconventional inputs," such as investments or expenditures for education, health and research, the effects of economies of scale resulting from the growth of all inputs, and the effects of changes in the effectiveness of resource use associated with changing degrees of monopoly power and of other restrictions on output or the most economical use of resources. In recognition of these ambiguities, the index of productivity produced by Kendrick and his predecessors has been dubbed by some a "measure of ignorance," and it is often referred to simply as the Residual.

In its very broad lines, Denison's method is similar. Like Kendrick, he combines labor input and capital input, weighting each by its base-year earnings, to obtain an index of total factor input whose meaning is the same as that of Kendrick's. And, like Kendrick, he obtains an index of productivity by dividing an index of real national product by his index of total factor input. Denison's measures of labor and capital input, however, are differently constructed, and the Residual is broken down in an attempt to reveal its constituent elements. He substitutes a measure of the gross (that is, undepreciated) capital stock for measures of the net capital stock usually employed.[3] He rejects the procedure – of weighting man-hours in separate industries by their average hourly earnings – by which Kendrick tries to allow for the effect of shifts in the industrial composition of the labor force on the quality of labor input. Denison's procedure is more direct and, in a sense, more radical. He starts with a measure of the over-all contribution of aggregate man-hours and then adjusts it for changes in several specified elements of quality: the increased experience and better use of women; changes in the age-sex composition of the labor force; greater efficiency per man-hour associated with reductions in hours worked per week and year; and the rise in the level of education. The treatment of labor input goes a certain distance towards freeing the Residual from the impact of shifts in the quality of inputs associated with demographic changes and from unconventional inputs – in this case, expenditures for education. But Denison breaks open the Residual still more widely by making allowances for the effects of changes in various kinds of market restrictions on the movement of productivity, for economies of scale, and for the advance of knowledge.

The effect of these differences can be seen most clearly by displaying Denison's results in tabular form. Table 4.1, lines 1–8, shows the outcome of his analysis as it would have appeared had he stopped at the same stage as earlier writers had done. It shows the very large part of total output that remains to be explained by the Residual when the only inputs accounted for are capital[4] and undifferentiated man-hours and when the contributions of these inputs to growth are given

Table 4.1. *Allocation of growth rate of real national income among the sources of growth*

		Percentage points in growth rate		
		1909–29	1929–57	1909–57
1.	Real national income	2.82	2.93	2.89
2.	Increase in total inputs	1.63	.92	1.22
3.	Labor input (unweighted man-hours)	.88	.47	.65
4.	Employment	1.11	1.00	1.06
5.	Hours	−.23	−.53	−.41
6.	Capital	.75	.45	.57
7.	Increase in output per unit of input (The Residual)	1.19	2.01	1.67
8.	Ratio: 7 ÷ 1	.42	.69	.58
9.	Increase in total input (Kendrick)	1.96	1.10	1.46
10.	Output per unit of input (1 minus 9) (the Residual)	.86	1.83	1.43
11.	Ratio: 10 ÷ 1	.31	.62	.50

Sources: Lines 1–7: Denison, Table 19. Line 9: Based on Kendrick [4, Table A XIX]. Line 10: Line 1 minus line 9.

weights based on their base-period earnings.[5] For comparison, lines 9–11 provide figures based on Kendrick's input calculations and Denison's (that is, Department of Commerce) national income estimates. The difference betwen Kendrick's and Denison's estimates of the contributions of input – and the complementary difference between the contributions of the Residual – is not large. Such as it is, it derives in small part from the somewhat different procedures they use to estimate capital input. The major part of the difference, however, represents the fact that Kendrick's labor input is derived from a weighted sum of man-hours in a considerable number of industries, the weights being hourly earnings. The contribution of labor is, therefore, augmented by the shift of labor over time from industries in which average earnings were relatively low to those in which they were relatively high.

By contrast with this relatively simple set of figures stands Table 4.2 in which Denison summarizes his own work.[6] Comparison of the two tables reveals a number of striking differences. Most prominent is the large reduction in the apparent importance of the increase in output per unit of input to under half its former size. Three adjustments in labor input account for the bulk of the change. Two large adjustments are made to allow for the alleged effects of shorter hours and of the

Table 4.2. *Allocation of growth rate of real national income among the sources of growth*

	Percentage points in growth rate	
	1909–29	1929–57
Real national income	2.82	2.93
Increase in total inputs	2.26	2.00
Labor input, adjusted for quality	1.53	1.57
Employment	1.11	1.00
Hours	−.23	−.53
Effect of shorter hours on quality	.23	.33
Education	.35	.67
Increased experience and better use of women	.06	.11
Changes in age-sex composition of labor force	.01	−.01
Capital input	.73	.43
Nonfarm residential structures	.13	.05
Other structures and equipment	.41	.28
Inventories	.16	.08
U.S.-owned assets abroad	.02	.02
Foreign assets in U.S.	.01	.00
Increase in output per unit of input	.56	.93
Restrictions against optimum use of resources	NA	−.07
Reduced waste in agriculture	NA	.02
Industry shift from agriculture	NA	.05
Advance of knowledge	NA	.58
Change in lag in application of knowledge	NA	.01
Economies of scale – independent growth of local markets	NA	.07
Economies of scale – growth of national market	.28	.27

Source: Denison, Table 32. Certain lines in Denison's table constituting subtotals not reproduced. One line referring to the contribution of "Land" is omitted. Denison puts the contribution at zero on the ground that available land has been constant during the period covered.

rise in the level of education upon the quality of labor input per hour worked. A third, smaller, adjustment takes account of the fact that women in the labor force have come typically to represent a more experienced group employed at work which makes better use of their talents. The Residual, moreover, no longer seems just that. It has seven different parts, each with a name, the two largest of which are "economies of scale" and "advance of knowledge." Moreoever, even the items in Table 4.2 which have small numbers attached to them provide substantial pieces of information. They tell us that certain characteristics of the economy, which might have been deemed important for growth, in fact were not. Denison, in short, appears to have done what every economist concerned with the subject has hoped would be done, namely, broken down the Residual into its component elements. The inevitable question is whether his attempt is successful. I propose to tackle this question in brief comments on the major elements in Denison's adjustments.

Hours of work and labor productivity

Denison argues with considerable plausibility that when hours of work are very long, workers' output per man-hour is lower than it might be. Presumably they cannot work either as hard, as carefully, or as cleverly as they would were their daily, weekly, and annual stints shorter. Consequently, when hours are reduced, one may suppose that some parts of the potential loss occasioned by the reduction in hours are offset by greater productivity per man-hour, and this offset ought to be counted as an increase in labor input.

To implement this position, Denison adopts a specific formula which expresses the hypothesis that the productivity offset to a given reduction in hours varies inversely with the number of hours in the working year. He places the point at which a slight reduction in hours is just offset by the rise in output per man-hour at the level prevailing in 1929 (when the level was 2592 hours a year or 48.6 a week) and assumes that, at the level prevailing in 1957 (2069 hours per year or 39.8 per week), a slight change in hours was offset to the extent of 40 per cent by an opposite change in man-hour output. He interpolates between these years and extrapolates backward and forward. The result, as Table 4.2 indicates, is that the reduction in hours between 1909 and 1929 is treated as fully offset by an associated improvement in productivity, and that between 1929 and 1957 is treated as offset by slightly over 60 per cent. On this assumption, of course, the implications for the future are serious. Since productivity offsets are now much smaller than they were and are becoming still smaller, labor input is destined to follow the curve of man-hours more closely and future reductions in hours, to the extent that they occur, will weigh more heavily on our growth rate.

Denison, of course, is properly reserved about this calculation. He claims no more for it than that it constitutes a formula which *may* be reasonably correct. (". . . its merit is that it is consistent with the general pattern of expectations and is not, I think, demonstrably wrong"). It is not demonstrably wrong, but the fact remains that the theory on which Denison relies is no more than speculation and his special

formula no more than a guess. Granted that there has been an historical association between shorter hours and greater intensity of work, it
is plausible to argue that the underlying cause has been a stream of
innovations in technology, factory organization and discipline, layout
and flow of work, modes of remuneration (piece rates and bonus
schemes), selection and assignment of workers and other aspects of
personnel management which acted to speed the pace of work, to
control its quality, and to reduce waste in the use of materials and
equipment.[7] Innovations of this character have, of course, joined with
larger quantities of capital, cost-reducing technology and other forces
to raise the marginal productivity schedule for labor. On their side,
workers have reacted, partly through the collective processes of union
organizations, by taking a portion of their potential gains in greater
leisure. A priori, however, it is not at all clear that this part exceeds the
portion of the gain in labor's marginal product associated with those
improvements in management and technology which made for
greater intensity and quality of work. Yet it is only in so far as declines
in hours did pass this moving point that they could be said to have an
independent effect on output per man-hour. Denison's calculations
may, therefore, overstate the rise of labor input as much as the simple
identification of labor input with man-hours understates it.[8] These
views are, of course, no less – but possibly also no more – speculative
than Denison's. I am, therefore, led to take my stand with Denison at
another point, where he writes (p. 39): "Few studies offer more promise of adding to welfare and contributing to wise decisions in a matter
that may greatly affect the future growth rate than a really thorough
investigation of the present relationship between hours and output."

Education
Doubtless every economist who has looked at the large size of
the Residual in earlier studies has speculated on the possibility – indeed the probability – that a large part of the explanation might be
found in the rapidly soaring levels of education attained by representative members of the labor force. Denison has now attempted to measure the contribution made by education to our past growth.

His procedure begins with an estimate by Houthakker [3] (based on a
3⅓ per cent Census sample of males) of the mean incomes earned
before tax in 1949 by men classified in 8 groups according to age and
years of school completed. This Denison reduces to a set of typical
differentials by level of education for males of the same age. He treats
these differentials as preliminary indications of the difference which
specified amounts of schooling would make to the output of randomly
chosen individuals. It is only a preliminary indication, however, be-

cause the observed differences between mean incomes for various levels of schooling are not due to differences in education alone. There are good reasons to think that differences in schooling completed are correlated with ability, energy, and motivation, also with the education and income of parents, and with parents' occupations and age of marriage. (Some of these correlates, however, may themselves be partly attributable to education – or to education of an earlier generation – for example, motivation and parents' schooling.) Denison deals with these complexities forthrightly and assumes that only 60 per cent of the observed differences are due to differences in schooling.

He next combines the adjusted differentials for 1949 with estimates of the distribution at various past dates of males, 25 and over, by years of school completed. In this way, he obtains estimates of past change in average income due to the rise in education measured in school years completed. These estimates, however, remain to be adjusted to allow for the rise in the number of school days represented by each school year, a figure which has been rising as fast as the average number of school years completed. And Denison makes the necessary adjustment by assuming that increasing the number of days spent in school per year raised a man's contribution to production as much as did an equal percentage increase in number of years spent in school.

These calculations, on their face, indicate that the contribution of the rise in levels of schooling was very high indeed. They suggest that the rise in output per man due to education was proceeding at a pace of .93 per cent per annum from 1929 to 1957 (fully 1 per cent per annum from 1940 to 1950 and .99 per cent from 1950 to 1960). Allowing for the weight of labor's share in the national income (73 per cent), the indicated contributions of education to the growth of national product during 1929–57 would have been .68 percentage points, or 23 per cent of the growth rate of aggregate national product and 42 per cent of the growth rate in product per person employed. They indicate that the rising level of education contributed more than any other source to the rise in output per person employed since 1929, more even than the "advance of knowledge," and more than any single source, excepting only the increase in the labor force itself, to the increase in aggregate output. If we may trust the calculations, their implications for economic policy – at least when we have our eye on long-term results – are dazzling. My own reluctant conclusion, however, is that we cannot rest our faith in the importance of education for economic growth on these figures. They are subject to question at each important point.

First, the basic table of differentials by level of education is itself a weak basis for the calculation. At best, it gives us a reading on educational differentials at one point in time. The data on which it is based reflect "response errors which abound in the reporting of income and education in household surveys and censuses . . ." [6, p. 963]. The census data appear in the form of medians for age-education-income classes which need to be transformed by estimation into means. Variability of income around the estimated means for each age-group classified by educational level is large [3, Table 1]. Given the small size of the samples in many of the cells, the question arises whether the mean figures are, in fact, representative or biased by accidental differences due to type of education, quality of schooling, occupation and other factors.

Secondly, the adjustment to allow for the influence on the observed differentials of factors extraneous to education, while presumably necessary, is admittedly arbitrary. No one can say whether Denison's 40 per cent adjustment is too large or too small and by how much.

Thirdly, the distribution of the male population by level of education for years before 1940 is accomplished by cohort analysis based on 1940 Census reports in which it appears that older age-groups overstated their educational achievements to a degree that varies positively with age. Denison adjusts for this bias (which would have resulted in an understatement of the rise in the level of schooling) on the basis of its indicated importance in the decade 1940 to 1950. The indicated adjustment (0.81 percentage points per decade) amounted to 18 per cent of the calculated contribution of education to average earnings in the decade 1940–1950. But the importance of the adjustment in earlier decades, when the contribution of education to earnings change was smaller, would have been relatively still more important.[9]

Fourthly, the apparent importance assigned by Denison to the rise in level of education is approximately doubled by the fact that he treats the rise in school days per year on a par with the rise in number of school years completed. Denison offers no evidence to support his treatment, and I regard it as highly questionable.[10]

Fifthly, the Denison calculations are an incomplete accounting because they neglect changes in the quantity of on-the-job training and, more generally, of training outside formal educational institutions. Since the amount spent on such training is reported to be nearly equal to the amount spent on formal education,[11] changes in such expenditures would have a substantial bearing on the question.

Finally, whatever the accuracy and completeness of the Denison calculations, one should be clear that they take account of only that part of the return to education which is captured by individuals. Yet the difference between social and private product is probably very large and may be of the same order of magnitude as the private product itself. The progress of applied technology and the pace at which businessmen exploit it – including that part associated with the scale of markets – are surely significantly influenced by the number of scientists and the intensity of their schooling and by the level of skills in the population at large. The geographical mobility of the population and its adaptability to new forms or organization are also presumably substantial influences affecting the pace of progress which depend on the level of education in ways still hard to specify. Finally, the capacity of a democratic society to accomplish the transformation in its political institutions required to meet the evolving problems of a growing and rapidly changing economy also depends on the level of education of its people. Little of the return to education flowing through these channels can be captured by individuals. All of it is excluded implicitly or explicitly in Denison's calculations.

If these arguments are sound, we must conclude that Denison has probably not been successful in approximating the contribution made by the rise in the level of education to our past growth. His estimate of its private product is subject to a number of serious uncertainties and, perforce, he neglects the difference between its private and social product. According to his calculation, the contribution was very large; but it may have been much smaller or even larger, and we have no way now, so far as I can see, of saying what it really was.

Capital input

As is well known, the measure of capital input is among the most vexed in the entire calculation. Consistent with his general procedure, Denison tries to obtain a series of capital inputs which will be proportionate to the product of the base-period earnings of capital and an index of the real capital stock. And, logically, the real capital stock is taken to be the cumulative sum of resources, valued at constant prices, devoted to saving diminished by "appropriate" sums because of depreciation or retirement. Denison defines the objective of deflation in these terms (p. 94): "The value in base period prices, of the stock of durable capital goods (before allowance for capital consumption) measures the amount it would have cost in the base period to produce the *actual* stock of capital in the given year (*not* its equivalent in ability to contribute to production)." And, with regard to capital consumption, he quotes Pigou: "When any discarding has occurred, in order to make good the depletion of capital implied in it, *that quantity of resources must be engaged which would suffice in actual current conditions of technique to reproduce the discarded element*" (Denison's italics, p. 95).

The net result of this procedure, if it could be implemented, would be to make the stock of capital move with the cumulative sum of saving in real terms, after appropriate depreciation, leaving changes in the quality or efficiency of capital goods to influence changes in output per unit of input, rather than the index of capital input itself. The actual means available for translating this conception into numbers are, of course, seriously imperfect. Raw data on capital formation (and hence the stock to which they cumulate), the figures underlying estimates of capital consumption, and the price deflators for both, all have serious limitations. The enforced neglect of the growth of government capital, for which there is no way to estimate earnings, is still another difficulty. It is surely among Denison's most valuable contributions that he threads his way so surely over this rough ground and explains the trail so clearly in this and other writings.

I confine my comments to a single point of principle. This is whether Denison (like Kendrick and his colleagues) is right in excluding the effect of quality change from his index of capital input and, therefore, in the frame of his calculations, from the estimated contribution of capital.[12] It is chiefly from this exclusion, coupled with the assumption that average earnings per unit of capital express capital's marginal contribution, that the generally rapid rise in the capital stock nevertheless accounted for only some 20 per cent of the growth in total output. Earnings of capital, taken over five-year periods, have been consistently small compared with earnings of labor. This was true even though the return to entrepreneurship is intermingled with the return to property. In Denison's calculations of total input, therefore, the rapid rise of capital stock is given only a small weight. The implicit moral is that the progress of output per unit of labor (adjusted for the contribution of education, etc.) has depended chiefly on the pace of advance in knowledge, on the skill of enterpreneurs in finding the best opportunities to use capital and labor, and in the efficiency of capital markets in channeling savings to business firms which are exploiting the best opportunities. The pace of advance would not have been much slower – problems of demand generation being neglected – even if the level of capital formation had been much lower. By the same token, acceleration of growth in the future, if it were to be accomplished by higher levels of investment alone, would require relatively huge increases in investment quotas.

The economic model which underlies Denison's calculations stands in sharp contrast to the model with which Robert Solow has been experimenting in his attempts to develop an aggregate production function for this country [10]. Solow asks us to imagine an economy enjoying advances in knowledge, potential economies of scale, extensions and improvements in schooling, improvements in social and economic organization and other elements of progress, all at some constant rate. But he assumes that none of these advances can be exploited except through the use of newly designed durable capital equipment. On the other hand, each unit of capital equipment carries with it a certain factor of improvement compared with equipment of older vintages, and this improvement factor is independent of the level of investment in a given year. In such an economy, given the improvement factor, the pace at which labor productivity advances would depend on the pace at which old capital is retired and replaced by capital of modern design and on the amount of capital of latest vintage added to the stock. In short, it would depend on the volume of gross capital formation. In calculating a production function which gives quantitative expression to this interpretation of U.S. growth, Solow finds, in effect, that the contribution of capital input to output growth is much greater than Denison does. An issue of first-rate importance is, therefore, posed.

In the issue thus drawn, it is well to be clear about what Solow is saying. He is not contending that capital formation is a sufficient condition for growth. The advances of knowledge, the economies of scale, the longer schooling, the improvements in organization were all necessary. Given their existence, however, Denison would have it that we could have enjoyed the greatest part of the observed increase in national product per man even if net capital formation had been zero. On Solow's calculations, however, the growth of national product is very sensitive to the accumulation of capital. If it had proceeded more slowly, the pace of advance of national product would have been greatly retarded. Capital accumulation was not a substitute for anything, or anything much, but it was the vehicle of everything.

So far as I can see, the difference between these two views depends crucially on the question whether improvement from whatever source can impinge on output per man only through the mediation of capital equipment of new design. As to this, it is common ground that the requirement that all improvement be "embodied" is not literally valid, and Solow makes no claim that his econometric work constitutes a test of the relative merits of his and a Denison-type model. By contrast with the literal requirements of Solow's model, Denison offers the judgment that the largest part of the actual changes in equipment design has as its object changes in the character of final products whose contributions to economic welfare do not register in measured national product. Contrariwise, Denison argues that as much as one-half of the productivity change which takes the form of reductions in cost actually reflects managerial and

organizational improvements requiring little or no changes in equipment. Moreover, in so far as new capital was required to carry productivity change, it was a vehicle for somewhat less than one percentage point in the growth rate in recent decades, not for the whole
increase in man-hour productivity – some 2.5 per cent per annum –
as in Solow. The factual gap between the two views is, therefore,
profound and not really usefully attacked by speculation. Still further issues arise when we consider the implications of the Denison
and Solow analyses for growth policy [see below].

Output per unit of input

In earlier calculations of the kind Denison makes, the difference between the number of percentage points in the rate of growth
of the index of combined inputs and that in the rate of growth of
national product represented an unanalyzed residual. It was larger
than Denison's measure of productivity change because it included
the contribution of certain unconventional inputs which Denison has
isolated in the form of changes in the quality of labor associated with
the rise in the level of education and with that in intensity of effort.
But Denison does not leave even the smaller figure which he derives
as the difference between input growth and output growth as an
undifferentiated residual. He makes explicit allowance for two broad
classes of factors: changes in the efficiency of resource allocation and
economies of scale.

Denison treats changes in the efficiency of resource allocation under a dozen different heads. Each taken separately appears to have
had only a small influence on the growth rate in past decades. According to Denison's estimates, their effect would have been minor even if
they had all operated in the same direction. It appears, however, that
they did not, and in Denison's tables, their net effect during the last
three decades emerges as zero. I see no reason to doubt that Denison's estimates are of the right order or magnitude. For good or evil,
changes in the efficiency of resource allocation have not been an important growth factor in this country. It is worth remembering, however, that the kinds of factors Denison takes up as having a bearing on
resource allocation have other consequences for growth which may be
far more important, but which inevitably escape our statistical net.
Thus, in considering the tax structure, we cannot account for its impact on the level and composition of investment. In considering the
restrictions on competition, we have to neglect their influence on the
inducement to engage in research and to hunt out and exploit new
methods of production and improved final products. In considering
international trade restrictions, we have to pass over their significance

for competition and for the flow of information about production processes and methods of industrial organization. Denison does, indeed, make perceptive comments about all these influences, but, quite understandably, he finds no way to measure them, and he leaves them all to be reflected in his ultimate residual.

By contrast with resource allocation, the economies of scale appear, in Denison's tables, as a principal source of growth, accounting for some 37 per cent of productivity growth during 1929–57 and for fully 50 per cent during 1901–29. Unfortunately, the estimate for this undoubtedly important factor hardly bears discussion. The considerable figure Denison assigns to it is merely the numerical expression of an assumption that the economies of scale due to the growth of the national market yielded an advance in output equal to one-tenth that yielded by all other growth factors (that is, one-eleventh of the increase in measured national product) and that economies due to the independent growth of local markets were one-tenth as large. But this assumption is based on no empirical evidence whatever and, as Denison makes amply clear, constitutes no more than his own sober judgment. A good man's sober judgment is not to be spurned. I know of no theoretical or empirical considerations which render it doubtful, but, like Denison, I know of none which makes it seem particularly trustworthy. I take it that the explicit recognition of this factor in Denison's table chiefly serves to remind us that there is such a factor which needs to be taken into account when one considers the contribution to growth made by changes in other forces.

It is only after providing for the two classes of influences just mentioned that Denison comes to his ultimate Residual. He calls it the "Advance of Knowledge," but, of course, this category, which nominally accounts for just 20 per cent of total growth during 1929–57, is not in any meaningful sense a measure of that alone, and it may not be a measure chiefly of that. For, as a residual, it is the grand legatee of all the errors of estimate embodied in the measures of national product, of inputs conventional and otherwise, and of the economies of scale and other factors classified under productivity growth. Beyond this, however, several points of principle deserve notice and discussion.

First, as Denison clearly explains, the figure set down for the Advance of Knowledge is not the full contribution of that factor – whatever it may really be – to the growth of national product considered as a measure of economic welfare. For national product, as measured, neglects much or most of the change, conventionally taken to be improvement, in the quality of final products. Since such change does not affect the measure of inputs, any adjustment for quality change in the measure of national product growth would add the same amount to the measure of the Advance of Knowledge. Indeed, it is Denison's view that a very large part of that advance, particularly in the form of technical progress, is in fact devoted to the discovery and production of new final products not reflected in the national product estimates.

Second, the Denison residual still reflects the contribution of certain inputs, chiefly expenditures to support research and development activities and expenditures for education in so far as these help provide the scientific and technical personnel for research and the skilled labor whose presence encourages firms to exploit the advance of technology.

Finally, however, we have to recognize that, even apart from errors, the residual cannot be regarded as the contribution of the advance in knowledge in any meaningful sense. It is, in fact, nothing more and nothing less than the measure of the advance in productivity from every source other than those specifically identified elsewhere in Denison's calculations. The issue can, perhaps, be brought to a focus by considering the distinction made by Denison between what he calls the advance in knowledge and what he calls the "lag in the application of knowledge." The latter he considers can be measured by, though it is not identical with, the change in the average age of capital goods, a consideration which turns out to have been a negligible growth factor in recent decades. This identification for purpose of measurement, however, suggests that there is some stable relation between the techniques embodied in the capital stock added in a given year by firms who invest that year and the best techniques which are, in some sense, "available" in that year. What sense should the word "available" be given?

a. Is it to mean the best techniques which the basic principles of the physical universe as apprehended at a given time, together with the existing empirical information, make possible, regardless of the expense and work involved in translating the basic principles into appropriate applied forms and communicating that knowledge to all concerned, and regardless too of the institutional obstacles involved in obtaining finance and labor or of the will and incentive to overcome these obstacles?

b. Or is it to mean, say, the techniques adopted by the most advanced firms in each year (in the United States alone? anywhere?)? This criterion would take into account the existing problems of information, entrepreneurship, finance, labor supply, legal and market restrictions as faced by the most advanced firms in a given year.

c. Or is it to mean, as I think it does mean for Denison (and, in the present state of our estimates inevitably must mean) the techniques available to representative firms which actually do invest in a given year, having regard to the representative state of entrepreneurial capacities, drives and outlets and to representative conditions governing information, labor supplies, finance, and so forth.

It goes without saying that the last criterion is tautological since it identifies the Advance in Knowledge with the improvements actually made. Denison's ultimate residual is, therefore, inappropriately titled. Errors aside, the size of that residual must be taken to reflect the effective rate at which actual progress in techniques of production takes place in representative firms. Certainly its connection with the advance of knowledge conceived of as some disembodied stock of principles and factual information is indirect and uncertain.

No one who reads Denison on the sources of U.S. growth can fail to benefit. His discussion of the conceptual and statistical problems involved in estimating the contributions of various sources can only be described as a tour de force. So far as that goes, his book is an epitome of years of work and writing by himself and by many other students of national income and productivity measurement. In Denison's hands, the subject emerges again pithy, fresh and forceful. Nevertheless, it seems to me that the fruits of all this work have not yet ripened. The problem posed by Schmookler and by Kendrick and his National Bureau colleagues – namely, that to explain a very large part of the growth of total output and the great bulk of output per capita, we must explain the increase in output per unit of conventionally measured inputs – still remains. We can draw up a catalogue of the kinds of elements of which such an explanation must be composed: unconventional inputs, like labor intensity and education; economies of scale; and advances in knowledge of techniques and organization. Denison's attempts to attach numbers to these elements, however, still falls short of success. And this unfortunate fact is just the inevitable consequence of the present state of the art. The underlying data are weak, the various growth factors interact in a complex way (and expand along distressingly parallel lines), and experiments with the statistical derivation of production functions have really just begun.

The alternatives before us

In this review, I have followed the lead of Denison's title (which prints SOURCES in caps and Alternatives in caps and lower case) by devoting most of my space to Sources. It is probably true, however, that Denison's interest in the analysis of history is largely subsidiary to his interest in the formulation of policy. Nevertheless, I must now deal with the policy side of his work in summary fashion. I can, perhaps, do this the more easily because I can agree with so much of what Denison has to say.

If I read him right, Denison's general conclusion is that, for the United States, acceleration in growth cannot be sought only along a few very broad lines of policy. If we are to raise our measured growth rate significantly above the level it would achieve without deliberate social intervention, we must take action along a great many lines, each of which taken by itself can make only a minor contribution. In Denison's view, the country would be hard put to devise and implement a set of policies likely to raise our rate of growth per annum during the period 1960–80 by a full percentage point above what it would otherwise be. Yet, if we were determined, such a set could be found among the many alternative policies open. And a one percentage point increase would be no mean achievement since it would imply a rate of aggregate growth about one-third higher than Denison's projected autonomous rate and a 50 per cent rise in the rate of growth of per capita income relative to the same standard. Subject to some comments at the end of the paper, I agree with this general position, and I think its strength can best be brought out by reviewing Denison's appraisal of four lines of policy that have attracted attention.

One is to increase the rate of growth of the labor force. Since past births have already determined the native-born population from which the labor force can be drawn, only three possibilities remain: to increase participation rates, to slow down the decline in hours of work, and to increase the flow of immigrants. Maintaining conditions of full employment is often held out as likely to have a favorable influence upon participation rates and hours. However, Denison surely is right in saying that the difference between the average level of unemployment maintained since the war and that at which a successful employment policy might aim would have a small and uncertain effect on participation rates.[13] The opportunity to influence working hours seems brighter, and Denison considers that a successful full employment policy would help to reduce the anticipated decline in hours. We might make limited gains in this way. If we could reduce the anticipated decline by 25 per cent, or one hour per hour-week, this would increase our growth rate by 0.1 percentage point per annum. What we can do by way of immigration is, of course, entirely a matter for national choice. Yet, even doubling the rate of immigration would add only 0.1 point to the growth rate, allowing something for the generally lower quality of immigrant workers.

Education to improve the quality of representative members of the labor force is a second possible source to which many look for more rapid growth during coming decades. It seems clear, from Denison's calculations, however, that little can be expected from this source in so far as its contribution depends on the quantity of education. A crude calculation tells one reason why. From 1930 to 1960, when – by Denison's figures – increased levels of education were increasing output per man almost one per cent per annum, the average number of school days attended by workers in the labor force was rising about 20 per cent per decade. The projected increase in school days attended during the next 20 years is somewhat smaller, but still large, roughly 16 per cent per decade. The drop is due to a combination of an expected smaller increase in the number of years attended by representative youngsters now in, or expected to enter, school, and a still smaller increase in the length of the school year, counterbalanced by the entrance into the labor force during the next decades of many younger workers who benefited by the great extension of education during the last few decades. The result would be a rate of increase in output per man almost, but not quite, as great as in previous decades. However, as the effect of past educational reforms makes itself fully felt with the graduation of young people into the labor force, it will be increasingly difficult to maintain the contribution of longer schooling to labor output. The school year is already quite long. In the aggregate, the possibilities of extending the contribution of education at the high school level is running out because the percentage of young people completing high school is already very high. Thus the pace of advance would have to be sustained largely by a great expansion of college and university education alone. In the long run, it seems inevitable that the contribution of education to growth must fall.

Apart from the physical difficulties of continuing to raise the amount of schooling at even its old pace, the effect of additional schooling on labor output is a very long-run effect. What we do now to increase years of schooling will be of little consequence until, after some decades, a large proportion of the labor force with less schooling has been replaced by men and women with more. One need not accept Denison's estimates of the returns to schooling in order to see the force of these considerations which seem to me to be among the most cogently argued portions of his book.

All this is not to say that longer education would not benefit certain underprivileged groups greatly, or that expenditures to make more education more widely available are not of the greatest importance simply to sustain present growth rates during the next decades and to provide for a somewhat more rapid advance in the still longer run. It does mean, however, that if education is to make striking advances to accelerated growth of output, it probably will have to be through improvements in the quality of education, through better selection of the most able students for higher education, and through concentration on those courses of study the importance of which for increased output is particularly high.

An increase in the proportion of gross national product devoted to *capital formation* is regarded by many as the key to more rapid growth. Two questions arise: how to raise the level of investment; and how much benefit we might obtain from a given increment of investment.

Denison's discussion of the first question is knowledgeable and sophisticated, but not particularly novel. The way in which the brew of monetary policy, fiscal policy, redistribution of tax burdens, the treatment of depreciation, etc., might be mixed has engaged the attention of many cooks. Economists will find Denison's recipes carefully considered but familiar. They are unlikely to make anyone sanguine about the possibility of obtaining dramatic results. And dramatic results are what would be needed, for – as we already know – additional capital accumulation, according to Denison, is likely to contribute much less to growth than many suppose.

On this point, Denison's views are challenging. They flow simply and directly from the proposition – a deduction from marginal productivity theory – that, say, a one per cent increase in capital input will raise national product by only that fraction of one per cent which is given by the share of income going to capital. Since the share going to capital is small, while the capital stock is several times as large as the national product, it is obvious that the order of magnitude of the additional net investment required to increase national product by, say, one per cent is very large indeed. On Denison's calculations, additional net investment would have to be in the neighborhood of 13 or 14 per cent of national income if the composition of the new investment were similar to that of the existing stock.[14] This would involve raising the ratio of net investment to national income to 3.3 times its present level.[15] Simply to raise the growth rate by 0.1 per cent during the next 20 years would mean raising the net investment ratio by about 25 per cent. These figures reflect Denison's allowance for returns through economies of scale, but they make no allowance for diminishing returns. For massive injections of additional capital per worker, the allowance required on this latter account might well be substantial, as Denison points out, and even his large figures for the additional investment needed to raise growth rates would then be too small.

It is an implication of Denison's analysis that we might do much to stimulate growth without raising our investment quotas. We might

even permit them to sink, but in order to stimulate growth significantly through capital accumulation we should have to increase our
investment quotas enormously. The moral of Solow's view is just the
opposite. Pressed to the limit, nothing we might do to stimulate
growth would be effective without a good deal of investment. But if
we could merely maintain the rate of *potential* improvement opened
up by the advance of knowledge, the economies of scale, the extension of education, and whatever else contributes to the potential efficiency of resources, a fairly modest increase in rates of capital formation would provide large increases in our rate of growth. Additional
investment would embody additional quotas of each year's potential
productivity gains from all sources *pari passu*. But is Solow right?

We have already seen how the range of validity of his model depends
on the degree to which potential productivity gains, whatever their
source, require embodiment in capital of new design. As we look to the
possible gains from enlarged investment quotas, additional questions
arise, and Solow himself has identified them: ". . . a sharply higher
rate of investment may bring about premature scrapping of old equipment. . . . [T]here may be limits even in a mature economy to the
speed with which the system can adjust to large inflows of capital" 10,
p. 86.

It is evident that even in what Solow calls "the prosaic case of
tangible capital formation," we are still a long way from having quantitative estimates of the social return to resource input.

Finally, I note briefly, Denison's treatment of the potentialities of
expenditures for *research and development*. The great hopes that are
sometimes placed in the efficacy of enlarged expenditures for this
purpose are swiftly cut to more modest dimensions by Denison's
scalpel. How much, he asks, of the .58 percentage points in the measured growth rate which he assigns to Advance of Knowledge can be
attributed to organized R and D? The knowledge relevant to measured growth is that which lower costs, not that which yields new
final consumer goods. In large part such knowledge consists of managerial and organizational procedure rather than technology proper,
and some part of technology is an engineering by-product of ordinary
production activity. Suppose one-half the relevant advance is technological, that one-half of this stemmed from activity in the United
States, and that two-thirds of this came from organized R and D. Then
one-sixth of the .58 percentage points is assignable to R and D in this
country. The factor Denison applies is one-fifth, so his answer is .12
percentage points. Denison calculates that the expenditure which is to
be associated with this result may be gauged from the $5 billion for
privately financed research in 1960 of which some portion was de-

voted to style changes and other adaptations of only transient influence. Since Denison estimates that it would have required about $3.8 billion of net investment devoted to nonresidential capital to raise national product by the same .12 percentage points, he concludes that the social return on the two classes of expenditure was about the same and that neither was high.

Such calculations are, of course, only guesswork,[16] yet useful in establishing orders of magnitude. An important reason for this apparently modest return is that the bulk of R and D – perhaps four-fifths of private and virtually all government expenditures – is devoted to product improvement, which does not register in measured national product, but which we want. We, therefore, have every reason to encourage R and D, but little reason to expect dramatic results in terms of measured growth. This is all the more true if Denison is right in thinking that resources devoted to research operate subject to rapidly diminishing returns to scale. He finds no evidence that the pace of Advance of Knowledge has been growing even as fast as our population, much less as fast as the scientific personnel and capital specially involved.[17] On the other hand, there is no reason to accept the present outlay of funds devoted to applied research as even approximately as good as it might be. In an activity where the difference between private and social return is so great and where the returns private firms can capture are so heavily dependent on the size of firms, the character of markets, and the nature of the product, there is little reason to trust ordinary market incentives to guide the allocation of funds. Actual expenditures are, in fact, highly concentrated in relatively few industrial sectors, and in some are virtually neglected. There may well be opportunities to increase the productivity of resources devoted to research by a wider distribution of expenditures, as Denison cogently argues.

The general moral of Denison's book is that those who seek more rapid growth for the United States must pursue it along many lines. There are no three or four broad measures which, if taken, promise dramatic success. Denison himself offers a shopping list of 31 possible lines of action from most of which we should be hard put to extract an extra 0.1 percentage point for the growth rate. Some might be pressed for more, some do not offer even that much, some would affect only "true" rather than measured growth, some might be judged undesirable for one reason or another.

I suspect that this hard moral of Denison's book is sound. Yet it is also clear that the knowledge on which such a judgment is based is extremely weak. Denison has made a wholly admirable effort to reduce the problem to quantitative terms, and the authority with which he handles the data, the skill and judgment with which he uses them, are evident from first to last. Yet, on close inspection, I think the figures fall apart at almost every important point. In spite of the author's careful and candid exposition, there is a certain air of reliability and precision about his estimates which the state of our knowledge today simply does not support.

We are, indeed, just at the beginning of serious work on the subject of economic growth in the United States. Denison's important contribution is to have pulled the many parts of the problem together and built a structure with such shape and solidity as the materials now permit. Doubtless as the work advances, more complex and subtle models of our economy will be designed, and statistical estimation will have to rest on more advanced econometrics than Denison employs. The pace at which useful work can proceed will depend in good part on the appearance of more reliable and detailed information. There is, in fact, almost everything yet to be done, but those who want to contribute to the subject can hardly do better than to take their start with Denison.

Notes

1. F. C. Mills [7] did the first work of this kind at the Burear followed by Fabricant [2] and the present writer [1], both of whom took advantage of Kendrick's work then in progress.

2. Troubles from this source were minimized by Kendrick, and by Denison as well, since each first divided the long period they studied into subperiods and constructed separate indexes on inputs for the various subperiods, weighting by the relative earnings of the input classes in each subperiod. They then chained the subperiod indexes so derived to obtain a continuous index for the entire span of years they studied.

3. Like Kendrick, Denison distinguishes several classes of capital stock, which he combines by weights based on rates of return. But Denison's classification is by type of capital, Kendrick's by industry.

4. Denison's capital, as already noted, is an index of gross stocks in five categories weighted by rates of return.

5. It is worth a digression to notice that Denison's figures do not suggest any long-term retardation in the rate of growth of national income. The pronounced retardation in the growth of both labor and capital inputs is offset by an equally pronounced acceleration in the growth – from all causes – of output per unit of input. Kendrick's input calculations, taken in conjunction with the Denison (Commerce) income estimates, lead to the same conclusions. If one may regard the periods distinguished by Denison as suitably long and comparable, it would appear that current discussion of retardation in growth is actually concerned with the experience of a relatively few recent years, a period hardly adequate, in view of the unsteadiness of growth rates, to provide evidence of a secular drift. Kendrick's own estimates of net national product, which are based on Kuznets' work up to 1929 do, indeed, show some retardation between the period 1909–29, when the growth rate was 3.45 per cent per annum, and

1929–57, when it was 2.93. But again, this was entirely a question of retardation in the growth of labor and capital inputs, offset – but not completely – by acceleration in productivity growth.

6. There are some very small differences in individual figures since Table 4.1 is drawn from Denison's Table 19 and Table 4.2 from his Table 32. In the latter, figures are slightly adjusted to eliminate a portion of the increase in inputs considered not to be represented in the increase in measured national product.

7. In another connection Denison is led to write as follows: "It would be difficult to find technological innovations with an impact on production exceeding that of the introduction of interchangeable parts, or of the assembly line, or of time and motion study and all that has flowed from it. . . . The design of factory buildings has been radically changed to permit the easy flow of materials. . . . Improvements in work scheduling, [and] in personnel relations . . . are in this category . . ." [p. 232].

8. One minor point is that, though man-hours on the job itself fell, there were many years when true leisure time did not increase quite as much. Travel time tended to increase for all grades of labor, and work-connected activities outside of regular hours probably became more demanding for a larger group of salaried officials.

9. The relative importance of the same adjustment would have been 19.7 per cent for 1930–40; 24.6 per cent for 1920–30 and 30 per cent for 1910–20.

10. If I understand it, the procedure carries the absurd implication that a boy who completes eight years of elementary school today, when the number of school days per year is perhaps twice as large as it was on the average in 1910, has received the equivalent of a 1910 college education so far as effect on earning power is concerned.

11. T. W. Schultz reports this estimate by Harold F. Clark and adds: "About all that can be said about on-the-job training is that expansion of education has not eliminated it" [9, pp. 9 and 10]. Apart from industry, the armed forces are an important locus of voational training outside the schools.

12. There are other points which challenge discussion and, perhaps, debate, but alternative procedures would not greatly alter Denison's results and lack of space prohibits comment. These issues include Denison's use of estimates of "gross" rather than net capital stock as an index of capital input, his reliance on measures of the capital stock available rather than on that employed, and his classification of the reproducible durable stock into three groups: farm, nonfarm residential, and other nonfarm, each weighted by its own earnings.

13. Denison (pp. 661–66) argues persuasively that J. W. Knowles' view [5] that, if unemployment rates are maintained at 3 per cent rather than 5 per cent, the labor force might grow at 1.9 rather than 1.5 per cent per annum, greatly exaggerates the possibilities. If Knowles were right, the 1975 labor force would be 5.9 million persons, or 6.5 per cent larger if the unemployment rate stayed at 3 per cent in the interim than if it stayed at 5 per cent. But this would imply an enormous difference in the participation of women and elderly persons, since there is little room for variation in the participation of males in their prime working years.

14. The figure would be in the neighborhood of 10 per cent if none of the additional investment were devoted to housing for which the return is low.

15. If none of the increment went to housing the required multiple might be lower – 2.7, according to Denison.

16. One possible flaw in the argument, however, may be worth notice. If there is any substantial lag between R and D expenditure and its results, the contribution of .12 percentage points to the growth rate should not be associated with the expenditures of the same date. Five years earlier, such expenditures in current prices were one-half as

large and ten years earlier perhaps one-fifth as large. The difference in constant prices would have been smaller.

17. This is a judgment manifestly subject to the ambiguities surrounding Denison's identification of his Residual with Advance of Knowledge.

References

1. Moses Abramovitz, *Resource and Output Trends in the United States Since 1870.* National Bureau of Economic Research Occasional Paper 52. New York 1956.
2. Solomon Fabricant, *Basic Facts on Productivity Change.* National Bureau of Economic Research Occasional Paper 63. New York 1959.
3. H. S. Houthakker, "Education and Income," *Rev. Econ. Stat.*, Feb. 1959, *41*, 24–28.
4. J. W. Kendrick, *Productivity Trends in the United States.* Study by the National Bureau of Economic Research. Princeton 1961.
5. J. W. Knowles, "Potential Economic Growth in the United States," Study Paper No. 20, prepared for the Joint Economic Committee in connection with the study *Employment, Growth and Price Levels*, 86th Cong., 2nd Sess. Washington 1960.
6. H. P. Miller, "Annual and Lifetime Income in Relation to Education," *Am. Econ. Rev.*, Dec. 1960, *50*, 962–86.
7. F. C. Mills, *Productivity and Economic Progress.* National Bureau of Economic Research Occasional Paper 38. New York 1952.
8. Jacob Schmookler, "The Changing Efficiency of the American Economy, 1869–1938," *Rev. Econ. Stat.*, Aug. 1952, *34*, 214–31.
9. T. W. Schultz, "Capital Formation by Education," *Jour. Pol. Econ.*, Dec. 1960, *68*, 571–83.
10. R. M. Solow, "Technical Progress, Capital Formation and Economic Growth," *Am. Econ. Rev.*, Proc., May 1962, *52*, 76–86.

5
Manpower, capital, and technology

There are two standard ways of viewing the process of economic growth. One sees it as the outcome of capital formation and technological and organizational progress, including progress made possible by enlargement of scale; the other as a process of transformation in the use of a country's resources, principally in the size, intensity of use, and training of its labor force and its occupational and industrial structure. The two views are sometimes regarded as competitive, sometimes as supplementary. The truth is, however, that manpower development, capital formation, and technological progress are so closely allied and so interdependent as almost to confound analytical separation.

The purpose of this essay is to elaborate and illustrate the theme of interdependence and to sketch some of the main lines of connection between manpower development on the one side and capital formation and technological progress on the other. This is an expository paper, making no claim to originality. The factual assertions on which the argument depends mainly refer to the United States, although some have a wider application. For the most part, they are in the public domain, reducing the need to make a show of empirical support, but not guaranteeing accuracy. These notes are, therefore, provisional and, even in respect to their factual content, subject to verification.

Conventional versus total capital formation

The very distinction drawn between manpower development and capital formation rests in part on a conventional, but basically arbitrary, definition of the latter concept. Conventionally, capital formation refers to the use of resources to add to the stock of tangible reproducible goods useful in production. The fundamental idea underlying the con-

Reprinted by permission from *Human Resources and Economic Welfare: Essays in Honor of Eli Ginzberg*, ed. by Ivar Berg. New York: Columbia University Press, 1972, pp. 50–70.

ventional definition, however, has to do with any deliberate use of resources in ways which increase our potential productive capacity. In this more basic sense, it comprehends any deliberate employment of income to increase the productivity of resources, including uses which are not tangible but rather embodied in the knowledge, skills, energy, strength, location, or other qualities of people.

If we consider capital formation in this controversial but more truly basic sense, the most important category is, of course, expenditure on education, including both formal schooling and on-the-job training. There are, however, other important categories as well, including some expenditures for health care and recreation and for domestic and international migration and resettlement. The expenditures for education and training are themselves of the first order of magnitude. Indeed, Professor Simon Kuznets has estimated that, while the typical share of conventional capital formation in developed countries in the postwar period was about 30 percent, private and public consumption taking the other 70 percent, if one allows for "investment in man" through formal schooling and on-the-job training, the capital-formation proportion rises to 47 percent of the revised GNP, leaving only 53 percent for consumption.[1]

Needless to say, such estimates of investment in man rest on a number of shaky assumptions, variations in which might change the numbers significantly. In a final calculation, one would need to reduce the capital-formation share because not all the expenditure for education is either intended to or has the effect of raising the productive capabilities of people. On the other hand, the expenditures on education do not by any means exhaust our current investments in man. Expenditures for health care, public, household, and corporate, are partly undertaken to increase productivity. So are some of our expenditures nominally for recreation, including some significant part of the cost of supporting newspapers, television, and other communications media. Educational investment expenditures themselves might be expanded to include a large part of corporate and professional expenditure for travel, meetings, and trade and other professional literature. Perhaps most important, one would need to allow for the costs of migration and resettlement as workers and their families move within and between countries in their efforts to enlarge their own earning power and, by implication, the productive capacity of the economy.

Figures, as they now stand, can do no more than show that in a comprehensive accounting, industrialized countries now use a significant part of their total output for investment in man and that such investment forms a very large part, if not a major fraction, of capital formation, tangible and intangible. The Kuznets estimates do that sufficiently well. One can add that, in preindustrial times and in the earlier stages of development in countries now industrialized, investments in man were much less important both as a share of total output and as a share of the much smaller part of output used for capital formation. Expenditures for formal education were tiny; the industrially relevant part of literature or of other means of communication was insignificant. Travel and migration were restricted by the expense, difficulty, and dangers of transportation. All these avenues for using income to increase personal effectiveness were gradually enlarged in the course of the last century, and it is tempting to attribute the recorded acceleration in the pace of productivity growth during the last hundred years in good part to the enlargement of investment in man. This is too difficult a question to be pursued here.[2] Taking for granted the importance of such enlarged investment, how can we explain why people, acting individually and through public agencies, were willing to devote increasingly large portions of their personal income and of the government's revenue to the development of their productive capabilities, be it their own, their children's or those of other families? I shall try to look at this question from several angles and at the same time develop other connections among manpower development, capital formation, and technical progress.

The implications of demographic change

The very small share of investment in man during the early stages of industrialization, roughly from the last third of the eighteenth to the last third of the nineteenth century, corresponds to two broad characteristics of that period. First, the demand for schooled personnel was small, which itself restricted this most important avenue of investment. (How it came to be larger is a question taken up in a later section.) With the supply of educated people also limited, the earnings premium enjoyed by the fortunate was large, yet this did not induce a large responsive educational effort. For one thing, incomes were low, education was costly, and access to finance for most people close to nonexistent. But second, even a large earnings premium for schooled people did not necessarily signify a large return to an investment in education. In the same way, earnings differentials between countries or between places in a given country or between occupations, all of which were considerable in preindustrial times, did not necessarily offer a large return to geographical or occupational movement. One reason for this lay in the demographic conjuncture during preindustrial and early industrial times.

It is a commonplace that, during that period, both mortality rates and birth rates were high and that the difference between them – the rate of population growth – was small. The decline in mortality rates, concomitant in most industrialized countries with the onset of industrialization, is usually considered chiefly for its influence in accelerating the pace of population and labor-force growth. It is less commonly appreciated that the same decline in mortality rates was probably one of the forces behind the expansion of educational effort and the growing mobility of people across space and between occupations.

The high level of mortality rates a century and more ago meant not only that infant mortality was high, but also that the chance of survival through adolescence was smaller and life expectancy thereafter much shorter than it is today. Crippling morbidity was also more common. All these conditions effectively reduced the prospective rewards to investment in man. To spend eight or ten years in school beyond the age when earnings might otherwise begin, to forego these earnings, and to bear the other expenses of schooling was obviously less attractive when the remaining span of working life was, say, twenty-five years, on the average than it is today, when it is forty or forty-five years. In the same way, the lengthening span of working life must have made people more ready to accept the risks and costs of seeking their fortunes in distant places and in new occupations.

A special consideration applies to women. Their chance of enjoying a material reward from schooling or other personal improvement was obviously limited so long as families were as large as they were through much of the nineteenth century. They were limited still more because high levels of infant and childhood mortality required more pregnancies for each surviving child. Smaller families and the decline in infant and child mortality together were forces helping to release many women to work outside the home and consequently to change traditional views about education for women.

Technological and organizational progress and the sex-composition of the labor force

In most industrializing countries, declining death rates were followed by declining birth rates, and these, together with the extension of life, meant a shift in the age structure of the population. The population of working age rose relative to the total population. In the United States, this change supported a rise in labor force relative to population during at least the half-century from 1870 to 1920 and perhaps longer and, by the same token, the growth rate of output per head. It would not have done so, however, had not the proportion of people of working age who were gainfully employed remained essentially stable. It did, however, remain stable – short-term fluctuations apart – even until the present time, in short, for at least a century.

A full discussion of the reasons for this remarkable example of secular stability would take us far afield. Its two chief elements, however, have in a sense already been introduced. Increased investment in man meant, among other things, more schooling. It required an ever-rising average age for entry into the labor force and, therefore, an ever-falling proportion of young people at work. By and large, the withdrawal of young people from work was offset by the entry of older women. Though each development had its peculiar causes, they also had common sources in the nature of technological and organization progress, in the vast enlargement in the scale and urban concentration of economic life and in the accompanying rise in incomes during the last hundred years and more. I can best pursue my main theme by focusing sharply on these common causes.

I begin with the rise in the participation of women. We have already seen how fewer pregnancies and smaller families helped to release women from the home. Their release was also furthered by the appearance of labor-saving equipment for the household, by rising incomes and financial facilities which helped families buy such aids and by commercial substitutes for homemade food and clothing and for home laundering and cleaning. Progress in food preservation and packaging, the reorganization of retailing and the use of automobiles were, at least until recently, additional savers of women's time. Women have been pushed to work by the need to provide extra family income to support longer periods of schooling for children and even for husbands – a direct and obvious reflection of the forces supporting investment in man. Their way to employment has been eased by the availability of part-time jobs and by the general shortening of the working day and working week. Although the rise in men's wages tended, indeed, to reduce the need for married women to work, the higher wages the latter could earn if they did work proved even more important in drawing women into employment.[3]

All this is, in many ways, a twice-told tale. What needs to be stressed is that virtually every aspect of this story stems in one degree or another from a transformation in the nature of jobs. On the one hand, this transformation was itself a reflection of shifts in the scale of industry and of the urban concentration of activity and population, of technological progress and greater use of capital and of higher incomes. On the other hand, it gave women a chance to compete with men over a far wider range of employment and, in many types of work, to outdo them.

From the viewpoint of opportunities for employment of women, the transformation can be characterized as a growth of soft-handed at the expense of hard-handed occupations. It reflected four interconnected developments central to economic growth given the nature of technological progress during the last century:

1. With the rise of incomes, there was a shift in the composition of final demand toward the output of the service industries – principally education, health care, travel, and other forms of entertainment and recreation – in which soft-handed, or white-collar, jobs are relatively abundant.

2. The rise in productivity on which the increase of incomes depended, itself rested on technological progress of a particular character. This involved a huge increase in the overall scale of the economy, a much higher degree of specialization and a more intense articulation of functions which expressed itself, *inter alia*, in a heavy concentration of population in metropolitan communities. To support this particular technological structure, there was required an impressive relative growth of commercial services, specifically those of trade, finance, communications, and, most of all, governmental regulation and the provision of a wide range of auxiliary public services required for the operation of large cities. These again are employment sectors in which soft-handed jobs predominate.

3. The new technology meant not only this growth of social overhead, but also a growth of private overhead functions. Large-scale, heavily capitalized and roundabout methods of production required heavier expenses within individual firms for administration, finance, sales, intrafirm communications, supervision of production, personnel management, and the provision of services to improve the selection and retention of increasingly skilled and expensive workers.

4. Finally, though the demand for the output of overhead functions grew relatively rapidly, the productivity of labor supplying these functions rose relatively slowly, at least until quite recent years. Indeed, the whole process may be regarded as one in which overall productivity was increased by substituting soft-handed for hard-handed workers as a necessary adjunct to the adoption of the modern American technological mode. At all events, it was a process in which jobs suitable for both women and men replaced jobs suitable only for men.[4]

Economic growth and the rise of education

Of all the manpower developments of the present century, the great increase in the length of schooling enjoyed by people before beginning work is surely the most prominent. On the one side, the extension of schooling has meant a great reduction in the proportion of persons under 20 or 22 years old who work during most of the year. On the other side, the prolongation of formal schooling and the changes in school curricula have presumably made a significant, if uncertain, contribution to the rise of productivity and incomes.

That longer schooling has made a useful contribution to the effectiveness of workers is rarely questioned, however much the size of that contribution is disputed. In the same way, few doubt that the prospect of financial rewards associated with extended training induced people to seek longer schooling for themselves and their children, however hard it may be to specify the exact weight to give this consideration. Other forces were doubtless at work. The democratization of politics and of society would have made for an extension of schooling apart from any change in prospective earnings. So would the extension of life, the rise of incomes, and the enlarged access to credit facilities which wider segments of people have enjoyed. It remains true, nonetheless, that the costs of schooling beyond the primary grades, still more beyond secondary school, were and are very heavy in terms of fees and foregone earnings, and it is implausible to suppose that the great mass of Americans would willingly have borne these costs and supported the enlarged public expenditures for expanded school facilities had they not expected a large private return in terms of careers, incomes, and status.

My aim is not to settle these questions of weight and measure. I focus rather on a central fact on which the apparent contributions of longer schooling to labor efficiency, whatever that may have been, and the apparent financial attractiveness of longer schooling, both rest. This fact is the large earnings premiums which people with longer schooling have enjoyed, on the average, over people with shorter school experience. Viewed as indexes of the additional effectiveness of people with longer education, the premiums are the bases for approximative measures, however uncertain these may be, of the contribution of additional schooling to output and labor productivity. Viewed as a measure of additional earning power associated with longer education, they were the visible symbol of the prospective financial rewards which induced individuals to seek more schooling for their children and to support larger public expenditures for education.[5] The question I ask, therefore, is: why have persons with relatively more schooling continued to command attractively large earnings premiums even though so many of them have joined the labor force since the beginning of the century? Unless there had been an offsetting rise in the demand for more highly educated people, one would have expected such a large increase in relative supply to have been accompanied by a significant decline in the premium for longer schooling. Young people leaving high schools, colleges, and universities would have been generally disappointed by the advantages in occupations, careers, and incomes opened to them by schooling: and their discontent would long since have brought the secular boom in education to a close. Perhaps some decline in earnings premiums did occur in the earlier decades of the century. The data are too scant to permit a firm judgment. Yet as late as 1940, the spread of earnings associated with length of schooling was still wide, and since that time it has not contracted notably, although the rise in the educational level of the labor force accelerated.

An explanation for the persistence of the premium for education comes in two parts, and both reveal the obtrusive influence of technological progress and of the shifts in occupation which flow from it. We look, first, to the large change in the occupational composition of employment since at least the beginning of this century. The proportion of people employed in occupations characteristically filled by people with relatively long schooling has grown in importance; and rough calculations suggest that this shift accounts for something between a third and a half and perhaps more of the rise in the average school-level of the employed labor force since 1900. Some part of this shift may, indeed, have been due to a decline in the relative price of educated workers resulting from an increase in their supply. If so, it is presumably a small part since 1940, for the relative price of educated workers has fallen little if at all since that time. Before 1940, there may well have been a relative price decline which encouraged the growth of "education-intensive" occupations. Yet both before and since 1940, forces were clearly at work on the demand side which contributed substantially to sustaining the reward for schooling.

We note first that, among the principal industrial divisions of the economy, those in which the level of labor-force schooling is above average have been increasing their share of employment at the expense of those in which the level of workers' schooling is below average. In the latter group are the industries primarily concerned with the extraction, fabrication, and movement of goods, that is, farming, mining, construction, transport, and manufactures. In the former are the auxiliary industries concerned with distribution, coordination, and regulation as well as with furnishing those things the demand for which tends to grow rapidly with income – trade, utilities and communications, services, finance, and civilian government. Since 1948, and perhaps even earlier, the shift has rested in part on an increase in relative output. Before and since 1948, however, the shift has reflected a more rapid rise in labor productivity in industries directly concerned with the handling of tangible commodities compared to the service-producing or auxiliary sectors. A number of forces have combined to produce these results, but two are outstanding. First, the technology of power and machinery has so far proven

more effective in saving the less well-educated blue-collar labor dominant in the goods-producing sectors and less effective in saving the
white-collar, "education-intensive" labor which is dominant in the
service-producing industries.[6] Second, the increase in scale, specialization, and articulation, on which the application of this technology
rests, itself required an increase in the activity of those sectors providing regulation, communication, coordination, and finance.

Next, we note that these shifts in the occupational-composition of
employment have been associated not only with changes in the industrial distribution of output and workers, but also with changes within
firms and industries. Even in mining, transportation, and manufacturing, the white-collar, education-intensive jobs concerned with administration, record-keeping, communication, sales, and finance have
grown at the expense of jobs more directly concerned with the handling of goods. And again, this was partly because efficiency gain
called for enlargement in the scale of establishments and firms which
was costly in terms of the overhead functions served by education-
intensive, white-collar workers. It was partly because the larger scale
of firms made profitable, and so encouraged, the growth of other
education-intensive activities, like research and development, advertising, and employee-training. And it was partly because technical
progress has, so far, been less effective in saving white-collar than
blue-collar labor.

The second part of the answer is connected with the rise which
occurred in the educational qualifications attached to most occupations. Some of this rise almost certainly has its origin in the extension
of education itself. Employers depend on school records and diplomas to help them select applicants who are likely to meet their standards of intelligence, industry, and responsibility. When only 75 percent of all youngsters finished elementary school and only 40 percent
were graduated from high school, an elementary school diploma
could qualify its holder to be a clerk while a high school graduate
might become a private secretary. When virtually every boy and girl
finishes elementary school and three out of four obtain high school
diplomas, mere maintenance of old standards means that clerks must
have finished high school, and the boss demands that his own secretary have a junior college certificate or even a B.A. How far the increase in supply goes to account for an inflation of schooling requirements, we do not know. It may be, probably is, a major element of an
explanation.[7] At the same time, developments have been taking place
in both the worlds of work and of education which are manifestly
calculated to raise the real value of schooling in the production of
goods and services.

Some categorical assertions must suffice to put the case. From the side of industry, the content of jobs changed in ways which made formal schooling more useful. The machines which displaced labor became themselves more sophisticated and required more of the common school skills of reading and reckoning for their operation and maintenance. The enlargement of plants and firms meant not only more administrators and clerks, it demanded more paper work in all operations. Gas station attendants handle credit cards, check stock, and requisition supplies, and even the simplest mechanical operations have acquired peripheral record-keeping and communications functions. Manifestly, the expansion of the need for the clerkly skills has been all the greater at the higher occupational levels of larger organizations in which administration has more and more taken the form of consultation and decision on the basis of records, reports, analyses, committees and interpersonal and, in a sense, impersonal communications.

At the same time, the curricula of schools, colleges, and universities have come to include more that is of vocational, commercial, and professional interest and use. The high schools – partly in order to engage the interest and keep the attention of a much larger population of students, of whom only a minority were preparing for higher education or had a disinterested concern with impractical academic subjects – enlarged their program of vocational courses. Universities, led by the state universities, gradually embodied their goal of service to the whole community, in an ever-broader program of instruction in industrial subjects – for example, in agriculture, nursing, engineering, forestry, and mining.

The curriculum reforms were also a consequence of the growth of knowledge generally and of the increasing degree to which industry, commerce, and other activities, including education itself, have been made the subjects of formal disciplines and of the larger extent to which industry has come to rest on applied science. Professional training has become more complex and more rigorous as the scientific bases of the professions have become better established. Courses in engineering and medicine, including internship, to take just two examples, have, therefore, been extended and much more frequently involve postgraduate work. New disciplines came into being and gradually won a place in the esteem of students and their prospective employers. Business administration became the subject most frequently studied by college students, and the list includes journalism, public health, and education itself. Nor did this development stop at the level of professional training in normal four-year colleges and universities. The advance of science and its increasing application in industry have not only opened up many new technical and subprofessional occupations, they have also deepened the training regarded as useful in older occupations. These, in some cases, have so changed in character as to assume new names: kitchen managers have become nutritionists; dental assistants, hygienists; and masseurs, physical therapists. Training for these occupations has gradually been made the subject of classroom or laboratory study, and they have become the basic concern of the growing number of two-year community and junior colleges.

I conclude, therefore, that the rise in the level of schooling characteristic of most occupations is only in part an inflation of requirements due to an increase in supply. The rest, like the expansion of employment in education-intensive occupations, is associated with technical progress, with the enlargement of scale it has entailed and with the evolution of applied science, the professions and their auxiliary specialities. These have made for a true expansion in the training which jobs demand and in the capacities of schools to impart useful skills.

Education and technological and organizational progress

We now have to close the circle of interdependence between manpower development and technological progress. The advance of technology, by its effects on the scale of activity, the character of jobs, the level of income and the span of life has made for an increase both in the demand for, and in the number of, people with higher levels of schooling. At the same time, the enlarged number of educated people has itself fostered the advance of technology. This is manifestly the case insofar as larger numbers of scientists, engineers and administrators are directly concerned with the creation of new products, including new mechanical, electrical, chemical, and biological devices, and with exploring and improving the technology and organization by which they are produced. It is equally manifest insofar as the efforts of these professionals are better supported by larger numbers of auxiliary technicians. It is also widely appreciated that a generally educated population is better prepared, both as workers and consumers, to adapt to, and so to adopt, the novel products and services, the novel work routines, and the new locations which technical and organizational advance entails. Their adaptability lowers the costs and the risks of innovation.

The fundamental connections between manpower development and technological progress, however, are at once wider and less immediately apparent. If we assume that the character of our technological advance is given, we may well view the rise of educational effort, the withdrawal of the young from the labor force, and the offsetting entry of women as simply responses to the demands of an emerging technology with its implied requirements for "overhead" labor in the broad meaning we have given this term. As we grope uncertainly toward an understanding of technological change, however, it becomes more apparent that its pace and character are not facts entirely fixed by the nature of the physical universe and the state of basic science. On the contrary, they are themselves, at least in part, adaptations to the tastes and life styles of the people they serve and to the relative resource costs that they entail.

A more adequate view of the matter seems to proceed from the proposition that nature presents us, in each successive era, not with a singular path of technical progress, but with a choice among a variety of paths. Some entail much capital, little production labor, but much administrative effort; some involve a different mix of these elements. Some can be operated with small producing units and small firms; others require large establishments organized in still larger firms. Some can be successfully applied by producing units working at a distance from other units in the same industry and with little help from an auxiliary complex of establishments providing repairs, storage, distribution and advertising, finance and accounting; others require the full panoply of metropolitan business services and facilities. Some, therefore, entail a great development of government services; others would do so to a lesser degree. And in the same way, some paths depend on a very wide extension of literacy and on an intense development of technical and professional skills, while others would be less demanding of formal education.

The path which this country has followed during the last century clearly has been a labor-saving, capital-using path – where labor means unskilled labor and capital includes not only the tools used by workers in direct production, but also the "social" capital required for urban population concentration and for administration, transportation, communication and finance and, perhaps most of all, the very large capital investments in schooling and on-the-job training. Compared with other countries, we early chose a capital-intensive and education-intensive technology and social organization, in part because it was cheaper in a country where labor – unskilled labor – was relatively expensive and where at least elementary schooling was relatively widespread.[8] We developed this technology and organization in part because a practice, once established, becomes, for a time, the object of progressive improvement.[9] More and more, we apprehend that technical and organizational advance is, to some extent, a matter of continuing exploration based on experience, a matter of learning-by-doing. Since the established mode of production and organization, in the history of U.S. industrialization was a capital- and education-intensive mode, it was the one in which we chiefly gained experience and tended to advance.

In part, however, we have followed the capital-using and education-intensive path because it appeared to be cheaper than it actually was. The full costs of a technology based on large and very dense metropolitan concentrations and on great expenditures for transport, communications, and administration are gradually revealing themselves: and it would be surprising if the direction of development in the future did not bend away from this path and toward one based on less dense population concentrations, on labor-saving in administration, and on some economy in social and private overheads. If so, this itself will have an impact on the need for schooling in preparation for work.

The full costs of an education-intensive technology are also now gradually revealing themselves as the period of schooling is extended and as entrance into the work force is postponed from the fourteenth to the eighteenth and now to the twenty-second, twenty-fourth, and twenty-sixth years, not for 6 or 10 percent but for 30 and 40 percent of the population of young people. It is not only that the expansion of public subsidies for education is being increasingly resisted as the aggregate size of the expenditure increases. It is also that the private costs, psychological as well as financial, of ever more protracted periods of schooling and hence of dependency come to be seen as out of balance with the physical and emotional maturity of the bulk of young people. Thus, it may be that for several reasons – from the sides of both demand and supply – we shall be slowing down the pace of education-using technical advance, even evolving a new path which is education-saving. Doubtless any attempt to assess the future relations of education and technological progress is in the highest degree uncertain. The character of technological and organizational progress may prove to be highly resistant to alteration. The schools themselves may finally learn to do their jobs of educating young people and of screening talent more expeditiously and cheaply, which would encourage the further development of technique and organization dependent on the use of people with more formal schooling. Nonetheless, one may well ask whether we are not now witnessing something of a climacteric in the trend of investment in man, at least in the United States. Needless to say, one should not expect to see our schools contract like the steel rail or the freight car-producing industries of earlier decades, but their long secular boom may well be over.

Notes

1. The distribution according to the conventional definition of capital formation is based on unweighted arithmetic means of shares in fifteen countries, usually for

1950–58. The magnitudes for "investment in man" are based on T. W. Schultz' estimates of the cost of schooling in the USA in 1956. Kuznets' revised shares are calculated after reestimation of standard GNP data to eliminate intermediate output properly excluded. The stages in his calculations are indicated in the following figures:

	Shares of GNP components, percent	
	Private and public consumption	Gross capital formation
National accounts definition	77	23
Omitting intermediate products	70	30
Allowing for investment in man but excluding income foregone from capital formation and GNP	58	42
Adding income foregone in formal education and on-the-job training	53	47

See S. S. Kuznets, *Modern Economic Growth, Rate, Structure, and Spread* (New Haven: Yale University Press, 1966), Table 5.2.

2. See the paper by the author and Paul A. David, "Economic Growth in America: Historical Parables and Realities," *De Economist* 121, no. 3 (1973), 251–72.

3. Cf. Jacob Mincer, "Labor Force Participation of Married Women," in *Aspects of Labor Economics, A Conference of the Universities – National Bureau Committee for Economic Research* (Princeton, N.J.: Princeton University Press, 1962), pp. 63–97.

4. It is perhaps only an incidental matter, though one of some importance, that, in many of the enlarging sectors, particularly in trade, finance, office work of many types and in some health care, educational, and recreational activities, part-time and intermittent employment proved tolerable for firms and effective, therefore, in attracting a supply of useful female workers with competing household demands on their time.

5. I am not arguing that the premiums can be wholly attributed to what schooling does to raise a person's effectiveness as a worker. So far as the contribution of schooling to productivity is concerned, it is enough if a substantial part of the earnings differentials associated with education can be so explained. So far as the inducement to seek more schooling is concerned, it is enough if people merely believe that the premiums are a measure of rewards of education.

6. Cf. Victor Fuchs, *The Service Economy* (New York: Columbia University Press for National Bureau of Economic Research, 1968).

7. This is a view emphasized and documented by Ivar Berg, *Education and Jobs: The Great Training Robbery* (New York: Praeger, 1970).

8. Cf. H. J. Habakkuk, *American and British Technology in the Nineteenth Century: The Search for Labour-Saving Inventions,* (Cambridge: At the University Press, 1967).

9. That technological progress tends to be capital-saving or labor-saving over a period of time because we gain experience in the kind of technology chosen in the past is an idea I owe to my colleague, Paul David. I have ventured here to give it a wider application than he himself might be disposed to do.

6

Rapid growth potential and its realization: the experience of capitalist economies in the postwar period

Dramatic statements about the remarkable growth of the industrial-ised market economies are by now superfluous. The forces which account for this notable experience, however, still challenge explana-tion. And without a well-tested explanation, we are in a poor position to say whether rapid growth has now come to an end or whether it is likely to be resumed. Equally, we are in a poor position to suggest what policies might regenerate and sustain rapid growth were that an agreed aim of public policy.

Although, as said, we do not as yet have a well-tested explanation, a good deal of ground has been cleared, and the elements of a general understanding of the causes of rapid growth have begun to come into view. This being the case, I think it will be useful to try to draw these together as well as I can. This may help us discover how much agree-ment there is about the factors underlying postwar growth. And it may help us see where the empirical basis of our theories is especially weak and where, therefore, future work ought to be directed.

Reprinted by permission from *Economic Growth and Resources*, vol. 1, *The Major Issues*, ed. by Edmond Malinvaud. Proceedings of the Fifth World Congress of the Interna-tional Economic Association held in Tokyo, Japan. London: Macmillan, and New York: St. Martin's Press, 1979, pp. 1–30.

I should like to acknowledge the help I have had from Paul David. This paper has benefited not only from his critical reading, but also from his insights, shared during a long collaboration.

I must also acknowledge special intellectual debts to many contributions to the postwar growth literature. These include the growth-accounting calculations of John Kendrick, Edward Denison, Dale Jorgenson and others; the historical and analytical studies of Europe and Japan by Angus Maddison, of Japan by Ohkawa and Rosovsky, of France by Carré, Dubois and Malinvaud, and of Italy by G. Fuá, as well as still unpublished studies of the UK by Matthews, Feinstein and Odling-Smee, of Sweden by R. Bentzel and of Germany by Bombach and Gerfin; also the studies of structural change and the role of labour supply by Kuznets, Kindleberger and Kaldor and the collaborative Brookings volumes on the postwar economies of Britain and Japan.

187

Both the breadth of this assignment and the limits of my own competence require that I restrict attention to the experience of the industrialised market economies as a group, and, correspondingly, to the common causes which I see behind it. A general view of this experience should help us understand the differences among countries in their rates of growth, in so far as those differences have a systematic character. But I do not try to account for the utterly extraordinary speed of Japanese expansion or what is, from some perspectives, the equally divergent relative slackness of the British pace.

In this paper, I confine attention to one aspect of growth: namely, labour productivity as measured by output per worker. I treat the forces determining rapidity of productivity growth as falling into two classes: those governing the potential for productivity growth during the postwar era and those controlling the pace at which that potential was exploited. By the potential for productivity growth, I mean, first, the opportunity for progress which is presented by the enlargement in technological and organisational knowledge which took place in the course of the postwar period. I mean, second, the opportunity for productivity growth which exists when a country, relatively advanced in the state of its political, commercial and financial institutions and in its degree of technical competence, nevertheless finds itself behind the industrial leader in the level of achieved productivity. In that case, the country's degree of initial backwardness in productivity can be regarded as the rough measure of a gap between existing and potential productivity, and therefore, of the advance potentially open to it in the course of capital turnover and expansion and accompanying economic reorganisation. On the other hand, the absorption and application of potential advances in productivity – whether these are contemporaneously generated or available from a pre-existing, still unexploited stock of knowledge – involve several responsive economic actions: accumulation of both tangible and human capital per worker, together with a change in design of structures and equipment and content of education; enlargement of the scale of production, accompanied by greater specialisation of productive establishments, worker tasks and machine designs; change in the industrial distribution of labour, capital and output; and research and development effort to adapt new techniques to the resource endowments and scale constraints of particular markets and economies. The pace of exploitation of potential productivity growth should, therefore, be viewed as controlled by the speeds at which these economic responses take place and, at the next remove, by the conditions governing those speeds of response.

My paper's general thesis is simply stated. A special, but transitory, set of circumstances made the postwar potential for productivity growth strong and enabled developed countries to exploit that potential rapidly, in concert and over a long period. Some of the favouring circumstances arose from the Second World War itself, some from the frustration of normal growth caused by war, political upheaval and depression during the longer period beginning in 1914; some reflected the stage of development which a number of industrialised countries had reached; and some rested on national and international political and economic arrangements which have now broken down. Of course, there are other forces – an expanding technological frontier, rising education, growing managerial competence – which continue to work steadily for material progress. However, the importance of the essentially transitory influences in postwar development and the fact that these have now weakened and, in some cases, disappeared make the prospects for an early renewal of the postwar growth drive at the same rapid pace uncertain and dubious. Though it is not directly argued in the present paper, that seems to me to be the somewhat gloomy implication of my analysis. Are those prospects more dubious and uncertain than they were in 1950? That is, in a sense, the more hopeful question which our considerable ignorance still permits us to entertain.

Postwar potential

As already said, the potential for productivity growth during a period has two elements: first, the current pace of advance of productive knowledge; and, second, the initial gap between existing and best practice. I take these up in order.

Acceleration in the growth of productive knowledge

There are no direct measures of the stock of productive knowledge, so no one can make secure judgements about its rate of advance. It is a question basic to our subject, however, and one must adopt some view about it, however provisional. In this very tentative spirit, I argue that the pace of progress in productive knowledge during the postwar years was at least as fast as in any earlier, comparably long period. Indeed it may well have been more rapid. Two sorts of considerations support this position.

First, it is consistent with many impressions and observations about the contemporary world – that there has been a speed-up in the pace of scientific progress generally; that levels of education are higher; that the numbers and proportions of scientists and engineers in industry or concerned with industrial applications have grown; that science-based industry has become more important; that business administration has become more systematic and is staffed with better-trained people; that the enlarged scale of economic activity, in the postwar period itself provided a wider basis of experience and, therefore, of improvement.

Second, it is consistent with the only aggregate measures we have – indirect and uncertain as these may be – namely, the residuals in the growth-accounting calculations. For this purpose, the relevant accounts are those for the U.S. That is not because America is the source of all technological progress, but because, as Denison and Chung say, 'it seems unlikely that in the U.S. economy . . . the rate at which advances were incorporated departed much from the worldwide rate of new advance'.[1]

Proceeding from this assumption, we may note, first, that estimates for 'conventional'[2] total factor productivity growth, made with different bodies of data and by different students, suggest that such advance was distinctly faster in the postwar period or, more generally, since the 1920s than it was before the First World War.[3] Denison's growth accounts, which go further and allow for intensity of work, longer schooling, better resource allocation and economies of scale, also suggest a similar acceleration in his final residual which he himself names 'Advances of Knowledge'.[4] The difference is of the order of 1 percentage point or somewhat more in comparisons between the postwar years and the decades immediately preceding either the 1920s or the First World War. And since, for most of the western industrialised countries, the intervening years constituted something of a growth hiatus imposed by great wars, political upheaval and major depression, this is the relevant comparison.

It is perhaps unnecessary to recite all the reasons which make such residuals unreliable measures of technological progress.[5] So far as they go, however, they are not contradicted by other evidence, and they are consistent with the idea that contemporaneously generated productive knowledge helped provide a strong potentiality for rapid postwar productivity growth among industrialised countries.

Greater 'backwardness' in Europe and Japan

When the postwar period opened, the actual levels of labour productivity in Japan, north-west Europe and Italy were especially low compared with those which their technological tradition, human skills and governmental, commercial and financial institutions were capable of supporting. This gap between capability and achievement constituted a second source of potentially rapid postwar growth.

To establish orders of magnitude, we can compare labour productivities in the various industrialised countries with that in the U.S.

One can determine the relative levels in 1950 on the basis of two closely related sets of figures. One set, provided by Denison,[6] is based on the well-known OECD/Gilbert comparisons of output with uniform U.S. 1955 price weights. This set includes the U.S. and eight European countries. The other is an extrapolation back to 1950 from a 1965 comparison by Angus Maddison[7] which is itself an extension of the same OECD/Gilbert data. This set includes the same countries covered by Denison plus Japan and Canada. Differences between the two sets of figures for 1950 are negligible for the kinds of uses to which I put them.

Since the Maddison data cover two additional countries, I have used them as the basis for further extrapolation back to 1913 and forward to 1970 using figures for output per man in which outputs are aggregated with national price weights.[8] See Table 6.1.

According to these figures, the average labour productivity of the ten other countries in 1913 was about 60 per cent of the U.S. level. The variance was wide. These figures reflect the high level at which the U.S. had started its own industrialisation some 75 to 100 years earlier and the varying number of decades which then intervened before the industrialisation process had become well launched elsewhere. Between 1913 and 1950, the average productivity relative fell by about 20 per cent as a result of the combined effects of the First World War, the Second World War and the political and economic disturbances in the immediate aftermath of both wars. The rise in the relative during the Depression was illusory gain. Compared with potential, progress in almost all countries slowed down, but since under-utilisation of manpower was so much greater in the U.S. than elsewhere, there is a false appearance of catch-up.

The measured decline between 1913 and 1950 in productivity relative to potential was, in a sense, greater than these measures suggest. The U.S. advantage in 1913 rested in part on a favourable man-land ratio which other countries, except Canada, presumably could never match. By 1950, proportions of employment devoted to farming had become smaller throughout the group and very much smaller in the U.S.[9] The U.S. productivity advantage in 1950, therefore, rested more nearly completely on its larger stock of reproductible capital per man and on the various elements underlying the efficiency of labour and capital in regard to which it is open to other countries to overtake it sooner or later.

The figures, next, carry the strong suggestion that the large productivity gap of 1913 and its enlargement during the disturbed years between then and 1950 did, in fact, constitute a strong potentiality for rapid postwar growth in the less advanced countries. In the next

Table 6.1. *Output per worker in 1965 $U.S. measured at U.S. relative prices, 1913–70 (means and relative variance of the relatives of nine or ten countries compared with the U.S. (U.S. = 100)*

	1913	1929	1938	1950	1955	1960	1965	1970
9 countries excl. Japan								
Mean	65.1			51.7	53.9	59.8	62.3	70.6
Relative variance	0.053			0.048	0.044	0.026	0.017	0.014
9 countries excl. Germany								
Mean	59.8	54.3	58.5	48.5				
Relative variance	0.102	0.068	0.036	0.109				
10 countries								
Mean	61.2			48.4	50.8	57.0	60.1	69.8
Relative variance	0.096			0.096	0.078	0.053	0.029	0.014

Means and variances calculated excluding the U.S.
Source: See note 7, p. 213. Maddison-based table of relatives with employment of women in agriculture adjusted to share in non-agriculture.

twenty years, these countries' productivity grew distinctly more rapidly than did that in the U.S., although American labour productivity was rising as fast as ever and much more rapidly than before 1913. The mean productivity relative of the other countries rose from about 50 per cent to about 70 per cent of the U.S. level between 1950 and 1970. At the same time, the variance among the follower countries declined by more than five-sixths (by seven-tenths excluding Japan). In general, the less productive the country in 1950, the more rapidly its productivity rose.[10]

The same results emerge from measures of rank correlation between countries' labour productivity growth rates during successive periods and their initial relative productivity levels. The association is highest ($\rho_r = -0.9$) for the two decades 1950–70 taken together, somewhat less high ($\rho_r = -0.8$) for 1950–60 and lower ($\rho_r = -0.6$) for the 1960s alone. (See Table 6.2)

That the association should be closer over two decades than over either one is not hard to understand. Some countries recovered from the war and its aftermath more quickly and launched themselves into their postwar growth process sooner than others. Those which did relatively less well in the first decade by comparison with their initial standing tended to do better in the next. That the association of growth with initial standings should have been weaker in the 1960s than in the 1950s is again what one should expect. The potentiality which backwardness affords for growth may be thought to weaken as catch-up proceeds (though, as we shall see, that is not necessarily so). More important, the differences among the backward countries had become much smaller by 1960 than they had been in 1950. The relative variances of Table 6.1 provide one indication. According to Denison's estimates, the productivity indexes of five of the six north-west European Continental countries in 1960 fell within a range running from 56 to 61 per cent of the U.S. level – under 10 per cent of their mean level. No one can suppose that differences so small are indicative of significant differences in growth potential. Moreover all the industrialised countries except Canada continued to gain on the U.S. And the remaining broad differences among countries in relative productivity levels – as between Japan, Italy, north-west Europe, Canada – were accompanied by growth-rate differences which varied consistently and markedly in the inverse order as expected.[11]

The record of postwar growth, therefore, appears to be consistent with the view that relative backwardness, for countries with the proper apparatus of governmental and commercial institutions, with educated and skilled populations and advanced technological capabilities, is an important aspect of growth potential which shaped the

Table 6.2. *Coefficients of rank correlations between the labour productivity growth rates and relative productivity levels of eleven countries*

A Growth rates 1950–70 and relative levels in 1950	
1 Maddison-based levels, adjusted	−0.91
2 Maddison-based levels, unadjusted	−0.91
3 Denison levels	−0.89[a]
B Growth rates 1950–60 and relative levels in 1950	
1 Maddison-based levels, adjusted	−0.80
2 Maddison-based levels, unadjusted	−0.82
3 Denison levels	−0.80[a]
C Growth rates 1960–70 and relative levels in 1960	
1 Maddison-based levels, adjusted	−0.61
2 Maddison-based levels, unadjusted	−0.67
3 Denison levels	−0.65[a]

[a]Denison did not provide estimates of productivity levels for Japan and Canada. They were given arbitrary ranks of 1 (lowest) and 10 (next to the highest) respectively according to the showing of the Maddison-based data. There is no reason to think that direct estimates would have yielded any different result.

Source: The ranks of countries according to their productivity levels were obtained from the sources cited in notes 6 and 7 and further described in note 8 (pp. 213–14). See also note *a*, above.

The ranks of countries according to their productivity growth rates are based on OECD data for output and employment with extensions as follows:

Output (gross domestic product) obtained by linking data for 1950 (or earliest available date) through 1968 from OECD, *National Accounts, 1950–68* to later data for 1968 through 1970 from OECD, *National Accounts, 1960–71*.

Employment: In general, data for 1957–8 from OECD, *Labor Force Statistics, 1957–68* were extrapolated forward to 1970 by the movement of data from OECD, *Labor Force Statistics, 1961–72* and backwards as far as possible by the movement of data from OECD, *Manpower Statistics, 1950–62*. In a few cases, other data were used, as follows:

France: 1955 OECD data extrapolated back to 1950 by data from Carré, Dubois and Malinvaud, *French Economic Growth* (Stanford: Stanford University Press, 1975) Appendix Table 4.

Italy: 1955 OECD data extrapolated back to 1950 by data from Fua (ed.), *Lo Sviluppo Economico in Italia*, vol. III, Table XII–2.4.

Switzerland: 1960 OECD figure was extrapolated directly to 1950 by data from OECD, *Labour Force Statistics, 1956–66*.

Canada: The 1957 OECD was extrapolated to 1950 by data from Canadian Statistical Review, 1963 Supplement, *Historical Summary*, Table 14 augmented by members in the Armed Forces from Historical Statistics of Canada, Series C–48.

postwar record. I have already argued, however, that it is only potential, a permissive not sufficient condition for rapid growth. The force of this distinction is apparent when we consider the common observation that, if relative backwardness were by itself the governing determinant of growth, one would expect that the labour productivity growth rates of the follower countries would decline as the U.S. lead was gradually reduced. But there is no evidence of a general marked retardation in postwar labour productivity growth before the 1970s.

The proximate cause of this is now apparent. As Christensen, Cummings and Jorgenson have now made clear, the 1960s saw a great investment boom in Europe and Japan in which growth rates of capital stock per worker rose above the high rates of the 1950s and in which the composition of capital shifted toward higher-yielding assets. The effect was to raise or sustain labour productivity growth in the fast-growing countries, a growth which would otherwise have declined markedly in the European countries, and risen by little in Japan, even if total productivity growth had been unaffected by slower capital accumulation.[12] I shall argue below, however, that the pace at which countries can exploit their potential for productivity advance is itself governed by investment and growth of capital. If the investment boom of the 1960s had been less pronounced, total factor productivity growth would also have been slower.

In addition to the speed-up in capital accumulation per worker, other developments took place in the course of the postwar period which helped to quicken the pace at which potential productivity could be realised. These emerge in the next section, Sources and Processes. I contend, therefore, that the retardation which one might otherwise expect to accompany catch-up was avoided during the 1960s by conditions which favoured capital investment and by these and other developments supporting more rapid exploitation of opportunities for modernisation.

Sources and processes

We can learn something more about backwardness as potential by considering the proximate sources from which the relative productivity gains of the poorer countries were obtained. This will also help us identify the processes through which catch-up and, indeed, contemporaneously generated progress operated and so enable us to go on to consider the factors which permitted those processes to run at a rapid pace.

My point of departure is the calculation of 'sources of growth' car-

Table 6.3. *Sources of differences in growth rates of national income per person employed between U.S. 1948–69 and Japan 1953–71 and between U.S. and three European countries,[a] 1950–62*

Excess over U.S. (in percentage points per annum)	Three European countries,[a] 1950–62	Japan, 1953–71[b]
1 Standardised growth rate	2.18	4.79
2 Total Inputs	0.29	1.82
(a) Hours and age-sex composition	0.20	0.66
(b) Education	−0.15	−0.07
(c) Non-residential reproducible capital[c]	0.49	1.26
(d) Dwellings and other capital[d]	−0.24	−0.02
3 Improved allocation[e]	0.79	0.65
4 Total input and improved allocation	1.08	2.47
5 First residual [= line (1)−(4)]	1.09	2.32
(a) Economies of scale (A) (U.S. prices)[f]	0.23	0.64
(b) Economies of scale (B) (associated with income elasticities)[g]	0.66	0.88
6 Second residual	0.17	0.80
(a) Advance of knowledge and n.e.c. in U.S.[h]	0	0
(b) Changes in the lag in the application of knowledge, general efficiency, errors and omissions,etc.	0.17	0.80
7 Sum of 3 sources associated with catch-up [line 3 + line 5(b) + line 6(b)]	1.62	2.33
8 Standardised growth rate less line 5(a) [see text]	1.95	4.15
9 Ratio: line 7 ÷ line 8	0.83	0.56

[a]Average of France, Germany and Italy. Growth of national income and sources were combined by unweighted arithmetic averages.
[b]Compared with U.S. in 1948–69.
[c]Non-residential structures, equipment and inventories.
[d]Includes international assets and land.
[e]Includes contraction of agricultural inputs, non-agricultural self-employment and reduction in international trade barriers.
[f]Effects of expansion of national markets measured in U.S. prices and independent growth of local markets.
[g]See text for explanation.
[h]Assumed to be the same in other countries as in U.S.
Sources: 1950–62: From country tables in Denison, *Why Growth Rates Differ*, Chapter 21. German figures (for standardised growth rate adjusted downward to reflect Denison's estimates of the contribution in 1950–5 of 'capital balancing' and the difference between 1950–62 and 1955–60 in the change in the lag in application of knowledge, etc. Figures

ried out by Denison (Table 6.3). His tables include three classes of contributions which are plausibly associated with backwardness itself. His 'improved allocation of resources' includes the effects of shifts of labour from agricultural to non-agricultural employment and from non-farm self-employment to dependent employment in larger factories and commercial establishments.[13] His 'economies of scale associated with income elasticities' measures one part of the gain from borrowing the more advanced technology of richer countries, a part which is supposedly dependent on the expansion of the market for consumer goods with income-elastic demand. His 'changes in the lag in application of knowledge, general efficiency and errors and omissions' includes the effects of non-scale-dependent modernisation either in the course of capital replacement and expansion or by the borrowing of technology not necessarily embodied in tangible capital. (This last is, for the countries behind the U.S. Denison's ultimate residual.) These three sources together generally accounted for more than half and in France, Germany and Italy more than three-quarters, of the excess of productivity growth in the poorer countries over that in the U.S.

These figures are, in one sense, lower bounds on the contribution to fast productivity growth from catch-up-connected sources because they allow nothing for the support which opportunities for catch-up lent to rapid capital accumulation by supporting the rate of return to capital. If, say, half the excess contribution of growing capital per man in the poorer countries over that in the U.S. were so attributable, virtually the whole of the differential productivity growth rate would be accounted for. The figure for France, Germany and Italy together would be 95 per cent and that for Japan, 71 per cent.

The Denison figures suggest that there was not merely an empirical association between productivity levels and rates of growth, but that the proximate sources of rapid growth are plausibly connected with relative backwardness. Viewed as a guide to the processes involved in

Notes to Table 6.3 (cont.)

for the U.S. were adjusted to reflect Denison's later revisions. See his *Accounting for U.S. Economic Growth*, Table S–2.

Japan, 1953–71: Denison and Chung, *How Japan's Economy Grew So Fast*, Table 5–1.

U.S., 1948–69: Denison, *Accounting for U.S. Economic Growth, 1929–69*, Table 9–7.

Note that the table above follows Denison in subtracting the extraordinary gains enjoyed by Germany between 1950 and 1955 due to 'balancing' its capital stock and because in that early period it was still overcoming inefficiencies connected with the aftermath of war. With these sources included, Germany's rate of catch-up would appear considerably more rapid and the average rate for the three countries somewhat more so.

exploiting productivity potential, however, Denison's sources also present certain difficulties.

To my mind, these centre in his ingenious estimates of 'economies of scale associated with income elasticities.' Denison's calculations[14] proceed from the well-established observations that shares of different kinds of products in the consumer expenditures of different countries are inversely related to their relative prices and that patterns of both prices and expenditures converge as the incomes of poorer countries rise relatively. Denison attributes the convergence of expenditure patterns to the similarities of income elasticities of demand and the convergence of price structures to the increasing ability of the faster-growing poorer countries to exploit the scale-dependent technologies earlier discovered and applied by the richer countries. As Denison's calculations of 'economies of scale associated with income elasticities' are constructed, this source contributes so much of the productivity growth of the pursuing countries that little remains in his ultimate residuals to be attributed to 'changes in the lag in the application of knowledge, general efficiency . . .' etc.

There is, however, another explanation for the convergence of price structures.[15] Consider the well-known difference between the prices of tradable and non-tradable goods in open economies with fixed exchange rates. Subject to the usual qualifications, the absolute prices of tradables are everywhere the same. Fixed exchange rates, however, ensure that average money wage rates are higher in the more productive countries, a difference which is necessarily reflected in the relative prices of labour-intensive, low productivity non-tradables. These tend to be relatively high in the high money-wage rich countries. Since such countries consume relatively more of the tradable durables than of the non-tradable, labour-intensive, low-productivity products, this helps account for the characteristic differences between price and expenditure structures and for the convergence of price structures as productivity levels converge.[16] The increasing ease of *scale-dependent* technological borrowing is no necessary part of this story.

I do not regard this hypothesis as an exclusive alternative to Denison's view, which I think carries part of the truth. The alternative does suggest, however, that Denison may have relied too much on his own interpretation of the convergence of price structures. If so, there is more room for a significantly large contribution from 'changes in the lag in the application of knowledge' – that is, for productivity growth connected with technological modernisation in the course of capital replacement and expansion without scale-constraint, as well as with other sorts of technical and organisational diffusion.

Denison's treatment of this subject may also be misleading in another way. His hypothesis makes economies of scale a function of the scale of consumer *expenditures*. The direct and true connection, however, is between efficiency and scale of *production*. Manifestly, there is a relation between patterns of consumer expenditure and of production. Changes in production structure, however, are responsive to more than the income elasticity of consumer demand. They also respond to the growing demand for capital goods in the course of development, to an increasing need for intermediate goods of industrial origin and, perhaps most important, to shifting comparative advantage which, by import substitution and export expansion, enables developing countries to move into those industrial sectors in which scale-dependent technology is important.[17] When, therefore, we consider what causes may have permitted the process of technological diffusion to proceed rapidly since the war, we should keep in mind these broader aspects of structural change.

We can, then, summarise the story to this point, by saying that the potentiality for rapid postwar productivity growth arose from rapid contemporaneous advance in knowledge and from enlarged initial gaps between actual and possible productivity. This potentiality was exploited through several channels:

1. Substitution of more advanced for obsolescent methods in the course of capital turnover and expansion or, if improved capital goods are unimportant ingredients, simply in the course of reorganising production routines. The opportunity to apply both new and borrowed advanced techniques was, to some extent, scale-dependent. It arose in part, perhaps in substantial part, in connection with the establishment and growth of those industries in which the demand for products is income-elastic. The Denison hypothesis about 'scale economies associated with income elasticities' itself connects with Verdoorn's Law and with Kaldor's emphasis on scale-dependent technical progress associated with industrial growth.[18] The unbalanced growth which is basic to all these hypotheses, however, goes beyond that envisaged by Denison's theory about the high income elasticity of certain classes of consumer goods. It also comprehends the expansion of industries producing machinery and equipment and intermediate goods serving as industrial and agricultural raw materials. It also goes beyond the unbalanced industrial growth generated by the composition of domestic consumption and capital formation and extends to that which rests on import substitution and export expansion. The process underlying the exploitation of available scale economies, therefore, involves the entire range of structural changes normally

accompanying productivity growth which are described and rational-
ised by Kuzents[19] and adopted by Kaldor.

2. Reallocation of labour, and presumably capital as well, from low
productivity employment in agriculture and petty trade to more productive occupations in industry and larger-scale commercial establishments. This transfer is again associated with the process of structural
change already mentioned.

3. Capital accumulation, which entered the process in three ways.
The first, which represents capital's own, so to speak independent
contribution, consists in the increase of productivity associated with
an increase of capital per man in an otherwise unchanging economy.
Additional capital was also required, however, to permit the adoption
of relatively capital-intensive techniques associated with large-scale
production and with industrial compared with agricultural employment. Finally, the rate of capital accumulation influenced the pace of
technical advance in so far as that rested on the replacement of capital
goods, whether to modernise existing establishments or to reorganise
production in larger or more specialised units or to establish or expand new lines of production.

Conditions controlling the pace of development

I turn now to the behaviour of the economic agents which mediate
between productivity potential and the pace of realization. Having in
mind the processes of growth just described, I take up three subjects,
considering each in relation to this question: What conditions and
developments supported the rapid, general and sustained exploitation of the postwar periods' large potential for productivity growth?

Improved facilities for technological innovation, diffusion and adaptation

The practical application of existing technology demands,
first awareness, then appraisal, then commercial acquisition, then
adaptation from the form in which it may have been cast in the place
of first application to one better suited to the resources, skills, scale of
market and style of products of the firms and places to which it is to
be spread. Having defined the problem in this way, one can see a
number of developments which favoured more rapid diffusion and
adaptation than had existed before the Second World War.[20]

First, when the Second World War ended, the human capabilities
for absorbing and using more advanced technology were better developed. General levels of education were higher, engineers and technicians were more numerous and their relative numbers kept rising

during the postwar period itself. Further, as a reflection of the new importance of science-based industry, the need for highly trained engineers and scientists in industry became manifest, and they were more often drawn into leading positions. Longer experience with large-scale enterprise brought more systematic organisation of management. The increasing dependence on schools of business and engineering as training grounds for industrial administrators in America encouraged European countries and Japan to follow a similar practice.

The growing professionalisation of both administrative and technical leadership in business was matched by better facilities for the rapid diffusion of information. The technical and business press at the opening of the postwar period was already larger than it had been, and it expanded rapidly thereafter. The Marshall Plan, with its arrangements for the exchange of American and European productivity missions, was a rapid refresher course for both sides. Thereafter, the perfection of air travel sustained intense international communication.

The restoration of trade and capital movements to something like pre-1913 levels was also important. Revived trade provided practical demonstrations of new products and materials. Foreign competition, encouraged by the liberalisation of trade and payments, the opening of the Common Market and EFTA and the successive rounds of tariff reductions, was a spur to modernisation. When restrictions on capital and other payments had been reduced and when the potentialities of the European and Japanese markets had become clear, U.S. industry became interested in obtaining a share of the business through patent licences, contracts for the transfer of technology, joint ventures and foreign subsidiaries. The Common Market encouraged the same sort of activity among European countries. By contrast with the portfolio investment which had dominated capital transfer to other industrialised countries before 1913, these methods were both carriers of technological knowledge and goads pressing domestic firms to modernise.

Finally, the increasingly scientific basis for industrial technology encouraged the establishment of research facilities by industrial concerns and associations, as well as by governments. These pioneered in the exploration of original advances and also worked to keep firms abreast of developments elsewhere and to adapt them to local circumstances. As time passed, moreover, firms became better aware of the problems involved in maintaining a proper connection between their R & D establishments and the commercial sides of their business, on the one hand, and the more basic engineering and scientific work of the universities on the other.

Besides helping to explain the generally rapid progress of the postwar years, these developments may provide another group of reasons why the high growth rates established by the mid-1950s should have been sustained for so long instead of suffering the retardation which catch-up is usually supposed to entail. Larger scale of markets and a relative cheapening of capital goods clearly favoured adoption of capital-using technological advances. But it was also true that conditions favoured a speed-up in the spread of information, in the transfer of know-how, and in the work of adapting it to local conditions, as well as increasing European and Japanese participation in original innovation.

Conditions facilitating structural change

Transformation in the composition of output and employment holds a well-established place in the standard view of the development process. Kuznets has taught us that shifts between the broad sectors are founded on intersectoral differences in the income-elasticity of consumer demand; on the expanding roles of the industrial sector as producer of capital goods and of both the industrial and tertiary sectors as producers of intermediate goods and services; and on the advanced countries' growing comparative advantage in the production of industrial products. In these respects, structural change emerges as a necessary concomitant of productivity growth, if not for each country individually, at least for the industrialised countries as a group. In the earlier argument of this paper, however, it also appeared as a direct source of growth in two respects: by providing opportunities for transferring low productivity workers to more productive employments; and by furnishing relatively poor countries with a better chance to borrow technology as their production patterns converge towards those of richer countries in the course of catching up.

The process of structural change proceeds at a pace governed by both demand and supply conditions; and it seems that developments on both sides may have favoured easy and rapid adaptation to the structural requirements of development after the Second World War.

1. Domestic markets for manufactured goods in Japan and the fast-growing European countries were especially strong and responsive to income growth. This was particularly true of those consumer and producer durables which typify the kinds of goods which had been used in quantity and which were relatively cheap in the U.S. and which, therefore, held out a particular promise of rapid, scale-dependent productivity growth if produced in large quantities in the advancing countries. The special strength and responsiveness of these markets rested on several grounds. Stocks were badly depleted at the

end of the Second World War. The widespread use of the new consumer durables – motor vehicles and household and other consumer equipment – had been developing in America since the First World War, but the economic and political disturbances from 1913 to 1950 had inhibited their spread to other countries. Once the more well-to-do countries of north-west Europe had regained and surpassed pre-war income levels, households could afford to adopt the new durables. Finally, in Italy and Japan, the same process was favoured by the dual structure of these countries. Average incomes in both were, indeed, very low. Had earnings been more evenly distributed, the development of markets for the more durable and expensive types of consumer goods might have proceeded more slowly. Families with a member employed in the modern sectors, however, had incomes and consumption standards which soon approximated north-west European levels. So, in these countries too, the markets for complex consumer manufactures expanded rapidly. In some ways, the markets for producer durables were affected by similar influences, and I comment on that sector later.

2. The establishment of domestic industries in all the industrialised countries to satisfy the demand for consumer and producer durables and more generally, for heavy industrial products had taken place well before the Second World War. In Europe the beginnings go back into the nineteenth century. There were, however, two noteworthy developments during the decades between 1913 and 1950 when, in an aggregate sense, the gap between Japan and Europe and the U.S. widened. In Japan, Italy and Germany, heavy industries were rapidly expanded as part of these countries' military programmes. In France, though output itself was restricted, technical preparation went forward.[21] The postwar period, therefore, opened with an industrial framework which required, indeed, to be fleshed out with modern equipment, but was otherwise better prepared to expand the output of durable goods and other heavy industrial products than had been true in the 1920s and earlier.

3. In most of the industrialised countries, the modern non-agricultural industries had access to large supplies of cheap labour, flexibly responsive to additional demand. In some countries, these reserves of unemployed and of low productivity labour in agriculture and petty trade were even larger in 1950 than they had been before the war.[22] In others, as in France, there had been a slowdown in rural-urban migration during the Depression and the Second World War which, having regard to the secular trend of population movement toward the city, must have built up the pool of potential migrants. That pool was also fed by the rapid postwar pace of labour-saving technology on the

farms. Before the war, productivity growth rates on the farms were typically lower than in industry.[23] In the postwar period, they were much higher absolutely and in some countries matched or surpassed the high productivity growth rates in manufacturing. Finally, Germany, Switzerland, and, to a lesser extent, France and other countries enjoyed an augmented supply of labour from permanent or temporary immigration.[24]

Access to flexibly responsive labour supplies permitted the manufacturing and non-agricultural sectors generally to expand rapidly without provoking very large increases in wage rates. The increase in capital per worker associated with the relative growth of industry could more easily proceed without depressing the return to capital and checking the growth of profits. Wage restraint based on reserves of labour was also implicated in the process of structural change through its influence on international trade. Whether the increase in a country's domestic demand for durable manufactures is actually translated into expanded production must depend substantially on the course of change in the locus of its comparative advantage in trade. Given the rapid productivity growth associated with the expansion of industry, some shift of advantage towards industrial goods would be likely to occur. But the opportunity to combine productivity growth with additional cheap labour must have speeded up the process of industrial growth through import substitution and export expansion. This was further speeded for the faster-growing countries of Europe and for Japan, although not for the U.S. and the U.K., because exchange rates were fixed before the rapid growth potentials of the former countries were perceived. And it was still further speeded up by the notable advances towards trade liberalisation made in the 1950s and early 1960s.

Conditions encouraging and sustaining capital investment

Viewed from the standpoint of capital accumulation, the postwar period was an investment boom of unprecedented size both with respect to the rates of growth of stock and to the number of years these high rates were sustained. I have already emphasised the physical and technological opportunities for such a boom which were inherent in the depleted and obsolescent condition of capital at the end of the war. I now ask what postwar conditions facilitated the exploitation of these opportunities and helped to sustain the boom so long.

1. *Conditions stemming from growth itself.* Some of the more important of these conditions were created by the growth of output

and productivity itself. On the side of demand for capital, they were an indirect reflection of the profits promised by investment when capital is in short supply and obsolescent and by other conditions which facilitated modernisation, structural change and capital invest- ment itself. On the side of supply, high rates of household saving reflected the laggard adjustment of expenditures to fast-rising in- comes and also the efforts of households to protect cash balances from being eroded by growth-induced inflation. The conservative projec- tions of tax revenues in the fast-growing countries also made govern- ments an unusual source of savings.

I am not in a position to measure the impact of these forces. They are repeatedly cited in analyses of postwar investment and saving,[25] and I do not doubt their importance. Moreover, the strength of some of these factors developed gradually. They may, therefore, have played a part in sustaining investment as some of the conditions which created a great initial demand for capital weakened. None the less, they are, as said, secondary effects of rapid growth itself. They would have played their part whenever growth for other reasons accelerated. I believe, therefore, that in a paper whose main concern is with the causes of rapid postwar growth, I ought to direct attention to other matters.

2. The initial financial condition of firms and households. Invest- ment booms in the past typically took their start during recovery from serious depressions during which inventories were reduced, debts repaid and the financial structures of companies reorganised. As a result, the borrowing power of firms was strengthened. After the war, the financial environment also became immensely favourable to the development of a sustained investment boom. In all the indus- trialised countries, the real burden of debts had been substantially reduced compared with the value of physical assets, or even elimi- nated. In the Continental countries, and Japan, indeed, the wartime and postwar inflations essentially wiped out the financial indebted- ness of firms and households. As soon as financial markets were reorganised, therefore, firms were willing and able to borrow with little concern for debt burden, and lenders were correspondingly will- ing to extend credit. In most countries, therefore, credit rationing, rather than concern for credit-worthiness, was the effective constraint on finance in the early postwar period. This initial freedom from debt served to support investment for many subsequent years. It was an underpinning for an investment boom clearly analogous in a qualita- tive sense to that afforded by the post-depression origins of earlier booms, but it was quantitatively of a higher order of magnitude.[26]

It is harder to generalise about later experience. Certainly, after an initial period of high profits and reliance on retained earnings, the debt ratios of corporations began to rise and, in some countries – France, for example – dependence on short-term borrowing increased. The significance of this change is, however, hard to gauge. As Carré and his collaborators say, 'it may be that the development observed is a return to a "normal" situation rather than the gradual establishment of an unfavourable economic condition.'[27]

There is no basis for comparing the postwar financial development systematically with that in earlier investment booms. There is some presumption, however, that the cumulation of debt which normally takes place during a period of heavy investment and serves, after a time, to check expansion, did not reach serious levels in the postwar period.

3. Government support for investment. In all the industrialised market economies, private business firms were the dominant agents of capital formation, but governments participated in different ways and to varying degrees. In Germany, the government's role does not appear to have been very different after the war from what it had been before the advent of the Nazis, possibly because large-scale industry in Germany was already better established than in other countries except for the U.S. Moreover, German industry had enjoyed a relatively recent period of profitable expansion during the 1930s and during much of the war under the stimulus of Nazi military preparation and war production. Elsewhere, however, large-scale industry was less developed. France and, to a lesser degree, Italy had suffered longer periods of stagnation more recently. Those countries, and still more Japan, had traditions of regulation and protection which gave governments postwar roles of particular importance.

To appreciate that influence, one must recall that, at the outset, expectations of rapid growth were not common. Few people in Japan or in the Continental countries appreciated the growth potentials of their economies.[28] In the initial atmosphere of uncertainty and indecision, governments acted to provide a necessary impetus to investment. Schumpeter stressed the role of New Men as the entrepreneurial galvanisers of his classic investment booms before the First World War. After the Second World War, there were again New Men, who got their chance in the train of war and defeat and who operated in and through government. France is the type case. Spurred by Jean Monnet and the group who established the Plan, the government committed itself to unprecedentedly large programmes to expand and

modernise transport, power and heavy industry generally. Its ability
to carry through this programme was strengthened because the scope
of state-owned industry had been enlarged by the postwar nationali-
sations and because it had sufficient control over finance and trade to
give effective priority to other heavy industry not directly owned.[29]
In Italy, there had also been an enlargement of the public sector
because of the government takeover of industrial facilities both under
fascism and after the war. Grouped in ENI and IRI and led by forceful
and energetic new personalities, these government-directed corporations also took the lead in supporting the early enlargement of capital
investment.

In Japan, the government made itself felt chiefly through the Ministry of International Trade and Industry. The Ministry's purpose and
effect appear to have been to provide guidance and to reduce the risks
of innovation and investment faced by Japanese business in venturing
into so many new lines on such a large scale. It operated by selecting
sectors for development, by supporting tariff protection, by choosing
firms as instruments for the importation and exploitation of foreign
technology and by helping to arrange the industrial combinations
needed to ensure a proper scale of operation. Together with other
government agencies, its activities served to raise the sights of private
business.[30]

These considerations explain something about the otherwise puzzling disjunction between catch-up and sustained rapid growth.
Private-sector investment went forward boldly only as the growth
potential of the postwar economies became clearly revealed. Governments, therefore, played a crucial role in providing early impetus,
which was carried forward later by the rising confidence of private
business. Partly for this reason, the investment of the earlier years
was somewhat more heavily concentrated in the sectors under government ownership and special influence: that is, transport, power and
heavy industry generally. These demanded heavy forward-looking
investment which yielded its returns relatively slowly. The private
investment of subsequent years could be more largely applied to
equipment which both raised the utilisation rate of basic capacity and
yielded more immediate returns.

4. *Flexible labour supplies again.* I have already indicated how
access to cheap labour acted to facilitate structural change. I must add
some brief comments concerning the influence of flexible labour supplies on the level, the sustained duration and the international diffusion of the investment boom.

Movement of workers from the farms, from petty trade and from less developed countries in Europe and Africa provided very large fractions of the growth of employment in the more advanced non-farm sectors of the industrialised countries.[31] The availability of this supply of cheap labour must have inhibited the rise in non-farm wages and so sustained the rate of return to investment in the face of large expansions of capital stock. By permitting large productivity gains to be achieved in the industrial sector without provoking an unduly rapid rise in wages, it also encouraged the expansion of industry through import substitution and export growth and, in this way, enlarged the scope for capital investment. On both counts, therefore, the level of investment must have been raised and the boom protracted instead of being cut short by the need to intensify capital-labour substitution.

The need, of course, could not be avoided forever. Reserve labour pools were being drained during the 1960s, and resistance to foreign workers was growing. I have already indicated how the sustained increase of productivity in that decade came to depend on an accelerated rate of rise of capital-labour ratios. Such dependence, however, has its limits, and if the investment boom had not been cut short by other causes – as it was – a tightening labour market might soon have imposed a slowdown.

There was a noteworthy difference between the pattern of international migration in the postwar period and that before 1914 when such movements last were large. Before the First World War, the movement was from Europe to the U.S., Canada and other countries of recent settlement. One may, therefore, say that the non-farm sectors in both Europe and overseas countries formerly were fed in part from a common reserve pool of labour on the European farms. Sustained investment booms in the U.S. and other overseas areas were marked by heavy emigration from Europe and, in part for this reason, they were associated with less active home investment in the U.K., Scandinavia and, to a lesser degree, Germany. Growth in the industrialising west, therefore, moved in a seesaw pattern. Decades of rapid development overseas alternated with decades of rapid development in the U.K. and Europe. In the postwar period, however, immigration restriction in the U.S., Canada and elsewhere made these countries only limited rivals for the supply of European reserve labour. Instead, the overseas countries, aided by large increases in agricultural productivity, drew heavily on their own farm populations. At the same time, European industry gained labour by immigration from the less developed countries bordering the Mediterranean. The obstacle which population flows among the industrialised countries posed to simultaneous expansion on both sides of the Atlantic was, therefore, largely removed. Since, as I shall next argue, another obstacle which used to be raised by international flows of capital and monetary reserves was also lowered, a vigorous and sustained investment boom in the U.S. and Canada could be accompanied by a still more vigorous investment boom in Europe.

5. International accounts and supplies of money. The considerations already discussed bear on the investment boom from the real side. The boom also had a monetary side.

It is a necessary element in a sustained investment boom that real money stock should grow roughly in proportion to the accompanying growth of aggregate real output. In principle, of course, any growth rate of nominal money stock could satisfy this requirement if the rate of price-change were sufficiently accommodating. A long-term decline in prices, however, was neither practical economics nor practical politics in the postwar years. In the U.S., for example, the release of suppressed wartime inflation made a large postwar price-rise inevitable, and the Korean War caused renewed inflation. Considering the price expectations so generated, it was something of a triumph of monetary management that the subsequent rate of increase of U.S. consumer prices was no more than 1.3 per cent a year from 1952 to 1965 and the rate of increase in wholesale prices no more than 0.5 per cent.

One may, I believe, take this to be about the slowest rate of increase consistent with avoiding protracted stagnation in the U.S. If so, the money stock growth needed in the industrialised world at large must have been considerably faster than real output growth itself. The reason is that in a fixed exchange rate system, the process of balance of payments adjustment forces up money wages faster in countries whose productivity growth is relatively rapid than in countries where it is slower. Further, since differences in productivity growth are concentrated in the production of traded goods whose product prices move in a similar way everywhere, the relatively fast rise of money wages means relatively fast rise of prices of non-tradables and, therefore, of general price indexes in countries with rapid productivity growth.[32] It follows, then, that even when U.S. prices were stable, prices in the more progressive remainder of the industrialised world had to be rising. The necessary growth rate of nominal income was, therefore, even faster than that of real output. And, while it might have been possible for a rise in velocity to have substituted for growth of money stock, that, in fact, did not occur (except, to some degree, in the U.S. itself).

The necessary growth of money stock demanded a rapid, but by no means equal, growth of monetary reserves and, considering the exigencies of fixed exchange rates, a large part of these reserves had to have international currency. And since the world stock of monetary gold was itself expanding only slowly, that need could only be satisfied by redistribution of the initial U.S. gold holdings and, still more, by the adoption of some internationally acceptable supplementary reserve asset. The Bretton Woods scheme and the economic strength of the U.S. made that asset short-term claims on dollars.

Monetary growth, therefore, came to depend on an arrangement of considerable delicacy. Successful operation over a protracted period demanded simultaneous fulfilment of two basically contradictory conditions: first, a chronic U.S. deficit and, therefore, the cumulative deterioration of the U.S. reserve position; second, continued faith in the ability of the U.S. to maintain convertibility and the par of exchange, thereby avoiding both a flight from the dollar and a U.S. monetary policy tight enough to produce serious constriction in the U.S. and secondarily in the rest of the industrialised countries.

Needless to say, it did not prove hard to maintain a chronic deficit. The system, indeed, worked as designed. By 1970, the U.S. had lost $13.5 billion in gold, $2 billion in other international reserves and accepted some $41 billion of additional short-term liabilities. Meanwhile, the international reserves of other countries had risen by some $52 billion and those of developed countries alone by $42 billion – a rough quadrupling of their 1949 holdings.[33]

This process, by which the monetary side of the European and Japanese investment booms was supported for over two decades by U.S. balance of payments deficits and by cumulative gold losses and deterioration of her international reserve position, constitutes a basic difference between the postwar and earlier periods. In earlier times, when investment booms and growth spurts overseas led to a deterioration of Britain's reserve position, losses even a fraction as large as those of the U.S. in the postwar period would have caused the Bank of England to impose severe checks on monetary expansion and capital exports. The dollar basis of the postwar boom proved as durable as it did because of several peculiarities of the postwar economy:

1. The dollar was initially extremely strong. The U.S. had at first an enormous stock of gold and other international reserves and few liquid liabilities. There was then an excess demand for dollars. The actual deficit was discretionary – not only planned, but perceived to be planned.

2. Although short-term claims on dollars cumulated, some part of them were willingly held as working balances to support a growing trade in which debts and credits were denominated and settled in dollars.

3. The U.S. proved politically capable of exercising monetary and fiscal restraint for some dozen years after the end of the Korean War. By accepting a certain degree of underemployment, it limited the size of its deficits. As indicated, it reduced its own rate of inflation to a practical minimum and, by the same token, limited the rate of inflation in the rest of the world.

4. When, finally, the U.S. international position came to be viewed unfavourably, other countries were faced with a dilemma: whether to continue to accumulate dollar claims and to accept an increasing risk that these would eventually be devalued, or, by demanding gold at once, to precipitate an immediate devaluation and, perhaps, the demonetisation of gold as well. The two dangers being equally unacceptable, countries chose to postpone rather than to hasten the event. By continuing to accumulate dollar claims, the life of the system was extended for some years.

The pressures of two political developments then joined to bring the process to a halt. First, the politics of the Vietnam War ultimately imposed on the U.S. government a policy of inflationary war finance. The rate of U.S. inflation rose. The size of the U.S. balance of payments deficit increased both on that account and because of speculation against the dollar. In so far as European and Japanese authorities monetised the claims arising from the mounting U.S. deficit, the U.S. inflation was duly exported. In so far as they tried to sterilise the claims, they discovered that the process was costly, since it involved deflationary fiscal or monetary policy. And in so far as such sterilisation succeeded in curbing inflation, it was hard to maintain. For then dollar claims of dubious future value mounted all the faster. Dollar devaluation and the realignment of exchange rates followed. Finally, the formation of OPEC and the rise in the price of oil completed the downfall of the postwar system of monetary growth and, at least for a time, brought to a halt the generalised investment boom which that monetary growth had supported.

Notes

1. Edward F. Denison and Wm. K. Chung, *How Japan's Economy Grew So Fast* (Washington, DC: Brookings Institution, 1976) p. 79.

2. By 'conventional' total factor productivity I mean an estimate of output per unit of total factor input in which inputs are not adjusted for differences in 'quality'.

3. *U.S. growth rates of total factor productivity, private domestic economy (% per annum)*

	Kendrick Compound Rates			Abramovitz-David	
	Net weighted (1)	Net unweighted (2)	Gross weighted (3)		Gross unweighted (4)
1889–1919	1.3	1.65		1800–55	0.3
1919–48	1.8	2.03		1855–1905	0.5
1948–66	2.5	2.84		1905–27	1.5
				1927–67	1.9
Trend rates					
1889–1916	1.03				
1916–29	2.29	2.2			
1936–66	2.33	2.7	2.09		
1948–66	2.33	2.6	2.09		

Sources: Columns (1), (3) and trend rates Column (2): Kendrick, *Postwar Productivity Trends in the United States, 1948–1969* (New York: Columbia University Press for NBER, 1973) Tables 3–2 and 3–4. Compound rates Column (2), *ibid.*, Table A–19b, extrapolated on the basis of Kendrick, *Productivity Trends in the U.S.* (NBER, 1961) Table A–XXII, Supplement. Column (4), M. Abramovitz and P. A. David, 'Economic Growth in America: Historical Parables and Realities,' *De Economist*, 121, no. 3 (1973) Tables 1 and 2.

'Net' figures combine labour and capital inputs with net share weights; 'gross' figures use gross share weights; 'weighted' figures combine labour and capital inputs by industry with weights proportionate to average net compensation per unit; unweighted figures are based on simple aggregations of man hours and net capital stock.

4. Making use of Edward F. Denison's estimates for 1909–29, 1929–48, and 1948–69 and adjusting them for comparability yields the following estimates of the effect of advances in knowledge actually incorporated into production in the U.S. on the growth rates of national income per worker (figures in per cent per annum):

Line:	1909–29	1929–48	1948–69
(1) Denison-based estimates	0.15	0.62	1.19
(2) Alternative estimates	0.82	1.36	1.72

Source: Line (1): For 1929–48 and 1948–69, the figures are from E. F. Denison, *Accounting for U.S. Economic Growth, 1929–69*, (Washington, DC: Brookings Institution, 1974) Table 9–4, Columns 2 and 3. For 1909–29, the original figures were taken from Denison's *The Sources of Economic Growth in the U.S.* (New York: Committee for Economic Development, 1962) Supplement Paper No. 13, Table 32, Column 1. These were adjusted by the present writer to make them comparable with the estimates for later years. For this purpose, I made use of a comparison provided by Denison for 1929–57 between estimates of sources of growth based respectively on the data and procedure used in his earlier volume and those used in his later volume (see, *Accounting for U.S. Economic Growth*, Appendix S and Tables S–1 and S–3).

Line (2): The Alternative estimates' in this line are intended to test whether the acceleration of knowledge indicated by the Denison-based figures derive from some of the more controversial elements in the Denison calculations. The 'Alternative', first, eliminates his 'efficiency offset for decline in hours' (including his 'shift offset to hours decline'). Next, Denison's estimates of the contribution of longer schooling continue to be questioned. Recent work (cf. Paul Taubman and T. Wales, *Higher Education and Earnings*, New York: NBER General Series 101) implies that the Denison figures overestimate the contribution of education by failing to make enough allowance for the effect of differences in 'ability' and other correlates of education. The 'screening model' presents a rival theory which makes educational earnings differentials a basis for a private return to longer schooling but not for a social return. My 'alternative' recognises these doubts by reducing the Denison-based contribution by one-half. Third, doubts have been raised as to whether the contribution of economies of scale are to be associated only with output growth due to factors other than advance of knowledge itself or whether, as Denison contends, they should be associated equally with output growth from all sources. The 'alternative' reduces the contribution of scale economies. Finally, the 'alternative' recognises that, for the period 1909–29, there is a rival figure for the growth rate of national income based on the estimates of John Kendrick, who built on Kuznets' earlier work. The Kendrick-based growth rate is significantly higher than the Department of Commerce figures used by Denison. (See Denison, *The Sources of Economic Growth in the U.S.*, Table 32, Footnote 1.) I do not contend that the 'alternative estimate' of the contributions of advance of knowledge is better than the Denison-based figures. I merely note that adjustments of the latter to allow for controversial elements do not change the conclusion to which they point: the increase in the effect of advance of knowledge on output growth between 1909–29 and 1948–69 remains approximately 1 percentage point.

5. I have in mind not only the sensitivity of residuals to errors in reported data, but also serious uncertainties of principle. Are Denison's estimates of gains from longer schooling or better allocation sound? How much should really be allowed for economies of scale, and should the allowance be constant over time? Do Denison's figures allow adequately for the effect of change in the composition of capital by durability and other characteristics affecting true social rates of return? (Cf. L. R. Christensen and D. W. Jorgenson, *Measuring the Performance of the U.S. Economy, 1929–69*, Social Systems Research Institute, University of Wisconsin, February 1973.) How much of the contribution of technological progress itself is hidden because the estimates rely on an assumption that such progress is Hicks neutral? (Cf. Abramovitz and P. A. David, op. cit.)

6. Edward F. Denison, *Why Growth Rates Differ* (Washington, DC: Brookings Institution, 1967) Table 2–5, p. 23.

7. Angus Maddison, 'Comparative Productivity Levels in the Developed Countries', *Banco Nazionale del Lavoro Quarterly Review*, no. 83 (December 1967).

8. I have developed tables of relatives of output per worker based on U.S. price weights starting from the Maddison estimates on two bases. One starts from Maddison's 1965 figures in which his estimates for employment are adjusted to make the proportion of women employed in agriculture conform to the female share of employment in non-agricultural industries (op. cit., Table 16). These are the basis for the summary figures in Table 6.1 of this text. The other starts from Maddison's 1965 relatives based on unadjusted employment data (op. cit. Table 9, with relatives converted to the base, U.S. = 100). Maddison obtained his 1965 productivity relatives by extrapo-

lating the OECD/Gilbert 1955 figures for output with U.S. price weights according to the movement of output with national price weights as estimated by OECD, and then dividing by estimates of employment based on figures from OECD sources. I moved the Maddison 1965 figures back to 1960, 1955 and 1950 and forward to 1970 according to the movements of OECD output with national price weights and OECD employment data. The results of further extrapolations to 1913, shown in Table 6.1 of this volume were based on output and employment figures from national sources.

Denison (*Why Growth Rates Differ*, Tables 2–5) has worked out a third set of estimates of output per employed worker with 1955 U.S. price weights for 1950, 1955, 1960 and 1964. Denison used the OECD/Gilbert *et al.* estimates of output for 1950 and, with the exception of consumer goods, also for 1955. He provides the following description of his method of deriving the proper figures for consumer goods output in 1955 and for total GNP in 1960 and 1964:

"Gilbert and Associates brought their 1950 estimates in United States prices forward to 1955 by a quite summary procedure. The 1950 national product in United States prices of each of the European countries was divided into twelve broad product categories including a five-way breakdown of consumption. For each category they assumed the percentage change from 1950 to 1955 to be the same in constant United States prices as in the constant prices of the country concerned. I have used their methodology in this study to obtain estimates for 1960 for components other than consumption. Instead of reweighting consumption on a five way basis, I used an indirect procedure to approximate the difference between the 1950–60 movement of consumption valued in United States and in national prices." (Denison, *Why Growth Rates Differ*, p. 20; his 'indirect procedure' is described in his Section II, Chapter 17.)

The three sets of figures are much alike. The rank order correlation coefficients between the relative standings of the several countries in 1950 according to the several sets of estimates are, as follows:

	Coefficient
Maddison-based adjusted and unadjusted	0.97
Denison and Maddison-based unadjusted	1.0
Denison and Maddison-based adjusted	0.95

At the same time, the levels and movements of the three sets of relatives were very similar. The figures in the table that follows show the unweighted means of the relatives of the various countries and, in parentheses, the relative variance among the relatives. The U.S. is excluded uniformly.

	1950	1960	1970
Ten countries			
Maddison-based adjusted	48.4 (0.096)	57.0 (0.053)	69.8 (0.014)
Maddison-based unadjusted	47.4 (0.109)	55.5 (0.058)	67.6 (0.014)
Eight countries			
Denison	49.9 (0.040)	56 (0.017)	–
Maddison-based adjusted	49.2 (0.029)	57.5 (0.017)	70.4 (0.017)
Maddison-based unadjusted	48.1 (0.036)	56.2 (0.017)	68.5 (0.012)

9. The share of workers engaged in agriculture in the U.S. fell from 32 per cent in 1910 to 12 per cent in 1950 (Kuznets, *Modern Economic Growth,* Table 3.2). The average share in nine other advanced countries fell from 35 per cent at various dates in the first decade of the century to 21 per cent at various dates between 1947 and 1952 (ibid., except Japan, for which see Ohkawa and Rosovsky, *Japanese Economic Growth,* Basic Statistical Table 15).

10. The rise in the mean relative standing, as measured in Table 6.1, may exaggerate somewhat the true rise as this would appear in figures consistently valued at constant U.S. relative prices, but the qualitative conclusion holds.

In Table 6.1 the relative productivity standings of 1950 with output measured with U.S. price weights are, in effect, extrapolated to 1970 by the movement of national productivity figures with national price weights. Since, in general, the output growth rates of poorer countries with output weighted with national price relatives are higher than those calculated from output weighted consistently with U.S. price weights, the rise in the productivity relatives as shown in Table 6.1 is biased upwards. We can get an idea of the importance of the bias from the results of the new study by Kravis and Associates (*A System of International Comparisons of Gross Product and Purchasing Power,* Baltimore: Johns Hopkins University Press, 1975, Table 1.6) which, for three of the countries of concern to us, repeats for 1970 the work of Gilbert and Associates for 1950. The new study provides a comparison of relatives of output *per capita* in 1950 and 1970 with outputs measured with own price weights and U.S. weights respectively. The percentage increase in the average of the *per capita* relatives for France, Germany and Italy with U.S. weights was 69 per cent of the increase with outputs measured in own weights. (The Kravis study also provided information for the U.K., but since its change was so small, it seemed better to neglect it.) We may use this ratio to adjust the rise in the average productivity level in Table 6.1. If we did, the 1970 relative in Table 6.1 would have been 63.4 instead of 69.8.

11. Since growth rates are calculated as rates of increase between standings at terminal dates, errors in the estimates of such standings will generate errors in the derived growth rates. If errors at both terminal dates were random and if those at the end-year were independent of those at the initial year, the inverse correlations between initial-year standings and subsequent growth rates would be biased upward. The high coefficients we observe would be too high and the lower coefficient for 1960–70 might not be significant. But if errors at both dates were random and independent, there would on that account be no tendency for the variance of standings about the mean to decline between initial and end-year dates. The error bias would then run against the very marked decline in variance which we observe. I conclude, therefore, that there was, in fact, a strong, significant inverse correlation between initial year standings and subsequent growth rates.

12. I depend on the following estimates for the growth of output per man and of the contributions of growing capital intensity and total factor productivity derived from L. R. Christensen, Dianne Cummings and D. W. Jorgenson, *Economic Growth, 1947–1973: An International Comparison,* Harvard Institute for Economic Research, Discussion Paper No. 521 (December 1976) Tables 11, 12, 13 and the various country tables in the Appendix. Quality of capital refers to an estimated change in capital service per unit due to shifts in the composition of capital stock between asset classes with characteristically different gross rental rates. Labour quality represents an allowance for the rise of labour service associated with longer schooling. Growth rates of labour and capital services are weighted by gross income shares (I have omitted figures for Korea, which the authors also estimate, because that country is not otherwise considered in the present paper. Its record is similar to that of the other fast-growing countries):

Contributions to growth of real private domestic product per worker
(percentage points per annum)

	Product per worker (1)	Capital stock per worker (2)	Quality of capital (3)	Capital services per worker (4) = (2) + (3)	Hours and quality of labour (5)	Total fact-or pro-ductivity (6)
Japan						
1952–60	4.1	−0.2	0.5	0.3	0.5	3.4
1960–73	8.2	2.4	1.2	3.6	−0.1	4.5
Change	4.1	2.6	0.8	3.4	−0.6	1.1
Italy						
1955–60	4.3	0.6	0.1	0.7	0.3	3.4
1969–73	4.0	1.6	0.2	1.8	−0.4	2.6
Change	−0.3	1.0	0.1	1.1	−0.7	−0.8
Germany						
1950–60	6.0	1.8	0.0	1.8	−0.6	4.7
1960–73	5.6	2.7	0.2	2.9	−0.4	3.0
Change	−0.4	0.9	0.2	1.1	0.2	−1.7
France						
1950–60	5.1	1.5	0.3	1.8	0.3	2.9
1960–73	5.3	1.9	0.5	2.4	−0.1	3.0
Change	0.2	0.4	0.2	0.6	−0.4	0.1
The Netherlands						
1951–60	4.1	1.0	0.4	1.4	0.4	2.3
1960–73	4.8	1.6	0.9	2.5	−0.3	2.6
Change	0.7	0.6	0.5	1.1	−0.7	0.3
U.K.						
1955–60	3.3	1.3	0.4	1.7	0.2	1.5
1960–73	4.0	1.7	0.2	1.9	0.2	2.1
Change	0.7	0.4	−0.2	0.2	0.0	0.6
Canada						
1947–60	4.0	1.6	0.7	2.3	0.0	1.7
1960–73	2.9	0.7	0.5	1.2	−0.1	1.8
Change	−1.1	−0.9	−0.2	−1.1	−0.1	0.1
U.S.						
1947–60	2.1	0.8	0.2	1.0	−0.3	1.1
1960–73	1.9	0.3	0.3	0.6	0.0	1.1
Change	−0.2	−0.5	0.1	−0.4	0.3	0.0

13. It also includes the effect of reduction of international trade barriers, but, in Denison's estimates, that is a tiny source.

14. See Denison, *Why Growth Rates Differ*, pp. 239–45 for a description of his procedures.

15. Denison himself considers but rejects still another, quite different alternative

explanation based on a convergence in the supplies and prices of capital relative to labour as incomes *per capita* converge.

16. Cf. Ronald I. McKinnon, 'Monetary Theory and Controlled Flexibility in the Foreign Exchanges', *Studies in International Finance*, Princeton (1971).

17. See Hollis B. Chenery, 'Patterns of Industrial Growth', *American Economic Review*, 50 (September 1960).

18. Nicholas Kaldor, *Causes of the Slow Rate of Economic Growth of the United Kingdom* (Cambridge University Press, 1966).

19. Simon Kuznets, *Modern Economic Growth Rate, Structure and Spread* (New Haven: Yale University Press, 1966), Chapter 3.

20. My comments in this section are supported by evidence and appraisals from a variety of sources. See in particular, OECD, *Gaps in Technology, General Report* and *Analytical Reports* (Paris, 1968); OECD, *The Conditions for Success in Technological Innovation* (Paris, 1971); L. Nabseth and G. F. Ray (eds), *The Diffusion of New Industrial Processes* (London: Cambridge University Press, 1974) Chapters 1, 2, 11 and *passim*; Carré, Dubois and Malinvaud, op. cit., pp. 208–21, Chapters 9, 14 and p. 495 ff.; Ohkawa and Rosovsky, op. cit., pp. 39–43; 204–16, and Chapter 9; Merton S. Peck and Shuji Tamura, 'Technology', in H. Patrick and H. Rosovsky (eds), *Asia's New Giant* (Washington, DC: Brookings Institution, 1976) Chapter 9.

21. Carré *et al.*, p. 501: 'The depression and the war probably interrupted growth in the relevant industry groups [i.e., the 'industries with a future']. But engineers and technicians continued to work on new techniques, and were ready to develop them rapidly after the war.'

22. Ratios of unemployed workers to the sum of non-agricultural wage and salary workers including the unemployed in 1950 were (in percentages):

Belgium	7.0	Netherlands	3.1
Denmark	6.7	Norway	1.0
France	2.6	Italy	17.6
Germany	11.1	UK	1.5

Source: Denison, *Why Growth Rates Differ*, Table 5–1A.

In Japan, the agricultural labour force was 14.3 million, or 44 per cent of the total number of workers in 1940. In 1950, the number was 17.3 million, or 48 per cent of the whole labour force. (Ohkawa and Rosovsky, op. cit., Basic Statistical Table 15.) Territorial change makes comparison difficult for Germany, but it seems likely, given the large inflow of refugees from East Germany and from Polish occupied territory to West Germany immediately after the war, that the West German farm population had also grown. On the slowdown of rural-urban migration in France from 1930 to 1950, see Carré *et al.*, op. cit., Chapter 3, Table 6.

The following illustrate the level of the reserves in 1950:

	France	Germany	Italy	Japan
Farm employment as per cent of total employment	29.3	24.8	42.8	48.3
Self-employed and unpaid family workers as per cent of civilian non-farm employment	21.4	15.7	31.3	–

Sources: France, Germany, Italy: Denison, op. cit., Table 16.4 and 16.5; Japan: Ohkawa and Rosovsky, op. cit., Basic Statistical Table 15.

23. In France, the productivity growth rate in agriculture was 1.6 per cent per year from 1896 to 1929; in manufacturing, 2.7 per cent. From 1949 to 1963 the rates were 6.4 per cent and 5.0 per cent respectively. (Carré *et al.*, op. cit., Table 3.10). There was a similar development in Germany according to figures supplied by H. Gerfin, based on Hoffman and the reports of the Sachverstandigenrat. In Japan, the non-agricultural productivity growth rate rose from 2.1 per cent in 1917–37 to 10.1 per cent in 1956–62. The growth rate in agriculture went from 1.5 per cent to 5.4 per cent. (Ohkawa and Rosovsky, op. cit., Table 2.7)

Needless to say, measured productivity growth in agriculture reflected the rapid withdrawal of low-productivity farm workers to satisfy the growing demand for non-farm labour. But consolidation of holdings, mechanisation, fertilisers, chemical insect controls and better seeds were also driving up the productivity of the remaining farm workers.

24. Between 1945 and 1948, Japan received some 6.1 million persons (half-civilian, half-military), amounting to 7.6 per cent of the 1948 population and almost 18 per cent of the gainfully occupied. Between 1945 and 1950, West Germany received some 9 million refugees from the east (C. P. Kindleberger, *Europe's Postwar Growth; The Role of Labour Supply*, Cambridge, Mass.: Harvard University Press, 1967, p. 30). Between 1955 and 1961, about 150,000 workers per year came to West Germany from the east, accounting for 27 per cent of the labour force growth in that period (OECD Economic Survey of Germany, 1962). France repatriated 350,000 persons from Algeria in 1962 and had net immigration of 180,000 per year in 1964–8. (Carré *et al.*, op. cit., Chapter 2 and Appendix Tables III and IV). Germany, Switzerland and other northern countries enjoyed a large net immigration of foreign guest workers during the entire postwar period. The proportion of foreign workers in the German labour force rose from 1.3 per cent in 1960 to 10 per cent in 1971 (Statistiches Bundesamt, *Bevolkerung u. Wirtschaft*, 1872–1972, pp. 115, 116).

25. See Ohkawa and Rosovsky, op. cit., Chapters 6 and 8; Henry C. Wallich and Mabel Wallich, 'Banking and Finance', in Patrick and Rosovsky (eds), op. cit., pp. 256–64; Carré *et al.*, op. cit., Chapter 9.

26. Carré *et al.*, op. cit., pp. 313 and 501.

27. Ibid., pp. 320–1, and Chapter 10, *passim*.

28. Ibid, pp. 278–9, 471; Ohkawa and Rosovsky op. cit., pp. 232.

29. Carré *et al.*, op. cit., p. 477; also pp. 274–6. The more general influence of the Plan and of French planning is described and appraised in Chapter 14.

30. Ohkawa and Rosovsky, op. cit., Chapter 9.

31. I have already cited evidence about the importance of inflows of workers from abroad. See note 24, above.

I have estimated that migration of workers from farms accounted for the following percentage rises in non-farm employment:

Countries	1950–60	1960–70
U.S.	28	20
U.K.	17	52
Germany	41	62
France	95	60
Italy	53	148
Japan	58	59

The underlying data are derived from OECD *Manpower Statistics, 1950–62*, Tables II and III and OECD *Labour Force Statistics, 1960–71*, Tables 3 and 6. To estimate farm-worker migration, I assumed that in the absence of migration, farm employment would have increased in the same proportion as total employment. An estimate of worker migration from farms was, therefore, obtained by subtracting actual end-of-decade farm employment from the hypothetical figure obtained by applying the percentage increase in total employment to the beginning-of-decade farm figure. The estimate understates the contribution of farm migration to domestic non-farm employment to the extent that natural increase on the farms exceeds that in the towns. It overstates such migration to the extent that immigration was included in total employment increase and if migrants from farms went abroad. The latter bias was important for Italy and helps account for the fact that estimated farm worker migration exceeded the rise in Italian non-farm employment from 1960 to 1970.

32. McKinnon, op. cit., explains this process more fully and shows that differences in national price trends were consistent with these views.

33. U.S. gold and U.S. and other country international reserves from *Economic Report of the President* (February 1971) Tables C–91 and 92. Short-term liabilities of the U.S. from U.S. Bureau of the Census, *Historical Statistics of the U.S., Colonial Times to 1970,* Bicentennial Edition, Part 2, Table U–37.

7

Catching up, forging ahead, and falling behind

Among the many explanations of the surge of productivity growth during the quarter century following World War II, the most prominent is the hypothesis that the countries of the industrialized "West" were able to bring into production a large backlog of unexploited technology. The principal part of this backlog is deemed to have consisted of methods of production and of industrial and commercial organization already in use in the United States at the end of the war, but not yet employed in the other countries of the West. In this hypothesis, the United States is viewed as the "leader," the other countries as "followers" who had the opportunity to catch up. In conformity with this view, a waning of the opportunity for catching up is frequently advanced as an explanation of the retardation in productivity growth suffered by the same group of followers since 1973. Needless to say, the size of the initial backlog and its subsequent reduction are rarely offered as sole explanations of the speedup and slowdown, but they stand as important parts of the story.

These views about postwar following and catching up suggest a more general hypothesis that the productivity levels of countries tend to converge. And this in turn brings to mind old questions about the emergence of new leaders and the historical and theoretical puzzles that shifts in leadership and relative standing present – matters that in some respects fit only awkwardly with the convergence hypothesis.

Reprinted by permission from *Journal of Economic History*, vol. 46, no. 2 (June 1986), 385–406.

The author acknowledges with thanks critical comments and suggestions by Paul David and Knick Harley. The present paper is the revision of a draft read to the Economic History Association at its New York meeting in September 1985. This, in turn, was a greatly abbreviated version of a longer paper since published. See "Catching Up and Falling Behind," Fackföreningsrörelsens Institut för Ekonomisk Forskning (Trade Union Institute for Economic Research), Economic Research Report No. 1 (Stockholm, 1986).

The pertinence of all these questions to an understanding of modern economic growth obviously demands their continued study. The immediate occasion for this paper, however, is the appearance of Angus Maddison's new compilation of historical time series of the levels and growth of labor productivity covering 16 industrialized countries from 1870 to 1979.[1] These data enable us to observe the catch-up process in quantitative terms over a much longer span of time than was possible hitherto. At the same time, the evidence of Maddison's tables raises again the historical puzzles posed by productivity leadership and its shifts.

The catch-up hypothesis

The hypothesis asserts that being backward in level of productivity carries a *potential* for rapid advance. Stated more definitely the proposition is that in comparisons across countries the growth rates of productivity in any long period tend to be inversely related to the initial levels of productivity.

The central idea is simple enough. It has to do with the level of technology embodied in a country's capital stock. Imagine that the level of labor productivity were governed entirely by the level of technology embodied in capital stock. In a "leading country," to state things sharply, one may suppose that the technology embodied in each vintage of its stock was at the very frontier of technology at the time of investment. The *technological* age of the stock is, so to speak, the same as its *chronological* age. In an otherwise similar follower whose productivity level is lower, the technological age of the stock is high relative to its chronological age. The stock is obsolete even for its age. When a leader discards old stock and replaces it, the accompanying productivity increase is governed and limited by the advance of knowledge between the time when the old capital was installed and the time it is replaced. Those who are behind, however, have the potential to make a larger leap. New capital can embody the frontier of knowledge, but the capital it replaces was technologically superannuated. So – the larger the technological and, therefore, the productivity gap between leader and follower, the stronger the follower's potential for growth in productivity; and, other things being equal, the faster one expects the follower's growth rate to be. Followers tend to catch up faster if they are initially more backward.

Viewed in the same simple way, the catch-up process would be self-limiting because as a follower catches up, the possibility of making large leaps by replacing superannuated with best-practice technology becomes smaller and smaller. A follower's potential for growth weakens as its productivity level converges towards that of the leader.

This is the simple central idea. It needs extension and qualification. There are at least four extensions:

1. The same technological opportunity that permits rapid progress by modernization encourages rapid growth of the capital stock partly because of the returns to modernization itself, and partly because technological progress reduces the price of capital goods relative to the price of labor. So – besides a reduction of technological age towards chronological age, the rate of rise of the capital-labor ratio tends to be higher. Productivity growth benefits on both counts. And if circumstances make for an acceleration in the growth of the capital stock its chronological age also falls.[2]

2. Growth of productivity also makes for increase in aggregate output. A broader horizon of scale-dependent technological progress then comes into view.

3. Backwardness carries an opportunity for modernization in disembodied, as well as in embodied, technology.

4. If countries at relatively low levels of industrialization contain large numbers of redundant workers in farming and petty trade, as is normally the case, there is also an opportunity for productivity growth by improving the allocation of labor.

Besides extension, the simple hypothesis also needs qualification.

First, technological backwardness is not usually a mere accident. Tenacious societal characteristics normally account for a portion, perhaps a substantial portion, of a country's past failure to achieve as high a level of productivity as economically more advanced countries. The same deficiencies, perhaps in attenuated form, normally remain to keep a backward country from making the full technological leap envisaged by the simple hypothesis. I have a name for these characteristics. Following Kazushi Ohkawa and Henry Rosovsky, I call them "social capability."[3] One can summarize the matter in this way. Having regard to technological backwardness alone leads to the simple hypothesis about catch-up and convergence already advanced. Having regard to social capability, however, we expect that the developments anticipated by that hypothesis will be clearly displayed in cross-country comparisons only if countries' social capabilities are about the same. One should say, therefore, that a country's potential for rapid growth is strong not when it is backward without qualification, but rather when it is technologically backward but socially advanced.

The trouble with absorbing social capability into the catch-up hypothesis is that no one knows just what it means or how to measure it. In past work I identified a country's social capability with technical competence, for which – at least among Western countries – years of education may be a rough proxy, and with its political, commercial, industrial, and financial institutions, which I characterized in more qualitative ways.[4] I had in mind mainly experience with the organization and management of large-scale enterprise and with financial institutions and markets capable of mobilizing capital for individual firms on a similarly large scale. On some occasions the situation for a selection of countries may be sufficiently clear. In explaining postwar growth in Europe and Japan, for example, one may be able to say with some confidence that these countries were competent to absorb and exploit then existing best-practice technology. More generally, however, judgments about social capability remain highly problematic. A few comments may serve to suggest some of the considerations involved as well as the speculative nature of the subject.

One concerns the familiar notion of a trade-off between specialization and adaptability. The content of education in a country and the character of its industrial, commercial, and financial organizations may be well designed to exploit fully the power of an existing technology; they may be less well fitted to adapt to the requirements of change. Presumably, some capacity to adapt is present everywhere, but countries may differ from one another in this respect, and their capacities to adapt may change over time.

Next, the notion of adaptability suggests that there is an interaction between social capability and technological opportunity. The state of education embodied in a nation's population and its existing institutional arrangements constrains it in its choice of technology. But technological opportunity presses for change. So countries learn to modify their institutional arrangements and then to improve them as they gain experience. The constraints imposed by social capability on the successful adoption of a more advanced technology gradually weaken and permit its fuller exploitation. Thorstein Veblen said it this way:

There are two lines of agency visibly at work shaping the habits of thought of [a] people in the complex movements of readjustment and rehabilitation [required by industrialization]. These are the received scheme of use and wont and the new state of the industrial arts; and it is not difficult to see that it is the latter that makes for readjustment; nor should it be any more difficult to see that the readjustment is necessarily made under the surveillance of the received scheme of use and wont.[5]

Social capability, finally, depends on more than the content of education and the organization of firms. Other aspects of economic systems count as well – their openness to competition, to the establishment and operation of new firms, and to the sale and purchase of new goods and services. Viewed from the other side, it is a question of the obstacles to change raised by vested interests, established positions, and customary relations among firms and between employers and employees. The view from this side is what led Mancur Olson to identify defeat in war and accompanying political convulsion as a radical ground-clearing experience opening the way for new men, new organizations, and new modes of operation and trade better fitted to technological potential.[6]

These considerations have a bearing on the notion that a follower's potential for rapid growth weakens as its technological level converges on the leader's. This is not necessarily the case if social capability is itself endogenous, becoming stronger – or perhaps weaker – as technological gaps close. In the one case, the evolution of social capability connected with catching up itself raises the possibility that followers may forge ahead of even progressive leaders. In the other, a leader may fall back or a follower's pursuit may be slowed.

There is a somewhat technical point that has a similar bearing. This is the fact, noticed by Kravis and Denison, that as followers' levels of per capita income converge on the leader's, so do their structures of consumption and prices.[7] R.C.O. Matthews then observed that the convergence of consumption and production patterns should make it easier, rather than more difficult, for followers to borrow technology with advantage as productivity gaps close.[8] This, therefore, stands as still another qualification to the idea that the catch-up process is steadily self-limiting.

The combination of technological gap and social capability defines a country's *potentiality* for productivity advance by way of catch-up. This, however, should be regarded as a potentiality in the long run. The pace at which the potentiality is realized depends on still another set of causes that are largely independent of those governing the potentiality itself. There is a long story to tell about the factors controlling the rate of realization of potential.[9] Its general plot, however, can be suggested by noting three principal chapter headings:

1. The facilities for the diffusion of knowledge – for example, channels of international technical communication, multinational corporations, the state of international trade and of direct capital investment.
2. Conditions facilitating or hindering structural change in the composition of output, in the occupational and industrial distribution of the workforce, and in the geographical location of industry and population. Among other factors, this is where conditions of labor supply, the existence of labor reserves in agriculture, and the factors controlling internal and international migration come in.
3. Macroeconomic and monetary conditions encouraging and sustaining capital investment and the level and growth of effective demand.

Having considered the technological catch-up idea, with its several extensions and qualifications, I can summarize by proposing a restatement of the hypothesis as follows:

Countries that are technologically backward have a potentiality for generating growth more rapid than that of more advanced countries, provided their social capabilities are sufficiently developed to permit successful exploitation of technologies already employed by the technological leaders. The pace at which potential for catch-up is actually realized in a particular period depends on factors limiting the diffusion of knowledge, the rate of structural change, the accumulation of capital, and the expansion of demand. The process of catching up tends to be self-limiting, but the strength of the tendency may be weakened or overcome, at least for limited periods, by advantages connected with the convergence of production patterns as followers advance towards leaders or by an endogenous enlargement of social capabilities.

Historical experience with catching up

I go on now to review some evidence bearing on the catch-up process. The survey I make is limited to the 16 countries covered by the new Maddison estimates of product per worker hour for nine key years from 1870 to 1979.[10] The estimates are consistently derived as regards gross domestic product and worker hours and are adjusted as regards levels of product per worker hour by the Kravis estimates of purchasing power parities for postwar years. I have compressed the message of these data into three measures (see Tables 7.1 and 7.2).

1. Averages of the productivity levels of the various countries relative to that of the United States, which was the leading country for most of the period. (For 1870 and 1890, I have also calculated averages of relatives based on the United Kingdom.) I calculate these averages for each of the nine key years and use them to indicate whether productivity levels of followers, *as a group*, were tending to converge on that of the leader.[11]

2. Measures of relative variance around the mean levels of relative productivity. These provide one sort of answer to the question of whether the countries that started at relatively low levels of productivity tended to advance faster than those with initially higher levels.

3. Rank correlations between initial levels of productivity and subsequent growth rates. If the potential supposedly inherent in technological backwardness is being realized, there is likely to be some inverse correlation; and if it works with enough strength to dominate other forces the coefficients will be high.

Table 7.1. *Comparative levels of productivity, 1870–1979: means and relative variance of the relatives of 15 countries compared with the United States (U.S. GDP per manhour = 100)*[a]

	(1) Mean	(2) Coefficient of variation[b]
1870	77 (66)	.51 (.51)
1890	68 (68)	.48 (.48)
1913	61	.33
1929	57	.29
1938	61	.22
1950	46	.36
1960	52	.29
1973	69	.14
1979	75	.15

[a]1870 and 1890. Figures in parentheses are based on relatives with the United Kingdom = 100.
[b]Standard deviation divided by mean.
Source: Calculated from Angus Maddison, *Phases of Capitalist Development* (New York, 1982), Tables 5.2 and C.10.

The data I use and the measures I make have a number of drawbacks. The data, of course, have the weaknesses that are inherent in any set of estimates of GDP and manhours, however ably contrived, that stretch back far into the nineteenth century. Beyond that, however, simple calculations such as I have made fail, in a number of respects, to isolate the influence of the catch-up hypothesis proper.

To begin with, my measures do not allow for variation in the richness of countries' natural resources in relation to their populations. Labor productivity levels, therefore, are not pure reflections of levels of technology. In the same way, these levels will also reflect past accumulations of reproducible capital, both physical and human, and these may also be independent of technological levels in one degree or another. Further, the measured growth rates of labor productivity will be influenced by the pace of capital accumulation. As already said, differences in rates of accumulation may reflect countries' opportunities to make advances in technology, but rates of capital formation may also be independent, to some degree, of countries' potentials for technological advance. Finally, my measures make no allowance for countries' variant abilities to employ current best-practice technology for reasons other than the differences in social capability already dis-

Table 7.2. *The association (rank correlation) between initial levels and subsequent growth rates of labor productivity (GDP per manhour in 16 countries, 1870–1979)*

	Shorter periods		Lengthening periods since 1870	
	(1)	(2)		(3)
1870–1913	.59		1870–1890	−.32
1870–1890		−.32	−1913	−.59
1890–1913		−.56	−1929	−.72
			−1938	−.83
1913–1938	−.70		−1950	−.16
1913–29		−.35	−1960	−.66
1929–38		−.57	−1973	−.95
			−1979	−.97
1938–1950	+.48			
1950–1979	−.92			
1950–60		−.81		
1960–73		−.90		
1973–79		−.13		

Source of underlying data: Maddison, *Phases*, Tables 5.1, 5.2, and C.10.

cussed. Their access to economies of scale is perhaps the most important matter. If advanced technology at any time is heavily scale-
dependent and if obstacles to trade across national frontiers, political
or otherwise, are important, large countries will have a stronger potential for growth than smaller ones.

There are many reasons, therefore, why one cannot suppose that
the expectations implied by the catch-up hypothesis will display themselves clearly in the measures I present. It will be something if the
data show some systematic evidence of development consistent with
the hypothesis. And it will be useful if this provides a chance to
speculate about the reasons why the connections between productivity levels and growth rates appear to have been strong in some periods and weak in others.

Other countries, on the average, made no net gain on the United
States in a period longer than a century (Table 7.1, col. 1). The indication of very limited, or even zero, convergence is really stronger than
the figures suggest. This is because the productivity measures reflect
more than gaps in technology and in reproducible capital intensity,
with respect to which catch-up is presumably possible. As already
said, they also reflect differences in natural resource availabilities
which, of course, are generally favorable to America and were far

more important to America and to all the other countries in 1870 than they are today. In 1870, the agricultural share of United States employment was 50 percent; in 1979, 3½ percent. For the other 15 countries, the corresponding figures are 48 and 8 percent on the average. The declines were large in all the countries.[12] So the American advantage in 1870 depended much more on our favorable land-man ratio than it did in 1979. Putting it the other way, other countries on the average must have fallen back over the century in respect to the productivity determinants in respect to which catch-up is possible.

In other respects, however, one can see the influence of the potential for catching up clearly. The variance among the productivity levels of the 15 "follower" countries declines drastically over the century – from a coefficient of variation of 0.5 in 1870 to 0.15 in 1979. Not only that: the decline in variance was continuous from one key year to the next, with only one reversal – in the period across World War II. In the same way, the inverse rank correlation between the initial productivity levels in 1870 and subsequent growth rates over increasingly long periods becomes stronger and stronger, until we reach the correlation coefficient of $-.97$ across the entire 109 years.[13] (Again there was the single reversal across World War II when the association was actually – and presumably accidentally – positive.)

I believe the steadily declining variance measures and the steadily rising correlation coefficients should be interpreted to mean that initial productivity gaps did indeed constitute a potentiality for fast growth that had its effect later if not sooner. The effect of the potentiality became visible in a very limited degree very early. But if a country was incapable of, or prevented from, exploiting that opportunity promptly, the technological growth potential became stronger, and the country's later rate of advance was all the faster. Though it may have taken a century for obstacles or inhibitions to be fully overcome, the net outcome was that levels of productivity tended steadily to even out – at least within the group of presently advanced countries in my sample.

This last phrase is important. Mine is a biased sample in that its members consist of countries all of whom have successfully entered into the process of modern economic growth. This implies that they have acquired the educational and institutional characteristics needed to make use of modern technologies to some advanced degree. It is by no means assured – indeed, it is unlikely – that a more comprehensive sample of countries would show the same tendency for levels of productivity to even out over the same period of time.[14]

This is the big picture. How do things look if we consider shorter periods? There are two matters to keep in mind: the tendency to converge *within* the group of followers; and the convergence – or lack of it – of the group of followers vis-à-vis the United States. I take up the second matter in the next section. As to the convergence *within* the follower group, the figures suggest that the process varied in strength markedly from period to period. The main difference was that before World War II it operated weakly or at best with moderate strength. For almost a quarter-century following the war it apparently worked with very great strength. Why?

Before World War II, it is useful to consider two periods, roughly the decades before 1913, and those that followed. In the years of relative peace before 1913 I suggest that the process left a weak mark on the record for two reasons, both connected with the still early state of industrialization in many of the countries. First, the impress of the process was masked because farming was still so very important; measured levels of productivity, therefore, depended heavily on the amount and quality of farmland in relation to population. Productivity levels, in consequence, were erratic indicators of gaps between existing and best-practice technology. Secondly, social competence for exploiting the then most advanced methods was still limited, particularly in the earlier years and in the more recent latecomers. As the pre-World War I decades wore on, however, both these qualifying circumstances became less important. One might therefore have expected a much stronger tendency to convergence after 1913. But this was frustrated by the irregular effects of the Great War and of the years of disturbed political and financial conditions that followed, by the uneven impacts of the Great Depression itself and of the restrictions on international trade.

The unfulfilled potential of the years 1913–1938 was then enormously enlarged by the effects of World War II. The average productivity gap behind the United States increased by 38 percent between 1938 and 1950; the poorer countries were hit harder than the richer. These were years of dispersion, not convergence.

The post-World War II decades then proved to be the period when – exceptionally – the three elements required for rapid growth by catching up came together.[15] The elements were large technological gaps; enlarged social competence, reflecting higher levels of education and greater experience with large-scale production, distribution, and finance; and conditions favoring rapid realization of potential. This last element refers to several matters. There was *on this occasion* (it was otherwise after World War I) a strong reaction to the experience of defeat in war, and a chance for political reconstruction. The postwar political and economic reorganization and reform weakened the power of monopolistic groupings, brought new men to the fore, and focused the attention of governments on the tasks of recovery and growth, as Mancur Olson has argued.[16] The facilities for the diffusion of technology improved. International markets were opened. Large labor reserves in home agriculture and immigration from Southern and Eastern Europe provided a flexible and mobile labor supply. Government support, technological opportunity, and an environment of stable international money favored heavy and sustained capital investment. The outcome was the great speed and strength of the postwar catch-up process.[17]

Looking back now on the record of more than a century, we can see that catching up was a powerful continuing element in the growth experience of the presently advanced industrial countries. The strength of the process varied from period to period. For decades it operated only erratically and with weakened force. The trouble at first lay in deficient social capability, a sluggish adaptation of education and of industrial and financial organization to the requirements of modern large-scale technology. Later, the process was checked and made irregular by the effects of the two world wars and the ensuing political and financial troubles and by the impact of the Great Depression. It was at last released after World War II. The results were the rapid growth rates of the postwar period, the close cross-country association between initial productivity levels and growth rates, and a marked reduction of differences in productivity levels, among the follower countries, and between them and the United States.

Looking to the future, it seems likely that this very success will have weakened the potentiality for growth by catching up among the group of presently advanced countries. The great opportunities carried by that potential now pass to the less developed countries of Latin America and Asia.

Forging ahead and falling behind

The catch-up hypothesis in its simple form does not anticipate changes in leadership nor, indeed, any changes in the ranks of countries in their relative levels of productivity. It contemplates only a reduction among countries in productivity differentials. Yet there have been many changes in ranks since 1870 and, of course, the notable shift of leadership from Britain to America towards the end of the last century.[18] This was followed by the continuing decline of Britain's standing in the productivity scale. Today there is a widely held opinion that America is about to fall behind a new candidate for leadership, Japan, and both Europe and America must contemplate serious injury from the rise of both Japan and a group of still newer industrializing countries.

Needless to say, this paper cannot deal with the variety of reasons – all still speculative – for the comparative success of the countries that advanced in rank and the comparative failure of those that fell back.[19] I focus instead on a few matters that help illustrate the ramifications of the catch-up process and reveal the limitations of the simple hypothesis considered in earlier sections.

The congruity of technology and resources: United States as leader

Why did the gap between the United States and the average of other countries resist reduction so long? Indeed, why did it even appear to become larger between 1870 and 1929 – before the impact of World War II made it larger still? I offer three reasons:

1. The path of technological change which in those years offered the greatest opportunities for advance was at once heavily scale-dependent and biased in a labor-saving but capital- and resource-using direction. In both respects America enjoyed great advantages compared with Europe or Japan. Large-scale production was favored by a large, rapidly growing, and increasingly prosperous population. It was supported also by a striking homogeneity of tastes. This reflected the country's comparative youth, its rapid settlement by migration from a common base on the Atlantic, and the weakness and fluidity of its class divisions. Further, insofar as the population grew by immigration, the new Americans and their children quickly accepted the consumption patterns of their adopted country because the prevailing ethos favored assimilation to the dominant native white culture. At the same time, American industry was encouraged to explore the rich possibilities of a labor-saving but capital- and resource-using path of advance. The country's resources of land, forest, and minerals were particularly rich and abundant, and supplies of capital grew rapidly in response to high returns.[20]

2. By comparison with America and Britain, many, though not all, of the "followers" were also latecomers in respect to social capability. In the decades following 1870, they lacked experience with large-scale production and commerce, and in one degree or another they needed to advance in levels of general and technical education.

3. World War I was a serious setback for many countries but a stimulus to growth in the United States. European recovery and growth in the following years were delayed and slowed by financial disturbances and by the impact of territorial and political change. Protection, not unification, was the response to the new political map.

The rise of social democratic electoral strength in Europe favored the expansion of union power, but failed to curb the development and activities of industrial cartels. Britain's ability to support and enforce stable monetary conditions had been weakened, but the United States was not yet able or, indeed, willing to assume the role of leadership that Britain was losing. In all these ways, the response to the challenge of war losses and defeat after the First World War stands in contrast to that after the Second.

Points (2) and (3) were anticipated in earlier argument, but Point (1) constitutes a qualification to the simple catch-up hypothesis. In that view, different countries, subject only to their social capability, are equally competent to exploit a leader's path of technological progress. That is not so, however, if that path is biased in resource intensity or if it is scale-dependent. Resource-rich countries will be favored in the first instance, large countries in the second. If the historical argument of this section is correct, the United States was favored on both counts for a long time; it may not be so favored in the future. Whether or not this interpretation of American experience is correct, the general proposition remains: countries have unequal abilities to pursue paths of progress that are resource-biased or scale-dependent.

Interaction between followers and leaders

The catch-up hypothesis in its simple form is concerned with only one aspect of the economic relations among countries: technological borrowing by followers. In this view, a one-way stream of benefits flows from leaders to followers. A moment's reflection, however, exposes the inadequacy of that idea. The rise of British factory-made cotton textiles in the first industrial revolution ruined the Irish linen industry. The attractions of British and American jobs denuded the Irish population of its young men. The beginnings of modern growth in Ireland suffered a protracted delay. This is an example of the negative effects of leadership on the economies of those who are behind. Besides technological borrowing, there are interactions by way of trade and its rivalries, capital flows, and population movements. Moreover, the knowledge flows are not solely from leader to followers. A satisfactory account of the catch-up process must take account of these multiple forms of interaction. Again, there is space only for brief comment.

Trade and its rivalries. I have referred to the sometimes negative effects of leading-country exports on the economies of less developed countries. Countries in the course of catching up, however, exploit the possibilities of advanced scale-dependent technologies by

import substitution and expansion of exports. When they are successful there are possible negative effects on the economies of leaders.
This is an old historical theme. The successful competition of Germany, America, and other European countries is supposed to have
retarded British growth from 1870 to 1913 and perhaps longer.[21]
Analogous questions arise today. The expansion of exports from Japan and the newer industrializing countries has had a serious impact
on the older industries of America and Europe, as well as some of the
newer industries.

Is there a generalized effect on the productivity growth of the leaders? The effect is less than it may seem to be because some of the trade
shifts are a reflection of overall productivity growth in the leader
countries themselves. As the average level of productivity rises, so
does the level of wages across industries generally. There are then
relative increases in the product prices of those industries – usually
older industries – in which productivity growth is lagging and relative declines in the product prices of those industries enjoying rapid
productivity growth. The former must suffer a loss of comparative
advantage, the latter a gain. One must keep an eye on both.

Other causes of trade shifts that are connected with the catch-up
process itself may, however, carry real generalized productivity effects. There are changes that stem from the evolution of "product
cycles," such as Raymond Vernon has made familiar. And perhaps
most important, there is the achievement of higher levels of social
capability. This permits followers to extend their borrowing and adaptation of more advanced methods, and enables them to compete in
markets they could not contest earlier.

What difference does it make to the general prospects for the productivity growth of the leading industrial countries if they are losing
markets to followers who are catching up?

There is an employment effect. Demand for the products of export-
and import-competing industries is depressed. Failing a high degree
of flexibility in exchange rates and wages and of occupational and
geographical mobility, aggregate demand tends to be reduced. Unless
macroeconomic policy is successful, there is general unemployment
and underutilization of resources. Profits and the inducements to
invest and innovate are reduced. And if this condition causes economies to succumb to protectionism, particularly to competitive protectionism, the difficulty is aggravated.

International trade theory assures us that these effects are transitory. Autonomous capital movements aside, trade must, in the
end, balance. But the macroeconomic effects of the balancing process may be long drawn out, and while it is in progress, countries

can suffer the repressive effects of restricted demand on investment and innovation.

There is also a Verdoorn effect. It is harder for an industry to push the technological frontier forward, or even to keep up with it, if its own rate of expansion slows down – and still harder if it is contracting. This is unavoidable but tolerable when the growth of old industries is restricted by the rise of newer, more progressive home industries. But when retardation of older home industries is due to the rise of competing industries abroad, a tendency to generalized slowdown may be present.

Interactions via population movements. Nineteenth-century migration ran in good part from the farms of Western and Southern Europe to the farms and cities of the New World and Australasia. In the early twentieth century, Eastern Europe joined in. These migrations responded in part to the impact on world markets of the cheap grains and animal products produced by the regions of recent settlement. Insofar they represent an additional but special effect of development in some members of the Atlantic community of industrializing countries on the economies of other members.

Productivity growth in the countries of destination was aided by migration in two respects. It helped them exploit scale economies; and by making labor supply more responsive to increase in demand, it helped sustain periods of rapid growth. Countries of origin were relieved of the presence of partly redundant and desperately poor people. On the other hand, the loss of population brought such scale disadvantages as accompany slower population growth, and it made labor supply less responsive to industrial demand.

Migration in the postwar growth boom presents a picture of largely similar design and significance. In this period the movement was from the poorer, more slowly growing countries of Southern Europe and North Africa to the richer and more rapidly growing countries of Western and Northern Europe.[22] There is, however, this difference: The movement in more recent decades was induced by actual and expected income differences that were largely independent of the market connections of countries of origin and destination. There is no evidence that the growth boom of the West itself contributed to the low incomes of the South.

Needless to say, migrations are influenced by considerations other than relative levels of income and changing comparative advantage. I stress these matters, however, because they help us understand the complexities of the process of catch-up and convergence within a group of connected countries.

Interaction via capital flows. A familiar generalization is that capital tends to flow from countries of high income and slow growth to those with opposite characteristics or, roughly speaking, from leaders to followers. One remembers, however, that that description applies to gross new investments. There are also reverse flows that reflect the maturing of past investments. So in the early stages of a great wave of investment, followers' rates of investment and productivity growth are supported by capital movement while those of leaders are retarded. Later, however, this effect may become smaller or be reversed, as we see today in relations between Western leaders and Latin American followers.

Once more, I add that the true picture is far more complicated than this idealized summary. It will hardly accommodate such extraordinary developments as the huge American capital import of recent years, to say nothing of the Arabian-European flows of the 1970s and their reversal now underway.

Interactions via flows of applied knowledge. The flow of knowledge from leader to followers is, of course, the very essence of the catch-up hypothesis. As the technological gaps narrow, however, the direction changes. Countries that are still a distance behind the leader in average productivity may move into the lead in particular branches and become sources of new knowledge for older leaders. As they are surpassed in particular fields, old leaders can make gains by borrowing as well as by generating new knowledge. In this respect the growth potential of old leaders is enhanced as the pursuit draws closer. Moreover, competitive pressure can be a stimulus to research and innovation as well as an excuse for protection. It remains to be seen whether the newly rising economies will seek to guard a working knowledge of their operations more closely than American companies have done, and still more whether American and European firms will be as quick to discover, acquire, and adapt foreign methods as Japanese firms have been in the past.

Development as a constraint on change: tangible capital
The rise of followers in the course of catching up brings old leaders a mixed bag of injuries and potential benefits. Old leaders, however, or followers who have enjoyed a period of successful development, may come to suffer disabilities other than those caused by the burgeoning competitive power of new rivals. When Britain suffered her growth climacteric nearly a century ago, observers thought that her slowdown was itself due in part to her early lead. Thorstein Veblen was a pioneer proponent of this suggestion, and Charles Kin-

dleberger and others have picked it up again.[23] One basis for this view is the idea that the capital stock of a country consists of an intricate web of interlocking elements. They are built to fit together, and it is difficult to replace one part of the complex with more modern and efficient elements without a costly rebuilding of other components. This may be handled efficiently if all the costs and benefits are internal to a firm. When they are divided among different firms and industries and between the private and public sectors, the adaptation of old capital structures to new technologies may be a difficult and halting process.

What this may have meant for Britain's climacteric is still unsettled. Whatever that may be, however, the problem needs study on a wider scale as it arises both historically and in a contemporaneous setting. After World War II, France undertook a great extension and modernization of its public transportation and power systems to provide a basis for later development of private industry and agriculture. Were the technological advances embodied in that investment program easier for France to carry out because its infrastructure was technically older, battered, and badly maintained? Or was it simply a heavy burden more in need of being borne? There is a widespread complaint today that the public capital structure of the United States stands in need of modernization and extension. Is this true, and, if it is, does it militate seriously against the installation of improved capital by private industry? One cannot now assume that such problems are the exclusive concern of a topmost productivity leader. All advanced industrial countries have large accumulations of capital, interdependent in use but divided in ownership among many firms and between private and public authorities. One may assume, however, that the problem so raised differs in its impact over time and among countries and, depending on its importance, might have some influence on the changes that occur in the productivity rankings of countries.

Development as a constraint on change: intangible capital and political institutions

Attention now returns to matters akin to social capability. In the simple catch-up hypothesis, that capability is viewed as either exogenously determined or else as adjusting steadily to the requirements of technological opportunity. The educational and institutional commitments induced by past development may, however, stand as an obstacle. That is a question that calls for study. The comments that follow are no more than brief indications of prominent possibilities.

The United States was the pioneer of mass production as embodied in the huge plant, the complex and rigid assembly line, the standard-ized product, and the long production run. It is also the pioneer and developer of the mammoth diversified conglomerate corporation. The vision of business carried on within such organizations, their highly indirect, statistical, and bureaucratic methods of consultation, plan-ning and decision, the inevitable distractions of trading in assets rather than production of goods – these mental biases have sunk deep into the American business outlook and into the doctrine and training of young American managers. The necessary decentraliza-tion of operations into multiple profit centers directs the attention of managers and their superiors to the quarterly profit report and draws their energies away from the development of improved products and processes that require years of attention.[24] One may well ask how well this older vision of management and enterprise and the organiza-tional scheme in which it is embodied will accommodate the problems and potentialities of the emerging computer and communications revolution. Or will that occur more easily in countries where educa-tional systems, forms of corporate organization, and managerial out-look can better make a fresh start?

The long period of leadership and development enjoyed by the United States and the entire North Atlantic community meant, of course, a great increase of incomes. The rise of incomes, in turn, afforded a chance to satisfy latent desires for all sorts of non-market goods ranging from maintenance in old age to a safe-guarded natural environment. Satisfying these demands, largely by public action, has also afforded an ample opportunity for special interest groups to ob-tain privileges and protection in a process that Mancur Olson and others have generalized.

The outcome of this conjuncture of circumstances and forces is the Mixed Economy of the West, the complex system of transfers, taxes, regulations, and public activity, as well as organizations of union and business power, that had its roots long before the War, that expanded rapidly during the growth boom of the fifties and sixties, and that reached very high levels in the seventies. This trend is very broadly consistent with the suggestion that the elaboration of the mixed econ-omy is a function of economic growth itself. To this one has to add the widely held idea advanced by Olson and many others that the system operates to reduce enterprise, work, saving, investment, and mobility and, therefore, to constrict the processes of innovation and change that productivity growth involves.

How much is there in all this? The answer turns only partly on a calculation of the direct effects of the system on economic incentives. These have proved difficult to pin down, and attempts to measure them have generally not yielded large numbers, at least for the United States.[25] The answer requires an equally difficult evaluation of the positive roles of government activity. These include not only the government's support of education, research, and information, and its provision of physical overhead capital and of the host of local functions required for urban life. We must remember also that the occupational and geographical adjustments needed to absorb new technology impose heavy costs on individuals. The accompanying changes alter the positions, prospects, and power of established groups, and they transform the structure of families and their roles in caring for children, the sick, and the old. Technical advance, therefore, engenders conflict and resistance; and the Welfare State with its transfers and regulations constitutes a mode of conflict resolution and a means of mitigating the costs of change that would otherwise induce resistance to growth. The existing empirical studies that bear on the economic responses to government intervention are, therefore, far from meeting the problem fully.

If the growth-inhibiting forces embodied in the Welfare State and in private expressions of market power were straightforward, positive functions of income levels, uniform across countries, that would be another reason for supposing that the catch-up process was self-limiting. The productivity levels of followers would, on this account, converge towards but not exceed the leader's. But these forces are clearly not simple, uniform functions of income. The institutions of the Welfare State have reached a higher degree of elaboration in Europe than in the United States. The objects of expenditure, the structures of transfers and taxes, and people's responses to both differ from country to country. These institutional developments, therefore, besides having some influence on growth rates generally, may constitute a wild card in the deck of growth forces. They will tend to produce changes in the ranks of countries in the productivity scale and these may include the top rank itself.

A sense that forces of institutional change are now acting to limit the growth of Western countries pervades the writings of many economists – and, of course, of other observers. Olson, Fellner, Scitovsky, Kindleberger, Lindbeck, and Giersch are only a partial list of those who see these economies as afflicted by institutional arthritis or sclerosis or other metaphorical malady associated with age and wealth.

These are the suggestions of serious scholars, and they need to be taken seriously. One may ask, however, whether these views take account of still other, rejuvenating forces which, though they act slowly, may yet work effectively to limit and counter those of decay –

at least for the calculable future. In the United States, interregional competition, supported by free movement of goods, people, and capital, is such a force. It limits the power of unions and checks the expansion of taxation, transfers, and regulation.[26] International competition, so long as it is permitted to operate, works in a similar direction for the United States and other countries as well, and it is strengthened by the development in recent years of a more highly integrated world capital market and by more vigorous international movements of corporate enterprise.

In the ranking of countries within the group of presently advanced industrial economies, their variant responsiveness to competition may be still another influence making for change in rank and relative level of productivity. As this group competes with the newly industrializing countries of the East and South, however, the pressures of competition on their institutional development, as distinct from their impact on particular industries, should help the older group maintain a lead. There are, however, still more solid grounds for a renewal of productivity advance in both Europe and the United States and for the maintenance of a substantial lead over virtually all newcomers. These are their high levels of general and technical education, the broad bases of their science, and the well-established connections of their science, technology, and industry. These elements of social capability are slow to develop but also, it seems very likely, slow to decay.

Finally, it is widely recognized that the process of institutional aging, whatever its significance, is not one without limits. Powerful forces continue to push that way, and they are surely strong in resisting reversal. Yet it is also apparent that there is a drift of public opinion that works for modification both in Europe and North America. There is a fine balance to be struck between productivity growth and the material incomes it brings and the other dimensions of social welfare. Countries are now in the course of readjusting that balance in favor of productivity growth. How far they can go and, indeed, how far they should go are both still in question.

Concluding remarks

This essay points in two directions. It shows that differences among countries in productivity levels create a strong potentiality for subsequent convergence of levels, provided that countries have a "social capability" adequate to absorb more advanced technologies. It reminds us, however, that the institutional and human capital components of social capability develop only slowly as education and organization respond to the requirements of technological opportunity and to experience in exploiting it. Their degree of development acts to limit the strength of technological potentiality proper. Further, the pace of realization of a potential for catch-up depends on a number of other conditions that govern the diffusion of knowledge, the mobility of resources and the rate of investment.

The long-term convergence to which these considerations point, however, is only a tendency that emerges in the average experience of a group of countries. The growth records of countries on their surface do not exhibit the uniformly self-limiting character that a simple statement of the catch-up hypothesis might suggest. Dramatic changes in productivity rankings mark the performance of a group's individual members. Some causes of these shifts in rank are exogenous to the convergence process. The state of a country's capability to exploit emerging technological opportunity depends on a social history that is particular to itself and that may not be closely bound to its existing level of productivity. And there are changes in the character of technological advance that make it more congruent with the resources and institutional outfits of some countries but less congruent with those of others. Some shifts, however, are influenced by the catch-up process itself – for example, when the trade rivalry of advancing latecomers makes successful inroads on important industries of older leaders. There are also the social and political concomitants of rising wealth itself that may weaken the social capability for technological advance. There is the desire to avoid or mitigate the costs of growth, and there are the attractions of goals other than growth as wealth increases. A reasonably complete view of the catch-up process, therefore, does not lend itself to simple formulation. Its implications ramify and are hard to separate from the more general process of growth at large.

Notes

1. Angus Maddison, *Phases of Capitalist Development* (New York, 1982). Maddison's estimates of productivity levels are themselves extrapolations of base levels established for most, but not all, the countries by Irving B. Kravis, Alan Heston, and Robert Summers in their *International Comparisons of Real Product and Purchasing Power* (Baltimore, 1978) and in other publications by Kravis and his associates.

2. W.E.G. Salter, *Productivity and Technical Change* (Cambridge, 1960) provides a rigorous theoretical exposition of the factors determining rates of turnover and those governing the relation between productivity with capital embodying best practice and average (economically efficient) technology.

3. *Japanese Economic Growth: Trend Acceleration in the Twentieth Century* (Stanford, 1973), especially chap. 9.

4. Moses Abramovitz, "Rapid Growth Potential and its Realization: The Experience of the Capitalist Economies in the Postwar Period," in Edmond Malinvaud, ed., *Eco-*

nomic Growth and Resources, Proceedings of the Fifth World Congress of the International Economic Association, vol. 1 (London, 1979), pp. 1–30.

5. Thorstein Veblen, *Imperial Germany and the Industrial Revolution* (New York, 1915), p. 70.

6. Mancur Olson, *The Rise and Fall of Nations: Economic Growth, Stagflation and Social Rigidities* (New Haven, 1982).

7. Kravis et al., *International Comparisons;* Edward F. Denison, assisted by Jean-Pierre Poullier, *Why Growth Rates Differ, Postwar Experience of Nine Western Countries* (Washington, D.C., 1967), pp. 239–45.

8. R.C.O. Matthews, Review of Denison (1967), *Economic Journal* (June 1969), pp. 261–68.

9. My paper cited earlier describes the operation of these factors in the 1950s and 1960s and tries to show how they worked to permit productivity growth to rise in so many countries rapidly, in concert and for such an extended period ("Rapid Growth Potential and Its Realization," pp. 18–30).

10. The countries are Australia, Austria, Belgium, Canada, Denmark, Finland, France, Germany, Italy, Japan, Netherlands, Norway, Sweden, Switzerland, United Kingdom, and United States.

11. In these calculations I have treated either the United States or the United Kingdom as the productivity leader from 1870 to 1913. Literal acceptance of Maddison's estimates, however, make Australia the leader from 1870–1913. Moreover, Belgium and the Netherlands stand slightly higher than the United States in 1870. Here are Maddison's relatives for those years (from *Phases,* Table 5.2):

	1870	1890	1913
Australia	186	153	102
Belgium	106	96	75
Netherlands	106	92	74
United Kingdom	114	100	81
United States	100	100	100

Since Australia's high standing in this period mainly reflected an outstandingly favorable situation of natural resources relative to population, it would be misleading to regard that country as the technological leader or to treat the productivity changes in other countries relative to Australia's as indicators of the catch-up process. Similarly, the small size and specialized character of the Belgian and Dutch economies make them inappropriate benchmarks.

12. Maddison, *Phases,* Table C5.

13. Since growth rates are calculated as rates of change between standings at the terminal dates of periods, errors in the estimates of such standings will generate errors in the derived growth rates. If errors at both terminal dates were random, and if those at the end-year were independent of those at the initial year, there would be a tendency on that account for growth rates to be inversely correlated with initial-year standings. The inverse correlation coefficients would be biased upwards. Note, however, that if errors at terminal years were random and independent and of equal magnitude, there would be no tendency *on that account* for the variance of standings about the mean to decline between initial and end-year dates. The error bias would run against the

marked decline in variance that we observe. Errors in late-year data, however, are unlikely to be so large, so an error bias is present.

14. See also William J. Baumol, "Productivity Growth, Convergence and Welfare: What the Long-run Data Show," *Amer. Econ. Rev.*, 76 (Dec. 1986), pp. 1072–85.

15. See Abramovitz, "Rapid Growth Potential and its Realization."

16. Olson, *Rise and Fall.*

17. Some comments on the catch-up process after 1973 may be found in Abramovitz, "Catching Up and Falling Behind" (Stockholm, 1986), pp. 33–39.

18. If one follows Maddison's estimates (*Phases*, Table C.19), the long period from 1870 to 1979 saw Australia fall by 8 places in the ranking of his 16 countries, Italy by 2½, Switzerland by 8, and the United Kingdom by 10. Meanwhile the United States rose by 4, Germany by 4½, Norway by 5, Sweden by 7, and France by 8.

19. The possibility of overtaking and surpassing, however, was considered theoretically by Edward Ames and Nathan Rosenberg in a closely reasoned and persuasive article, "Changing Technological Leadership and Industrial Growth," *Economic Journal*, 72 (1963), pp. 13–31. They conclude that the troubles connected with leadership and industrial "aging" that doom early leaders to decline in the productivity scale are not persuasive. They hold that outcomes turn on a variety of empirical conditions, the presence of which is uncertain and not foreordained.

20. These arguments are anticipated and elaborated in Nathan Rosenberg's fertile and original paper, "Why in America?", in Otto Mayr and Robert Post, eds., *Yankee Enterprise: The Rise of the American System of Manufactures* (Washington, D.C., 1981).

21. See also R.C.O. Matthews, Charles Feinstein, and John Odling-Smee, *British Economic Growth, 1856–1973* (Stanford, 1983), chaps. 14, 15, 17. Their analysis does not find a large effect on British productivity growth from 1870 to 1913.

22. The migration from East to West Germany in the 1950s was a special case. It brought to West Germany educated and skilled countrymen strongly motivated to rebuild their lives and restore their fortunes.

23. Charles P. Kindleberger, "Obsolescence and Technical Change." *Oxford Institute of Statistics Bulletin* (Aug. 1961), pp. 281–97.

24. These and similar questions are raised by experienced observers of American business. They are well summarized by Edward Denison, *Trends in American Economic Growth, 1929–1982*, (Washington, D.C., 1985), chap. 3.

25. Representative arguments supporting the idea that social capability has suffered, together with some quantitative evidence, may be found in Olson, *Rise and Fall;* William Fellner, "The Declining Growth of American Productivity: An Introductory Note," in W. Fellner, ed., *Contemporary Economic Problems, 1979* (Washington, D.C., 1979); and Assar Lindbeck, "Limits to the Welfare State," *Challenge* (Dec. 1985). For argument and evidence on the other side, see Sheldon Danzigar, Robert Haveman, and Robert Plotnick, "How Income Transfers Affect Work, Savings and Income Distribution, *Journal of Economic Literature*, 19 (Sept. 1982), pp. 975–1028.; and Edw. F. Denison, *Accounting for Slower Economic Growth* (Washington, D.C., 1979), pp. 127–38.

26. See R. D. Norton, "Regional Life Cycles and U.S. Industrial Rejuvenation," in Herbert Giersch, ed., *Towards an Explanation of Economic Growth* (Tübingen, 1981), pp. 253–80; and R. D. Norton, "Industrial Policy and American Renewal," *Journal of Economic Literature*, 24 (March 1986).

Part III

Long swings in economic growth

8

The nature and significance of Kuznets cycles

Two forms of general economic change have long been accepted by most economists as systematic features of industrialized economies organized under capitalist institutions. One is persistent long-term growth; the other is the business cycle.

Both are generalizations of apparently irregular behavior. Total output rarely rises or falls at the same rate for two consecutive months, and it seldom moves in the same direction for many months together. These irregular movements, however, are not without pattern. The month-to-month movements are, for periods of time, predominantly upward, and these periods of expansion are succeeded by other periods in which movements are predominantly downward. These are the *business cycles* of capitalist economic life. They are fluctuations of aggregate output in which other aspects of economic activity join; they are widely diffused through the many sectors of the economy; and they recur at intervals which are as long as ten to twelve years but are normally less than five or six. And when we consider periods longer than those of business cycles, there emerges a persistent underlying tendency for output to rise. Although the rate of growth is not constant, the average level of output during any business-cycle period is normally higher than that attained during the preceding cycle period. The persistence of growth is one characteristic of the *primary secular trend* of output in capitalist countries in the era of industrialization.

The existence of business cycles and of irreversible primary trends is supported by considerable bodies of evidence. Both types of movement are widely regarded as at least partly, perhaps chiefly, systematic in nature, and both are the subject of intensive investigation.

Economists, however, are not generally agreed that these are the

Reprinted by permission from *Economic Development and Cultural Change*, vol. 9, no. 3 (April 1961), 225–48.

only systematic, or quasi-systematic, movements which the record of economic change presents. There are recurrent suggestions of waves, of reversals in levels or rates of change of output, with durations longer than business cycles. As regards duration, these suggestions essentially span the spectrum of possibilities. They include a relatively short wave of eight to eleven years, the so-called Juglar cycle, a very long wave of 40 to 60 years, the so-called Kondratieff cycle, and a wave of intermediate length, between 15 and 25 years in duration.

Considering the span of years for which output records are available, it is hard to see how waves longer than the Kondratieff could be at all separated, however tentatively, from the primary trend itself. And considering the admitted variability of the shorter movements, it is hard to see how more than two, if even two, other systematic waves could be fitted between the business cycles at the short end and the Kondratieff at the long end of the spectrum.

Useful discussion of the relative validity of these several hypotheses is beyond the scope of this article. It must suffice to start from the assertion that continuing study has tended to cast doubt on the usefulness of the Kondratieff and Juglar hypotheses and has concentrated attention on the postulated wave of intermediate length.[1] For this reason, the present article proposes to give some account of the chief features of these intermediate waves, and to discuss their probable nature and significance.[2]

This subject is especially appropriate for treatment in the present volume because Simon Kuznets was one of the discoverers of this wave. Kuznets, no doubt, must share honors with others whose pioneering work helped to establish the general importance of the wave. More than others, however, Kuznets has continued to investigate its properties and to defend its significance. W. A. Lewis has suggested that we recognize this long record of work by referring to the 15–25 year general waves in economic change as *Kuznets cycles,* and I propose to accept this suggestion with the understanding that the use of the term "cycles" is not meant to prejudge the question whether these waves are significantly self-generating, a matter about which Kuznets is dubious and which the present writer regards as unsettled.[3] Following Kuznets' own practice in recent writings, it may be better to substitute "swings" or "waves" for "cycles."

I

Kuznets first encountered his cycles in the course of his early work on long term trends which he published in 1930.[4] Here Kuznets showed that production and price series, with primary trends eliminated and the influences of business cycles attenuated or smoothed by moving averages, exhibited pronounced wave-like undulations. He called them "secondary secular movements."[5] Kuznets' measurements suggested that the average duration of the cycles had been about 22 years in the production series and 23 years in the price series.

Although Kuznets apparently believed that the swings he observed in the output and prices of individual commodities appeared at about the same time in many different activities, he made no systematic attempt in his early work to establish the existence of long swings in aggregate economic activity. This matter was settled, at least for the United States, by Arthur F. Burns. Burns studied a large sample of United States production series for the years 1870–1930. From his original data, he calculated rates of growth during successive overlapping decades displaced five years. These he expressed as deviations from the trend rate of growth. He called the fluctuations of the corrected decade rates of growth "trend-cycles."[6] Burns argued that "if a set of common causes, variable in time operate uniformly through the trend-cycles of individual industries, their effects will be registered in the movements of the averages of the trend-cycles, even though random factors operate simultaneously with the set of common causes."[7] Burns' findings left little doubt that a set of common causes had been operating. He found that the median rates of growth of the industries in his sample traced out definite oscillatory movements, that the pattern of these movements ran through the entire system of series, that irregularities were confined chiefly to the agricultural sector, that the waves in the median rates of growth were matched by the trend-cycles of indexes of total industrial production and of major industrial groups and that the same was true of trend cycles in other aspects of the economy, prices, money in circulation, the monetary stock of gold, real earnings, business failures, and patents issued. Burns felt able to conclude that the concurrence of trend-cycles in the various branches of non-agricultural production and their consilience with trend-cycles in other aspects of economic life created a "strong presumption that a long-term rhythm has been pervasive in the American economy since the Civil War. . ."[8]

These indications have been bolstered in more recent years by the appearance of Kuznets' long-term estimates of national product. Kuznets first published his extended estimates in the form of averages for overlapping decades displaced five years (1869–78, 1874–83, etc.). Since such decade averages may be presumed to accomplish a substantial smoothing of business cycles, rates of change between overlapping decade averages may be thought to constitute approximations to rates of secular growth. Such rates display wave-like fluctuations which succeed each other at intervals of about twenty years. Their maxima and minima correspond sufficiently closely with those previously determined by Burns and, still earlier, by Wardwell so that there can be little doubt that all three were revealing the same phenomenon.[9]

Kuznets cycles in the rate of growth of output have been found in a number of countries besides the United States.[10] Kuznets cycles, moreover, are not confined to output growth. In addition to the various facets of economic life already mentioned above, they are particularly prominent in building and other forms of construction. Kuznets cycles, therefore, can be thought of as the more general manifestation of the well-known long cycles in building and of the "transport-building cycle" revealed by Isard.[11] Such cycles are, further, clearly apparent in the great waves of immigration before the 1930's. These were naturally accompanied by similar, though smaller, swings in the rate of growth of the labor force and population. The long swings in population and labor force growth, however, were never wholly the result of immigration waves, and since World War I, their chief source has been in the fluctuations of marriage and birth rates, and, in the case of labor force growth, in those of participation rates. The illumination of the demographic aspects of Kuznets cycles has, indeed, been one of Simon Kuznets' more important contributions to the subject.[12]

The participation of immigration waves in the Kuznets cycles of the USA and of other "new" migrant-receiving countries in the 19th and early 20th centuries suggests that Kuznets cycles in the new countries may have had an inverted relation to Kuznets cycles in the "old" countries of emigration. Such inversion was established so far as Great Britain is concerned, by the work of Brinley Thomas, Cairncross and others.[13] Thomas also showed that the waves of British population migration were accompanied by similar waves of capital exports,[14] and it can now be added that the Kuznets cycles in British capital exports are matched by similar waves in US capital imports and by inverse swings in the US balance of payments.[15]

Finally, the present writer[16] has shown that at least in the United States, Kuznets cycles in output growth have arisen from the swings in almost all the elements into which output growth can be resolved. Waves in the rate of change in output have been accompanied – with certain characteristic differences in timing – not only by swings in additions to the labor force, but also by fluctuations in additions to the capital stock, in the rate of increase of output per unit of resources employed, and in indicators of the intensity of resource-utilization. Such waves were not confined to the period since 1870 to which the studies by Burns, Kuznets, and Lewis and O'Leary were restricted. For the United States, at any rate, there is evidence of general Kuznets fluctuations, going back at least to the 1830's and perhaps earlier and suggesting, therefore, the presence of a phenomenon which persisted over a very considerable period of time.

This review of earlier work leads me to the following general conclusion. In the United States and in at least some other growing economies, development during the nineteenth and early twentieth centuries took the form of a series of surges in the growth of output and in capital and labor resources followed by periods of retarded growth. The duration of these waves in the United States was roughly 15–20 years.[17] These waves in the growth of physical resources and activity were accompanied by generally similar swings in other aspects of economic life – in gold movements, in the growth of money supply and in the rate of change in prices, and in the balance of payments and international capital flows to mention only some of the more prominent features of the movements. Whatever their underlying nature, therefore, the Kuznets swings represent pulses of economic life which ramified widely through the developing economies of the past century or more and, on that account alone, they deserve close study.

II

What kind of phenomena are these swings? In particular, do they reflect principally a fluctuation in the rate of growth of the economy's capacity to produce as determined by the rate of growth of labor and capital resources and by the productivity of resources optimally employed, or do they also, and perhaps chiefly, reflect a fluctuation in the intensity with which resources are utilized? When one considers the primary trend of aggregate input, one thinks chiefly of the factors that control the growth of capacity to produce. When one considers business cycles, one thinks chiefly of factors that control the intensity of resource utilization and one is concerned principally with fluctuations in the determinants of effective demand. Have the Kuznets cycles been capacity or demand phenomena, or have they partaken of the nature of both?

One might suppose that, if one proceeds by applying moving averages or other smoothing devices to crude data with the purpose of eliminating the fluctuations associated with ordinary business cycles, and if one defines Kuznets cycles, in a rough fashion, as the fluctuations in the level or rate of growth of data so smoothed, one has eliminated the effects of fluctuations in the intensity of resource utilization. This, however, would be an unjustified inference, and this section argues, first, that Kuznets cycles have been compounded of fluctuations in the intensity with which resources are used, and, secondly, that the fluctuations in resource growth and in utilization rates have been interconnected causally. A long swing in the volume of additions, perhaps even in the rate of growth of additions, to the stock of capital, that is, in capital formation, is likely to involve a fluctuation in effective demand and thus to generate an alternation between states of relatively full and relatively slack employment. A long swing in unemployment rates in turn appears to have been among the chief causes of Kuznets cycles in the volume of additions to the labor force and, perhaps, in capital formation. It has also shaped the patterns formed by the waves in measured productivity growth so that it becomes difficult to say whether a wave in output per unit of resources employed at standard rates of utilization has actually been present. The evidence on which I base these conclusions is drawn from a study of long swings in U.S. development.

To help establish these points, I present a table of figures derived from data presented on an earlier occasion.[18] Table 8.1 purports to show the peaks and troughs of Kuznets cycles in output growth and in some of the major elements into which output growth can be resolved: productivity growth, additions to labor force and capital stock, growth in the input of resources and an indicator of the intensity of resource utilization. The sources of the data on which the table is based are described in source notes attached to the article in which the data originally appeared. Kuznets cycles in such series as addition to the labor force and additions to capital stock (i.e., capital formation) were isolated by calculating averages of annual data for periods bounded by successive pairs of ordinary business-cycle peaks and then for periods bounded by pairs of troughs. These two sets of averages were then intermixed to form a series of averages for overlapping business-cycle periods. We may think of the result as indicating how these series would have stood in the absence of ordinary business cycles (but not, according to the argument below, as the series would have stood in the absence of extraordinarily long or severe business-cycle movements). The Kuznets cycles in such series as the rate of growth of output or of productivity were isolated by calculating average rates of change between average standings for business cycle periods.[19] Again the resulting series of rates of growth are to be interpreted as indicating how the series would have grown in the absence of normal, but not abnormal, business cycles.

We have no way of measuring the intensity of resource utilization or its changes that is even roughly reliable before 1900. Even after that date such figures are confined to joblessness and do not touch fluctuations in the utilization of employed workers and of the stock of capital. To help show that there were changes in the intensity of resource utilization in the course of Kuznets cycles and to help indicate the phases of such cycles in which the turning points of changes in the rate of utilization probably occurred, we simply list the peaks preceding the beginning of protracted depressions and the troughs preceding the beginning of sustained recoveries from such depression. By protracted depressions we mean deep contractions of general business activity sustained over periods longer than ordinary recessions, or periods in which recoveries, if they occur, do not bring the economy back to full employment or do so only transiently. In the latter event *stagnation* may be the better term to employ. The periods so selected will be seen to include the classic periods of deep depression or stagnation in the United States. Some question, no doubt, may be raised about the periods 1853–8 and 1907–14, but I believe the weight of the evidence justifies my treatment.[20]

There are a number of uncertainties about Table 8.1 of which the reader ought to be aware. First, the swing in the rate of growth of output, 1911–21, was a movement connected with World War I in which the normal relations between swings in the rate of growth of output and those in other aspects of the economy were upset. War demand caused output growth to speed up and unemployment to drop, but these conditions, which in peacetime normally saw a rise in immigration, labor force growth, and in residential and other civilian construction, were accompanied by a drop in all these variables under the unusual strains and restrictions of war. It was a short and peculiar Kuznets cycle, if indeed it should be thought one at all, and it ended in a depression in 1920–21 which, while severe, was hardly protracted. Secondly, there is a peculiarly short period of alternation between acceleration and retardation in the late eighties and early nineties. The very short duration of this swing and some of its internal characteristics[21] make it questionable whether it is useful to recognize the acceleration 1886–1890 as more than a cyclical interruption of the retardation which began in the early 1880's. The use of ten-year moving averages, rather than the shorter business-cycle averages, as a device for smoothing out business cycles would wash out both the short movement in the late 80's and the short and mild movement connected with World War I. There may well be grounds for using the more radical smoothing provided by decade averages, but no substantial point in the argument that follows turns on the choice of smoothing methods or on such difference in chronologies as would flow from that choice. It may be of interest to note, however, that the two movements referred to immediately above are the only "extra" movements which turn up as a result of using our less radical smoothing

Table 8.1. *A chronology of the peaks and troughs of Kuznets cycles in selected aspects of the US economy*

	Rates of change in:						Volume of additions to:		
GNP per member of labor force	Gross physical output per unit of input	Gross physical output	Economic activity or gross national product	Industrial and commercial production	Total input of labor and capital	Labor force	Capital stock (= capital formation)	Years preceding the beginning or end of protracted depression or "stagnation"
–	–		1814	–	–	–	1815–18	1815
–	–		1834	–	–	–	1836–37	1836
–	–		1846	–	–	1851.5	1854–55	1853
a	–		1864.25	1864.25	–	1871	1871	1873
–	–		1881	1881	–	1884.5	a	1882
1890	–		1889.75	1888	–	1893.5	1892–93	1892
1899.75 b	1896.5 b	1899 b	1899	1899	1900	1906.5	1906	1907
			1914.5	1913.25	b	a	1919	1920
1923.25c	1923	1923	1923	1923	1923	1924.5	1927–28	1929
1943.75	1938.5	1936.75	1938.5	1938.5	1938.5	a	a	a

Long swing peaks

Long swing troughs

–	–	–	1819	–	–	–	1821–4	1821
–	–	–	1840	–	–	–	1842–4	1843
–	–	–	1858	–	–	1859.5	1862–4	1858
–	–	–	1874.25	1874.25	–	1874.25	1877–8	1878
–	1886.5	–	1886.5	1884	*a*	1886.5	*a*	1885
1892.25*d*	1893	1892.25*d*	1892.25	1892.25	1893.75	1896.5	1895	1896
1913.5	1906.75	*b*	1911	1906.75	*b*	1919.5	1912–13	1914
b	*b*	1920.25	1920.25	1920.25	1920.25	*a*	1921–2	1921
1927.5	1930.25	1930.25	1930.25	1930.25	1930.25	1935.5	1933	1932

Note: Dates expressed in whole years refer to years with midpoints at June 30. Dates expressed in whole years plus fractions have midpoints later than June 30 by the specified fraction of a year. Dash (–) data not available.

a Turning point skipped or, at end of table, not yet reached.
b Extra movement makes comparison with GNP impossible.
c Value at this date was the same as that at 1921.75.
d Tentative selection: Earlier data if available might suggest that the turning point was reached at an earlier date.

device. Including these two short movements in our chronology makes the average durations of Kuznets cycles in this country slightly under 14 years while their elimination would make their average duration almost exactly 18 years, a figure long associated with building cycles and closer to the durations of Kuznets' earlier "secondary secular movements" and Burns' "trend-cycles." There is, however, no one right method of smoothing to eliminate business-cycle fluctuations, and we can only try to remain aware of the differences which variant smoothings can make in our results.

While a mere chronology of turning points cannot persuasively establish the relations among time series, our table suggests a far-reaching and interesting conclusion, namely, that the long waves in the rate of growth of output[22] are the reflection of underlying long waves in almost all the measurable elements into which output growth can be resolved. Our table suggests, first, that there were long waves in additions to resources, both labor force and capital stock. However, since the long waves in resource growth lag far behind those in output growth, it appears that the earlier turning points in output growth must be traced in the first instance to a concomitant or still earlier change in the rate of growth of output per unit of resources available. So far as concerns labor, we have direct evidence of this connection in the turning points of output per member of the labor force.[23]

The growth of output per unit of resources can itself be resolved into two elements. One is the part contributed by changes in output per unit of input used at standard intensity, or, for short, per intensity unit. We may think of this part as the growth of "true" productivity. The other is the part contributed by changes in the number of intensity units employed per unit of resources available, that is, by changes in the rate of employment, or more generally, the rate of utilization of available resources. Changes in the utilization rate will occur not only because of changes in the unemployment rate for labor or because of changes in the number of hours worked, but also because of change in the intensity with which employed labor and available capital are used.

There is no completely satisfactory measure of either true productivity change or of changes in utilization rates. There is, however, a substantial quantity of evidence that changes in utilization rates have been a regular concomitant of Kuznets cycles and that they probably account for a considerable share in the apparent changes in the growth of output per unit of available resources.

We begin with the observation, documented elsewhere by the present writer, that each period of retardation in the rate of growth of output has culminated in a protracted depression or in a period of stagnation in which business cycle recoveries were disappointing, failing to lift the economy to a condition of full employment or doing so only transiently.[24] Because such protracted depressions or stagnation periods have occurred only once in each of the long swings or Kuznets cycles and always at the same phase of each successive swing, their effects cannot be smoothed out or eliminated completely by moving averages with a period substantially less than that of the Kuznets cycles themselves, say, fifteen to twenty years. And since averages with such a long period would presumably smooth out the Kuznets cycles also, it is not practicable to aim at eliminating, at least by moving averages, the extraordinary depressions or stagnations which have marked the boundaries between successive long swings. Not only is it impracticable to smooth away these episodes fully, it would be wrong to do so because, as the argument below suggests, the occurrence of protracted periods of abnormally high rates of unemployment and underemployment of labor and capital probably forms an essential part of the Kuznets-cycle mechanism.[25]

That the behavior of important economic indicators which display Kuznets cycles still reflect the effects of a long swing in unemployment and, presumably, underemployment is attested by evidence both direct and indirect. The direct evidence consists of the time-patterns formed by annual estimates of the percentage of the labor force unemployed, after smoothing to eliminate ordinary business cycles. For the limited time such data are available, they give a clear picture of a Kuznets cycle in unemployment rates for non-farm workers. Thus, the percent of the non-farm employees out of work stands at around 12 percent in the mid-1890's. From this high level, the percentage falls to around five percent in the middle of the next decade, then rises again to approximately 10 percent in the period 1907–1915. By the early 1920's, the rate is down again to about 6 percent. The curves then display the huge rise of unemployment associated with the Great Depression. In the smoothed data, the peak level for this last swing is reached in the mid-1930's, and, thereafter, unemployment rates fall until the late 1940's with some indications of a very mild rise since that time.[26]

In addition to these more or less direct evidences of Kuznets cycles in utilization rates, we must interpret the behavior of the series representing the growth of output, input, and output per unit of input, the turning points of whose Kuznets cycles are shown in Table 8.1. Note, first, that in every case in a line going back to the early part of the 19th century, the trough in output growth occurred during a period of sustained depression or stagnation. We note, secondly, that in most cases, the peak in output growth occurred within a few years after the beginning of sustained recovery from depression or stagnation. The three exceptional cases, when the peak in output growth did not occur until some years after the beginning of recovery, fell in 1834, when the basis for an estimate of output growth is most unreliable, in 1864, when the economy operated under the strain of war production and disturbance, and in 1889, during a movement whose qualifications for inclusion in a list of Kuznets cycles is doubtful. In five other cases, the peak in output growth appears to have fallen no more than three years after the beginning of sustained recovery.[27] In one other case, 1938–39, the peak growth rate comes 6 or 7 years after the beginning of sustained recovery, dating the latter from 1933. There can be no doubt, however, that in this case, the peak in the rate of growth of output was associated with the reemployment of idle resources, which, as I shall now argue, is the moral of these figures.

I have already argued that the substantial lead of the turning points in output growth relative to those in additions to labor force and capital stock implies that the former must be associated with turning points in growth of output per unit of available resources. Now, the fact that the turning points in output growth occur in association with sustained depressions and stagnations and with recovery therefrom strongly suggests that the turning points in growth of output per resource unit are to be associated with turning points in the rate of change of resource utilization.

This interpretation is supported by consideration of the behavior of Kuznets cycles in three comparable series provided by Fabricant on the basis of Kendrick's estimates.[28] The series refer to gross physical output, to the associated total input of labor and capital and to output per unit of total input. To interpret these series, we should remember that the input series does not represent the number of intensity units utilized. It makes no allowance for changes in the utilization rate of plant and equipment. Moreover, although the input of labor is measured in manhours, it is doubtful whether the hours estimates Kendrick had to use fluctuate as widely as hours actually do. Finally, the input estimates make no allowance for changes in the flow of work per hour to either production workers or salaried employees, many of whom obviously are kept on the job through both slack and busy periods. It follows that output per unit of measured input can vary either because of changes in output per intensity unit or because of changes in the intensity of utilization.

Allowing for some differences in amplitude (input and output per unit of input fluctuate less widely than their product, gross physical output), the Kuznets cycles in the growth of all three series resemble one another closely, and all three resemble closely the Kuznets cycles in gross national product.[29] The only serious divergence occurred during World War I, when input growth slowed down, but output per unit of input accelerated while output growth itself followed an intermediate course. For the time the series are available, however, (since 1890) the turning points in the rates of growth of the three series bear the same relation to the development of, or recovery from, protracted depression or stagnation as those in the rate of growth of total output for a longer period. This association suggests that turning points of Kuznets cycles in input growth are connected with fluctuations in the growth or decline of unemployment. We may surely assume, further, that the intensity of utilization of capital and employed labor will move inversely with unemployment. Recalling now that the movements of output per unit of measured input will reflect the effects of variations in the utilization rate for employed resources, it is plausible to think that the conjunction of the turns of Kuznets cycles in output per unit of input with those in input itself and of both series with the onset of depression and recovery is due to changes in rates of utilization.

We turn now to several other features of the Kuznets swings which seem to be most easily explained if we may assume that there is a Kuznets swing in the level of unemployment. The first is the Kuznets swing in immigration. Kuznets and Rubin have shown that the waves in aggregate immigration were formed from generally similar waves of migration from many different countries of origin. The considerable degree of international diffusion in immigration waves points clearly to some variation in conditions in the United States as the common cause influencing movements from different countries.[30] Granted this inference, it seems plausible to point to the ease or difficulty of finding employment as the specific common cause directly responsible.

This hypothesis is quite consistent with Jerome's well-known observation of a correlation between migration and business cycles.[31] It is also consistent with the relation between the Kuznets swings in the volume of immigration and long swings in unemployment rates for the period since 1890 when estimates of unemployment begin.[32] Finally, the troughs and peaks in the Kuznets swings in immigration are consistent in their timing with the occurrence of the periods of protracted depression or stagnation which punctuated U.S. development. The troughs of the Kuznets swings in immigration regularly occurred toward the end of periods of depression or stagnation, while the peaks in immigration occurred toward the close of periods of sustained growth. From all this, I infer that the very large Kuznets waves in the level of immigration are evidence supporting the belief that there were Kuznets waves in the rate of unemployment.

If this be accepted, then one may add, parenthetically, that a considerable portion of this responsibility for the pre-World War I swings in the growth of the labor force and of population are also to be attributed to the occurrence of protracted periods of unemployment and of recovery therefrom. For a large part of these fluctuations consisted precisely in fluctuations in the volume of immigrants. One should also note that immigration is not the only demographic variable that displays Kuznets swings. They are to be found in marriage and birth rates, in rates of household formation and in the labor-force participation rates of various native-born groups. Fragmentary data suggest that at least a partial explanation of these waves may also be found in the postulated long swing in unemployment rates.[33]

Finally, we must consider the fact that, among the several elements of the general Kuznets swing is a long wave in capital formation. This wave derives in part, though not entirely, from the well-known long cycles in railroad construction, in residential building, and in construction of associated community facilities and consequently is associated with the wave in population growth and household formations just noticed. The wave in total capital formation manifestly has implications for the hypothesis that the general Kuznets swing involves a fluctuation in effective demand. In some cases, the down phase of these waves has consisted only in a marked retardation – lasting longer than an ordinary business cycle – in the rate of growth of capital expenditures. In other cases, there is evidence of a protracted period of at least mild decline between one business-cycle period and another.[34] In either event, we should expect such behavior to be accompanied by abnormally high unemployment rates for periods longer than ordinary business cycles. And if as they do, these protracted periods of slow growth or decline in capital expenditures coincide with periods which have, on other grounds, been identified as periods of depression or stagnation, we may take the observation of a Kuznets cycle in total investment as another piece of indirect evidence that the general Kuznets wave has been characterized by a fluctuation in effective demand which expresses itself in a swing in the rate of unemployment of labor and in the utilization of resources generally.

The evidence and its implications run to the conclusion that general Kuznets swings have regularly involved alternations in effective demand and in the rate of resource utilization. Before going on, however, a short digression may be desirable to deal with a scruple, or qualm, which readers may harbor. If our own observations of the long swings still manifest fluctuations in the intensity of resource utilization, does this not mean simply that we have not "smoothed-out" business cycles successfully, so that to isolate long swings in economic growth from business cycles, we ought to employ a more radical smoothing technique? This question may occur to readers with especial force in connection with the technique which lies back of Table 8.1, a technique designed to smooth out "ordinary" business cycles (that is, those identified by the National Bureau of Economic Research), but which does not pretend to smooth out completely the alleged "major" or "Juglar" cycles.

To this question, there are two answers. First, no reasonable smoothing technique which depends essentially on some variant of the moving average device will eliminate employment fluctuations or their effects. For example, the use of ten-year moving averages and decade rates of growth leaves unchanged the observations and arguments made above in every essential point except one. Specifically a fluctuation of significant size still appears in a ten-year moving average of unemployment rates running back to the 1890's. Moreover, we may take it as probable that such a moving average of unemployment rates would stand at lower levels in the mid-eighties than in the mid-nineties and at higher levels in the mid-seventies than in the mid-eighties. Further, the timing of peaks and troughs in the decade rates of growth of output, input and productivity bear the same relation to one another and to the onset and end of periods of depression or stagnation as do the turning points revealed by the less radical smoothing technique that underlies Table 8.1.[35] Troughs in the decade rates of growth of these series occur in the early part of depression periods or in years just preceding depression, which indicates that they rest on a comparison between years when employment rates were high with years when they were low. Peaks in years marking recovery from protracted depression or recovery suggest that they rest on a comparison between years with opposite characteristics. A fluctuation in unemployment, finally, still remains the most plausible explanation for the long waves in immigration.

The one important difference which the use of ten-year moving averages makes in our picture of Kuznets swings is that there is no longer a clear and pronounced long swing in gross capital formation in the period between 1870 and 1914. One may still find a fluctuation in the rate of growth of investment, but it is less pronounced than that revealed by the less radical smoothing, the results of which were cited in footnote 34. I interpret this difference to be an example of the vagaries of moving averages. The behavior of the crude data, of business cycle averages, and of measures taken from one business-cycle peak to the next seem to me to be persuasive evidence of long periods when gross capital formation alternately grew at a rapid rate and then grew at a very low rate or actually declined.

If decade averages and rates of growth will not eliminate completely the effects of fluctuation in unemployment, it is plausible to think that no reasonable smoothing technique would do so. Moving averages of longer period would presumably remove a portion, perhaps a considerable portion, of the phenomenon we want to observe, particularly, if some examples of long swings are shorter than the 17 or 18 years which represented their average duration in the past. Given all the data and experience needed, it would, ideally, be possible to eliminate the effects of unemployment by direct measurement. A fully adequate study of Kuznets cycles would certainly employ such measures. But they could only be a part of the investigation since the full story of long swings appears to include a fluctuation in employment and utilization rates as both the effect and the cause of other prominent features of the general Kuznets cycles. As pointed out, a long swing in unemployment is at least a likely accompaniment of a pronounced wave in the rate of growth – still more in that of the level – of gross capital formation. It is the most plausible explanation of the observed long waves in the level of immigration, and it contributes to an explanation of waves in certain other demographic variables and of those in still other features of long swings not noticed in this paper.

The stress we place on the existence of a wave in unemployment and utilization rates as an integral feature of the general Kuznets cycle should not, of course, cause us to lose sight of the fact that such waves involve much more than an alternation in the intensity of resource use. They also involve waves in the growth of the supply of resources. And while the argument above suggests that the swings in the growth rate of resource supply stem at least in part from the occurrence of protracted periods of unemployment and partial failure of effective demand, it remains true that the growth of resources was alternately rapid and slow. In addition, there may have been waves in the growth of "true," as distinct from measured, productivity. While it seems clear that the waves in measured productivity growth take their form in part from a fluctuation in utilization ratios, it is an open question whether there may not have been underlying waves in the growth of output per intensity unit of input, that is, in true productivity. Since capital equipment is the material embodiment of technique, we expect each year's gross addition to the stock of capital to carry with it an advance in technology. It follows, then, that the rate of growth of true productivity depends in part on the ratio of gross capital formation to the existing stock of capital. Waves in gross capital formation should, then, tend to produce waves in true productivity growth. This is an expectation qualified by the fact that the Kuznets waves in the level of gross capital formation, as distinct from rate of change, were usually very mild. It is an expectation which, however, is to some degree heightened by Kuznets' observation[36] that, at least before World War I, the wave in total gross capital formation was the net result of two more pronounced, but partly offsetting, waves in what he calls "population-sensitive" capital formation (railroad investment plus urban residential building) and "other" capital formation. Kuznets argues, plausibly, that since the contribution of residential building to productivity growth is dubious and that of railroad building long-deferred, it is the wave in the residual which counts for productivity change in the context of the long swings. As stated, this is a more pronounced wave than that in total gross capital formation.

III

The general view of the long swings to which this argument leads is that they have a two-sided character. They involve first, an ebb and flow in the pace of economic growth in the basic sense that the development of our capacity to produce, of our supplies of labor and capital and, perhaps, of their productivity at optimum rates of utilization, has alternately proceeded faster and slower in waves that, in the past, have been longer than ordinary business cycles. Secondly, they involve swings in the intensity of resource use in which periods of relatively high unemployment, or low intensity of use, alternate with periods in which the labor market is tighter and capital is used more intensively. The two sides of the phenomenon interact and each stands in relation to the other both as cause and effect.

Granted the validity of this view, I should like to take a few pages simply to notice the variety of these interactions as they appear in the context of the long swings experienced in the United States. These examples of interaction between resource growth and intensity of resource use are also present in the more common business-cycle process, and some attention has been given to them in that connection. But chiefly because of the shorter duration of such movements, they are probably of lesser importance in business cycles. They appear in their full stature only in the longer movements. From the fact that there are interactions, we may anticipate that disturbances or movements in either direction will, for a time, gain strength cumulatively, while the important and moot question whether the Kuznets cycles are in any significant sense self-generating may, of course, also turn on the nature of the interactions.

A. Interactions via the relation between capital stock and income flow

For a number of reasons, the simpler capital-stock adjustment models with their implied requirements for balanced growth take on heightened interest when considered in the context of long swings rather than in that of shorter business cycles. First, insofar as these models treat investment as dependent in part on current or past changes in the demand for finished goods, there has always been justifiable skepticism about their applicability to durable equipment and structures, so long as the theory was supposed to illuminate investment movements in short cycles. Since investment in durables is made for long periods of time, it is doubtful whether it would respond readily to income change over short periods. This difficulty disappears, however, when we consider expansions lasting 8 to 12 years or more.

In the same way, we are unlikely to explain much of the fluctuations of investment in durables during short business cycles by appealing to fluctuations in the growth of capital stock. A. F. Burns has pointed out that in such cycles, there is little regularity in the relation between the growth of installed capital stock and business activity.[37] Because the lag between investment expenditure and the installation of equipment and structures is of the same order of magnitude as a business-cycle phase, because the lag may vary depending on the mix of investment and because the heights of peaks and troughs in investment vary widely, the curve of capital stock during business cycles when measured in physical units appears to follow a rising trend with random variations. The duration of the phases of long swings, however, overshadows the expenditure-delivery lag, and there is less reason to doubt that if there is a long swing in the level or rate of growth of capital formation, there will be an associated long swing in the rate of growth of capital stock or in the rate of change in such growth. In business cycles, the observed fluctuation in the ratio of capital stock to income would appear to arise systematically from the fluctuation in income. In long swings, however, it presumably arises both from income and capital stock movements.

Finally, the capital stock adjustment models stress the requirement that income and, therefore, investment, should grow at some critical rate in order to avoid the accumulation of excess capacity. So far as concerns fixed capital, however, it is no more than an implication of the argument above that the consequence of failure to meet this requirement is unlikely to be an important feature of short cycles. Given the lag between investment and installation, business cycle expansions reach peaks before excess capacity could seriously cumulate as a result of the investments made during the same cyclical phase. By contrast, the duration of long-swing expansions makes such cumulation, with its implications for protracted depression or stagnation, at least an interesting possibility.

B. Interactions through growth of population and labor force

Kuznets has taught us that long swings in the rate of economic growth are associated with long swings in additions to the population.[38] Before World War I, these population waves reflected principally the large waves in immigration. Since then, they have turned far more on a fluctuation in marriage and birth rates. As pointed out above, the most plausible explanation of these waves, apart from the effects of wars, is that they were responses to the occurrences of protracted periods of abnormally high unemployment and to the recovery from such periods. The long waves in population growth in turn operated through several mechanisms to aggravate and prolong periods of depression or stagnation and the periods of recovery and growth that followed.

In the first place, the long waves in population growth acted on the demand for residential housing and, presumably on that for related commercial, public utility and community facilities. The mechanism is not altogether simple because there is not a rigid proportional relation between population growth and household formation. The latter depends also on age composition and on changes in headship rates in each age group. Until the 1930's, however, headship rates remained relatively steady. The fluctuations in household formation were determined chiefly by the waves of immigration which accounted for most of the swings in population growth and at the same time so altered age composition as to cause household formation to increase and decline with the level of immigration.[39]

It is chiefly, though not entirely, to this fact that the well-known long waves in the national aggregate of urban residential building are to be attributed. We may, indeed, explain long cycles in local building activity on the basis of a cobweb process arising from long lags of building supply to changes in demand. In the absence of some common cause acting on all urban communities at about the same time, however, it is hardly likely that the local waves so engendered would run together to form national waves. Such a common cause is the long wave in population growth, which is widely diffused geographically because of its dependence on the state of the national labor market. In addition to unifying the local building waves, moreover, the swing in population growth must have acted to prolong them. A wave in building activity, once set in motion, must have tended to keep rising not only because of the lagged response of housing supply to the initial excess in demand, but also because of the further increase in demand caused by population growth so long as that kept rising.

The demographic response to change in the level of unemployment acts on the volume of capital formation not only through an associated wave in household formation, but also through an associated swing in labor force growth. As Easterlin has shown (*op. cit.*, note 33 in this chapter), swings in labor force growth are connected with the state of the labor market not only through the response of immigration, but also through changes in the participation rates of marginal groups (women, racial minorities and older workers), who enter or withdraw from the labor force in response to employment opportunities. An upswing in growth of capital formation which led to a tighter labor market was, therefore, strengthened and prolonged by the labor-force response to rising employment opportunities. For the rise in labor-force growth must have helped maintain the marginal productivity of capital and, therefore, the marginal efficiency of investment, in the face of an upsurge of investment.

C. Interactions through change in the composition of capital formation

Having divided total gross capital formation into "population-sensitive" (railroad capital expenditures plus residential building) and "other" investment, Kuznets[40] found in the period between the Civil War and World War I, that these two categories of investment tended to move inversely to one another, at least with respect to their rates of change, sometimes with respect to their levels. The result was a regular wave in the share of each category in total capital formation.

The observed alternation in the shares of "population-sensitive" and "other" investment is presumably not a perfectly satisfactory characterization of the fluctuations in the composition of capital formation since the "other" category is a heterogeneous grouping whose components did not always behave uniformly. For this reason alone, it is impossible to account briefly for the causes of the swing in the composition of investment. Part of the explanation, however, is probably to be traced to the wave in the level of unemployment and capacity utilization. If, as we suspect, the onset of a tight labor market and of near-capacity utilization of plant helps account for retardation in the growth of output, it can also help explain retardation in the growth, perhaps even a decline of those parts of "other" gross capital formation the demand for which is linked to output growth – for example, inventory investment and some branches of producer durables and non-residential construction. By contrast, a tight labor market stimulates immigration and otherwise encourages household formation and, therefore, the demand for residential building. To say this much is not to explain the observed shift in the composition of investment satisfactorily, but it is, perhaps, enough to identify another important connection between the intensity of utilization and the character of economic growth.

Granted that there was a characteristic change in the composition of capital formation of the general nature described by Kuznets, we may look for its significance in at least two directions. In the first place, it presumably influences the growth of productivity in the fashion alluded to above. Kuznets, indeed, suggests that the shift in the composition of capital formation may be the chief reason for the observed wave in productivity growth.[41]

The shift in the composition of investment is also connected with the question of financial ease or stringency. The argument is, briefly, as follows. Each category of real investment generates its own characteristic types of financial assets. These differ from one another in liquidity, risk, maturity, and other qualities which reflect the type of issuer and the kind of liabilities he feels able to undertake, given the nature of his business and the durability and liquidity of the real assets in which he is sinking his capital. The terms on which business can obtain finance, therefore, depend in part on how readily the public is willing to change the composition of the financial assets they absorb along with the change in the composition of real investment, or on the willingness and ability of intermediate financial institutions to absorb the changing mix of securities offered by the "real" investors and to issue to the public a more attractive mix. Unpublished historical analyses by John Gurley and Edward S. Shaw indicate that at least on some occasions before World War I, the shift of real investment demand to Kuznets' "population-sensitive" types generated a mix of financial assets which did not easily satisfy the public's desire for liquidity. The result was a hardening of the financial markets which helped to check the growth of total investment and to bring on a period of underemployment.

The swing in the composition of investment has still another special aspect which I note below.

D. Interactions via the foreign balance, international capital movements, and the supply of money[42]

From the early part of the 19th century until World War I, each general Kuznets cycle was accompanied by an inverse movement in the current balance of payments. This, in turn, reflected chiefly, but not exclusively, a positive wave in merchandise imports. In the early part of this era, the swing in the balance of payments alternately aggravated and then alleviated a chronically negative current balance. In later decades, the level of the balance gradually rose, so that the wave produced an alternation between times when the balance was positive and those when it was negative.

Given a specie standard, such as obtained during most of the era, the prolongation of a period of rapid growth manifestly depended then on the country's ability to finance a rising payments deficit either by gold shipments or capital imports. Except in the unusual circumstances of the years following the California discoveries, however, continued gold shipments in the size of the deficits would have brought rapid growth to a halt through monetary stringency and associated unemployment. Protracted periods of rapid development, therefore, implied rising capital imports such as did in fact accompany the rising phases of the Kuznets cycles. Finally, since these phases lasted for a number of years, sale of long-term securities was required and not merely the accumulation by foreigners of short-term claims. In short, foreigners, more particularly British investors, had to be offered securities they were willing to hold for some time. The question, therefore, is, what kinds of securities could foreigners be induced to accept as each upsurge of development generated its payments deficit. In the 19th and early 20th centuries the answer is clear. Only the securities of the railroads and those of the states (which were in turn issued in good part to finance railroad and canal building) were available. Throughout the century, these, in fact, constituted the bulk of the securities purchased by foreigners. The finance of the payments deficit, and, to that extent, the prolongation of general development, therefore, depended on recurrent upsurges of transport development.[43] It was, therefore, associated with the shift in the composition of capital formation to which Kuznets points.

Transport development, therefore, appears to have played three roles in the drama of United States development. First, the expansion of transport facilities enlarged our productive capacity. Secondly, the expenditures made in the course of railroad development, together with associated expenditures for farm and urban building, sustained the growth of demand during the upswings of Kuznets cycles. When the pace of railroad development declined, this contributed to retardation in the growth of total investment and so to the onset of protracted periods of unemployment and slow growth. Finally, the upsurges of transport development generated a flow of securities abroad which offset the accompanying rise in our payments deficit. When, however, the prospects for railroad profits became dimmer, this not only discouraged capital expenditures, it made for balance of payments difficulties. Manifestly, the competing pressures for finance of British home investment and of demands in other areas of the world played their parts in determining whether the United States could continue to finance a large deficit.

The mechanism by which the Kuznets swings in our payments deficit, together with those in the railroad industry, influenced our capacity to sustain rapid growth cannot be presented fully here. It may be interesting to point out, however, that waves in the rate of growth of the money supply and in the rate of change of prices accompanied the general Kuznets cycle, that during most of the period before 1914, the growth of the money supply depended on the expansion of the domestic stock of specie, and that changes in that stock depended on the relation between the level of our current balance of international payments and that of capital imports.[44] In the context of nineteenth century institutions, therefore, the swings in the profits prospects and in the rate of expansion of the transport system played a peculiarly important part in determining whether our international accounts and our monetary position would favor slow or rapid growth.

IV

The last two sections have argued and illustrated the thesis that the long swings were the outcome of interactions between the pace at which resources were developed, the generation of effective demand, and the intensity of resource use. If we accept this view, then one may contend that, at least for the United States and possibly also for other countries, they are the most useful historical experiences available in terms of which the problems of maintaining balanced growth and of the relations between growth and business cycles may be studied realistically. While the standard business cycles involve some of the interesting interchanges between resource growth and effective demand, particularly as regards inventories, such cycles run their course in too short a time to display the full range of response. The various interactions sketched in Section III manifestly do not constitute a model which displays the essentials of these problems in a comprehensive and systematic way. They do, however, suggest the range of interrelations which such a model would have to encompass. It would necessarily include not only the direct relations between capital stock and income flow normally built into such models but also the repercussions via growth of population and labor force, the composition of capital formation, the terms of finance, the balance of international payments, and the supply of, and demand for, money.

The various interactions sketched above are also relevant to a question which must lie at the heart of all work on long swings, the question whether the observed long swings are to be regarded as systematic self-generating movements or as the outcome of episodic shocks. Again, the considerations set forth above do not and cannot settle the question. They do, however, suggest that there are a variety of cumulative responses set off by recovery from a protracted depression and that these responses are of a type that do not exhaust themselves in a single standard business-cycle expansion. As a result, we may well consider that there were systematic reasons for the fact that the periods of protracted depression or stagnation which punctuate the successive Kuznets cycles do not follow one another as frequently as do minor recessions.[45]

In addition, there is reason to think that some of the responses to recovery from protracted depression are of a type likely to push activity in some directions to unsustainable levels or rates of growth. This is true in part because recovery goes forward at first with the help of a general inventory build-up and without the restraints imposed by capacity ceilings. As full employment and capacity are approached, however, such restraints gradually force a reduction in the pace of output growth; and this also serves to dampen the pace of inventory accumulation and perhaps that of other kinds of investment which may be tied to output growth. The same sort of difficulty will arise in part because periods of protracted depression or stagnation are years in which the fulfillment of normal aspirations or plans is blocked, plans, for example, to immigrate, to marry, to establish separate households or to undertake far-reaching industrial ventures. Recovery, when it comes, is sustained by the renewed opportunities it affords to carry out such deferred intentions. When, however, the various backlogs have been worked down, investment demand is likely to decline or to grow less rapidly. Further, the kinds of investment important in the long swings – notably construction, including railroads and public utilities construction – are notorious examples of sectors in which supply responds only slowly to change in demand and often only in large, indivisible lumps. There is, therefore, ample opportunity for investment to be overdone and for supply of capital to overshoot requirements. Finally – at least as a matter of history – our surges of growth involved deterioration in our current balance of payments, while the finance of that balance depended largely on the sale to foreigners of securities whose attractiveness rested on the profits prospects of a comparatively narrow sector of the economy, viz., railroads. As with any single sector, it is hard to imagine that those profits prospects should advance in even a roughly steady fashion.

It is, therefore, not difficult to find reasons for believing that the progress of a developing economy, particularly one in which spurts of growth have their beginnings in periods of underemployment, should develop hindrances and obstructions. We do not know, however, how powerful these checks are or what offsetting and stabilizing forces they may release. At the present time, therefore, we may be justified in contending no more than that the long swings are quasi-self generating, in the limited, but important sense that:

1. They involve certain forces which operate cumulatively for a time to strengthen a surge of development following a protracted period of relatively high unemployment and so to prevent the early recurrence of another such period;
2. They generate checks and obstacles which, after a time, generally longer than a single business cycle, render the economy more vulnerable to another period of depression or stagnation.

To say this much is, of course, not to say that episodic factors were not important, nor is it to say that the cumulative and self-reversing tendencies, such as they are, have remained generally constant. Episodic factors were clearly important in determining the course of the successive surges of development. Financial panics have aggravated depressions. Accumulations of deferred demands have arisen during wars as well as depressions. Monetary policy and gold discoveries as well as capital imports and the current balance of payments have influenced the supply of money. Capital imports have been affected by events in Europe as well as by profits prospects in this country. However important their systematic mechanism, the course of Kuznets cycles in the United States has clearly been disturbed by extraneous influences to a very considerable degree.

Moreover, the systematic mechanism has clearly changed during the last century and a quarter in which the swings can be observed. The character of capital formation has changed from investment chiefly designed to extend the settled and cultivated area of the country to investment designed chiefly to extend capacity to provide manufactured goods and services. The speed with which capacity responds to demand must have altered a great deal in consequence. Residential construction has declined in importance. Decision-making units, which were chiefly farm households 125 years ago, are now giant corporations. Immigration is now a minor factor in the growth of population and labor force, but this change has apparently been accompanied by an increased sensitivity of our native-born elements to influences affecting internal migration, marriage, household formation and labor-force participation. The country now stands on a capital-exporting rather than a capital-importing basis, and the supply of money is now at least partially managed. In a variety of ways the sensitivity of income to declines in investment has been dulled.

These changes and many others will, no doubt, have altered the relations between economic development and intensity of resource use. If, however, this problem, which is the same problem as that of maintaining balance between capacity and effective demand, is to be studied empirically over a reasonably long stretch of history, these difficulties must be accepted. The Kuznets long swings appear to have been the phenomena in terms of which this problem manifested itself in the USA and, indeed, in several other countries in the past. Historical and analytical studies of these swings in a number of countries should, therefore, enrich and test the models designed to help us understand the problem of maintaining balance in growth as this old problem is faced both by advanced and backward countries in a modern setting.

Notes

1. For critical appraisal of Kondratieff cycles, see G. Garvy, "Kondratieff's Theory of Long Cycles," *Review of Economic Statistics*, XXV, No. 4 (November, 1943), 203–20; also A. F. Burns and W. C. Mitchell, *Measuring Business Cycles* (New York, 1946), Ch. 11. On the Juglar movements, see *ibid.*, Ch. 11, and R. C. O. Matthews, *The Business Cycle* (Chicago, 1959), Ch. 12. Representative literature on the intermediate wave is cited below.

2. Readers will, I hope, understand that what I propose is in the nature of a preliminary rather than a definitive discussion.

3. W. A. Lewis and P. J. O'Leary, "Secular Swings in Production and Trade, 1870–1913," *Manchester School of Economic and Social Studies*, XIII, No. 2 (May, 1955), 113–52.

4. Simon Kuznets, *Secular Movements in Production and Prices* (New York, 1930), Ch. III–VI.

5. Kuznets was not the first to publish empirical evidence suggesting the existence of general long swings of 15–25 years duration. Three years before Kuznets' book appeared, C. A. R. Wardwell announced the discovery of fluctuations in economic time series with a duration longer than business cycles but definitely shorter than the alleged Kondratieff cycles. Apparently Kuznets' work was already fairly far advanced when Wardwell published. Indeed, Wardwell and Kuznets studied each others' unfinished

manuscripts. Both were aware of having turned up evidence of the same new type of fluctuation, and Wardwell, though taking cognizance of Kuznets' work then in progress, did not claim priority on account of his earlier publication (C. A. R. Wardwell, *An Investigation of Economic Data for Major Cycles* [Philadelphia, 1927], pp. 14–15). Wardwell's evidence was less elaborate than Kuznets' in that it included fewer time series, a much shorter time period and fewer countries. In at least one respect, however, Wardwell went further than Kuznets. He asserted that the major peaks and troughs of his American series appeared in well-defined clusters suggesting that long swings were characteristics of the economy at large as well as of individual activities.

6. A. F. Burns, *Production Trends in the United States Since 1870* (New York, 1934), Ch. V. Burns' procedures were somewhat more complicated than this statement suggests. Interested readers should consult Burns' book for details of his methods and for the size and composition of his sample of production.

7. *Ibid.*, pp. 179–180.

8. *Ibid.*, pp. 174–5.

9. Simon Kuznets, "Long Term Changes in National Income of the United States since 1870," in Simon Kuznets, Ed., *Income and Wealth, Series II* (Cambridge, 1952), Tables 3 and 4; also Chapter 3 of this volume, Figure 3.1, pp. 138–9. There are differences in the dates of the peaks and troughs determined by each writer and even an "extra" cycle in Burns' waves, but there is little doubt that these differences can be traced to differences in the data they used and the manner in which they treated them.

10. See W.A. Lewis and P. J. O'Leary, *op. cit.*; also Simon Kuznets, "Quantitative Aspects of the Economic Growth of Nations, I, Levels and Variability of Rates and Growth," *Economic Development and Cultural Change*, V, No. 1 (October, 1956).

11. See W. Isard, "A Neglected Cycle: The Transport-Building Cycle," *Review of Economic Statistics*, XXIV, No. 4 (November, 1942), 149–58. Burns' measures (in *op. cit.*) seem to suggest that the trend cycles of building activity did not have a regular connection with his more general trend cycle in output. The tables in Kuznets' forthcoming book (Simon Kuznets, *Capital in the American Economy: Its Formation and Financing*, see Chapter 3, note 2) carry the same suggestion. The irregularity, however, is only apparent: it stems in part from the fact that the rate of change of building activity from the Civil War to World War I tended to lag behind that of output at large in the course of Kuznets cycles and in part from the fact that, in the special circumstances of World War I, the pace of total output growth accelerated while building activity was understandably depressed.

12. Simon Kuznets, "Long Swings in the Growth of Population and in Related Economic Variables," *Proceedings of the American Philosophical Society*, CII, No. 1 (February, 1958), 25–52.

13. B. Thomas, *Migration and Economic Growth* (Cambridge, 1954); also A. Cairncross, *Home and Foreign Investment, 1870–1914* (Cambridge, 1953).

14. Cairncross, Thomas, and others have also shown that Kuznets cycles in British foreign investment were accompanied by inverse, but not completely synchronous, waves in British home investment. The partially compensating character of these two investment waves apparently masked the Kuznets cycle in over-all British activity, while their *incomplete* compensation caused total investment to move in a wave with a period of about ten years. It appears, therefore, that while Juglar cycles dominate U. K. statistics on a superficial view, the underlying movements are connected with Kuznets cycles. Cf. Matthews, *op. cit.*

15. See Jeffery G. Williamson, *American Growth and the Balance of Payments* (Chapel Hill, University of North Carolina Press, 1964).

16. Moses Abramovitz, Statement in United States Congress, Joint Economic Committee, *Employment, Growth and Price Levels, Hearings* (86th Congress, 1st Session), Part II (Washington, 1959), 411–66. (This paper will be cited hereinafter as "Joint Economic Committee Statement.")

17. In making this statement about duration, I assume that it is appropriate to neglect two short and mild movements which appear in some indicators of activity – one, running from roughly 1914–21, associated with World War I, and one in the middle eighties associated with a serious decline in railroad construction and the accompanying business contraction in 1882–85. But see also Table 8.1 and accompanying text.

18. See my Joint Economic Committee Statement, Tables 9 and 11.

19. The rates of change were calculated between average standings for non-overlapping cycle periods and then intermingled to form a series of rates of change during over-lapping inter-cycle intervals.

20. The factual material underlying the selection is described in my Joint Economic Committee Statement, especially Table 10 and its notes and pp. 427–8.

21. The acceleration of 1886–1890 represents a recovery from a very low rate of growth associated with the unusually long and somewhat severe contraction of 1882–85 in which railroad building declined sharply while urban residential construction continued to rise. This was the only notable instance in which these two great sectors of construction parted company for very long during the nearly three-quarters of a century in which railroad building was important.

22. Readers may be puzzled by at least some of the dates assigned to peaks and troughs in output growth. They may, for example, resist the suggestion that the rate of growth in output was at a low point in 1930–31 (1930.25) and at a high point in 1938–39 (1938.5). They should, however, remember two points. First, the dates are themselves merely the midpoints of the interval between the midpoints of two business-cycle periods and are a short-hand device to refer to the interval between the two periods. To say that the rate of growth was at a trough at 1930.25 is a short-hand device for saying that the output change between the level reached during the business-cycle period 1926–29 and that reached during the period 1929–37 was lower than that in the intervals between the two preceding and following business-cycle periods. Similarly, the high rate of output growth at 1938.5 refers to the change between the output level of the period 1932–38 and that of the period 1938–45. Secondly, while the fluctuations in rates of growth during Kuznets cycles may be supposed to be free of the influence of business cycles of ordinary duration and amplitude, they do reflect changes in the severity of business cycles, as the argument in the text below suggests at greater length.

23. It is not, however, a very satisfactory measure since the underlying annual data of labor force are based in part on interpolations of participation rates for which there was evidence only at 10-year intervals.

24. Abramovitz, Joint Economic Committee Statement, pp. 427–8. Cf. the somewhat similar statement of Burns, *op. cit.*, p. 251: "We may therefore conclude from our analysis of American experience since 1870: first, that periods of sharp advance in the trend of general production, which are characterized invariably by considerable divergence in production trends, have been followed invariably by severe depressions; second, that most of the business depressions of marked severity have been preceded by a sharp advance in the trend of general production and considerable divergence in the trends of individual industries."

The present writer's statement is based upon experience running back to 1816 while Burns' is based on experience since the 1870's. The difference in the form of the statements, however, is due chiefly to the difference in the methods by which Burns and the present writer treated their data to smooth out business cycles – Burns by computing

decade rates of growth for decades displaced five years, the present writer by computing rates of growth between the average standings of series during periods bounded by
business-cycle turning points, both peak-to-peak and trough-to-trough. At the time of
writing, Burns considered his trend-cycles to be substantially free of changes in rates of
unemployment and thought of the observed serious depressions as phenomena substantially separate from his measures of cycles in "secular rates of growth." He subsequently altered his view.

25. This view seems to be accepted also by Lewis and O'Leary, *op. cit.* Noting that
the high phase of Kuznets cycles (as they measure them, in trend-adjusted but otherwise unsmoothed, form) lasted longer than the low phase, they write: "The fact that
prosperity outlasts depression is not without significance. One may be tempted to deny
that there is fundamentally a Kuznets cycle, and may prefer to say that all that happens
is that once every twenty years one of the Juglar depressions gets out of hand, and lasts
six to eight years, instead of lasting one or two years only. Even such regularity as this,
however, deserves the name of cycle: there is no reason why the number of years of
prosperity and of depression in a cycle should be equal to one another."

26. The estimates in question are those presented by Stanley Lebergott, "Annual
Estimates of Unemployment in the United States, 1900–1954," in *The Measurement and
Behavior of Unemployment* (A Conference of the Universities – National Bureau of Economic Research) (Princeton, 1957), p. 215, from 1900 on, pieced out by figures collected
by Kuznets for the 1890's, and published in *Capital in the American Economy*, Chart VII-8.
Essentially the same results, aside from some differences in the timing of peaks and
troughs, are obtained whether the annual data are smoothed by a ten-year moving
average or by averages for successive periods bounded by the peaks and troughs of the
National Bureau chronology of business-cycle turning points.

27. This statement is, of course, subject to the inaccuracy unavoidable when crude
smoothing procedures have been applied to data.

28. Solomon Fabricant, *Basic Facts on Productivity Change* (National Bureau of Economic Research, Occasional Paper 63) (New York, 1959), Table A.

29. See my Joint Economic Committee Statement, Chart 7.

30. Cf. Simon Kuznets and Ernest Rubin, *Immigration and the Foreign Born* (National
Bureau of Economic Research, Occasional Paper No. 46) (New York, 1954); also Richard
A. Easterlin, "Influences in European Overseas Emigration Before World War I," *Eco-
nomic Development and Cultural Change*, IX, No. 3 (April, 1961), 331–51.

31. See Harry Jerome, *Migration and Business Cycles* (New York, 1926). A high inverse
correlation between migration and unemployment was also found by Mr. Belton
Fleisher in his still unpublished study of Puerto Rican migration to the United States
since World War II. I am grateful to Mr. Fleisher for making his early results available to
me.

32. The worth of this evidence is, of course, qualified by the fact that unemployment
figures are not very dependable before quite recent years.

33. Space does not permit review of the evidence here, but see R. A. Easterlin,
Population, Labor Force and Economic Growth: The American Experience (National Bureau of
Economic Research, 1968).

34. By way of support for this assertion, I cite the following figures calculated from
Kuznets' estimates of gross capital formation.

A. Rates of growth between averages of annual data in successive business-cycle
periods:
(Dates refer to midpoints of intervals between the midpoints of successive non-
overlapping business-cycles measured alternately from trough to-trough and peak-to-
peak.)

	Percent		Percent		Percent
1874.25	6.94	1899	5.89	1920.25	−6.21
1877.75	6.34	1900	5.53	1921.25	−1.24
1881	4.71	1903	3.16	1923	8.75
1884	3.91	1904	3.01	1924	8.10
1886.5	4.27	1906.75	1.13	1926	2.27
1888.75	6.13	1907.75	0.82	1927.5	−5.46
1889.75	11.74	1910	2.57	1930.25	−10.56
1891	6.83	1911	2.17	1932.25	−6.72
1892.25	−0.60	1913.5	2.24	1936.75	8.64
1893.75	−1.35	1914.5	3.65	1938.5	10.16
1895.25	1.87	1917.25	6.00		
1896.5	3.93	1918.25	2.00		

B. Rates of growth (exponential) between peaks of successive short cycles in gross capital formation:

	Percent				Percent	
1873–81		6.37		1906–09	−0.54	
1881–87	3.49			1909–13	3.39	
1887–90	9.07			1906–13		1.69
1890–92	10.40			1913–16	6.21	
1881–92		6.23		1916–19	2.23	
1892–95	−4.09			1913–19		4.20
1895–99	2.40			1919–23	0.91	
1892–99		−0.43		1923–26	3.76	
1899–03	6.03			1926–29	0.32	
1903–06	6.10			1919–29		1.58
1899–06		6.06		1929–37		−0.10

Both sets of calculations tell substantially the same story. They reveal the relatively high rate of growth of investment in the 1880's; the decline and slow growth rate in the middle nineties; the rapid growth of the early 1900's; the slow growth of the period between 1907 and the beginning of the war; then after the rapid rise in the war and the collapse in 1920–21, the relatively rapid rise in the early and mid-twenties and finally the collapse and recovery of the thirties. Only the figures for the 1870's seem inconsistent with the view that this decade witnessed a very serious depression. Kuznets gross national product estimates in general seem to belie this view, and they call for closer examination.

35. If one defines Kuznets swings as the fluctuation in a ten-year moving average of annual data or in decade rates of growth, it is, of course, true that the chronology of the peaks and troughs of Kuznets swings is altered. In particular, two movements displayed in Table 8.1 are eliminated, viz., the period of acceleration in the late 'eighties and early 'nineties and the period of retardation associated with the depression of 1920–21. With these movements removed, Table 8.1 would show seven instead of nine swings from peak to peak. Their average duration would be between 17 and 18 years corresponding closely to the duration of the familiar building cycles. There may be some reason to work with the more radical smoothing and the chronology it yields. But there are also losses, and one is unlikely to remain satisfied with the results obtained from any smoothing technique so crude as a moving average.

36. *Capital in the American Economy, op. cit.*

37. A. F. Burns, "Keynesian Economics Once Again," reprinted in *The Frontiers of Economic Knowledge* (Princeton, 1954), p. 234, fn. 13.

38. Kuznets, "Long Swings in the Growth of Population. . . ," *op. cit.*

39. In this connection, see a forthcoming Stanford dissertation prepared by Burnham Campbell (*The Housing Cycle and Long Swings in Residential Construction: A Statistical and Theoretical Analysis*, doctoral dissertation, Stanford University, 1961).

40. *Capital in the American Economy, op. cit.*, Ch. VII.

41. *Ibid.*

42. I base this section mainly on the results of Jeffery Williamson's research (see note 15).

43. I do not mean to say that foreigners necessarily had to buy the new issues of expanding railroads. This was doubtless the case in early decades when the float of outstanding securities was small. Later, the capital imports might be covered by sale of old securities. In either case, however, financing the deficit implied a period when prospects for railroad (or canal) profits were bright and seemed to justify expansion.

44. Domestic gold production was, of course, another important element – in some years a dominant one.

45. There are, indeed, more reasons than the processes touched on in Section III can suggest.

9

The passing of the Kuznets cycle

In America, as Evelyn Waugh tells us, and particularly in California, where I now live, *The Loved One* who has "gone to his reward" is with lavish display, with appalling sentiment and with unbelievable expense tearfully interred and "laid to rest" by his "nearest and dearest". And even in what you would regard as the civilized world, the man or woman who has "joined the majority" is decently buried by his relatives. But in the world of scholarship and science, things are different. Defunct hypotheses and theories are usually pushed into their graves by their enemies or, at best, by strangers, while their parents, guardians and friends rush about, kicking and screaming and insisting that the corpse is still very much alive, in fact never better – though perhaps he could use a few new kidneys, a heart or some other transplants. I suppose, therefore, that in coming before you today to argue that the Kuznets cycle (those 15 to 20-year growth fluctuations, roughly associated with long cycles in building), with whose care and feeding I have had something to do,[1] has passed away, I shall be thought to be acting in bad taste by not conforming to the behaviour properly expected of me. But I offer the following defence.

First, I shall not be arguing that Kuznets cycles never existed – that this generalization about the form that growth used to assume in the United States and elsewhere was misconceived. I simply contend that it is a form of growth which belonged to a particular period in history and that the economic structure and institutions which imposed that

A Special University Lecture delivered at the London School of Economics and Political Science, February 27, 1968. The lecture is printed substantially as read with the addition of footnotes supplied by the author.

Reprinted by permission from *Economica*, new series, vol. 35, no. 140 (November 1968), 349–67.

form on the growth process have evolved, or been changed, into something different. My purpose is to try to guard the integrity and usefulness of the Kuznets-cycle hypothesis for interpreting development in the United States, Canada and Western Europe from about the 1840s to 1914 by shielding it from an inappropriate confrontation with the different form which the growth process in these countries is taking, and is likely to take, in the contemporary world.

Second, I shall not be contending that we are no longer likely to experience fluctuations in growth with periods distinctly longer than common business cycles. What I do wish to argue is that the specific set of relations and response mechanisms which were characteristic of pre-1914 "long swings" in growth are unlikely to be characteristic of future long swings. These will be of a different sort and may, indeed, not have much in common with one another in, say, their durations, amplitudes or internal structure.

Thirdly, I should like to suggest that the study of Kuznets cycles, though these belong to history, has, nevertheless, taught us some things of importance about the growth of industrialized countries which should not be lost as we try to understand contemporary spurts and retardations in growth. Here I think particularly about the importance of population growth both as a source of additions to the labour supply and of demand for certain kinds of new capital goods; next, about the need to regard population change and labour force change, both in the aggregate and in their geographic distribution, not as wholly autonomous phenomena, but as at least partly responsive to economic developments themselves; finally, about the relations between spurts in output growth on the one hand and the current balance of payments and international capital flows on the other and about the way these responses can act to permit individual countries to pursue independent paths or constrain them to keep in step.

Needless to say, these are very large themes to develop in the course of a single lecture, and to make even a stab at them, I need to do two things. First, I must try to define what I regard as the essential characteristics of the Kuznets cycles of the era from roughly 1840 to 1914 and relate these characteristics to the economic structure and institutions of the time. Second, I need to show that the contemporary economy is no longer built on these lines and that contemporary growth fluctuations – whatever their superficial resemblances to older swings – are actually reflections of a different, even if related, set of stimuli and response mechanisms. To do so much, I shall have to proceed with desperate brevity. I shall have to generalize about past episodes, which certainly were not replicas of one another, to a degree which leaves me uncomfortable. I hope a large part of my argument proceeds from a familiar factual base, but not all of it does. And in the absence of a full panoply of empirical support, which I have neither the time nor means to put before you, I can only suggest that you reserve judgement until more adequate evidence can be presented. Finally, I shall not have time to make acknowledgements of intellectual debts as I go along. Let me, therefore, make a general acknowledgement now – not only to Professors Cairncross, Thomas, Kuznets and Burns to whom everybody who has worked on these matters owes so much, but also to my students, Burnham Campbell[2] and Jeffrey Williamson,[3] and to Richard Easterlin,[4] whose studies are making a fundamental contribution not only to our understanding of Kuznets cycles but to the entire subject of the interrelations of economic and demographic change.

Essentials of the Kuznets cycle in the United States, 1840–1914

What I say now is a description – what Wesley Mitchell would have called an "analytic description" – of the typical or characteristic elements of Kuznets cycles in the US between 1840 and 1914. I say nothing about the roughly inverse patterns of growth rates in Great Britain, Germany and Scandinavia, except as this inverted behaviour was of importance for the pattern of American development.

1. When series representing aggregate industrial output are smoothed to eliminate ordinary business cycles, one finds 15 to 20-year waves in the growth rates of the smoothed series. The same is true of GNP growth rates after 1880 when industrial production becomes the dominant sector. There were four such waves from 1840 to 1911; they varied from 16 to 19 years in duration.

2. These waves in growth rates are the smoothed reflection of the fact that at intervals of 15 to 20 years, the US economy suffered either a severe and protracted depression or else a period of pronounced stagnation in which business-cycle recoveries were disappointing and did not return the economy to full employment. In the intervening years, the economy experienced only mild and short recessions with expansions vigorous enough to make unemployment low at business-cycle peaks. One way to state the problem of the Kuznets cycles, therefore, is to ask why it was that America suffered unusually severe depressions, or protracted periods of milder recessions with disappointing recoveries, only at these long intervals, while in the interim employment remained at high levels subject to short mild recessions.

3. Because the Kuznets cycles were punctuated by severe depres-

sions whose reflections we see in the output growth-rate waves, those waves are best understood by dividing them into three phases:

i. *Rebound from depression.* During this phase, the growth rate of output was accelerating to a maximum. It was a relatively short phase. Measured from the trough of depression to the year when smoothed output was at a maximum, this phase consumed only three years in three of the four episodes. In a fourth when the Civil War intervened, it lasted six years.

ii. *Steady growth.* In this phase, the smoothed growth rate was high enough to keep the labour force well employed. It was interrupted by short mild recessions, but at cyclical peaks the demand for labour pressed on supply. But though the growth rate was high, it was also falling, and, as we shall see in a moment, I regard this as raising a central analytical problem in the long swing mechanism. This phase of Steady Growth at full employment was the longest of the three phases. Measuring from the mid-point of the interval in which the growth rate reached its maximum until the year before the economy entered a serious depression (which we may call the peak of the Boom), the phase lasted from seven to eleven years.

iii. *Depression or stagnation.* In this phase, actual output always fell sharply; smoothed output usually declined or at best grew very slowly. Unemployment was, of course, high and remained so for several years. If there were cyclical expansions during the period of stagnation, they were "disappointing". It took from four to seven years from the peaks of the Booms to the troughs from which Rebounds started.

I pass on now to a description and interpretation of the events of the three phases.

4. Viewed from the side of supply, the characteristic feature of the Rebound, the first phase of accelerating growth, was an increasingly intensive utilization of resources; and the peak in output growth with which the phase ended was marked by the achievement of a high level of employment and followed by a slowdown in the speed with which the rate of resource utilization was being raised. There is some direct evidence to support this assertion, but the grounds for it are best appreciated if I argue by elimination. The end of output acceleration was not due to retardation in the growth of labour force or capital stock or to a slowdown in technical progress. Labour force growth did not reach its peak at this time; indeed, labour force additions kept growing until nearly the end of Phase II. And the same was true of the growth rate of capital stock, since the levels of net and gross capital formation continued to rise until the peak of the Boom. True, the growth rate of measured productivity reached a peak at about the same time as did output growth, but this is far more plausibly connected with more intensive use of employed labour and capital than

with a sudden three-year spurt in technological progress; and this is
the view I take of it.

The increasingly intensive use of resources, which is the central
feature of the Rebound on the side of supply, is itself to be attributed
to a vigorous revival of demand after the interruption of a period of
depression. I shall not pause to explain it. We have all of standard
business-cycle theory to fall back on. It is enough to say that the
recuperative processes usually attributed to a period of depression
took place. Confidence in credit markets was restored after the financial panic which was a feature of every major American depression.
The growth industries of the time doubtless felt increasing pressure
on their capacity to produce. The capital stock in most sectors became,
to a degree, obsolete. Any revival in these conditions would be more
vigorous and more protracted than usual – more vigorous because it
was based on an upswing in all branches of investment, inventories
and fixed capital alike; more protracted because it took its start in
conditions of severe underutilization of labour and capital, so that
output ceilings were less rapidly attained.

5. By contrast with the Rebound, the long phase of Steady Growth
rested visibly on growth in supplies of resources. As said, the growth
rate of the labour force continued to rise for years after the Rebound
had ended, while the growth rate of the capital stock, reflecting a rising
level of capital formation, increased till nearly the beginning of the
succeeding phase of Depression. Meanwhile, the retardation in the
growth rates of output and of measured productivity, in conditions of
high and even rising employment rates, carries the strong if not conclu-
sive suggestion that the economy was running out of unused and
under-used resources. If we accept this view tentatively, we may say
that as the phase wore on, perhaps till close to its end, the growth rate
of output, while supported by a speed-up in supplies of productive
factors, was being ever more closely confined within limits imposed by
such resource growth and by the rising level of technology.[5]

6. I now need to say something about the increasing pace of
growth of labour force and capital stock during the second phase,
since that, it seems to me, was the heart of the old Kuznets cycle.

The speed-up in the growth of the labour force was based on an
increase in the level of immigration. During the era with which we are
now concerned, 1840–1914, a large portion of both population change
and labour force growth in the United States consisted of immigrants.
From 1870 to the First World War, the portion due to migration was
approximately 20 per cent. More to the point, the accelerated growth
of population and labour force, characteristic of the second phase
of Kuznets cycles, was always traceable predominantly, sometimes

wholly, to an increased volume of immigrants. Never less than 50 per cent. of the changes in the pace of population growth after 1870 and often the entire change between successive periods (and much more) was due to a change in the number of immigrants.

Now the rising wave of immigration which came to a climax in the course of the second phase of Kuznets cycles was connected with developments in both America and Europe. Recall that the migrations of the nineteenth century were, in their broad lines, movements from European farms partly to overseas countries, chiefly America, and partly to European cities and towns. An economist is bound to begin by saying that these migrations were based on an apprehension by many people that the long-term prospects of income for themselves and their children were sufficiently better in America or in home cities than they were in home rural areas to offset the substantial psychic and material costs of moving. When the level of income in the United States rose relatively to that in Europe, as it did in the second Kuznets-cycle phase of steady growth, this *may* conceivably have raised the income expectations of potential migrants. What it *clearly* did, however, was to reduce the costs of migration. For the chief costs were transport and the transitional loss of income between departure from home and obtaining a suitable job in America. These costs were considerable and all the more serious because it was so hard for migrants to find finance. When, however, the labour market in America grew tight, men could migrate confident of finding a job in America quickly. And under the same conditions, it was easier to obtain the support of relatives and friends already in America to finance the costs of a steamer ticket and a few days or weeks of job-hunting. It was, therefore, the very tightening of the labour market, itself the cause of retardation in output growth, which led to a responsive upswing in population and labour force growth and so produced the supply conditions permitting continued rapid expansion of output.

This was the American influence. There was also a European influence – not, during the period with which we are concerned, a push of population pressure,[6] but rather a weakening in the competitive pull of the European cities. For, as a general rule and in a rough way, European waves of industrial growth ran inversely with the American.[7]

And here let me say the little I can say in this paper about the European-American inversion. It was founded chiefly, but not wholly, on the immigration response itself. Full employment in the US drew off workers who were potential migrants to European cities. It therefore cut the growth of the European industrial labour supply and, by analogy with what I shall say in a moment about America, it reduced the demand for new urban building. This was, I believe, the fundamental matter. But there were other things as well. The American booms, as we shall see, competed for European capital, and this may have been a depressing influence on domestic capital formation both in Britain and on the continent.[8] The retardation or decline of British home investment must have affected Britain's demand for imports, and there is a suggestion that this slowed down industrial growth elsewhere.[9]

Turning now to the capital stock, it is just short of obvious that its growth rate must have continued to rise until nearly the end of the second phase of Steady Growth. For the growth rate of the capital stock is simply a ratio between the level of net capital formation and the size of the stock. And net capital formation must have risen (as it did) at a rapid, even if gradually falling, pace until the end of the Boom. Had it not, a failure of demand would almost certainly have caused unemployment to begin to rise and the phase of Steady Growth would have been cut short. So the increasing growth rate of the capital stock is implicit in the rise of capital formation which was itself a virtually necessary condition for a long phase of steady growth at full employment.[10] But one must still explain the protracted rise of capital formation.

Here there is a *prima facie* difficulty to which I alluded earlier. The phase of Steady Growth was a phase of *retardation* in the growth rate of output reflecting the increasingly stern constraints of general and specific output ceilings. To anyone approaching the matter along multiplier-accelerator lines, the problem is obvious. What sustained the continued growth of investment for seven to eleven years after output growth had begun to decline? Not expenditures for producer durables; conforming to simple Hicksian expectations,[11] the growth rate of such expenditures either dropped to low levels early in the second phase or they even declined absolutely. Not inventory investment: although we have no adequate direct evidence about aggregate inventory investment before 1914, it is a virtual certainty that such investment declined along with the growth rate of output [but see the "Correction" at the end of this chapter]. The answer, of course, was construction and, above all, residential building and railway construction. Together, these accounted for 50 to 60 per cent. of total construction during the period 1840–1914 and, if we add in the portion of non-residential urban building associated with house building, for still more. Both forms of construction exhibited towering long waves in the *level* of construction activity and expenditure.[12]

As between the two, residential building was the more important. Its waves were doubtless influenced by many factors: by income change and finance, by rural-urban migration which also moved in waves associated with Kuznets cycles, by speculation and by the under- and over-shooting inherent in any lagged capital-stock adjustment process. Accepting all that, however, Burham Campbell has shown that by far the bulk of the variation in house building was associated with population change weighted by what he calls "headship rates", that is, by the propensity of people in different age groups to form independent households. And because immigration was the chief source of change in population growth and was heavily concentrated in age groups in which headship rates were high, it was the wave of immigration which was the dominant influence on house building.[13]

The railway building wave, for its part, may be understood as a consequence of the fact that in a growth industry – as this was before 1914 – and in one with huge capital requirements, the level of building depended on the magnitude of profits, both as a direct source of internal finance and because the ability of railways to raise external funds depended on the market's view of their profits prospects. Operating profits were controlled by the ratio of traffic to installed capital stock, a fact which was itself the consequence of the heavy weight of overhead in railway costs. The rapid growth of traffic in the phase of Rebound, therefore, produced a large increase in profits and set in motion a boom in construction. The size and complexity of railway construction projects, however, caused building contracts to lag behind profits, actual building to lag behind building contracts and the installation of completed facilities to follow on even later. There was, therefore, a considerable period in which operating ratios and profits were rising and setting in motion still larger expenditures.[14] As the phase of Steady Growth wore on, however, the retardation of output growth held back the growth of traffic while the pace at which new facilities were coming into use increased. So the boom in railway investment was gradually brought to a halt and turned about.

7. These were the major forces that sustained a long period of steady growth at full employment viewed in terms of the real elements of capacity growth and of demand. But there were also essential concomitants in the balance of payments and in the money supply.

With regard to the balance of payments, there were two characteristic developments. One was that the Rebound and phase of Steady Growth – being demand-led and accompanied by retardation in Europe – generated a large upswing of imports and a consequent deterioration in the current balance. In the earlier nineteenth century, when the United States current account was chronically in deficit, this meant a more severe deficit. Later, when the current account was in balance on the average, it meant a shift from surplus to deficit. In either case, the deterioration of the current account would sooner or later have implied serious losses of specie and a decline – at best a retardation in growth – of the money stock were it not offset by an enlargement of capital imports: for during most of the era, the United States was on a specie standard, specie was a chief element in bank reserves and there was no Central Bank. Failing an upswing in capital imports, therefore, the upswing in output would have been cut short by a constriction of the money supply.[15]

There was, however, an enlargement of capital imports. It was big enough not only to offset the deterioration in the current account, but also, in an irregular fashion, to provide for improvement in the overall account and to permit some specie inflow. The wave of capital imports, therefore, was a necessary permissive element allowing imports of goods and services and the money supply to expand in the fashion required by a sustained spurt of real income growth.

The upswing in capital imports in turn was connected with the swing in railway profits. Railway securities were, in this era, the chief variable element in British and continental holdings of American securities, and the same causes which accounted for the boom in railway construction were involved in the international flow of capital. And again the generally inverse pattern of British demand for home investment must have acted to augment the flow.[16]

8. But, finally, there were Depressions or periods of stagnant growth, which I have called the Third Phase. They were connected with episodic causes, like the silver controversies of the 1890s, but also with systematic influences reflecting developments in the phase of Steady Growth. Waves of immigration, feeding in part on a backlog deriving from the previous Depression, tended to level out and even decline. We may well suppose, subject to empirical test, that the consequent decline in the growth rate of the labour force made for higher labour costs, reduced the growth of profits, discouraged investment, prejudiced the country's competitive position in international trade and so influenced specie flows and the growth of the money supply. The analogy with contemporary experience in countries suffering from tight labour markets and inelastic labour supply is suggestive. Next, both house building and railway building are good examples of lagged capital-stock adjustment processes. There is evidence of over-shooting in both. Finally, the economy was less stable in response to income decline than it has since become. The ratio of wage earners to salaried workers was still high; the built-in stabilizers were still in the future; and most important, the American banking system was vulnerable to runs; every Depression had its Financial Panic.

It is important to realize, however, that Depressions not merely brought each Kuznets cycle to a close; they had an important role to play in preparing the ground for the next upswing. By sharply reducing the level of immigration, they discouraged house building in almost all localities at once and also brought the waves of house building and railway building into phase with one another and with industrial building in many industries. The resulting backlogs of repressed aspirations to migrate, to form independent households and to invest in railway and industrial expansion ensured that, when the Rebound came, it released a general upswing of capital expenditure in many sectors and regions which might otherwise have risen or fallen more nearly independently, each in response to influences peculiar to itself.

9. This review and interpretation of the events of the Kuznets cycles in the United States before 1914 enables me to state somewhat categorically what I believe to have been the essentials of the economic structure and institutions which produced them: (1) A considerable proportion of population and labour force growth had its source in immigration, and the migrants were themselves drawn from a fairly concentrated area abroad itself experiencing industrialization. (2) Chiefly because of the role of immigration in population growth, but partly because of rural-urban migration, the waves in house building rose and fell according to the state of the labour market. (3) Territorial expansion was proceeding rapidly on the basis of an expanding railway network. Capital formation in railways was, therefore, important. At the same time, the large stock of railway securities outstanding offered foreigners a convenient and attractive vehicle for investment in America. (4) Total demand was almost entirely private. The expenditures, and correspondingly the tax receipts of the Federal government, were insignificant. (5) The country adhered to a specie standard, except for the years 1862 to 1879. (6) The economy operated on the basis of a fractional reserve banking system composed of a large number of relatively small banks without benefit of central bank controls or reserves and without security of deposits. (7) The system was cyclically unstable in other respects than its monetary system for reasons already stated.

Was the output swing since the Second World War a Kuznets cycle?

The question which now arises is whether the model I offer of the old Kuznets cycle, or any reasonable facsimile thereof, can help us understand contemporary developments or whether, as I think, the economy's underlying structure and institutions have so changed as to render the old model defunct.

1. Let me note, first of all, that the economy of the United States since the Second World War *has* experienced a fluctuation in output growth rates with a duration longer than an ordinary business cycle.[17] Since virtually full employment was rapidly attained after a few months of demobilization and reconversion, we might regard the country as entering the post-war period in the situation I have attributed to Phase II of the older Kuznets cycles. We then, quite consistently, enjoyed output rates which, though declining, were until the mid-Fifties, sufficiently rapid to keep the labour force fully employed at business-cycle peaks. Subsequently, the growth rate dropped markedly. The business-cycle expansion of 1958–60 was insufficient to bring the unemployment rate below 5.5 per cent., and the average rate of unemployment in the four years from 1958 through 1961 was 6.1 per cent. From 1961 onwards, however, the United States enjoyed an expansion of unprecedented duration and, after 1962, of great vigour – to outward appearances, a Kuznets-cycle Rebound.

There were indeed other familiar symptoms of a Kuznets-cycle process. As in earlier episodes, the period of relatively rapid growth from 1948 to the mid-Fifties was supported not by inventory investment nor by expansion of expenditure for producer durables, but by an enormous residential building boom which subsequently tapered off and receded. Business investment, especially business construction, rose rapidly during the early Fifties, and the best interpretation of its subsequent decline attributes it to an over-accumulation of installed capacity compared with requirements.[18] As for the balance of payments, the United States had, of course, graduated to a capital-export basis, but the outflow was smaller in the rapid growth period of the early Fifties and grew larger during the retardation of the later Fifties. This inverse wave of capital exports might be thought to correspond to the older positive wave of capital imports – and it has been so interpreted. Finally, the Rebound of the sixties was accompanied by a pronounced upswing in labour force growth. Indeed, were I talking about Europe, I should add that a rapid growth of the industrial labour force from immigration or from rural-urban migration – such as supported United States growth before 1914 – also played a part in promoting postwar industrial capital formation and productivity growth in a number of European countries and in Japan; that the absence of such support constrained growth in Britain; and that the gradual exhaustion of such sources of labour force growth contributed to European retardation in more recent years. It is observations such as these which I think have inclined some writers to speak of the post-war period as a long swing, presumably similar in its essentials to the older Kuznets cycles – and I now ask whether this is really useful.

2. Let us consider, first, the demographic concomitants of the post-war output swing.[19] In the old days, both population growth *and* labour force growth speeded up when the growth rate of output was high. The ratio of labour force to population, therefore, remained fairly steady, and Easterlin has shown us why. Labour force and population moved almost *pari passu* because the dominant source of increased population growth was an increased flow of adult immi-grants, *not* an enlarged crop of babies. Moreover, the responsiveness of immigration to increased demand for labour was itself the cause of pronounced steadiness in the birth rates of the native-born. Though a tighter labour market tended to improve the economic position of all workers and so encouraged marriages and births, the influx of young, adult immigrants enlarged the supply of labour in the most marriage-able and fertile age classes. The two forces were roughly offsetting and kept native birth rates on a stably declining trend. Immigration, in short, was a cushion which protected the young native population from fluctuations in demand for labour and muffled its own latent responses to changing economic conditions.

The post-war history, however, has been very different. Its origins go back to the 1920s. Births had been low during the Twenties, partly as a reflection of a long established trend, partly because of an un-usual conjuncture of circumstances affecting not only the native white urban population in the fertile ages, but still more the foreign-born and rural groups. And this was followed by the disaster of the Thirties which pushed birth rates down further still. With immigration under tight control since the mid-Twenties, it was now fore-ordained that labour force would grow especially slowly in the Forties and Fifties whatever the labour-market pressure, and that pressure, of course, proved intense. These very facts, however, produced a pronounced response of births. With demand for labour booming and new en-trants to the labour force few, the excess demand for young adult workers was especially large; their economic position improved rap-idly even by comparison with older workers. A striking decline in age of marriage and a large rise in fertility followed. In the post-war pe-riod, therefore, we experienced a very *slow* increase of the labour force combined with a very *rapid* increase in the population. The ratio of labour force to population dropped rapidly. And this bears on the familiar fact that per capita growth rates in the United States were no more rapid in these years than earlier in spite of faster growth in productivity per man. Had the ratio of labour force to population even

remained constant, the per capita growth rate of output, other things
being equal, would have been 0.5 percentage points or one-third
higher than it actually was.

It is clear that the old mechanism of labour force and population
response, operating through immigration, is now gone. In that old
process, labour force growth moved in swings corresponding to demand. In its place, we now have the possibility (no more!) of long
swings in labour force growth which are echoes of birth-rate fluctuations 20 years earlier. But whether these echo effects are then coinci-
dent with periods of rapid growth and tight labour markets or of slow
growth and slack labour markets becomes a matter of chance. The
labour force echo of the baby boom of the Forties and Fifties reached
the labour market in the mid-Sixties when it operated to support and
reinforce a period of rapid growth of demand for output. This was
coincidental, and it is unlikely soon to be repeated in further echoes.
The current meeting of high demand for labour with a large supply is
not calculated to make the economic position of young adults especially favourable, and it has not done so; it is not calculated, therefore,
to produce another bulge in births, and, in fact, birth rates have been
falling.

There is another, less important, aspect of the demographic response to labour-market conditions which I can only mention. When
immigration responded sensitively to demand for labour, the labour
force participation rate – that is, the ratio of labour force to population
of working age – remained quite steady. Since the Thirties it has risen
and fallen with the employment rate. These responses were not
enough to offset the effect on the labour force of fluctuations in the
population of working age, but they have shown themselves to be a
source of labour-force response to the changing balance between demand and working-age population which is large enough to be significant. They are the source of hidden increases in unemployment when
demand for labour declines, and they need to be taken into account in
projections of the growth of labour force and of production and productivity when employment rates are changing. We can better appreciate the role such participation rate responses play in the contemporary growth process because of our knowledge of older conditions
when immigration permitted our labour force to be still more responsive to fluctuations in demand.

3. What I have already said about recent population changes tells us
clearly enough that the huge house building boom of the early Fifties
was not based, as older booms were, on a demographic development.
Quite the contrary. Had simple population change weighted by stable
household headship rates been in control, we should have had a

slump. Instead, for the first time of which we have knowledge, we had a great house building boom based predominantly on an unprecedentedly large change in the propensity of people of all ages – but particularly of young adults – to form independent households.[20] This large change in headship rates is plausibly attributable to two causes: the backlog of aspirations to marry and form independent households repressed by the depression and by wartime housing shortage, and the large relative rise in the economic position of young adults whose sources I have already described.

A boom due to such causes was bound to run out of steam. Building reached a peak in 1955, and its subsequent decline contributed to the retardation of the late Fifties.

Looking to the future, we cannot expect changes in headship rates to continue to dominate building activity. Population change will come into its own again. But, as we have seen, the building waves connected with such changes will be more largely echoes of past fluctuations in birth rate than responses to current conditions. As such, they will tend to lag behind fluctuations in labour force growth by some years – instead of roughly coinciding, as in the past – because the age-gradient of labour force participation rates rises more steeply in young adult age groups than does that of household headship rates.[21] This means that the labour-supply and building-demand effects of population growth will no longer clearly reinforce each other as in the past, and, of course, since they are no longer responses to current demand neither may fit neatly into such general waves in output growth as we may experience.

4. In the past, railway-building booms shared with house-building booms the burden of supporting growth of demand and full employment for long periods in the face of rapid but declining output growth. Railway investment, however, has now become an almost negligible part of total capital formation. It has been replaced by investment in a miscellany of public utilities – telephones, electric power, road transport, airlines. Investment in all these, as well as in general industrial construction, is, like that in railways, doubtless subject to some kind of lagged capital-stock adjustment process which is capable both of prolonging booms in the face of retardation in output growth and of generating periods of excess capacity due to over-shooting.

But there are differences. The very variety of industries gives greater play to influences peculiar to each; so the investment waves of individual industries are less likely to move in phase with one another, and on that account the amplitude of the aggregate wave will tend to be smaller. The amplitude of long waves in total *industrial* construction was, indeed, far smaller than that of waves in railway building before 1914. Lags between planning and installation of new capacity are probably shorter, on the whole, in other industries than they were in railways. Booms based on miscellaneous public utility and business investment, therefore, are unlikely to last so long after aggregate output approaches a ceiling. By the same token, over-shooting should be less pronounced and the consequent slumps less severe and prolonged – which again should provide greater opportunities for influences specific to individual industries to diversify investment behaviour and to make aggregate capital formation more stable.

5. In the post-war period, moreover, the United States has had to reckon, not only with fluctuations of private investment, but also with those of Federal government expenditure. Before 1914, no branch of government was an important source of expenditure; since the Second World War both the State and Local governments and the Federal government have each absorbed between 8 and 10 per cent. of GNP. And while the growth rate of State and Local expenditures has been quite steady, that of the Federal branch, chiefly under the impact of changing military pressures, but also in response to economic stabilization policies, has varied widely.[22]

The role of changing Federal expenditures, however, since they are a tool of stabilization policy, must be assessed, not in isolation, but in the light of concomitant variation in tax liabilities and of private investment expenditure. The expenditure – tax balance is best measured by estimating the so-called full employment surplus. Rough estimates suggest that this hypothetical surplus may have declined, in per cent. of GNP, by no less than five to six percentage points between 1948 and 1953. It then rose by perhaps four points from 1953 to 1957 and by still another point between 1957 and 1960. Finally, it was reduced by two or two-and-a-half points from 1960 to 1966. When we consider that private gross saving is highly stable in reasonably prosperous peacetime years at about 15 per cent. of GNP, we can appreciate that such large changes in the Federal fiscal impact would require correspondingly large variations in the volume of private investment generated at full employment to offset them.

With this in mind, and having regard to the state of private investment, the following observations seem justified:

i. During the early post-war years, when Federal expenditures vaulted in the midst of a great private investment boom, there was an inappropriately small rise in potential tax liabilities. The economy was put under great strain, and there was a large rise in prices which helped set the stage for the balance-of-payments problems which complicated economic policy after 1957.

ii. The full-employment surpluses of 1956 and 1957 were not out of line, given the private investment boom of those years.
iii. After 1955, however, Federal expenditures were kept level until 1961 – in part because of a felt need to counter balance-of-payments pressures – and tax rates were not significantly altered. The result was an upward drift in potential full-employment tax receipts as incomes rose, and, given the state of private investment demand, an inappropriately high full employment surplus. The Federal government's fiscal policy in those years must, therefore, bear a large share of responsibility for American retardation and unemployment from 1957 to 1962.
iv. By the same token, the rise in Federal expenditures after 1961 and the subsequent tax rate reductions must be assigned a fair share of credit for the remarkably long and vigorous Rebound of the first half and more of the Sixties.

The implications of the new situation seem to me, as to many others, fairly obvious. We must expect continued sharp changes in Federal expenditures so long as military pressures remain so intense; and we cannot expect taxation wholly to offset these changes. For the foreseeable future, therefore, fluctuations in the Federal government's fiscal impact will remain an important cause of variations in the growth rate of total demand, and this, in turn, will have its reflection in the swings in growth of capacity.

6. Coming now to the post-war swing in international trade and capital flows, there is again, as I have pointed out, an appearance of resemblance to older patterns. In the early post-war period of relatively rapid growth, the United States balance of payments remained roughly stable at a moderate deficit level because a reduction in capital exports offset a decline in the current account. In the subsequent retardation of the later Fifties, just the reverse was true. Indeed, the improvement in the current account was then more than offset by an increase in capital exports. The over-all deficit became larger. Monetary policy then hardened, and this might be taken to be analogous to the more direct effects of specie outflows during periods of depression or stagnation before 1914. Again, however, the resemblances to the older processes are superficial.

First, the deterioration of the United States current balance in the early Fifties was *not* due to relatively rapid, demand-led growth in America, still less to acceleration in the United States matched by retardation in Europe. That kind of systematic inversion has gone out with the disappearance of free immigration. The decline of the United States current balance in the early Fifties was, as we all realize, due to the rapid restoration of Europe's productive capacity in the course of a remarkable episode of export-led growth. In the same way, the offsetting decline in capital exports did not reflect the increasing attraction of a booming domestic economy for United States capital. It was, rather, a decline in government transfers connected with the phasing out of the Marshall Plan.

Second, the enlargement of American capital exports in the second half of the Fifties did *not* represent simply an increased outflow of private capital. About half the increase consisted of government grants and loans, chiefly to developing countries, and had a political motivation. Another quarter, consisting of private funds, invested in Europe, was *not* an outflow chiefly spurred by cyclical retardation in America and cyclical boom abroad. It started in 1956, too early to be a reaction to United States retardation; we were then enjoying an intense domestic investment boom. And from the angle of current European developments, it started too late. In the later Fifties, Europe's growth began to slow down and its condition of intense capital scarcity began to ease. The basic cause of the enlarged flow of American private capital to Europe was a changed view among United States corporations and security holders about the size and secular growth prospects of the European market and about the advisability of direct footholds to exploit those prospects. The timing of the wave of United States investment was also determined partly by the removal of restrictions on the transfer and repatriation of capital and income and by the establishment of the Common Market. It was a secular, not a cyclical response. And the basic correctness of this interpretation is attested by the fact that American private capital exports not only remained large but grew still larger during the Sixties, when growth in the United States accelerated and retardation in Europe became more pronounced.

Third, the pressure on the dollar, to which the United States became subject in the later Fifties, and the restrictive monetary and fiscal policies which were then invoked to counteract it, were only in some part responses to the then current change in the state of our international accounts. Rather they were the result of a cumulative change in the United States position in process since 1950 and of the market's belated appreciation of the fact that the dollar's super-strength had been gradually sapped by the recovery of Europe's capacity both to satisfy her own needs and to export.[23]

A number of considerations support this view: (i) the United States had in fact suffered a chronic over-all payments deficit since 1950. Its cumulative size from 1950–56 was 10.5 billion dollars. For years, however, this had caused no concern because it was believed, and, to a large extent, it was true, that there was an underlying excess demand for dollars, and our export surplus could be whatever we chose to finance. (ii) In these circumstances, the American deficit of the early Fifties should be regarded as a planned deficit. Capital transfers were set high enough to enable European countries to accumulate international reserves and so to permit the eventual liberalization of trade and capital movements. The United States authorities could easily plan such deficits, and markets could tolerate them, because both were conscious of the underlying United States export strength and of the country's extremely large reserves, reserves which the deficits were, indeed, designed to redistribute. (iii) The change in view and the outbreak of dollar pressure then arose when it was finally realized that Europe had recovered her productive and export capacity and that the cumulation of planned deficits had produced its designed result. The excess of United States gold stock over short-term liabilities to foreigners declined just 90 per cent. in 11 years – from 18 billion dollars in 1948 to 1.8 billion dollars in 1959.

Finally, this being the nature and extent of the change in the United States position, the dollar pressure continued in even more severe form during the Rebound of the Sixties. Yet, that pressure did not dominate monetary and fiscal policy, both of which were reversed and made expansive after the Kennedy administration came to power.

7. This bit of history carries, I think, some lessons for the future. The first is that the adaptive variation in the flows of capital funds, which, before 1914, made possible regular divergent fluctuations in the growth rates of Europe and the United States, may well continue to operate in the future. But it will probably be called on to operate only sporadically; not regularly. For with the disappearance of the migration link, the chief cause of regular divergent fluctuation between the two halves of the Atlantic Community has been removed.

The second is that the importance of capital flows of the old sort – direct and portfolio – in permitting divergent fluctuations has declined. With the disappearance of the true specie standard and the rise of national central banking and supra-national banking, countries now have far more freedom of action in the face of either favourable or unfavourable developments in their current balances.

8. Finally, there is the matter of serious depressions, a point I need to mention but hardly need to argue. Partly because of changes in the structure of investment already reviewed, but mostly for a variety of reasons familiar to us all, the vulnerability of the American economy to serious depression has been sharply reduced. If one grants this point and remembers the function that depressions used to perform in creating general backlogs of aspirations and plans and in bringing the investment fluctuations of different industries, localities and regions into

phase with one another, one must, I think, conclude that another vital cog in the old Kuznets-cycle mechanism has been removed.

To summarize a paper which is itself a frantic summary would be fatuous. Let me simply utter a few solemn words in farewell. The Kuznets cycle in America lived, it flourished, it had its day, but its day is past. Departed, it leaves to us who survive to study its works many insights into the kinds of connections and responses which go together to make for spurts and retardations in development. We are the wiser for its life, but it is gone. *Requiescat in pace*. Gone but not forgotten.

A correction

On page 282 there occurs the following passage: "What sustained the continued growth of investment [in successive long swings] for seven to eleven years after output growth had begun to decline? Not expenditures for producer durables: conforming to simple Hicksian expectations, the growth rate of such expenditures either dropped to low levels early in the second phase [that is, soon after the onset of retardation in total output growth] or they even declined absolutely. Not inventory investment: although we have no adequate direct evidence about aggregate inventory investment before 1914, it is a virtual certainty that such investment declined along with the growth rate of output."

A review of the evidence since submitting the lecture for publication suggests to me that, so far as the statement concerns producer durables, it is not a valid generalization of the facts now available for the period between 1870 and 1914. For example, the growth rate of the output of producer durables – as judged from Kuznets' estimates smoothed to allow for business cycles – though declining after the peak in total output growth around 1899, continued to be high until the onset of stagnant general business conditions after 1907.

In the 1880s, which was the next preceding decade of rapid growth, the situation is, at best, cloudy because it is hard to fix on a single acceptable dating for the relevant peak rate of total output growth. According to Kuznets' estimates of GNP, smoothed for ordinary business-cycle movements, there were two peaks, one in the mid-Seventies, another at about 1889. Frickey's index of Industrial Production also displays two peaks, one at about 1881 and a second more pronounced peak at about 1889. Finally, according to Gallman's estimates of non-perishable commodity output, there was but a single peak in the period 1888–1892. The behaviour of producer durables output was or was not consistent with the description in the statement quoted above according as we accept one or another of these dating schemes. This "correction" also applies to note 5, below.

Notes

1. "Statement" in United States Congress, Joint Economic Committee, *Employment, Growth and Price Levels, Hearings,* 86th Congress, 1st Session, Part II, Washington, 1959, pp. 411–66; "The Nature and Significance of Kuznets Cycles", *Economic Development and Cultural Change,* vol. IX (1961).

2. B. O. Campbell, *The Housing Cycle and Long Swings in Residential Construction: A Statistical and Theoretical Analysis,* doctoral dissertation, Stanford University, 1961.

3. J. G. Williamson, *American Growth and the Balance of Payments, 1820–1913,* University of North Carolina Press, Chapel Hill, 1964.

4. R. A. Easterlin, "The American Baby Boom in Historical Perspective", *American Economic Review,* vol. LI (1961): "Economic-Demographic Interactions and Long Swings in Economic Growth", *American Economic Review,* vol. LVI (1966); also his *Population, Labor Force and Long Swings in Economic Growth,* National Bureau of Economic Research, New York, 1968.

5. The text makes no assertion about the role of technology in accounting for the retardation of productivity growth except that the pace of technical progress, whatever it was, was overborne by the declining margin for more intensive use of employed resources. It is possible, however, that the rate of progress in the application of superior techniques was itself slowing down. As we shall see, during this phase the level of investment in producers' durable equipment either declined or grew only slowly, while that of investment in housing, railway building and other construction rose rapidly. The composition of investment, therefore, tended to shift away from those kinds of capital which yield returns rapidly and which presumably are the major carriers of new technology towards goods with opposite characteristics.

The text also makes no allowance for the possibility of an independent retardation in the growth of demand as a cause of slowdown in output growth. The matter is hard to test because it is difficult to isolate those changes in desired expenditures which reflect restrictions in the growth of potential output from those which reflect other causes.

6. See R. A. Easterlin, "Influences in European Overseas Emigration before World War I: Some Findings on the Historical Pattern," *Economic Development and Cultural Change,* vol. IX (1961), pp. 331–51.

7. For the relation between Britain and America, the standard source is Brinley Thomas, *Migration and Economic Growth,* Cambridge, 1954. For Sweden and the US, M. Wilkinson, "Evidences of Long Swings in the Growth of Swedish Population and Related Economic Variables 1860–1965", *Journal of Economic History,* vol. XXVII (1967), pp. 17–38. For other countries, W. Arthur Lewis presents suggestive evidence in *Growth and Fluctuations, 1870–1913,* Geo. Allen and Unwin, London, 1978, chapter 1.

8. The inverse relation of British home investment with British foreign investment and thus with American long swings is well known. Thorwald Moe, preparing a Stanford dissertation on Norwegian long swings, has found evidence that Norwegian shipbuilding was positively related to capital imports from Britain and inversely related to British capital exports in the aggregate.

9. Wilkinson's study of Sweden leads him to make the following tentative suggestions: "It would be very convenient to place the source of the swings in Swedish manufacturing in the growth of the British economy. There is considerable evidence of

long swings in significant sectors of the British economy. Furthermore, the turning points of the British long swings are provocatively close to the turning points of the Swedish long swings. Swedish exports do indeed give some support for this line of thinking. Prior to 1900, the growth of Swedish exports exhibits swings which consistently lead the swings in manufacturing. This pattern is temporarily broken during the war years, after which time the turning points of the swings in exports and manufacturing are synchronized." *Op cit*. p. 38.

10. The argumentative character of this paragraph is intended to bolster whatever weaknesses there may be in the statistical evidence that capital formation did, indeed, continue to rise at a rapid, even if declining pace, until the end or close to the end of Phase II. The qualifying phrases "Just short of", "almost certainly", "virtually" are inserted in recognition of other, distinctly less probable alternative bases of a continued rise in aggregate demand. I have seen no evidence, though some might be found, of favourable shifts in the propensity to consume. Exports, of which agricultural products were an important component, displayed no regular relation to long swings in this era. Imports *rose* more rapidly during the upswings of Kuznets cycles. Public expenditures were not a large element in the GNP and, apart from local construction, were not related to the long swings.

11. By "simple Hicksian expectations" I mean those we might form by reference only to the endogenous variables in Professor Hicks' trade-cycle model. Hicks himself might well argue that the elements impounded in his "autonomous investment" are intended to allow for developments which might sustain a boom for a long time in the face of retardation in output growth. As indicated in the text that follows, my own contentions are that waves in investment components treated as exogenous in Hicks' model were indeed characteristic features of the second-phase of United States Kuznets cycles before the First World War, that the elements in question can be at least roughly defined and that an explanation of their behaviour can be subsumed within a broader model.

12. In the interests of brevity and sharpness, I argue in this paragraph and in those that follow as if we can make a clear distinction between expenditures for equipment, closely controlled by the current growth rate of output, and those for construction, controlled only by other influences. But, in fact, I do not think the distinction is so sharp as this suggests.

13. Campbell's results are set forth in detail in his dissertation cited above. For a convenient summary see his "Long Swings in Residential Construction: The Postwar Experience", *American Economic Review*, vol. LIII, (1963), pp. 508–18.

14. If profits were determined simply by the relation between the *physical* volume of traffic and cumulative capital investment, the relevant lag would be that between profits and the time when expenditures on associated building projects reached a peak. Fishlow has estimated that two years was the typical interval between the beginning of construction and the peak of expenditures. Even this long period is presumably only a minimum estimate of the relevant lag since there was probably an interval between the time when profits increased and that when construction began. Further, since profits were influenced by railroad rates as well as traffic volume, the relation between transport demanded and facilities actually in operation would have counted, and completion of facilities naturally lagged behind expenditures.

15. Cf. P. Cagan, *Determinants and Effects of Changes in the Stock of Money, 1875–1960*, National Bureau of Economic Research, New York, 1965. Of the three proximate determinants of the money supply, that is "high-powered money", the ratio of currency held by the public to the total supply of money and the ratio of reserves held by banks to deposit liabilities, Cagan finds that changes in high-powered money were the domi-

nant sources of changes in the total money stock running across business cycles. Similarly, before the establishment of the Federal Reserve System, changes in the monetary gold stock were the chief source of changes in high-powered money.

To say that the Kuznets cycle upswings would have been cut short by constrictions in the money supply does not imply that *secular* growth rates would necessarily have been lower, though this may have been the outcome. I mean only that the pattern of fluctuations in which growth took place would have been different.

16. On the behaviour of imports, the trade balance and capital flows, see Williamson, *op. cit.*

17. The same, of course, was true of the inter-war period. It would be interesting to consider how far the old model could still serve to illuminate the long swing in output growth in these years; but that is another long story.

18. Cf. B. Hickman, *Investment Demand and U.S. Economic Growth*, The Brookings Institution, Washington, D. C., 1965.

19. The works cited in footnote 4 contain the evidence and analyses supporting my argument regarding population and labour force growth.

20. Campbell, *op. cit.*

21. Easterlin, "Economic-Demographic Interactions . . .", *op. cit.*

22. The average annual percentage change in Federal purchases of goods and services, measured in 1958 prices, between successive business-cycle peak years ran, as follows: 1948–53 +39.0; 1953–57 −6.6; 1957–60 0; 1960–66 +4.2.

23. Cf. the similar views developed in W. Salant *et al.*, *The US Balance of Payments in 1968*, The Brookings Institution, Washington, D. C., 1963.

Part IV

Growth and welfare

10

Economic goals and social welfare in the next generation

The most important economic problem in any age is to know what we want, to define useful and worthy ends, and to balance our efforts among them in due proportion. In social affairs, even more than in private life, however, the conceptions of one era tend to persist into another, when circumstances have changed, and so to provide false guides for social policy. In the United States, the dominant purpose of economic policy has been, and still is, to foster economic growth; that is, to maximize the pace at which we enlarge our capacity to produce goods and services. But multiplication of goods and services no longer promises the large rewards it used to do. My purpose is to urge the need for reconsidering the high priority we assign to this objective and so for striking a new balance among the goals towards which our economic life is, in a broad sense, directed.

The achievements of economic growth in the last century

During the last one hundred years the output of this country per head of population approximately quintupled. This in itself, however, is not the measure of our economic success. Our success lies rather in the fact that economic growth was made to serve a number of purposes of first-rate importance.

The most significant was that a very large portion of our population, then living below or near poverty levels and under intense economic pressure, was lifted above the poverty line and placed in comfortable circumstances. Another large portion has been able to achieve a level of comfort, and even luxury, never before known by any large fraction of

Reprinted by permission from *Problems of United States Economic Development*. New York: Committee for Economic Development, 1958, pp. 191–99.

a country's people. At the same time the generally heavy character of physical labor was greatly lightened and the relation between working and leisure time was reversed. Further, while the great bulk of our additional output was left at the free disposal of income receivers to satisfy individual consumption needs, a margin was created and used by government to establish our basic social services including a large public education system. Finally, our great rise in income was not confined to our native-born population. Because immigration was, during most of the period, unrestricted, over 26 million people came to this country since 1850 and stayed to settle and share in its growing prosperity. Between 1850 and 1910, these settlers from abroad accounted each decade for between 10 and 23 percent of our population growth.

Starting from the low levels of output of a century ago, it goes without saying that these results could have been achieved only by growth of output per head. No scheme of redistribution would have been remotely adequate.

The erasure of so much poverty, the rise in the level of comfort, the lightening of work and increase of leisure extended over so large an increase in population, native and foreign-born, corresponded to our own aspirations and inspired people everywhere. Our success, and the free political and economic institutions on which it was based, became the admiration of the world and the foundation of our present international prestige insofar as that rests on grounds other than sheer physical power.

Growth and welfare in the next generation

So much for the past. So far as the outlook for the future goes, one important thing to grasp is that the growth of incomes experienced in the last century gives every evidence of constituting a stable trend subject to extension into the foreseeable future. Although the interruptions of wars and depressions have caused our rate of growth to vary from decade to decade, the expansion of per capita income during each successive generation has been remarkably like that of the preceding generation. Apparently the bases of material progress in this country are firmly laid, depending not on occasional striking developments, but upon the well-motivated, steadily applied and widely diffused activities of individuals of all classes and occupations. Decade by decade the process of capital accumulation has gone forward, technical advance has proceeded along myriad interlocking and reinforcing channels, eagerly followed by enterprising and competing business firms guiding a labor force unusually tolerant of the serious and often difficult readjustments of job and location which economic advance involves. It is hard to doubt that this process of advance is still in full tide.

A prudent evaluation of the future, therefore, may well rest on the conviction that the freely acting forces of the American economy will raise our incomes as much in the next generation as they have during similar periods in the past. This implies that average family incomes, now standing in the neighborhood of $5000 a year, will, a generation hence, stand in the neighborhood of $8500 a year in terms of the same prices. This is the level now enjoyed by only some 13 percent of all families. At the same time, a quarter of our families will probably earn incomes in excess of $12,000, a level now achieved by only some 6 percent of all families. Since these rough calculations are based upon rates of growth experienced in the past, they will, barring some drastic change in the progress of efficiency, be attained despite disturbances, economic, military or otherwise, on a scale comparable with disturbances and catastrophes suffered during past generations. If, as we hope, the impact of such difficulties is less pronounced in the future, it may well be that the next generation will bring us to even higher levels of income than those foreshadowed above.

But what of the significance of this growth? Can our prospective economic progress be made to serve purposes as important as those served in the past? This will be difficult, for the old pattern of uses to which increased income was devoted, chiefly the enlargement of private consumption and leisure, no longer has the importance it once did. On the other hand, the significant purposes which enlarged earnings might be made to serve cannot be fostered without a considerable change in the part played by government. Since any impediment to the free use of income by individuals may conceivably act to weaken the system of incentives on which economic growth depends, we have a choice to make. Let us examine the matter more closely.

The need for broadly distributed additions to private consumption is now far less urgent than it used to be. For the great mass of people in this country, what goods and services can do to provide nourishment, clothing, shelter, comforts and conveniences, recreation, even the stimulation of travel, is already being done on a fantastic scale, not only by the standards of the past or by those of other countries, but even by our own standards today. The result is that a considerable proportion of current consumption, not only of the rich, but of a large part of our people, satisfies only trivial or frivolous needs. We need only recall our homes with multiple television sets, the radio in almost every room, the automobiles whose sole purpose is to stand at the suburban railroad station to await their master' return, the over-obsolescence of durables, the silly elaboration of packaging. If no better use can be made of goodly portions of our present incomes to what futility shall we be reduced when our incomes stand nearly twice as high?

There are, indeed, peculiar difficulties in raising the level of material satisfactions of an entire population which affect a very rich country with special force. One is that a general rise of incomes is accompanied inevitably by a general rise of standards and expectations. Appetite grows with income, and, to this extent, the psychological pressures inherent in a gap between aspirations and fulfillment are not relieved. And since the areas in which aspirations are most expansible seem to be those into which consumption moves after primary needs for food, clothing, shelter, and the like, are satisfied, this is a difficulty which becomes more intense the higher the level of income already attained.

A second difficulty is still more obtrusive. As incomes rise, our individual consumption activities clash more frequently and more fiercely. The spread of the traffic jam and roar from the city, where it is stimulating, to the suburbs, where it is an intrusion, from the roads to lakes and coastal waters, from land to air, the overcrowded parks and beaches, the neon-lighted solitudes of the Sierras are grim examples of the partially self-defeating character of the mass search for something to do with higher income. There are, of course, still returns to be had from a rise in the disposable income of consumers at large. But in the context of the technology now in prospect, and given the slow pace at which we are creating the social facilities for travel and recreation and, most important, raising the cultural preparation of people for higher income, the returns are diminishing rapidly.

Nor can these returns be boosted appreciably by more rapid transformation of enlarged productivity into leisure rather than goods. Given the comparative lightness of most labor today, even the present work week – due in any event to become still shorter – constitutes little more than that modicum of purposive, disciplined activity which satisfies rather than burdens and which gives savor to the rest of our lives. Increase in leisure may be as much a problem as a benefit to most people.

In addition, the further general rise of incomes cannot be expected to make the same contribution it once did to the elimination of poverty. The residual poverty of the present is not only more limited in scope, it is more resistent to general income growth than the more widespread poverty eliminated in the last century. Our residual poverty is, in part, one of the costs of income growth. Some of the poor represent the people whose skills, jobs and places of work are rendered obsolete by the changes of technology and the migration of industry inescapably involved in the process of economic development. Another reason that residual poverty is resistant to general income growth is that it is, in part, relative. In American conditions an important facet of poverty is not so much the lack of minimal quantities of goods as it is the acute sense of deprivation which stems from inability to consume or possess the goods which people somewhat better off can have. This sense of deprivation is intensified as communication and advertising develop. Whereas only a rise of average income could eliminate the widespread poverty of a century ago, only redistribution of income can alleviate the poverty of relative deprivation. Finally, our residual poverty is, in part, selective, representing the difficulty of achieving satisfactory conditions with regard to particular aspects of our needs. Some of the trouble stems from the heavy cost of certain important items of consumption. So we continue to regard much of our housing as impoverished when the bulk of consumption is at satisfactory levels. And some of the trouble arises because, in the lower income groups especially, it is hard not to sacrifice long-run needs to immediate desires. In particular, education and health care are sacrificed to apparently more pressing demands.

Finally, although the significance of additional income for ourselves has declined, our willingness to share our present level of income with the people of other countries is less than it used to be. We have reduced the flow of immigration to a fraction of its level fifty years ago. We maintain a higher tariff. And we seem unwilling to give adequate recognition in our international economic relations to the obligation of the rich to aid the poor. Although we have made large contributions since the war, the present flow of public grants and loans for other than military purposes is small. There are, of course, obvious difficulties in the way of making such transfers politically acceptable and technically efficient. But no one can say that we have yet made a sufficient effort to overcome these obstacles. In all these circumstances, the foreign view of the United States has understandably changed. The palpable waste of income sufficient *in toto* to support the investment programs of a dozen impoverished countries is noted by people everywhere. And our intent pursuit of still higher incomes to spend in still more trivial ways arouses in them mingled resentment and contempt. The political implications of this widespread reaction are already quite apparent.

The uses of growth

In a democratic society, there are two ways for people to employ their income. One is to apply individual earnings to individual uses. The other is to arrange politically for the provision of facilities to be used in common or for the redistribution of individual earnings among the various classes of the population. If the continued growth of productive capacity is to be put to significant and worthy uses, it seems clear that a great deal will depend upon a further expansion in the amount, and possibly in the share, of goods and services obtained through governments and upon additional measures for the redistribution of income. This conclusion is implicit in the difficulties now preventing us from using additional income as productively as we used to do.

The present pattern of consumption yields diminishing returns. We can open up new realms of consumption, however, by raising the level of education, and we can soften the clash of our consumption activities by much wider provision of public facilities for recreation and movement.

The residual poverty of a rich country is resistant to a general rise in individual incomes. We can attack it directly by more generous public provision for the health, housing and education of the relatively poor and by further redistribution of the burden of taxation.

We show inadequate concern for the tensions created by great international differences in income levels. We can make an effort commensurate with our resources by freer immigration policies, by freer trade, and by a much larger program of financial and technical aid.

Our capacity to move in these directions is a challenge to the soundness of American values and the vigor of American political life. It will be a very limited capacity unless the great bulk of our people come to agree about the essential rightness of the objectives we must seek. Such agreement does not yet exist, and its absence is perhaps the chief obstacle to the significant use of prospective growth.

We must also recognize that a large increase in governmental activity, of government income disposal, and, therefore, of taxation constitutes some threat to the system of incentives on which the growth of productive capacity rests. Several considerations, however, qualify the force of this threat. Barring utter unreason in the conduct of affairs, we shall enjoy a substantial rate of growth regardless of our social policy. We must consider, moreover, that the bases of economic growth are still obscure. It is not clear how serious a threat to economic incentives a larger volume of government activity constitutes or whether the loss of this account would not be more than offset by the economic benefits deriving from a healthier and better educated population. Finally, and most important, we cannot escape the fact that the sheer expansion of productive capacity has lost much of its former significance. If we must risk some reduction in our rate of

growth in order to apply our expanding capacity to worthy and meaningful uses, it is a risk well worth while. If we refuse to accept it we
may discover that the economic progress of the next generation was
an empty achievement, not only in the eyes of people in other countries, but perhaps still more in our own.

11

Growing up in an affluent society

Religion apart, no aspect of human affairs has such pervasive and penetrating consequences as does the way a society makes its living – and how large a living it makes. And few societies have experienced such radical alteration in the level of their income and in the manner in which it is earned as has this country during the last seventy-five years. In this period, in common with most of the countries which share in the civilization of the Western world, America has been passing through the complex series of changes we associate, however vaguely, with industrialization. Wherever this process has held sway, the application of science to industry and the accumulation of capital have transformed the economic life of peoples. But in America, these forces have operated in a peculiarly favorable environment and the transformation in the modes of living and working have been especially profound.

Industrialization has reshaped our lives, not only during the years people work, but during those in which they are not yet old enough to work and during those in which they are too old. In this essay, however, I will try to write about the impact of industrialization, not on the whole of our mortal span, but rather on those peculiarly malleable, impressionable, and seminal years of youth – not "from the cradle to the grave," but from the cradle to the job. I will try to say something about the economic developments which have been transforming the position and prospects of American youth. And I will try also to say what I can about the significance of these changes, although this is far from clear. Indeed to descry this significance is a major challenge to study and insight so that we may, so far as we can,

Reprinted by permission from *The Nation's Children*, vol. 1, *The Family and Social Change*, ed. by Eli Ginzberg. Published for the Golden Anniversary White House Conference on Children and Youth. New York: Columbia University Press, 1960, pp. 158–79.

put ourselves in a position to understand our fate and, in some degree, to shape it.

The rise in income and the change in its distribution

The most obvious effect of industrialization upon the young has come through the change it has wrought in the incomes of the families in which they grow up. In terms of the dollar's purchasing power in 1957, the average income of American families in 1870 was roughly $1,750. This date does not represent the beginning of industrialization in this country, but it is the earliest date for which fairly reliable figures are available and it carries us back ninety years to a time when nearly three-quarters of our population was still classified as rural and when some 53 percent of those gainfully employed were still engaged in agricultural pursuits. By 1958, however, the level of living had risen beyond recognition. Average family income had increased about three and one-half times and stood at well over $6,000 per family. And since the size of families has declined – from slightly over 5 persons per family in 1870 to about 3.5 in recent years – family income today is devoted to the support of fewer children. Income per capita, in other words, has increased still faster than family income. During 1958 disposable income per head of the population stood at about $1,800, a figure five times as large as per capita disposable income in 1869 when measured in dollars with today's purchasing power.

The effects of this great rise in income upon the growth of the country ramify in many directions. Our children, like their parents, are far better fed, clothed, and housed than they used to be. This more generous provision for the physical necessities of life is reflected in their health and in that of their parents. It is well-known that the great increase in life expectancy at birth, which has risen some 50 percent since 1870, manifests itself most strikingly in the proportion of all children born who survive the dangers of infancy and childhood and live to enter adult careers. It is less well-known that the lesser, but still significant, improvement in the life expectancy of adults has significantly reduced the proportion of our children who must grow up in broken families. As late as 1900, approximately 1 out of 4 widows was under forty-five years of age. In 1956, the corresponding figure was 1 in 12.

No doubt the advance of medical science and of the scientific basis of public health has been a necessary condition for the improvement recorded in the health of children and of the population at large. But just as clearly, the rise of income has been required to provide the resources needed to support scientific work, to exploit its findings, and to spread its benefits to the mass of the population. Some portion of responsibility for the improvement of health is to be ascribed to the mere fact that a much larger portion of the population now enjoys the varied diet and the more sanitary living conditions which only the rich could afford a century ago. Some portion too must be assigned to the resources which richer communities can provide for safeguards against the contamination of water and food, against the spread of epidemics, for the sanitary disposal of waste, and for the extension of hospital and other medical facilities to every section of the population. Nor should we forget that, in contrast to conditions one hundred or even fifty years ago, very few children now grow up in families in which medical care, more especially hospital care, is denied them because of mere geographical isolation. Industrialization has implied urbanization and has bound even the most remote places to centers of population and of medical facilities with an efficient system of transport and communication.

The rise of income then has enlarged the potential of youth in the fundamental physical sense that it has contributed to a great increase in the proportion of infants born who survive throughout the entire span of childhood and adolescence and live to become adults. In short, one of the most important things about living in an affluent society is that children stand a better chance of growing up, at least in the minimal sense of reaching adulthood. The rise in income, however, has helped to enlarge the scope of youth in another, equally important, respect. Childhood and youth are vivid, active years of life, important in themselves; but they are also years of preparation for adult careers. Indeed, one of the more significant ways in which the period of youth may be defined is by the age at which a young person makes the transition from preparation for work to work itself and, by obtaining gainful employment, secures the prerequisite for a life no longer in dependence upon his parents.

In this sense too, industrialization has extended the period of youth for the mass of young people. It has done so in two ways: by placing a greater premium upon formal education as a qualification for successful participation in a career of work, and by providing the means by which a longer period of education could be extended to a larger portion of our youth.

The level of a country's income supports, or restricts, its educational system in two ways. It provides the resources from which the staffs of its schools and their physical facilities are supported, and it affords that necessary surplus of income which makes it possible to dispense with the contribution of children to the family budget. In this country, partly because the level of income was relatively high, provision for public education developed earlier than in many countries of Western Europe. Yet in 1900, while 96 percent of American children between six and fourteen were attending school, the percentage of those between fourteen and seventeen was only 15, while those attending colleges and universities were 4 percent of the population aged nineteen to twenty-two. Thus in 1900, we were well on the way to universal elementary education, but this was as yet hardly true of secondary education, while a college education was still restricted to a very few. Today, as we know, these figures are very different. The percentage of children between six and fourteen attending school in 1957 was 99; that for the youngsters of high school age was 89; and in addition, no fewer than 20 percent of those between eighteen and twenty-four were in school, the bulk attending some institution of higher learning. We have, therefore, reached a period when secondary education, while by no means universal, is the norm, and when college or university training has been put within reach of a very large and growing minority of young people.

Insofar, then, as we look on youth as a period of dependency and of preparation, the rise in income has brought us the means and also the need to extend the period of youth for the mass of the population. Both these aspects of the enlarged scope of youth call for our closest consideration. We have extended the years of dependency and postponed the age when young people, by earning their own living, assume a role of responsibility as well as of independence of their parents' guidance and control. But this portentous change is qualified by another which we have already noted. If the average period of dependency has been extended, so has the life expectancy of young people at the age at which they pass into the work force. The latter may not completely offset the former in the sense of keeping the proportion between years of preparation and years of activity constant, but there has been a substantial offset.

The other aspect of the enlargement of youth through education is perhaps more nearly obvious but not less fundamental. The extension of schooling means, on the whole, better formal training and, therefore, a larger range of ultimate opportunities for the much larger portion of our youth who share in them. As we shall see, however, the larger provision of education has been accompanied by a larger need, and, therefore, has aggravated the disabilities imposed on the substantial fractions of our youth who may be deprived of a chance to gain all the formal training from which they are able to benefit.

The great rise in average income during the last century has been accompanied during much of the period by a trend towards greater equality in the distribution of income. In the last thirty years, the money incomes of the relatively poor families have increased considerably more rapidly than those of the relatively rich. This was not clearly true of money incomes in earlier decades, but there is good reason to think that it was, nevertheless, true of real income. For the goods and services whose supply is especially cheapened by the introduction and improvement of power machinery and mass production are typically the kinds of goods consumed by the lower income groups. And to this we must add the considerable contribution of state services, chiefly in aid of the lower income groups, which has grown apace with the burgeoning role of government.

The more equal distribution of income is working together with the extension of education and with the change in conditions of work to make the conditions of adolescence and the prospects of youth of all classes more similar to one another than they have ever been before. The extension of education fits a larger proportion of youth for work of a type requiring formal training and makes this central experience of youth more nearly the same for large sectors of the population. At the same time, the reduction in the inequalities among their families' incomes makes their lives at home less different and brings them together in neighborhoods less divided in external appearance and in the character of the activities they harbor. The net result is presumably that youths share a more nearly similar outlook and a more nearly similar set of aspirations. It goes without saying that, in this country, the outlook and aspirations which are coming to be more widely shared are those of the middle class – but what this ever-growing, long-dominant sector of American society is becoming, thinking and aspiring to are matters I must leave to other writers.

The changing character of work

The rise in income about which we have spoken is the most obtrusive aspect of industrialization and certainly the one in which we can take the most unalloyed satisfaction. But industrialization involves many great changes in the mode of economic activity and in nothing so much as in the nature of the daily jobs we do.

The most general way to characterize this change is to say that it involves a shift from the relatively direct manipulation and fabrication of things to jobs concerned with the organization and regulation of production and distribution, from hard-handed to soft-handed work, from blue-shirt to white-collar occupations. We may see this first in the great decline of farming which in 1870 still engaged some 53 percent of those gainfully employed but in 1957 employed under 10 percent of our labor force. We see it next in the lesser relative decline of the other great "commodity-producing" industries – manufacturing, mining, and construction, and in the relative growth of those departments of the economy concerned with the organization and regulation of production and the distribution of its products – that is, the services, trade, finance, the professions, and government itself. Finally, we may see it in the great increase of clerical, administrative, and overhead activity within *all* branches of economic activity. For it is in the nature of the process of industrialization and the basis of its efficiency that productive activity becomes more specialized and that machines take on more of the physical work, while men become increasingly concerned with the supervision of machines, with the coordination of specialized productive activity and the routing of its product.

Two aspects of this change are especially noteworthy in their impact on the position and prospects of youth, and both fit in with and support the forces set in motion by the income changes already described. In the first place, the change in the nature of work from unskilled to skilled occupations, from blue-shirt to white-collar, from manual manipulation to distribution, administration and regulation involves a vast increase in our need for educated people and, therefore, in the opportunities our economy affords to the educated. With regard to the kind of education that is needed, it is clear that a highly industrialized and rich society needs people with education at every level, starting with mere literacy and going on to specialized and profound training of every kind and degree. It cannot prosper without it. The process, therefore, which has given us the resources to support a longer period of preparation for an ever larger portion of our youth, has also greatly increased our need for that kind of preparation, and one of the central social questions of our time is whether we have so used our resources as to make provision for education to match our need. Nor should we forget that if one side of the coin of industrialization is the greater opportunity which is afforded to skill and education, the reverse is the barrier it sets up against the employment and advancement of young people who are deprived of formal training. Individual development, no less than social, demands that adequate provision be made for the education of every young person who can use it and that each such person be put in a position to avail himself of the facilities provided.

The change in the character of work is also acting to soften the class divisions of our society. For in this country, the chief social boundary has been the line dividing the manual, or, if one likes, proletarian occupations, from the nonmanual. Those engaged in the latter, however important the differences due to income, are broadly associated with the business, or middle, class in our society and, in a general way, share a common set of attitudes and aspirations and identify themselves with one another. Since the most prominent change in the character of work has been to effect a vast enlargement in the proportion of our population engaged in nonmanual occupations, we may assume that a larger proportion of families now identify themselves with the middle class. And, therefore, on this account, as well as on account of the extension of education and the more equal distribution of income, their children are growing up under more nearly similar circumstances and coming to share the outlook and ambitions of the middle class to which their parents see themselves as belonging.

We may well believe that such a change in the class divisions of our society has effects of the most far-reaching character upon the position of the young, their prospects, and their aims. It is far less easy to guess what these effects are and to evaluate them. We may well speculate upon the increase in social mobility when many more young people feel themselves to be members of the same dominant class, and upon the ease with which they will see themselves as moving to occupations, regions, and social strata still strange to their parents. And we may think too about what this widespread identification portends for the stability of our economic and political system. But if these vague directions of speculation give rise to any feelings of satisfaction or complacency, we should think also about what the change signifies for the variety of life in our country. And we should, in particular, consider what it means for the division between those growing up with an outlook proper to what Thorstein Veblen called "industry," as distinct from "business."

Few aspects of living shape our values and our interests more powerfully than does the concrete nature of our work-a-day lives. *Industry* is the fabrication of goods. It provides an education in the relations between physical causes and effects. Those who are concerned with it learn the properties and possibilities of materials and tools. They take from it a matter-of-fact concern with the direct and unadorned adaptation of goods to their functions, and they are led to conceive the functions of goods in their relations to the more solid needs and wants of human beings. *Business* is the making of money. As a social institution, it is the basis of the complex mechanism by which our labor and capital are guided towards the production of the goods people demand – as these demands register in markets. To those engaged in business, however, it is only in part an education in the adaptation of goods to people's needs and in the design and operation of efficient productive organizations. It is also an education in the manipulation of our needs and in the restriction of output, in the arts of bargain and maneuver, of speculation and promotion. It is an experience in the strategies by which advancement is gained in large corporations and in the tactics by which income and wealth are preserved in the face of the vagaries of markets and the exactions of governments. As the characters of children are formed in their homes rather more than in their schools, we must be deeply concerned with the impact of the changing nature of work on the everyday concerns of their parents.

The new security in business and professional careers

In view of the growth of the middle class, as distinct from the manual worker, or proletarian, class, it is worth considering some of the important ways in which the differing economic and career outlooks of these classes are reflected in the patterns of life of the youths who belong to them. For, it turns out, the career outlooks of these classes have changed along with the change in their relative size.

One of the chief differences between proletarian and middle-class life used to be that a proletarian youth left school and got a job relatively early, and fairly soon thereafter achieved a secure status relative to the standards of his class. By contrast, a youth entering a middle-class occupation, unless he was very rich, took much longer to obtain a secure foothold. If he were going into business, he needed years in which to accumulate the capital with which to start the independent venture which was the normal form of business activity, and even if he were fortunate enough to have access to a small capital, a considerable period was needed to obtain the experience with which to use capital effectively. Similarly, if he were entering a profession, he not only faced many years of preparation but also an indefinite period of insecurity thereafter while he built up at least a modest private practice. As a result of this difference in the time-patterns of their careers, working-class youths courted and married relatively early, and they had more children and had them earlier than did youths going into business and the professions. In this respect, the working-class youth resembled the young people of very rich families – though for very different reasons.

This important point of differentiation between the life patterns of the different classes, however, has now changed both in its incidence and its character in the further course of economic development. On the one hand, a larger proportion of young men, as already noted, are destined for occupations associated with the middle class and, therefore, adopt middle-class standards with regard to the time and character of courtship and marriage and with regard to the number and spacing of their children. On the other hand, it is now possible to obtain a foothold in the more characteristic middle-class occupations earlier and more easily than used to be true. Business is now generally organized in the form of large coporations rather than in small independent ventures. Young businessmen, therefore, enter their careers at the lower levels of large firms and advance through their managerial bureaucracies. Capital is not required for entrance, and experience is gained on the job.

The prospects for young professional and semi-professional aspirants have similarly improved. For one thing, the demand for people with such training has in recent years far outrun the growth of supply. Independent practice is, therefore, more easily established. For another, the growth in the size of business firms in the scope and variety of governmental activities, in the importance and size of labor unions, and of medical, scientific and educational institutions, has created a host of professional and semi-professional posts within the staffs of these organizations. At the same time, what amounts to the corporate practice of professions has grown in importance. Thus, the problem of establishing an independent practice may now be bypassed by a large fraction of those entering the learned middle-class pursuits. On all these counts, the aspiring young businessman or professional may now look forward with unprecedented confidence to a secure career upon the completion of his training. Finally, although the period of training is now somewhat longer in several of the major professions than was the case a generation or two ago, it is now probably easier for a young man to obtain the means to support himself during his training. For this there are a number of reasons. The rise of incomes has made it easier for parents to provide liberal support for their children. At the same time, philanthropic and governmental support of education has provided more scholarship aid than used to be the case. Finally, students themselves, profiting by the rise of earning power, find it easier to supplement their funds by work. And when, as is not uncommon, they marry in the course of schooling, their wives can contribute to their support by exploiting new opportunities for women in industry.

The net outcome of this complex of supporting changes has been to place the future of men entering middle-class occupations upon a secure basis at a much earlier age than was true even a generation ago. As a consequence early courtship, marriage, and family foundation are now more feasible for this group. In this respect, as in others already noted, the attitudes and life patterns of middle-class youth have come to resemble those of the working class and of the very rich. It would, of course, be imprudent to assert that the relatively new patterns of high-school courtships, much earlier marriage, of larger numbers of children more closely spaced, which has become characteristic of middle-class youth, as well as of the young of other classes, can be accounted for entirely, or even chiefly, by the economic developments traced above. Whatever the contributing circumstances, however, we can be confident that so large a change in the life patterns of middle-class youth could not have taken place except upon a firm economic basis.

The new position of women

Because men have been, and still are, more closely concerned with economic activity than women, much of the discussion so far has been concerned more with the position and prospects of boys and young men, rather than with those of girls and young women. In the more recent development of our economy, however, the working life of women, with some inevitable differences, has come to resemble that of men more closely than ever before. This, in turn, has affected the prospects of women; it has had a significant impact on their activities as youths, and raised certain problems concerning their schooling and the course of their early careers.

In industrialized societies, it has long been normal for men, except for farmers, to work outside the home. Until recently, however, the great bulk of women in America have spent the major portion of their adult lives inside the home. It is true that it was common for unmarried girls to seek outside employment during the period between the end of their schooling and their marriage. And it is also true that widows, as well as married women in the lowest income groups, were forced to seek employment to help support themselves and their families. By and large, however, the great bulk of married women occupied themselves with household duties. In 1890, women made up only some 16 percent of those gainfully employed, and married women were only 14 percent of the total number of women at work. By 1958, however, women constituted 32 percent of the labor force and over 50 percent of the women at work were married. The role of work in the lives of women has, therefore, changed considerably. In former decades, girls worked, if at all, between end of school and marriage, and then confined themselves, as a rule, to household occupations. In recent years, however, they tend to remain in school longer and marry earlier, which restricts the frequency and length of premarital employment. On the other hand, as already noted, they have their children earlier, and they then enter the labor market in very large numbers as soon as the youngest of their children reach school age. And since the life-span of women is now longer than it used to be, many married women experience a long period of work outside the home.

This considerable transformation in the working life of women reflects the combined impact of a number of economic causes directly and indirectly. In the first place, there is the change in the character of work from manual labor to office work of various kinds, which has created a large number of jobs deemed suitable for women in our society. In addition, the early foundation and completion of families leaves women with reduced household duties at a time of life when they are still active and vigorous. Next, the wider spread of middle-class standards of living imposes on women the need to help their families sustain such standards both in ordinary consumption and in the education of their children. It is, perhaps, not too much to say that in former decades children left school early to make money to help support their parents at working-class standards. More recently, however, mothers feel impelled to leave their homes to make money to help provide consumption goods and schooling for their children at middle-class standards. We must add finally that the entrance of women, especially married women, into work has been substantially eased by the fact that hours of work are now shorter, leaving them a larger amount of time to devote to children and household duties than was previously available to a working woman, and that homes are now easier to manage, thanks to the improvements in household equipment and the transfer of many household tasks to the commercial economy.

The fact that many women now feel impelled to enter gainful employment for a substantial portion of their married lives and that opportunities to do so now exist has already had some effect on the upbringing and education of girls and presumably should have still more. We note, first, that the great bulk of girls now attend and finish high school and that a considerable fraction of them continue their education in college and beyond. Not only is secondary and higher education for young women more widespread, it is now conducted with an eye somewhat more intent on the occupational and professional implications of such education. It is by no means clear, however, that the process of modifying the upbringing and education of girls has as yet gone as far as it might in view of the working life which is now in prospect for a considerable fraction of women. At least two areas of possible action need to be studied. First, curricula for women both in high school and college which used to have dominantly nonoccupational aims need to be reconsidered to achieve a proper balance between the contribution they can make to the work careers of women and to the other objectives of education. Secondly, young girls and women need to be made more aware than they already are about the career choices now open to them, about the kinds of training they can obtain, and about the way in which premarital work experience can help fit them for the much longer period of work many of them will desire after their children have entered school.

The new standards of consumption and leisure

We have so far been concerned chiefly with the economic development of the country upon the lives of our youth as this has acted through the changes in work patterns and in preparation for work. But the great rise in income, of course, has accomplished a change not only in the working lives of the bulk of our families, but also in their lives outside of work. Two aspects of this change seem especially noteworthy. In the first place, the great majority of families now enjoy an income which provides a substantial surplus with which they can buy goods and services yielding pleasure, as contrasted with commodities required to meet the necessities of nourishment, clothing, and shelter. In the second place, we have chosen to transform our enormous rise in productivity only partly into higher incomes. In good part, we have chosen to substitute fewer hours of work and more hours of leisure for the still higher incomes we might otherwise have. Thus, in 1890, a representative worker in a nonagricultural job would have worked an average of some fifty-eight hours per week. Today, he works only some thirty-nine hours per week, a change which has approximately doubled the effective leisure time at the disposal of employed persons. By contrast with the situation two or three generations ago, adults now have more goods to enjoy and more leisure time in which to enjoy them. Pleasure, play, community affairs, and non-work activities in general, it may be said, have now become, perhaps for the first time, substantial parts of the daily lives of the ordinary run of men and women.

The full implications of this striking, almost revolutionary change in the character of ordinary life are still far from clear. Two aspects of the matter, however, are quite closely tied to the themes already sounded. One is that fathers, like mothers, can now be with their families for a considerable portion of each day and week. The result has been a quickening and intensification of family life, and the family is again the center of youth's activities to a degree not experienced in urban communities for several generations. The return of the father to the family, however, has been in a rather new role – not as breadwinner, but as participant in the leisure-time activities of the family. One may categorize the change, somewhat too strongly perhaps, by saying that it was characteristic of an earlier and poorer generation that a major concern of family life was the effort of fathers to stimulate and govern the early stages of their sons' work activities. It is characteristic of our own more abundantly provided generation that a major concern of family life is the effort by sons – and daughters – to stimulate and govern the leisure-time activities of their fathers. However this may be, there is little doubt that fathers now share much more fully in the daily lives of their families and that family activities are now more largely concerned with things other than work than ever before. It may well be worth thinking whether this change in the pattern of family life is not connected in a significant way with the recent trend toward early courtship and marriage and with the tendency of young couples to have larger families earlier in their married life.

The new patterns of consumption and leisure may also be playing an important part in forming the goals and ambitions of youth as they look toward their careers in business. A long series of students from de Tocqueville in the 1820s to Andre Siegfried in the 1920s concurred in the finding that an intense and wholehearted dedication to the life of business and the goal of making (more) money was a distinctive characteristic of the American middle class. More recently, however, a new shade has been detected in the outlook of middle-class youth. Determined as ever to win a place in the world of work and to invest a major effort in this sphere, their dedication to the notion that their own goal, like America's, is success in business is no longer unqualified. They still look forward to careers that will win for them a secure status at a level perhaps better in most cases than their parents enjoyed. But more frequently, they seek to do so in jobs that will not demand from them the same intense application that their fathers and grandfathers were willing, and even eager, to accept. They are concerned, rather, to achieve a more even balance between the portion of their lives devoted to business or professional work and that which they are free to devote to their families, to the leisure-time activities in which their wives and children share, and to the affairs of the communities in which they live. We are challenged to consider how this more balanced, but less intensely pursued, round of activities will alter the quality of the satisfactions yielded by their lives. And we must also think how this more qualified devotion of our energies to business may influence the further economic development of the country.

"The child is the father of the man." For better or worse, the attitudes towards work, leisure, and consumption which will give tone to American civilization during the next generations are now being formed in our children. Their values and aspirations are emerging from the experience they now share with their parents and peers as we all learn to enjoy – to use or dissipate – our still new-won prosperity. Our own lives, private and public, will tell whether the affluence we now enjoy and the still more abounding productive powers which our children will control will be worthily used or most thoughtlessly squandered.

12

The retreat from economic advance: changing ideas about economic progress

A vision of the possibility of economic growth lies close to the center of the idea of progress in general. Francis Bacon, the great precursor of the idea, proposed that progress could be founded upon a steady increase in knowledge gained by the application of experimental methods. But Bacon also held that the real and legitimate goal of the sciences is "the endowment of human life with new inventions and riches" and, in J. B. Bury's words, "the amelioration of human life, to increase men's happiness and mitigate their sufferings."[1]

Bacon's outlook immediately suggests how closely intertwined are the notions of progress and economic progress. They are not the same since progress broadly conceived includes intellectual, moral, and spiritual advance, as well as other satisfactions, which are not closely constrained by the supply of scarce goods. The starting point of their connection, however, seems to be the possibility of increasing our command over nature and the output of goods. At the same time, there is a strongly held and plausible idea that if we are to cultivate our nonmaterial, intellectual and spiritual, potentialities, we can do so only to the degree that we are relieved from elementary poverty and repetitive toil.

Considering how crucial economic progress is to the idea of progress generally, it is perhaps ironic that classical economics emerged as a source of skepticism and disbelief in the possibilities of progress rather than as a source of support. Malthusian population theory and Ricardian diminishing returns on the land made the outlook for an indefinite rise of the common man's living standards doubtful even though the "industrial arts" themselves might continue to improve. This skeptical outlook was orthodox academic doctrine during the

Reprinted by permission from *Progress and Its Discontents*, ed. by Gabriel Almond, Marvin Chodorow, and Roy Harvey Pearce. Berkeley and Los Angeles: University of California Press, 1982, pp. 253–80.

entire half-century between Malthus' *Essay* of 1798 and Mill's *Principles* of 1848. In Mill's words:

Hitherto . . . it is questionable if all the mechanical inventions yet made have lightened the day's toil of any human being. They have enabled a greater population to live the same life of drudgery and imprisonment, and an increased number of manufacturers and others to make fortunes. They have increased the comforts of the middle classes. But they have not yet begun to effect those great changes in human destiny which it is in their nature and in their futurity to accomplish. Only when, in addition to just institutions, the increase of mankind shall be under the deliberate guidance of judicious foresight, can the conquests made from the powers of nature by the intellect and energy of scientific discoverers become the common property of the species and the means of improving and elevating the human lot.[2]

This somber vision was originated and fostered by the political economists. But it was far from being merely academic. It largely dominated the views of educated and influential people in Britain and only to a lesser degree in the United States. Because it made the fate of common people depend largely on their own procreative tendencies, it was powerful support for conservative politics.

All this changed in the next twenty-five years under the experience of rising English and American incomes and falling birth rates. When Alfred Marshall, the still young but immensely sober ascendant head of Anglo-Saxon economics, wrote his essay "The Future of the Working Classes" in 1873, he was able to envisage an England very different from Mill's:

It is to have a fair share of wealth, and not an abnormally large population. Everyone is to have in youth an education which is thorough while it lasts, and which lasts long. No one is to do in the day so much manual work as will leave him little time or little aptitude for intellectual and artistic enjoyment in the evening. Since there will be nothing tending to render the individual coarse and unrefined, there will be nothing tending to render society coarse and unrefined. . . . every man will be surrounded from birth upwards by almost all the influences which we have seen to be at present characteristic of the occupations of gentlemen. . . .[3]

If achieved, could such a utopian state of affairs be maintained? It could be and it would be.

the only labour excluded from our new society is that which is so conducted as to stunt the mental growth. . . . Now it is to such stunting almost alone that indolence is due. . . . The total work done per head of the population would be greater than now, less of it would be devoted directly to the increase of material wealth, but far more would be indirectly efficient for this end. Knowledge is power; and man would have knowledge. Inventions would increase and they would be readily applied.[4]

Could such a condition then be achieved? It could be and, in fact, already was.

if we look around us, do we not find that we are steadily, if slowly, moving towards that attainment? All ranks of society are rising; on the whole they are better and more cultivated than their forefathers were; they are no less eager to do, and they are much more powerful to bear, and greatly to forebear. . . . In the broad backbone of moral strength our people have never been wanting; but now by the aid of education, their moral strength is gaining new life.[5]

Marshall's optimism represented a wave of opinion which spread and gained strength for decades. The spread was based on a growing faith in the possibilities of technological advance accompanied by falling, not rising, rates of natural increase of populations and by land rents which declined as a share of national income. So far as concerned the beneficence of such developments, one could observe in all the industrializing countries rising levels of nutrition, health, housing, and education and longer life expectancies. Successive technological marvels were seen as enlarging the scope and variety of people's lives, opening up new worlds of travel, communication, information, entertainment, and convenience. The belief became common that release from deep poverty, greater command over material goods, and lightening of labor would conduce to a more cultivated life for the common man. Charles Beard, writing at the depth of the Great Depression, catches the mood of a time that already seems somewhat distant:

in dealing with the effect of technology upon social evolution, we are not confronted by accomplished work alone, but also by a swiftly advancing method for subduing material things. . . . there is something intrinsic in technology which seems to promise it indefinite operation. . . . The solution of one problem . . . nearly always opens up new problems for exploration . . . the passionate quest of mankind for physical comfort, security, health and well-being generally is behind the exploratory organs of technology. . . .

Through the press, the radio, the railway, the post office and enormous educational plants, [technology] extends literacy, distributes information, widens the social consciousness. . . .

If no Saint-Pierres, Comtes, and Spencers appeared in the United States to give theoretical formulation to what was taking place, there was no doubt about the course of events. Immense energies, physical, intellectual, and moral were being applied to the conquest of the earth, with a view to raising the standard of life, decreasing the death rate, overcoming illiteracy, eliminating physical suffering and providing the comforts of a rational being.[6]

Needless to say, academic economists did not remain outside this mainstream of opinion. They gave it expression in the "older welfare economics." This connected economic growth with human welfare according to an argument which rested on Benthamite utilitarian conceptions.⁷ The argument starts from the notion of "total or social welfare," a vaguely defined entity identified with people's states of consciousness, a matter of how people feel, their levels of satisfaction. Welfare depends on people's command over goods and services but also on other things: friendship, family affections, love, and the like. It has a place for moral and aesthetic values and satisfactions. "Economic welfare" is "that part of total welfare that can be brought directly or indirectly into relation with the measuring rod of money."⁸ It reflects the satisfaction of human needs and desires for goods whose production requires scarce resources. The greater the supply of such goods per head, the greater, other things being equal, the level of satisfaction or welfare. The national product or national income, finally, was proposed as the objective measurable counterpart of economic welfare.

National product estimates were never regarded as ideal measures of output relevant to economic welfare. With some qualifications, they measure only those outputs which move through markets; they count as costs only those which must be paid for by private producers; and they value goods according to the prices which individual purchasers are willing to pay. Thus, conventional national product figures make no allowance for productive work that takes place at home or for the satisfactions that people obtain from their leisure time activities. The estimates take no account of the depreciation imposed by production on those parts of the national wealth which are not privately owned; so they do not subtract the costs of air and water pollution or of damage to other elements of the environment, which producers are permitted to use without charge. Similarly, the estimates neglect the losses which one person's consumption activity may cause to the satisfaction of others when he adds to the congestion in streets and roads or in the use of other facilities provided without a proper service fee. As a practical matter, though not in principle, national product estimates understate the growth of many services because, in effect, they neglect such increase as may occur over time in the productivity of the labor employed in some parts of the service sector. Finally, the estimates grossly understate the rise in effective output that takes the form of qualitative improvement in goods and services. The difference between treating pneumonia with penicillin instead of poultices nowhere appears in the national product figures.⁹

When economists deal with national product data carefully, they are inclined to say that they are adequate indexes of short-term – year to year or quarter to quarter – changes in the flow of goods and services but very uncertain guides to longer-term growth relevant to welfare. That is because the division of time between market work and home work or between work and leisure changes only slowly and continuously and may be neglected when considering the fluctuations in output which are prominent in the short run. And similarly with environmental damage and other "external" costs and with advance in quality. Such developments cumulate over longer periods, however, and may become important compared with measured output change over the decades and quarter-centuries which are of concern for long-term growth.

Economists, however, have not always been careful. Lacking better figures, they make the practical judgment that the conventional national product can be used as a rough-and-ready substitute for the long-term index they want. Comparisons of long-term growth between countries and over time were, and still are, often made as if conventionally measured national products per capita were fully satisfactory indications of comparative growth in economic welfare. When, therefore, the national product, usually in its gross version – the GNP – became a household word, the public also came to think of national product figures as satisfactory indexes of output relevant to welfare. Economic growth in popular parlance came to mean growth of GNP. It then emerged, as we shall see, that what are no more than criticisms of the conventional GNP figures as *measures* of growth serve as arguments to discredit economic growth itself.

The deficiencies of national product as a measure of long-term growth relevant to welfare inject an element of ambiguity into the debate over growth. Because national product growth, as conventionally measured, is the conception of economic growth that most people concerned with the issue have in mind, it is convenient to adhere to that meaning. We should not forget, however, that the underlying meaning of economic growth for economists is, as it should be for everyone, increase in a fully comprehensive measure of *net* output per head – net after allowing for the costs of all scarce resources (including the air, the water, the landscape, etc.) which may be used up in production, inclusive of the values produced in the home as well as in the market and adjusted for the improvement or deterioration of quality that accompanies quantitative growth.

Just as increase of conventional national product is an uncertain guide to the growth of economic welfare, so a rise of economic welfare may be obtained at the expense of noneconomic aspects of human satisfaction. Manifestly, the way income is earned and the way it is spent affect the very nature of people and the relations among them. The older welfare economists, however, argued that in the absence of special information, we are entitled to rely on a practical, if rebuttable, presumption that changes in economic welfare also change total welfare in the same direction, if not in the same degree. Economists' favorable appraisal of growth in per capita national product, therefore, rested on a series of practical judgments about the relations between national product and economic welfare and between economic and total welfare. Their appraisal was bolstered by considering the miserable levels of average income from which poor people were rising in each successive generation as well as by the broad indexes of advances in well-being, health, and education already mentioned as concomitants of growth.

A commonsensical Benthamite psychology of fixed wants, the satisfaction of which conduced to happiness, formed the sometimes explicit, always implicit, basis for this outlook. As theoretical welfare economics developed, however, it became more austere. When writing for one another, economists became anxious to empty their subject of entities like happiness, which they could neither define nor measure. They recoiled before the realization that a welfare interpretation of growth demanded interpersonal comparisons of satisfaction among gainers and losers and between populations of different membership at different times. Lacking a clear basis for such comparisons, welfare judgments in any rigorous sense entailing comparisons of experienced satisfaction were held to be impossible. Economic growth in the technical literature came to mean only a greater capacity to produce and, therefore, a wider range of choice among goods, between goods and leisure, and in the distribution of goods among people. What might then be chosen and what that might mean for people were other matters about which objective judgment was impossible.[10] In principle, one might say, if one wished, that enlarging the range of choice is itself a good thing; but one cannot say more than that. Economists' practical judgments, however, did not change. As with people generally, economists as a group continued to support the view that economic growth conduces to welfare. By and large, they still do, and the basis of their position is the series of practical judgments on which the older welfare economics rested. It is those judgments which are now increasingly in question.

Postwar emphasis and achievement

The opening of the postwar period may be taken to be the bicentennial anniversary of the idea of progress at large – if we think of the mid-eighteenth century as the time when optimism about the possibilities of meliorative change first became widespread. And it can be taken to mark the centennial, counting from about 1850, of the idea that technological progress and capital accumulation could be the basis for sustained progress in human welfare based upon growth in output per head. The quarter-century following World War II was remarkable in three respects.

In the first place, there was, for the first two decades of the period, a still more pronounced interest in economic growth.[11] Growth became the premier goal of social policy throughout the world. This heightened emphasis rested, at bottom, on all the considerations already advanced; but these obtained added support from a variety of special circumstances and influences. In many European countries, there had been a serious check to growth since the outbreak of the First World War, that is, for some thirty-five years. In those years, the United States had forged ahead in industrial power and wealth and established a new standard of affluent living for common people. Since it was widely realized that the gap between European and American incomes was much wider than could be justified by any differences in technological capacity or in experience with commercial, industrial, or governmental organization, there was a natural determination to reduce the income gap rapidly. In the Soviet Union, the same determination was spurred not only by great poverty but also by the reigning political doctrine, which held that the advance to a true communist order was dependent on the achievement of material plenty. In the new countries of the Third World, nationalist governments properly regarded commercial and industrial development as necessary conditions for establishing their fledgling states on stable foundations. In the Cold War between the Soviet Union and the United States, military and political power were, for a time, largely equated with GNP. Since the market economies of the West still lived in the aftermath of the Great Depression, the minimization of unemployment rivaled growth itself as an economic goal. Jobs for an expanding labor force then meant growth, at least in the aggregate, if not per capita. Given technological progress, it meant both. Finally, in both Europe and America, the working classes had become a much stronger political force. Their demands for higher incomes could be more easily met from the fruits of average growth than by redistribution. Their demands for higher levels of mass education, health care, and economic security – for the Welfare State – could be more easily accommodated if incomes were rising than if they were stagnant. In the United States there was also the special problem of the blacks. It seemed far easier to reduce discrimination and to open a better place for blacks in schools, jobs, and professions in an atmosphere of rapid growth and full employment than in a stationary or slowly growing economy.

The second, perhaps still more impressive, feature of the postwar decades was that the heightened interest in economic growth was matched by the achievement. During the twenty-five years from 1948 to 1973, American growth in labor productivity was faster than it had been in any earlier quarter-century in even this country's notable record. Increase of per capita output just failed to establish a new speed record but only because the share of working age people in the total population was declining. More to the point, however, the period passed without a serious depression, and output per head rose by 2.4 percent per year and real disposable income per head by 2.3 percent.[12] Average real incomes, therefore, rose by nearly 80 percent during the quarter-century. And in Western Europe and Japan, growth proceeded even more rapidly and steadily. The per capita rate in those countries averaged some 4 percent per year for the decades of the fifties and sixties.[13] With hardly a pause, their average level of per capita output, which had been under one-half the U.S. level in 1950, rose to almost 70 percent of the now much higher American level in 1973.[14] In that year average incomes in the other industrialized market economies were well above the unprecedentedly affluent American levels of the early fifties. The growth that was so ardently desired was therefore obtained. The American level of consumption became much higher, and large numbers of people in Europe and Japan began to live at the level and in the manner of American consumers. The rise of living standards in those countries reached all classes of people, and the welfare state became established.

The third feature of the postwar period was, therefore, all the more notable. As the experience with rapid growth proceeded, doubts emerged. In the United States and Western Europe, though not in the collectivist societies or in the impoverished Third World, a mood of disappointment in the achievement spread. A critical movement of opposition to future growth appeared and became more powerful. The mood and the movement are not yet dominant. Public policy is still, in principle, pro growth. But the opposition is widespread in intellectual and professional circles and in popular writing. Individual communities seek to bar population expansion, and they make industry and commerce unwelcome. Moreover, both the ordinary person's attitude and public policy itself have become ambivalent. They welcome growth but they resist its concomitants – environmental damage and congestion and the risks posed by new products, materials, and industrial processes. The transformation of opinion is as marked in Europe and Japan as in the United States. The recoil from growth is as curious as it is unexpected. The next section deals with its rationale.

The reappraisal of economic growth

The new attack on growth may be viewed as proceeding on four broad fronts. On the first – which this essay only mentions but does not develop – continued growth is said to be both impossible to sustain and dangerous to pursue. It is unsustainable because growing scarcities of food, basic raw materials, and means of disposing of waste products must eventually halt the growth of aggregate world output and then force a decline. Further advance of per capita output could then proceed only in the measure that population decline might outrun that of production. But pushing output to such limits is also dangerous because we may at any stage overshoot the mark by establishing levels of population and output, which later prove unsustainable. Rapid and catastrophic reductions of per capita income, accompanied by severe population pressure, would then ensue, leaving the world to face a truly Malthusian adjustment by war, famine, disease, and misery. This essay says no more about this ultimate, gloomy, but possibly very remote, prospect.

On the other three fronts, critics attack growth from several directions. They argue, first, that growth entails costs which national product does not measure; so real growth of net output relevant to welfare is slower than the national product accounts suggest. Next, growth affords but limited consumer satisfactions and benefits to already affluent people; the enhanced satisfaction we seek is a will-o'-the-wisp which vanishes as it is approached. Finally, growth is gained by dependence on a technology and mode of organization which rob work of interest and stimulus. It entails a system of rewards the justification of which is efficiency but whose outcome is injustice. It implies a society which poisons people's characters and the relations among them.

Unmeasured and badly measured costs – and benefits

If one starts from net national product as the conventional measure of economic growth, the first general criticism holds that the measure is a misleading guide to the growth of economic welfare. Its best known, but not necessarily most important, failing is that it neglects the external costs of production and consumption.[15] These costs are the losses of valuable and scarce resources, which, because they can be used as free goods by producers and consumers, fail to be subtracted from the aggregate net product. If such costs are rising, the true net growth rate is smaller than that of the conventional measure. Familiar examples of such uncounted external costs are the pollution of water and air by industrial activity, by automobiles, and by household heating and sewage. Congestion on the highways and streets is another.[16] Damage to wilderness areas and the depopulation or extinction of certain species of wildlife are still others.

No one knows how large these costs may be because no one is asked to pay for the right to do the damage he does. And no one is asked to pay – or, at any rate, asked to pay a rationally determined fee – because no one knows how to value the damage any individual or firm may do. To the dedicated environmentalist, the value of the damage seems beyond all price, and it would be worth the blockage of any incremental output to prevent the occurrence of the smallest increment of environmental harm. To the ordinary urban worker, the problem is the obsession of overly affluent, overly idle sentimentalists. So long as their own drinking water remains potable, many people's tolerance for smoky air and congested national parks is very great. They would sacrifice very little in the way of a pay raise to save the bald-headed eagle. And, in between, the generality of people have their own particular interests and unexamined valuations. We shall learn something more about the valuations as the cost of environmental protection comes to be more systematically studied and better known.

As things stand, few would say that the negative external by-products of production are growing at a rate which would offset as much as one-half percentage point of a per capita growth, which until recently was approximately 2 percent a year in the United States.[17] Any figure of that order of magnitude, however, is important. It is accepted principle that we ought to spend "what it is worth" to us to offset environmental damage. And the expenditure – except for capital equipment and for making good past, rather than current, damage – should be counted as a cost of production, not as part of current net output. In the nature of the case, the value of environmental damage cannot be objectively fixed, and the sum to be expended in environmental protection will remain as an issue to be settled politically, in the confused way that political issues are ever settled.

The measurement of net national product relevant to welfare is beset by still other troubles. Some, as critics emphasize, tend to overstate the conventional, measured growth rate, but others work the other way. Much of the cost of government is arguably devoted to supporting the private production and consumption activity, which turns out the goods we want and obtain from the private sector. It therefore represents "intermediate" production, like cotton yarn in the ladder of activity which yields us clothing. To include it is double-counting; and since government expenditure has been rising faster than the total, its inclusion exaggerates the measured growth rate. We should not forget, however, that much government, like some private, expenditure has positive, as well as negative, external effects. Education, for example, benefits not only the recipient but society at large in ways which go beyond the acquisition of productive skills. Its value is understated by its cost; and the educational effort has been rising fast.

National product neglects production that does not pass through the market. This includes housewives' services and other home production, which have been rising slowly because women have gone to "work" in increasing numbers and because standard hours of work-for-pay have been falling slowly. Including production at home would slow down the growth rate. So would including the value of leisure time activity since that has been rising only slowly. If we included the productive value of the time spent by working age students in school, however (because they are creating "human capital" by raising their skill levels), this would have operated to raise the growth rate during recent decades. So would an allowance for rising labor productivity in parts of the service sector, where productivity growth is neglected in the conventional measures. And, most important, so would an adequate allowance for improvement in the quality of goods and services, which is now almost entirely overlooked by the standard measures, or at least so most people would say.

For what is quality? The national product account yields a dollar total into which the myriad goods and services produced enter with dollar weights, which are their market prices. The prices reflect the relative values placed on products by consumers who are viewed as good judges of the capabilities of different things to satisfy each person's own needs and tastes. Similarly, workers' wages, which help to determine relative prices, are supposed to reflect their knowledge about the relative toilsomeness, unpleasantness, and dangers of their jobs. For most consumer goods and for most jobs, especially long-familiar goods and jobs, these are plausible assumptions. Until a few decades ago, all goods were made of homely materials – grains, cotton, wood, iron. Power for tools came from boiling water; it was transmitted by leather belts. When horses gave way to gasoline engines, a farm boy could still understand and fix a motor. But many modern products and processes have become mysterious entities. What we eat and what we use are now often in the realms of an incomprehensible chemistry, biology, and physics.

In our imaginations, and to some extent in reality, our goods and our jobs assault us with unseen emanations. They deposit unknown substances that cumulate within us and years afterwards visit us with life-threatening diseases. In one instant, we are carried aloft on a silent wind; in the next, we may be smashed and incinerated. People sense that their bargains for goods and jobs have become deceitful. New products and processes proclaim their benefits openly: larger harvests of less perishable foods, warmer houses, faster, more comfortable transport, better wages based on higher productivity in pleasanter circumstances. Innovations contract with us according to their visible promise, but they do not at the outset reveal the full terms of the arrangement. They permit us to discover when and as we can, perhaps years later, that they may exact an uncertain additional price. Just as the national product does not measure the improvements in automobiles or in medical diagnosis and remedy, so it does not measure the concealed costs of innovation. A vague terror of novel technology, therefore, has spread. Critics of growth work to foster distrust of consumer products and working conditions and to slow down the pace of innovation in order to uncover and reduce its risks.

When all is said and done, there may still be some presumption that growth of national product per head is an indicator of growth of output relevant to welfare. That, at any rate, is the suggestion of such efforts as have so far been made to construct more adequate measures than conventional product itself.[18] These efforts, however, still fall short of our needs, and no one can say with confidence what the growth rate of a fully comprehensive and accurate measure of output growth relevant to welfare would be. Better measures are possible, but some problems are, in principle, beyond solution. We shall never be able to assign values, comparable with ordinary goods, to the externalities of production and consumption, neither to the negative effects, like environmental damage, nor to the positive effects, like education. Nor shall we be able to take full account of the values of the qualitative improvements and of the hidden costs embodied in new goods and jobs. Critics of growth understandably focus on the hidden costs; proponents, on the unvalued benefits. We have to learn to use the dubious national product numbers we have, or the better ones we may contrive, without assuming that the story they tell is decisive.

The limited satisfaction from growth in consumption

There can be little doubt of the human values of growth where the common pattern is at or near subsistence and where the largest part of increased production is devoted to a gain in elementary physical well-being – reduction of morbidity and mortality. In that case growth is life-giving and life-saving, restorative if not redemptive, permissive if not creative. To question growth there is to question the value of life itself.[19]

But what about the uses of higher income when people are already well off? In the commonsensical approach to growth, as well as in the outlook of the older welfare economics, people have fixed needs, wants, and desires. Goods help to satisfy these wants. In that somewhat ingenuous view, neither the intensity of their needs and desires nor the capacity of goods to satisfy them is affected by other people's incomes. A larger command over goods for the average person, therefore, means a higher level of satisfaction, happiness, or "welfare." As people become richer, increments of goods may, it is true, serve to satisfy less urgent needs and, therefore, yield proportionately smaller increments of satisfaction: this is the well-known "law of diminishing marginal utility." But the direction of the effect is unchanged. More continues to be better.

This simple doctrine, however, is now widely disputed. For one thing, there appears to be some evidence that in a rich country like the United States, growth of average income is not accompanied by an increase in people's happiness as they themselves perceive it. The evidence comes from repeated surveys carried out in the United States by the Gallup Poll and the National Opinion Research Center. In these surveys, intermingled with other questions, some of which established the income level of the respondents, people were asked to say whether they were "very happy," "pretty happy" (or "fairly happy"), or "not so happy." The results of those surveys were brought together and analyzed by Richard Easterlin.[20] They suggest a striking and puzzling conclusion. Easterlin found a contradiction in the association between income and reported happiness. If one considers people in a given country at a given time – say, as they reveal themselves in any single survey in the United States – one finds, as expected, a strong, consistent, positive association between income and happiness. A much larger fraction of people in the upper income groups report themselves "very happy" than in the lower. This positive association across income groups runs through all the individual surveys. On the other hand, if one compares the reports over time during which average U.S. incomes have risen markedly, there is no associated rise in reported happiness. The percentages reporting themselves "very happy" remain about the same.[21] How can these paradoxical results be reconciled? There are several mutually supporting explanations.

The income relativity of aspirations. Easterlin's own explanation of his paradox is that the satisfaction a person gets from his income depends not on its absolute level but on its relation to those of others in the same community. If a person stands high on the income ladder, he is the happier for it. But if there is an increase in the level of income with no change in people's relative positions, nobody feels better off. The idea is commonplace and plausible; and it is consistent with age-old observations of social critics about the vanities of wealth and its self-defeating dissipation in competitive display and status seeking.[22]

The relative income hypothesis, moreover, also helps explain why it has proven so difficult to eliminate poverty as incomes rise. By any absolute standard, we have made great progress. The proportions which contemporaries regard as in poverty, however, tell a different story. As incomes rose, the level which the community regarded as tolerable, and which, indeed, was presumably needed for people to function as full-fledged community members, also rose. The rising poverty standard was embodied in the income tests used by state and private agencies to fix eligibility for welfare aid. The result is that welfare rolls in the United States did not decline as a proportion of the population for many years. And several studies, both in the United States over time and across countries, suggest that countries tend to set the poverty threshold at about one-half the median income in the country, whatever that happens to be.[23]

Habituation.

In prewar days well-to-do people had elaborate meals and had a number of servants to work for them. Now they have simpler meals and do their own work. After they have become accustomed to the new conditions, are they less happy than before? It is doubtful whether a moderately well-to-do man is appreciably happier now than he would be if transplanted back to the pre-railway age and attuned to the conditions of that age. . . .[24]

This quotation suggests a second hypothesis. Suppose that people's feelings of satisfaction depend not on the level of their incomes but on the novelty and stimulation of experiencing a higher income than they are used to – and the reverse with feelings of dissatisfaction. This helps explain the Easterlin paradox because higher-income groups are likely to contain a relatively large proportion of people whose incomes have recently risen whereas low-income groups will contain a relatively large proportion of those whose incomes have recently fallen. That difference would tend to produce the observed positive association between income level and reported happiness in comparisons across income classes at any given time and place. But if the proportions of recent arrivals in the various income groups remained fairly constant, there would be no change in the proportions who declared themselves happy in comparisons over time.

Tibor Scitovsky has shown how this limitation on the power of rising income to yield an increase in the average person's satisfaction can be deduced from contemporary psychological theory.[25] In the older psychology, needs and desires, if unfulfilled, cause tension, anxiety, and alertness, what psychologists would now call a raised level of *arousal*, which is uncomfortable. People try to reduce arousal by satisfying the desire which gave rise to it. The lower the level to which arousal can be brought, the greater the feeling of comfort or satisfaction. The older welfare economics incorporated the same idea.

Backed by much experiment, modern psychological theory proposes a different view. Arousal can fall too low. The comfort of fulfillment, initially satisfying, becomes boring. Animals and humans then find pleasure in action or experience that raises the arousal level, which is stimulating. The keys to stimulation are novelty, challenge, and risk, which provide new desires, experiences, or goals and which renew or heighten the interest in meeting them. Such stimulus is found in hard and challenging work, artistic creation or connoisseurship, in exploration of all kinds, and in sports when seriously pursued. People also find stimulus – and this is the immediately relevant point – in the *process* of satisfying a previously unfulfilled desire. There is pleasure, therefore, in exploring the novel possibilities of a higher level of income but not in its routine use. It is a theory that has a disturbing implication. It says that the level of satisfaction depends not – or at least not only – on the level of income but on its growth rate. Other things being equal, we should have to grow *faster* in order to be happier, and we should have to keep on growing in order to stay in the same place. Is it any wonder that some people find the pursuit of satisfaction from higher income self-defeating?

The rising prices of space and time. The built-in frustrations arising from the income relativity of aspirations and from habituation, it will be noted, rest on the structures of individual and social psychology. There are, however, frustrations which are more truly economic in origin. When people think about the concrete things they lack, the possession of which might make them happier, it is natural to envisage them in terms of the particular goods and services that form the lifestyle of people who already enjoy a larger income. Two lifestyle differences between relatively poor and relatively rich bear particularly on our problem. One is that the rich live more spaciously. They enjoy larger living quarters with larger grounds about their houses, their locations commonly afford easier access to the countryside, they can pay for comfortable transportation, and both at home and on holiday, they can, if they wish, have quiet, privacy, and seclusion. The other difference is that the rich can, or could, afford servants and, more generally, a large command over "services." If a family can raise its level of income relative to that of other families, it can, of course, adopt the style of life of the richer families to which it aspires. On the other hand, if a family's income rises together with everyone else's, that will not be the case. A general rise of incomes brings with it an increase in the prices of space and personal service. The average family with rising income cannot afford much more of these goods than they had before, certainly not as much as they had imagined they would; and many who used to command a great deal cannot afford as much. This is a third explanation of Easterlin's paradox.

It is, indeed, true that so far as space and related matters are concerned, there are countervailing considerations. Higher income has brought better housing to the average family. Automobiles have given ordinary people a wider choice of location, great freedom of movement, and easier access to mountains and seashore. On the other hand, as Fred Hirsch has emphasized, a large part of the rise of incomes with which people try to buy spaciousness, seclusion, quiet, a pleasing landscape, or an occasional taste of unspoilt wilderness is dissipated because the competition of more people for the same limited space has, in effect, raised the price of what they seek.[26]

There are also complications as regards servants and services. It is not true that the prices of all services rise with average income. There has been rapid technological progress in the production of some services. More knowledge, better diagnostic equipment, antibiotics, and so forth have made medical care more effective. On the other hand, servants have been virtually priced out of employment, productivity in the production of most services has lagged behind that in goods production, and their relative prices have risen steeply. Indeed, on the extreme assumption that the productivity of an hour's service remains constant, there is a neat paradox, which makes the issue clear.[27] The average person, no matter how rich he or she becomes, can never command the service of more than one other average person – even if he spends his entire income to buy it. In this respect the "poor" cannot ever hope to live like the "rich," no matter how rich they become.

The rise in the price of services is the form which the rising price of time takes in the marketplace. There is also the rising price of time at home, the price of time for productive activities around the house or for leisure time activities. This is the development which Stefan Linder has dramatized in *The Harried Leisure Class*.[28] Linder builds his case on the basis of an old proposition, which holds a central place in the relatively new economic theory about the allocation of time. This asserts that consumption consists, not in the purchase of consumer goods and services but rather in combining such purchased materials with a person's own time and effort to produce final utilities or satisfaction. As with ordinary production, consumers may combine purchased materials with labor (that is, leisure) time in varying proportions to produce the largest output of utility with the resources available. In the production of final satisfaction, consumers have a finite amount of time at their disposal, and this they must divide to best advantage between work, which provides purchased raw materials, and leisure or, better, leisure time activity, which is the source of value added in consumption.

What happens to this division? Year by year, in the course of economic growth, people have access to more goods. This has two counteracting effects. On the one hand, the value of extra leisure rises because there are more goods to use and to use up per leisure hour. On the other hand, the price of such time also rises because with the rise of labor productivity, more purchasable goods must be foregone if working hours are cut. There is, therefore, no clear presumption that working time will be reduced to afford more leisure to consume more goods. And there *is* a clear presumption that, even as work hours are reduced, the division of time will be made such that we consume more goods per leisure hour. It is true that over the whole course of industrialization, working hours have declined, but this was conspicuously not the case in the United States and in some other affluent countries in the postwar period. On a family basis, with regard to the larger participation of women in the labor market, the opposite was true. So we end up with Linder's vivid picture of a typical Scandinavian evening at home, the prosperous householder desperately reading the *New York Times,* listening to Italian opera, sipping Brazilian coffee and French cognac, and smoking an Havana cigar while still entertaining his beautiful Swedish wife as well as he can.

All this, of course, means that increments of ordinary net national product yield diminishing increments of satisfaction since the leisure time-goods ratio has declined – always provided that there has been no rise in our own consumption skills, that is, in our ability to convert goods into satisfaction per unit of time. And this source of diminishing marginal utility is over and above the source we usually have in mind, namely, that incremental goods serve to satisfy less and less urgent needs and desires.

The rising price of time may act to reduce the value of growth to affluent people in still another way toward which Scitovsky's ideas point. As goods become cheap compared with time, the pattern of consumption should shift away from activities which require much time for their pursuit and toward those in which lots of goods are used. Goods-intensive consumption is, by and large, directed to desires, which, when met, lower people's levels of arousal. Their routine satisfaction leaves us bored, dissatisfied, and in need of stimulus. But experience and activities that are sources of stimulation – the arts, literature, active sports, travel, companionship, and so forth – generally demand considerable preparation, training, and active involvement. They are time-intensive, but the rising price of time and the cheapness of goods seduce us to other more immediately comforting but ultimately unsatisfying habits.

Technology, organization, and "life"

The title of this section is pretentious. It has to be. The contemporary debate about economic growth reaches into realms usually inhabited only by English poets, German philosophers, and American sociologists. This is uncomfortable for an economist. The point of departure is the character of the technology, which is the basis of productivity growth, and the character of the organization needed to exploit the technology.

The technology which enables us to apply science to utilitarian ends demands both massive and specialized equipment and highly trained and specialized workers. The organization needed to make economical use of very large units of specialized physical and human capital consists of either great integrated companies (large factories served by large sales, purchasing, warehousing, financing, research and administrative divisions, themselves divided into still more specialized subdivisions) or functionally specialized companies, often very large (professional, service, finance, insurance, transport, etc.). In either case, the finely divided activities of individuals, groups, divisions, departments, and companies are brought into cooperation either by command and higher authority within firms or by the impersonal operation of trade and markets among firms. In the economy of industrialized society (this is the critical view), individuals are trained to perform narrow and repetitive tasks and, endowed with appropriate personal attitudes and goals, they are led by a self-interested commercial drive to cooperate toward the grand unperceived end of producing a large GNP. To the critics of growth, the analogy between industrialized society and the subhuman life of the anthill is inescapable. In the human anthill, however (this is again the view of the critics) the nicely articulated but unconsciously directed efforts of individuals do not conduce to the preservation and improvement of either the individual or the species. Rather they block the full development of the one and promote the destruction of the other.

Work

The older conception of industrialization, still shared by many, sees it as the basis of an immense improvement in the character of work. Viewed across the decades, work has become lighter, safer, cleaner, and conducted in more pleasant surroundings. Jobs are more secure and workers are better protected against the arbitrary authority of supervisors. With the most physically demanding work taken over by machines, the mental and, in a sense, the moral capabilities of people are more important and more actively employed. The great expansion in the ancillary functions of production (professions, trade, finance, services, government) supports this tendency. It opens the world of work more widely to women and provides a material incentive for the spread of education.

The critics have a different vision. Their ideal is preindustrial. They see a craftsman, owner of his own tools and master of his trade. He sets his own hours and his own pace. He works with or near his family to design and then himself to build a well-constructed, finely proportioned utilitarian object. It will function well, it will last, and it pleases the eye. Or they see the village peasant. He works hard, but his work is part of both a seasonal and communal round. He lives close to nature, consumes the produce of his own work, and is free of market pressures. He and his neighbors are friends and cooperators, not competitors or objects of each other's sales efforts.

Industrialization, the critics complain, destroys these humanly satisfying work patterns. The economic organization demanded by advancing technology cuts off work from the rest of life, removes its connection with home and family, deprives it of its communal character, and leaves it shorn of ceremonial, religious, or other mystic elements. Workers, from being masters of their own time and their own tools, become tenders of a company's machinery. Specialized in content, organized on a large scale, knowing neither its beginning nor end, work, for many people, is left simply a burden, increasingly calculated to render them isolated, insecure, and unfulfilled.

It is not hard to recognize this picture of preindustrial work and life as largely mythic and fallacious. Few preindustrial workers were masters of their own time and tools. Labor, both rural and urban, was brutally hard and long. It was shared by children and women. As Marshall tells us, it precluded schooling for the young and left adults without time or energy for "intellectual and artistic enjoyment in the evening." It rendered the individual and, therefore, society "coarse and unrefined."[29] The myth of preindustrial fulfillment in work, however, is hardy. Presumably it projects to the past a human need or desire still unsatisfied for many by contemporary working life.

Country and city

The great cities which grew up in the course of industrialization were the creatures of the more intense trade, professional services, abundant skilled labor, finance, and transport facilities, which were, in turn, needed to support specialized, large-scale production. After basic problems of concentrated populations were overcome – pure water, sewage disposal, police and fire protection – modern cities came into their own as centers of education, art, music, libraries, newspapers, restaurants and cafes, and of social life generally. They were seen to provide a stimulating background for living, a far better combination of facilities for both work and "life" than the dull and torpid village.

Matters, however, did not remain in balance. Ever-growing densities of population and their superconcentration in skyscrapers and in commercial and industrial lofts made business and homelife geographically incompatible. The interesting intermixture of living quarters, shops and cafes, which fills the memories of older Europeans, broke down. First, whole sections of cities became specialized to work, alive by day but dead at night. The commuter railway and the automobile carried the process further by making dispersal to suburbs possible. The city then changed its character. Its population tended to become polarized toward the few rich and the many poor. In the United States, the removal of the middle classes to the suburbs created a chronic financial problem for the cities, which made for physical deterioration. The life of the streets was cramped by growing crime. And the suburban dispersal of so many important elements of the urban community restricted its intellectual activity. In the eyes of its critics, economic growth had produced conditions in which people, seeking to better their individual lives, were destroying a great social asset.[30]

The compulsions of growth

Defenders of growth regard material advance as an enlargement of people's range of choice and, therefore, of their freedom. Critics regard it as an instrument of compulsion. Defenders of growth tend to take people's tastes and attitudes as fixed by human nature. Technological progress presents a set of opportunities for satisfying those tastes more fully. Markets, private enterprise, and the free search for profits and for remunerative occupations are the instruments that release people's energies to exploit the opportunities presented by technical advance. The speed of exploitation is determined by the rate of technical advance itself and by people's choices regarding the pace of capital accumulation, by how much present income they are willing to divert to the building of physical capital, to the training of youth, and to research. The outcome is a rising level of labor productivity that offers people the chance to have both more goods and more leisure in the combination that best pleases them, as well as a wider choice among an increased variety of goods and services.

Critics see the same facts as restricting rather than enlarging the realm of choice. The nature of technological progress, built on economies of scale, increasingly confines the goods that are supplied to the standardized products of mass production. It restricts the jobs that are available to specialized, subdivided, robotlike occupations. In these, people are reduced to analogues of mechanical parts, and for their effective nonabrasive meshing, they are subject to the psychological and social lubrication of corporate administration. At the same time, a portion of the potentialities of the human spirit are stunted. To the great loss of instinctive social sympathy, feelings of solidarity, and tendencies to cooperate, people are encouraged to think and to behave as if their only extrafamily relations were those of contract and trade, competition or authority. Deliberate manipulation, by advertising or otherwise, is not central to the process. The compulsions are implicit in the existence of an industrialized civilization. The social pressures of a society adapted by education, demonstration, and emulation to accepting the kinds of goods and jobs that mass methods imply are pervasive, thorough, and largely unnoticed by the people on whom they act. Behavior in conformity with these pressures is not only foreordained; it is even perceived as freedom by the generality of people. And it is only consistent with this state of affairs that those who may try to adopt an alternative pattern of work, consumption, and communal relations are regarded by the rest of society as "dropouts."[31]

Where are we?

Since this essay's main purpose is to present the rationale for the contemporary attack on the growth of per capita national product, it cannot also attempt an appraisal of the grounds for the attack. It is perhaps possible to say something about the present state and implications of a debate which now goes on not only explicitly but also implicitly in the political and bureaucratic processes concerned with environmental regulation, occupational and consumer safety, sources of power, income redistribution, and the like.

It helps one understand the place of the contemporary attack on growth to realize that little in it is new. An analysis of the "external effects" of growth, its unmeasured costs in terms of environmental damage and the like, was a central feature of the earliest writings on the economics of welfare.[32] It has always been understood that true growth had to be measured net of such costs. The preacher in Ecclesiastes knew all about the vanities of wealth. Adam Smith and J. S. Mill, to say nothing of Thorstein Veblen, said most of what needs saying about the income relativity of aspirations, and Pigou[33] was equally clear about the effects of habituation in eroding satisfaction from higher income. Contemporary complaints about the effects of specialization, subdivision of labor, or the workers' loss of control over tools and product stem from Marx. The separation of work from family and communal life was mourned by Oliver Goldsmith in *The Deserted Village*. John Ruskin, William Morris, and many others deplored the passing of the artisan and his craft. Thomas Carlyle aimed his strongest diatribes against the rise of industry and commerce because they involved people in trade and reduced personal relations to an exchange of monetary values, a cash nexus. Rousseau was the precursor of Marcuse and of all those who decry industrial civilization because, like any civilization, it shapes and constrains man's natural, supposedly benevolent, impulses.

These old arguments did not sway opinion seriously during the two centuries culminating in the 1960s when industrialization was spreading and becoming more intense. The belief that economic growth conduces to human welfare rested firmly on the widely accepted assumption that critical considerations might qualify but could not offset the solid benefits of a greater capacity to turn out goods. Somewhat elaborated, the old critical arguments are now the basis of a powerful attack in the richer, industrialized market economies. In those countries, a considerable shift of opinion has taken place and public policy has moved in many ways that limit the pace of growth. What happened to make the old arguments more persuasive to many, if not most, people? The answers are to be found partly in some elements of contemporary technology itself, partly in the widespread affluence and large populations it has brought into being, and partly in our cumulating experience with the unmeasured costs of measured growth and its social by-products. These have combined to change the balance of advantage and disadvantage that people achieve.

The level of affluence achieved is itself a main reason for the change. When the proportion of people living in poverty – as measured by past standards – has been drastically reduced, when large numbers have incomes which are not only comfortable but provide margins for education, recreation, and travel, the most obvious and obtrusive benefits of growth tend to fade from view. Growth then appears less, to use Lampman's words, as a "life-giving and life-saving" force.[34] It is no longer needed to free life for something besides toil. Questions about the possible contributions of higher incomes to happiness then seem more pertinent, and the frustrations which underlie Easterlin's paradox loom larger.

When per capita output has become high and populations large and increasingly concentrated, the external, unmeasured costs of growth become much more important. Rivers, lakes, and the atmosphere itself can carry off great masses of waste before there is a significant loss of purity. The wastes of still larger output and its necessary concentration in and around cities, however, reach and increasingly surpass these threshold capabilities. The external costs of production then rise disproportionately. A power technology based on burning fossil fuels aggravates the problem, and the affluent comfort achieved in other directions makes people more sensitive to atmospheric and other environmental discomfort.

There is a similar story in other spheres. Streets and parks can absorb a considerable rise of population and usage without the appearance of intense congestion and disturbing noise, but these limits are increasingly surpassed. And given the need for population concentration, it is hard to expand thoroughfares, parks, and other such facilities adequately. The spread of private motor vehicles compounds the difficulty within the cities and helps carry it to the countryside.

From another angle, as the technology on which growth is based becomes more powerful, it also becomes more mysterious to ordinary people. The science that gives rise to new materials and processes also reveals its concealed by-products, dangers, and risks. In their strangeness and apparent power to strike invisibly, at a distance and after long intervals, hidden dangers surround the new technology with a sense of pervasive threat. Again, as the urgency of need for still more goods declines, people's willingness to tolerate risks they have come to feel, but which they are unable to understand and appraise, also declines.

The attack on growth also reflects interests and feelings that transcend any appraisal of the direct benefits and costs of rising productivity. That is because its ability to generate the growth that people want is one of the main supports of capitalistic economy and bourgeois society. To an increasing number of people, that society lacks a moral basis, and others find its taste and style of life unattractive. People who hold these views and who, in one degree or another, have become members of an adversary culture, may then oppose growth for reasons whose real thrust is different from the considerations they advance. Their ostensible and sincerely held aim may be environmental protection or consumer safety. Their underlying, perhaps not quite explicitly formulated, purpose is to render less effective an economy and society which they find distasteful.[35]

An economy is a mode of social cooperation based on a system of rewards and incentives. The system may be regarded as just and legitimate or as unjust and immoral. The capitalistic economy, which relies on trade and markets to offer incentives and to determine rewards, found its traditional legitimacy in the Protestant Ethic and its view of work, thrift, and prudence, and both together as good in the eyes of God. The development of a highly complicated commercial economy and the emergence of large, bureaucratic corporations made the connection between work, thrift, and their rewards more remote and hard to discern. At the same time, the decline of the religious temper weakened the claim of work to be a mark of merit, to say nothing of the claim of wealth itself to be a sign of grace. Indeed, the most sophisticated defenders of capitalism, such as Friedrich Hayek, have abandoned any contention that capitalistic rewards are proportioned to merit, as the following bears witness:

Most people will object not to the bare fact of inequality but to the fact that differences in reward do not correspond to any recognizable differences in the merit of those who receive them. The answer commonly given to this is that a free society on the whole achieves this kind of justice. This, however, is an indefensible contention if by justice is meant proportionality of reward to moral merit. . . . The proper answer is that in a free society it is neither desirable nor practicable that material rewards should be made generally to correspond to what men recognize as merit. . . .[36]

Hayek's argument, one will notice, opposes a free society and a just society, and, as Irving Kristol has said: "men cannot accept the historical accidents of the marketplace – seen merely as accidents – as the basis of an enduring and legitimate entitlement to power, privilege, and property."[37] That the market's distribution of rewards and property may, in a generalized way, still be the basis for a wonderfully effective system of production and growth is, indeed, a powerful alternative justification. It is, however, only a pragmatic defense. It will not persuade those who are impatient with the merely pragmatic or those to whom distributive justice seems an attainable ideal or those who are, on other grounds, antipathetic to the bourgeois society which capitalism implies.

It is in this last regard that the attack on growth gains strength from tendencies in the contemporary culture. The culture in question is "high culture," that is, the feelings, sensibility, and style characteristic of leading circles in literature, the arts, and social criticism. This culture has for long been out of sympathy with capitalism and the bourgeois mode, as earlier references to Rousseau, Carlyle, Morris, and Ruskin have suggested. The bourgeois style is sensible, measured, steady, rational, functional, and optimistic. The high culture is expressive, romantic, tragic, heroic, idiosyncratic, and, more recently, anti-intellectual and instinctual.

The disjunction, to use Bell's term, between economy and culture gains in importance from the altered role of the adversary culture in contemporary society. In the nineteenth century, the adversary culture provided a refuge and living space for a tiny minority of eccentric spirits who had little connection with society at large. But the rise in levels of income and education has permitted and encouraged a much wider segment of the population to consume and enjoy the products of high culture, to identify with it, and to adapt it to the tastes and intellectual capabilities of still wider circles. In consequence, the high culture has tended to meld into a "mid-culture." The exponents of the former have become contributors to journals of large circulation. Journalists, movie makers, television writers and producers, fashion designers, and the like have adopted the outlook of the adversary culture and become its translators to a broader public. The result is a conflict in the minds of a large and influential wing of opinion, which seeks its occupation and rewards within the capitalistic economy but is, at the same time, predisposed to attack and hamper its operation and to thwart its effectiveness.

The shift of opinion regarding the benefits of economic growth has been matched by a transformation in the process by which social decisions regarding growth are taken. Until very few years ago, such decisions were made without apparent conflict. They were largely the unconscious outcome of private choices about work and saving and about the technological innovations profitable to introduce and develop. Markets determined the value which the consuming public gave to these decisions and, by fixing the rewards they would carry, either ratified or vetoed them. Decisions, it is true, were not wholly private and market-controlled. Government in the United States was involved especially through its support of education and by its role in the development of transportation. In continental Europe and Japan, governments took a still more active part. Yet even in public decisions, debate did not turn on the desirability of growth but rather on the effectiveness of alternative policies and their cost.

The largely unconscious process which, especially in the United States, governed the pace and nature of growth has now been transformed into a political struggle. This is inevitable. The government is now so large that its taxing and spending activities, regardless of their direct and immediate objectives, have a significant indirect bearing on private choices regarding work, saving, and enterprise. It is inevitable also because the attack on growth is largely concerned with the diffused physical and social by-products of production and consumption. People seek protection against environmental damage and against health risks whose dangers they cannot appraise. They seek to guard their communities against the intrusion of more people or against commercial and industrial activity. In many spheres, the market cannot give people the protection they want, and in others they do not trust it to do so. The debate ranges very widely and connects matters as seemingly trivial to our environment as the fate of the notorious snail darter with matters as patently vital to economic growth as the provision of electric power.

It is an awkward fact that the political struggle over growth is necessarily carried on with little, if any, knowledge concerning the trade-offs that are involved. By way of example, we lack any way of measuring the values which people derive from and attach to various degrees of air or water purity. Nor can we say how much the achievement of such purity costs us in terms of future income. We are, indeed, beginning to measure the costs of compliance with government standards for waste disposal and the like. But no one knows how much future growth is lost because of the delays, expenses, and risks which the regulatory process imposes on investment and innovation. Nor can we know what importance people would place on the extra income which they are, in effect, losing.

This last issue is of special importance because even in countries as rich as America, there are still families who live on the edge of poverty and who would be lifted above it by the growth of average income. For many more, the skeptical views flowing from the "happiness surveys" can hardly be decisive. Progress, as Frank Knight, the great economic philosopher of the twenties, was fond of saying, is less a question of happiness than of what it is that people are unhappy about. Many, therefore, would strongly prefer the disappointments and frustrations of living at a higher rather than at a lower level of income, even if they could be persuaded that they would be no happier in doing so.

Beyond these continuing private interests in higher income, growth enlarges our capacity to deal with social problems. Engaged in fierce international rivalries for mortal stakes, growth is the basis for an adequate national defense. Committed, as in general we are, to a more nearly equal chance in life for the relatively poor and their children, it is politically more practicable to try to provide it from the fruits of growth than by redistributing a stagnant total income. Anxious, as we have now become, to guard ourselves better against the risks of work, product failures, and environmental damage, we look to the growth margin to pay the costs of protection.

The fact that the very size of government, the physical and social by-products of growth, and the social questions dependent on its pace and direction have thrust economic growth squarely into the political arena is perhaps the most important aspect of the present conjuncture. We must rely on a highly imperfect political process, with its confusing struggle of special and general interests, acting with inadequate knowledge, to adjudicate immensely complex conflicts of values. For the foreseeable future, therefore, our limited political capabilities may well be the most binding constraint on our ability to achieve a pace and direction of growth compatible with true human progress.

Notes

1. J.B. Bury, *The Idea of Progress* (New York: Dover, 1955), p. 52.

2. It is easy to oversimplify and misrepresent the positions of Ricardo, McCullogh, Mill, and the others of the time. They were not, of course, enemies of progress, and they believed that the common man was best off in a "progressive state" of society, that is, in a state in which the "industrial arts" are flourishing and advancing and in which returns to capital are still sufficiently high to induce net accumulation. They did not think that these processes would soon come to a halt. On the other hand, they did not believe that technical advance and capital accumulation would continue at a rapid pace indefinitely or that even the pace of their own era, speedy as they thought it, was sufficient to outrun that of population growth and to permit a cumulative rise of general living conditions. Insofar as the idea of progress comprehends that of indefinite advance in material standards for ordinary people, they did not accept it. See John Stuart Mill, *Principles of Political Economy*, ed. W.J. Ashley (London: Longman's Green, 1909), p. 751. Kenneth Boulding's quip, "One has to be either a lunatic or an economist to believe in the possibility of indefinite economic growth," does not apply to the classical economists.

3. In *Memorials of Alfred Marshall*, ed. A.C. Pigou (London: Macmillan, 1925), pp. 110, 111.

4. Ibid., pp. 111, 112.

5. Ibid., p. 115.

6. Charles A. Beard, Introduction to Bury, *Idea of Progress*, pp. xxii–vi, xxxv.

7. My statement about the place of economic growth in the older welfare economics follows A. C. Pigou, *The Economics of Welfare* (London: Macmillan, 1932), Chap. 1.

8. Ibid., p. 11.

9. These issues and a number of others are defined and discussed in detail in *The Measurement of Economic and Social Performance*, ed. Milton Moss (New York: Columbia University Press, 1973). This volume also republishes the well-known experiment by Nordhaus and Tobin in providing a set of national product estimates which allow for

many of the deficiencies of conventional national product when viewed as an index of output relevant to welfare. Their "Measure of Economic Welfare," except on extreme assumptions, appears to confirm the common impression that conventional national product can serve as a rough index of long-term growth useful for welfare judgments.

10. Readers will find a thorough review of the subtle and sophisticated literature concerning the possibility of welfare judgments based on output comparisons in Amartya Sen, "The Welfare Basis of Real Income Comparisons: A Survey," *Journal of Economic Literature*, 17(1) (March 1979): 1–45.

11. A more elaborate explanation of the heightened postwar interest in growth along the general lines of the text may be found in H. W. Arndt, *The Rise and Fall of Economic Growth: A Study in Contemporary Thought* (Melbourne: Longman Cheshire Pty., Ltd., 1978). See also Moses Abramovitz, "Economic Growth and Its Discontents," in *Economics and Human Welfare*, ed. Michael J. Boskin (New York: Academic Press, 1979).

12. *Economic Report of the President*, transmitted to the Congress, February 1979 (Washington, D.C.: Superintendent of Documents, USGPO), Tables B-2, B-22.

13. These are unweighted average rates for countries based on the national product estimates of the Organization for Economic Cooperation and Development. Averages weighted by population would be still more impressive since they would give relatively great weight to the larger countries, Germany, France, Italy and Japan which were also the faster growing.

14. The 1950 figures are estimates by the present writer. They are extrapolated from data for 1965 worked out by Angus Maddison, "Comparative Productivity Levels in the Developed Countries," *Banca Nazionale del Lavoro Quarterly Review*, no. 83, December 1967, pp. 3–23. The Maddison figures translate European and Japanese incomes in 1965 into 1965 U.S. dollars by weighting outputs in different classes by U.S. relative prices. The 1965 figures were then carried back to 1950 using national growth rates. The 1973 comparisons are from Irving Kravis, Alan W. Heston, and Robert Summers, "Real GDP Per Capita for More Than 100 Countries," *Economic Journal*, 88(350) (June 1978): 215–42, Table 4, Col. 9.

15. A standard contemporary discussion is E. J. Mishan, *The Cost of Economic Growth* (New York: Praeger, 1967).

16. Ibid., Chap. 8.

17. Edward F. Denison, *Accounting for Slower Economic Growth* (Washington, D.C.: Brookings Institution, 1979), has estimated that total expenditure on reducing damage from air and water pollution has been offsetting about 0.25 percentage points in the growth rate since 1973. This figure, however, includes expenditures for capital formation to help reduce future pollution and to correct past damage. So it exaggerates the growth of resources to offset current costs. Since there is now a general belief that the levels of air and water pollution are no longer rising, Denison's figure may be a useful upper bound to growth costs of that nature. This, of course, would still take no account of other externalities, congestion, noise, damage to wilderness and wildlife, flood control, etc. To get a sense of orders of magnitude, one should consider that net national product in the mid-seventies was running at about $1,500 billion a year. To offset one-half percentage point in the growth rate, the annual *increment* to currently caused environmental damage would have had to be $7.5 billion. This could be the case if we valued total annual environmental loss at, say, 10 percent of current net output, that is, at $150 billion, and considered that the loss level was rising at 5 percent a year. These are both very large figures, which few would accept.

18. William Nordhaus and James Tobin, "Is Growth Obsolete?" in *The Measurement of Economic and Social Performance*, ed. Milton Moss (New York: Columbia University Press

for National Bureau of Economic Research, 1973), pp. 509–32. See also the discussion of the national product treatment of expenditures to control environmental damage and the like in Thomas Juster, "A Framework for the Measurement of Economic and Social Performance," in *Measurement of Economic and Social Performance*, pp. 25–84.

19. Robert J. Lampman, "Recent U.S. Economic Growth and the Gain in Human Welfare," in *Perspectives on Economic Growth*, ed. Walter W. Heller (New York: Random House, 1968), p. 158.

20. R. A. Easterlin, "Does Economic Growth Improve the Human Lot?" in *Nations and Households in Economic Growth*, ed. P. A. David and M. W. Reder (New York: Academic Press, 1974), pp. 89–125.

21. Easterlin also analyzed the results of a considerable number of cross-country surveys made both by the Gallup Poll and by Hadley Cantril, *The Patterns of Human Concerns* (New Brunswick, N.J.: Rutgers University Press, 1965), and found the same contradictory results – a strong positive association between income and reported happiness across income groups within given national surveys, but no significant association across countries among which average income levels varied a great deal. This result, of course, bolsters the intertemporal findings for the United States. One may well ask, however, whether the standard according to which an Italian would feel justified in reporting himself very happy is the same as that of a Swede. The same question may, in principle, also be addressed to historical comparisons within a single country, but it is surely a less disturbing problem.

22. I have presented a somewhat extended version of these views in "Economic Growth and Its Discontents."

23. Cf. V. R. Fuchs, "Redefining Poverty and Redistributing Income," *The Public Interest*, 8 (1967): 88–95.

24. A. C. Pigou, "Some Aspects of Welfare Economics," *American Economic Review*, 41 (June 1951): 294.

25. Tibor Scitovsky, "The Place of Economic Welfare in Human Welfare," *Quarterly Review of Economics and Business*, 13(3) (autumn 1973): 7–19; and his *The Joyless Economy* (New York: Oxford University Press, 1976).

26. Fred Hirsch, *The Social Limits to Growth* (Cambridge, Mass.: Harvard University Press, 1978).

27. I owe this point to Sir Roy Harrod, "The Possibility of Economic Satiety: Use of Economic Growth for Improving the Quality of Education and Leisure," in *Problems of United States Economic Development* (New York: Committee for Economic Development, 1958), I, 207–14. Of course, if productivity were constant in the production of everything, per capita incomes would not rise at all. What gives the apparent paradox its point is that productivity in producing services rises very slowly, even as productivity in other sectors rises fast.

28. Stefan B. Linder, *The Harried Leisure Class* (New York: Columbia University Press, 1970).

29. Marshall, *Memorials of Alfred Marshall*, pp. 110, 111.

30. Mishan, *Costs of Economic Growth*, Chap. 8.

31. Views of this sort fill the New Left literature. Representative references are Herbert Marcuse, *One-Dimensional Man* (Boston: Beacon Press, 1964); William H. Whyte, Jr., *The Organization Man* (New York: Simon & Schuster, 1956); and J. K. Galbraith, *The Affluent Society* (Boston: Houghton Mifflin, 1958).

32. A. C. Pigou, *Work and Welfare* (London: Macmillan, 1904).

33. Pigou, "Some Aspects of Welfare Economics."

34. Lampman, "Recent U.S. Economic Growth," p. 158.

35. Irving Kristol and Daniel Bell have published compact elaborations of the argu-

ment in this and succeeding paragraphs. See their essays in Bell and Kristol, eds., *Capitalism Today* (New York: Basic Books, 1970); and also Bell's *The Cultural Contradic-tions of Capitalism* (New York: Basic Books, 1976), Chaps. 1, 2.

36. Frederick Hayek, from his *Constitution of Liberty* (1960), as quoted by Irving Kristol, " 'When Virtue Loses All Her Loveliness' – Some Reflections on Capitalism and 'The Free Society,' " in *Capitalism Today*, p. 6.

37. Ibid., p. 9.

13
Welfare quandaries and productivity concerns

The early debates over the role of government in economic life, at least during the era of industrialization, took the form of a contest between *laissez-faire* and thoroughgoing socialism. In Western Europe and North America, however, the movement away from individualism followed a much less radical course, which John Maynard Keynes was one of the first to define. His famous lectures in the mid-1920s on *The End of Laissez-Faire* carried the following passage:

. . . a time may be coming when we shall get clearer than we are at present as to when we are talking about Capitalism as an efficient or inefficient technique, and when we are talking about it as desirable or objectionable in itself. For my part, I think that Capitalism, *wisely managed*, can probably be made more efficient for attaining economic ends than any alternative yet in sight, but that in itself it is in many ways extremely objectionable. Our problem is to work out a social organization which shall be as efficient as possible without offending our notions of a satisfactory way of life. [p. 53, emphasis added]

Keynes, as we can now see, was among the first writers to form a definite vision of the kind of system under which we have come to live during the last half century, the system we now call the Mixed Economy or Welfare Capitalism or the Middle Way. Like the much more individualistic, much less guided, system that preceded it, the Mixed Economy developed with the support of a broad consensus of opinion. That consensus, however, has now weakened. The economic role of government is again the subject of debate, attack, and

Presidential address delivered at the ninety-third meeting of the American Economic Association, September 6, 1980, Denver, Colorado. I am grateful to a number of friends who read early drafts and suggested improvements: Kenneth Arrow, Michael Boskin, Arthur Burns, Paul David, Solomon Fabricant, Eli Ginzberg, Bert Hickman, Milton Katz, Ronald McKinnon, Nathan Rosenberg, John Shoven, Robert Solow, and Tibor Scitovsky. Reprinted by permission from *American Economic Review*, vol. 71, no. 1 (March 1981), 1–17.

resistance far more intense than we have known for decades. The attack ranges over a wide spectrum. It questions the scope of government, the particular measures and policies through which government exercises its functions, and the political institutions which shape the measures and policies employed. A few voices call on us to move on to a more encompassing socialism, including the ownership of industry. Many more call for a drastic revival of market rule.

We all, I think, sense that we have come to a very difficult juncture in the development of our Mixed Economy. How we shall emerge is still in dim prospect. As in other illnesses, social crises often are surmounted and are followed by periods of renewed stable development. But sometimes not. We, therefore, ought to think where we are and what the nature of our troubles is.

I

There is no single, simple way to gather together all the threads of our present discontent, and I shall not try. One useful opening, however, is to consider the pronounced and worrisome retardation of productivity growth from which we now suffer. Productivity growth, I need hardly say, is the main source of measured per capita output growth. And per capita output, in turn, is a central component of economic welfare as we economists conceive it, many would say *the* central component. It is elementary, however, that per capita output growth and welfare growth are not the same thing. National product is not even an adequate long-term measure of net output relevant to welfare. It makes inadequate allowance for the quality and variety of goods. It excludes the household and treats all government expenditure as final product. It neglects the externalities of production and consumption and the costs of growth proper, for example, the dislocation of people. It makes dubious assumptions about people's ability to appraise and guard against the dangers carried by jobs and products. And there is much more to economic welfare than can be captured in any long-term measure of output: job stability, income security, a fair distribution of opportunities and rewards.

The economic role of government expanded during the last half century and more in large part in order to pursue the social objectives that are not comprehended in measured net national product. The result is the mixed economy or welfare state in which we now live and which is now the object of attack.

Productivity growth is a useful focus of discussion in relation to the current discontents and the accompanying reappraisal of our mixed economy for a combination of two reasons.

To begin with, productivity, viewed as a source of private earnings, exists in a state of uneasy tension with the other welfare objectives, which we pursue largely through the government. The causes of the tension need to be underscored.

First – an obvious point – the more income that is diverted to social uses, the less of any given aggregate remains under the private control of income earners for their own personal use.

Next, the size of the diversion and the way it is made and used affects the level of output and productivity, present and future. That is partly because a host of government activities are supportive of current output and productivity, and many activities, including some, like education, that are undertaken for generalized social objectives, are in the nature of capital formation.[1] In a still more basic sense, moreover, and one much neglected in current debates, the pace of growth in a country depends not only on its access to new technology, but on its ability to make and absorb the social adjustments required to exploit new products and processes. Simply to recall the familiar, the process includes the displacement and redistribution of populations among regions and from farm to city. It demands the abandonment of old industries and occupations, and the qualification of workers for new, more skilled occupations. The extension of education, with all its implications for shifts in social status, in aspiration, and in political power, is a requisite. Along the technological path which we have followed, growth also demands very large-scale enterprise which establishes new types of market power and alters the relations of workers and employers. Viewed from another angle, the dependent employment status of workers and the mobility of industry and people imply a great change in the structure of families and in their roles in caring for children, the sick, and the old. Because the required adaptations can and do alter the positions, prospects, and power of established groups, conflict and resistance are intrinsic to the growth process. To resolve such conflict and resistance in a way which preserves a large consensus for growth, yet does not impose a cost which retards growth unduly, a mechanism of conflict resolution is needed. The national sovereign state necessarily becomes the arbiter of group conflict and the mitigator of those negative effects of economic change which would otherwise induce resistance to growth.[2]

The enlargement of the government's economic role, including its support of income minima, health care, social insurance, and the other elements of the welfare state, was, therefore – at least up to a point – not just a question of compassionate regard for the unfortunate, and not just a question of reducing inequalities of outcome and opportunity, though that is how people usually think of it. It was, and is – up to a point – a part of the productivity growth process itself.

And yet, manifestly, there is another side to the story, the side that is so much to the fore today. The government's roles as referee and as mitigator of the costs of growth – as well as instrument for pursuing welfare goals supplementary to measured productivity – must be paid for. But it is essentially impossible to design a tax system that places no marginal burden on the rewards for productive effort, or a regulatory system that has no cost in measured output. Similarly, we can hardly design a transfer system which – up to a point – necessarily divorces income from work, but which yet does not qualify economic incentives. There is a presumption, therefore, that the tax-transfer-regulatory system, whatever its essential, long-term, indirect, supportive role, operates more immediately and directly to constrict work, saving, investment, and mobility – just how much is, of course, a question.

There is, therefore, an uneasy many-faceted tension between measured productivity growth and the private earnings it generates on the one side, and the pursuit of other welfare goals through government on the other side. The tension implies a difficult and delicate problem of choice and balance. A balance – certainly a wide acceptance of the pace and nature of our joint pursuit of different welfare goals – seemed to exist during the first two postwar decades when productivity growth was relatively rapid. That balance, if it was a balance, has, however, now been upset by the protracted retardation of productivity growth during the last dozen or more years. That is the second reason why productivity growth is a useful focus for examining the current dissatisfaction with our mixed economy.

I shall deal briefly with three matters:

1. What were the developments which were antecedent to (which stand in the background of) our present troubles and its accompanying discontent?
2. What can we now say about the causes of the current productivity retardation? In particular, to what extent is the retardation connected with the enlarged role of government and its pursuit of alternative social goals?
3. What is the outlook for productivity growth, and what are the implications of that outlook for the further development of our mixed economic system?

II

In the early part of the postwar period, economic growth, in the aggregate and per capita, established itself as a premier goal of economic policy – co-equal with "full" employment, perhaps of even higher priority. Besides the standard reason, that per capita growth raises average levels of consumption, there were special reasons. Growth was seen as the best way to overcome poverty without the social conflicts accompanying redistribution. It would create a favorable environment in which to open opportunities for blacks and other minorities. It would provide the resources for meeting still other social goals, for example, extended education and health care. Growth was also sought to maintain defense, to compete politically with a fast-growing Soviet Union and to assert continued leadership in our rapidly progressing alliance. Growth would enable us to help not only the poor in our own country, it would permit us to help the still more impoverished people of the less-developed world. Productivity growth was a goal distinguishable from full employment, but it was also seen – not necessarily correctly – as a condition of full employment. Unless we could hold our own in international trade, our foreign accounts would impose demand restraints on policy and make for chronic underemployment.

This growth, so ardently desired, was in fact achieved. For two decades, income per capita grew faster than ever before and output per hour much faster. At the same time, there was a rapid development of government in pursuit of other welfare objectives, and this was also eagerly sought. The Social Security system established in the 1930's was enlarged; education was rapidly extended; science was fostered; there were large programs for hospital building and housing. The proportion of the population living below defined poverty levels was reduced – the joint result of rising average incomes, and extended insurance and welfare provision. Partly because government was bigger, partly because the scope of progressive taxation was wider, partly because of old age and unemployment insurance and other forms of income maintenance, we enjoyed the benefits of a system of "built-in stabilizers." Recessions were milder and growth more steady than they had ever been before in American experience as an industrialized country.

The main point, however, is that in this period, productivity growth paid easily for the pursuit of other welfare goals. Although government grew faster than GNP, fast growth of productivity supported fast growth of per capita disposable income, of real spendable earnings of workers, and of average family incomes. [See Table 13.2, page 372.] Productivity growth was, therefore, the substantial basis on which the consensus of opinion supporting the development of the mixed economy rested.

III

Frank Knight liked to say that progress is not a question of happiness; it is a question of what people are unhappy about. Not surprisingly, therefore, the progress of the first two postwar decades was followed by a certain recoil from growth – a reordering, if not reversal, of priorities. This took several forms:

1. Whereas in the 1950's, measured growth was regarded as the main instrument for overcoming poverty, as the 1960's wore on the view took hold, with much justification, that future growth alone could not deal adequately with the poverty which past growth had left behind. Although technical progress, capital accumulation, and general education would continue to be important in the future, an increasing proportion of the "residual poor" had special handicaps. They had to be helped directly, principally by a fight against discrimination, by special education and training programs, and by new and expanded schemes for social insurance, income support, health care, and other transfers in kind. The impulse to fight poverty directly was fed by new information about the size and composition of the remaining poor population, by the indignation of social reformers and, most of all, by rising racial tensions.[3] "We cannot," said the Council of Economic Advisors, "leave the further wearing away of poverty solely to the general progress of the economy" (1964, p. 60).[4]

2. As individual income levels rose, people generally became more sensitive to their immediate surroundings. They found hospital and educational facilities inadequate and the urban physical plant shabby. Yet the demand for improvement had to be met in difficult circumstances which continue to plague and torment local government to this day. The relative price of public, like that of private, services was rising. Higher incomes and automobiles were transporting upwardly mobile families to the suburbs, carrying their tax base with them. The cities, increasingly abandoned to the poor, unable to tap the suburban affluence about them, could barely cope. Congestion on the highways and streets, noise, air and water pollution, all fed by growth itself, swelled, moved to the countryside and everywhere became more objectionable to otherwise more affluent people.

3. People discovered the terrors of technology – products, working conditions, and environmental changes that carried risks. The dangers feared were often invisible, they operated at a distance and cumulated over time, carrying both real and imaginary threats to health and life now and in generations to come. Technological progress, which for decades had been seen as the process by which problems and

dangers might be overcome, was now increasingly feared as a major source of our troubles.

These shifts in outlook had two important practical consequences. One was the very rapid expansion of government social welfare and civil rights programs which began in the mid-1960's and which developed and matured in the 1970's. Expenditures for "social welfare," which were 9 percent of GNP in 1950 and only 10 percent in 1960, rose to 15 percent in 1970 and to 20 percent in 1977.[5] The other was an "explosion" of public regulatory legislation and administration directed to the protection of the environment, and to the safety of workers and consumers.[6] The new legislation became the basis for strong, privately organized campaigns to limit growth and the application of new technology.

IV

The maturing of the Great Society programs in the spheres of welfare and civil rights, and the implementation and expansion of the social regulatory laws, brought our mixed economy to a new stage of development. There was a new distribution of emphasis among the different dimensions of economic welfare, and correspondingly a new distribution of economic power between the private and public spheres. The new development of the mixed economy, however, is now confronted by a changed and less-favorable growth environment.

Looking back, we can now see that a slower rate of productivity growth accompanied the institution and the maturing of the Great Society programs. To what extent the two developments were associated as effect and cause, however, is still an open question. So is a related matter; that is, the responsibility of transient as distinct from durable factors for bringing about the slowdown we observe. It would be wrong to pretend that there are now definite answers to these questions. The factual position, however, deserves description because it bears on the origins of our present discontents.

Beginning in the late 1960's, private-sector productivity growth fell back from the high speed it had reached in the years preceding. The retardation before 1973 was moderate. The new pace approximated that during the somewhat slack later 1950's. After 1973, however, the slowdown became much more serious. The upshot is that average productivity growth for the fourteen years between 1965 and 1979 ran at only one-half the pace of the years from 1948 to 1965; since 1973, it has risen at less than one-fifth that earlier pace.[7] The extent of the slowdown between the two rough halves of the postwar period, before and after 1965 – to say nothing of the post-1973 period by itself –

may be judged from the fact that the post-1965 productivity slow-down has been more severe than any of the retardations measured across major depressions going back to the 1890's. That includes the retardation from the 1920's to the 1930's. [See Table 13.1, page 371.] Yet, up to 1979 we had had no major depression.

In my judgment, the productivity retardation, at least since 1973, has been accompanied by a slower rate of improvement in material conditions of well-being. In some respects, and by some measures, there have even been significant declines. It is true that, because the labor force was rising rapidly in relation to population, the growth rate of real disposable income per capita was well maintained – at least if we depend on the deflator for "personal consumption expenditures"; not if we use the CPI. As perceived by many people, however, the welfare significance of even the more favorable measure is qualified. That is partly because the demographic changes that supported labor-force growth also made for a faster increase of households than of population, so to some degree expenses per head increased with income per head.[8] It is qualified also to the extent that women felt forced to take paid work to offset the slower rise or actual decline of their husbands' real earnings; to the extent that the proportion of persons living in pretransfer poverty has been tending to rise since 1968; to the extent that transfer incomes became a more important part of aggregate disposable income – to the disadvantage of income earners; and to the extent that the rise of noncash compensation reduced worker's discretionary take-home pay. The upshot is that in recent years, the average real cash incomes of workers have, depending on the measure, almost ceased to rise or begun to fall. The same is true of the average real total income of families, supported as that has been by transfer incomes and by the entry of second workers. The presumption is that the real earned income of representative single worker families, still more their cash income, has definitely declined. [See Table 13.2, page 372.]

The slowdowns in the growth rates of productivity, annual wages, and household incomes are, moreover, not the only disturbing elements in our economic situation. They are accompanied by rapid and volatile inflation which redistributes income and wealth in arbitrary and confusing ways. Taken together, these developments have disappointed peoples' expectations; they have robbed many people of the fruits of earlier work and saving, and made almost everyone unsure or fearful about their future.

These developments stand in the background of the current discontent with the operation of our mixed economy. They have led to a backlash against the earlier recoil from productivity growth. This backlash – perhaps justifiably, perhaps not – raises sharply the issue of maintaining a steady balance between the productivity growth that supports the rise of earned incomes and the pursuit of other vitally important social goals.

V

Our attitudes towards that issue would be clearer if we could know to what extent the current productivity retardation is actually due to the workings of our·mixed economy or to its past and current attempts to raise social welfare through government actions. Many believe that the welfare and regulatory programs are heavily implicated both in direct ways and because of their arguably plausible connection with the onset and persistence of an erratic and accelerating inflation. There is a concomitant fear that the welfare and regulatory programs may be a serious drag on future productivity growth. Opposition to these programs, is, therefore, rising. True, if future productivity growth is slow for whatever reasons, people will be less willing than they might otherwise be to bear the cost of pursuing alternative welfare goals. But if that pursuit were actually a significant cause of slower growth, the reluctance would be still stronger, as it then should be.

The causes of the current retardation, however, remain cloudy. A portion of the slowdown is, by general agreement, due to a virtual cessation of the shift of workers from small-scale inefficient farming and from self-employment in petty trade to higher productivity occupations in larger-scale urban enterprise. A portion too is assignable to the massive entry of workers – youth and women – since the mid-1960's. Finally, a small part of the retardation is attributable to the diversion of resources to comply with environmental regulation and safety requirements in ways that do not register in measured output, though, of course, they should. Serious students, however, offer widely different estimates of the contributions of other factors: the quality of schooling, conventional capital services, R&D, and the influence of cyclical or other forces affecting intensity of resource use. The impact of higher energy prices on the substitution of labor for capital in the operation of existing energy-using equipment and on the post-1973 slowdown of capital deepening is equally unclear, though possibly very important. Most analyses leave a substantial part of the retardation unconnected with any identified and measured contributory source, and they disagree about the time – whether after 1973 or as early as the latter 1960's – when that unspecified residual retardation made its appearance.[9]

In this state of factual uncertainty, it is not hard to propose esti-mates of the sources of retardation which assign substantial responsi-bility to factors connected with the government's welfare and regula-tory activities. We, therefore, find William Fellner asking: ". . . whether, directly or indirectly [the analyses of the retardation] do not suggest that the weakening of the productivity trend is attributable in part to changes in the socio-political environment that are of recent origin or that have cumulated to a 'critical mass' " (p. 4).

The suggested mode of operation of these factors is, first, through a decline in the rate of capital deepening; second, through a decline of worker effort symptomized by absenteeism and by a drop in hours worked relative to hours paid; third, by a disinclination for risky, innovatory effort, whose manifestation is the observed slowdown in the residual measures of total factor productivity growth; and fourth, through the diversion of resources to regulatory compliance, the bene-fits of which do not register in measured output even when they should.

These sources of retardation whether great or small – the "sus-pects," as Fellner calls them – are arguably associated with characteris-tic features of our mixed economy, even if they are not exclusively due to them. The first of those features is the widening difference between before- and after-tax marginal rates of return to work, sav-ing, investment, and risk taking. The magnitude of the rise in these rates is indicated by the overall increase of total government expendi-tures from 20 percent of GNP in 1947–49 to 28 percent in 1963–65 and again to over 32 percent in 1977–79.[10] The incentive effects of the tax increases are still imperfectly understood, but there is little reason to suppose they are not distinctly unfavorable.[11] Allied to the effects of rising tax burdens is the possible effect of the cumulating "social security wealth" of individuals on savings and that of other insurance and income-support programs on work.[12] Next, there are the effects of burgeoning regulatory activity. These go beyond the direct re-source costs of compliance already mentioned. There are also indirect costs and risks of obtaining administrative and judicial clearance for new projects, the diversion of R&D expenditure to meet environmen-tal and safety standards, and the hazards of possible future changes in regulatory requirements. Finally, there are the manifold effects of erratic and accelerating inflation.

Inflation belongs in this litany because our pursuit of alternative welfare goals has thus far also involved a tolerance, indeed a pres-sure, for chronic budgetary deficits, and an understandable political incapacity to employ monetary and fiscal restraint forcefully and con-sistently at the risk of elevated unemployment. Inflation, in conjunction with tax rules and accounting practices designed for a stable price regime, has meant very high marginal taxes on returns to capital. In the judgement of some public finance experts, it has also meant a differential burden on business investment compared with that on household borrowing, spending, and investing.[13] If there are fears of accelerated inflation in the future, they carry the prospect of still higher taxes and lower returns while the erratic nature of rapid inflation makes the future more difficult to discern and increases the sense of risk. And if the same fears give rise to a vision of price controls, the risks of investment and innovation are compounded. In any event, inflation compels – or threatens to compel – governments to reduce capacity utilization below its potential. Therefore inflation acts to diminish one of the inducements to invest, as the 1980 business contraction following on financial disorder illustrates. We should remember, moreover, that there is an element of vicious circularity in this aspect of our present conjuncture. Inflation has deleterious effects on productivity growth – and unexpected declines in productivity growth exacerbate inflation.

This range of considerations leads some students to the view that the pursuit of alternative welfare goals accounts for a very considerable part of the retardation. Fellner, whom I mentioned before, suggests that "the causes of at least 1 percentage point annual slackening of the trend in output per worker's hour can be found among the 'suspects' " (*op. cit*, p. 10). That loss is equal to one-half the observed difference between the private-sector productivity growth since 1973 and that during the quarter century between 1948 and 1973.

Such numbers and the argument that leads to them should be understood to be no more than what they are – a *prima facie* indication that something very substantial may be involved in the choices we make between productivity growth and alternative welfare goals. I would not mention them if I did not fear that there is much to the problem, if not as a cause of the recent abrupt retardation, then as a longer-term secular constraint. Yet, at the present time the argument is only speculative, and the estimated loss still more so. The theoretical and quantitative issues are unsettled and deserve our most urgent attention.[14]

VI

So much for the past. We must now try to look ahead. What general view of the future is it sensible to entertain? And what are its implications?

Since our understanding of the productivity retardation of the last dozen years is so clouded, conjecture about the future must be still more fuzzy. True, the negative impact of the recent big influx of inexperienced young workers is due to be reversed. In looking ahead, however, more basic questions need to be addressed. No one, indeed, ought to doubt the persistence of some substantial continuity in what Solomon Fabricant has identified as

the basic factors underlying economic growth in the United States: the tastes and preferences of the American people, the economic opportunities and alternatives open to them, the social framework within which they live and work together, and the relations of the United States with the rest of the world. Different assumptions would be contrary to all experience and could only lead to wild speculation. [So he concludes] The trend of national output per worker-hour will . . . continue to be upward. [p.1]

I agree; but, as Fabricant also asks, how fast will the trend line rise? A "substantial degree of continuity" is not the same as ironclad fixity, and much of this talk has already pointed to some change in Fabricant's basic factors. Within the country, preferences and goals have changed in the degree to which concern for income security, equality of opportunity, environmental protection, and consumer and worker safety sways votes and, to some degree, personal behavior. Corresponding to these shifts in tastes and concerns, the "social framework within which we live and work together" has been recast. The government has come to play a larger role in shaping the "economic opportunities and alternatives" open to us – while imposing burdens on our growth potential whose weight we can now suspect but cannot yet clearly assess. Partly because of higher incomes, partly because of changes in industrial and labor market organization, and partly because of government regulation and income support, there has been a decline in market flexibility – in the responsiveness of prices and wages to the balance of supply and demand, and of people's own responsiveness to price changes – the implications of which were sketched by Tibor Scitovsky (1980).

Our relations with the rest of the world have also changed in ways which I believe are dominantly, but not entirely, unfavorable to U.S. growth prospects. The economic rise of Europe and Japan has, indeed, brought those countries to the technological frontier in many fields. On that account, the effort and experience on which world technological advance rests now has a wider base. The United States, therefore, should now begin to profit more from other countries' technical effort even as other countries borrow from us. It remains to be seen, of course, whether we shall prove as successful at borrowing and adapting foreign technology as some other countries have been.

The advance of other countries, however, also has a darker side for us. The development of many industries in which this country has long been a leader is now threatened by the competition of other countries. This changes the prospects for U.S. productivity growth to our disadvantage. It is harder for an industry to push forward, or even to keep up with, the technological frontier when its rate of expansion slows down, still harder when it is contracting. It is an old story that, in the course of aggregate productivity growth, the rise of new, more rapidly progressing industries constricts the growth of the old. That is Schumpeter's "creative destruction," and it helps explain why retardation in the growth of output and productivity is the normal fate of individual industries within a country, while the growth rate of the aggregate remains constant or even speeds up. The reverse, however, is not necessarily true, nor even probably true. We cannot count on new, more progressive sectors stepping into the breach merely because the development of our old industries is constricted by foreign competition. Foreign success, of course, offers us cheap imports. Yet the experience of Britain from 1870 to 1913 presents this country with a worrisome historical question mark. As Britain's basic industries lost their leadership and markets to the United States, Germany, and other countries after 1870, Britain's labor productivity growth rate was halved compared with previous decades, and her average total factor productivity growth during the forty years after 1870 fell to zero.[15] The question is: Can we mount a more energetic and successful response to the challenge of newly rising foreign competitors after 1970 than Britain did after 1870?[16]

The relative decline of U.S. economic and political power carries with it other disadvantages, and not for ourselves alone. The leadership of the United States in the liberalization and stabilization of international economic relations was one of the bases for rapid world-wide productivity growth in the postwar years. We were able to assert that leadership because superabundant economic strength permitted us to propose arrangements beneficial to ourselves but generous to other countries, and because dominant political power persuaded sometimes recalcitrant partners to cooperate. Today, with U.S. influence reduced and U.S. as well as European industries under pressure, the world economy is threatened by a resurgence of protectionism, in which this country is itself taking part. The world-wide price discipline, which a relatively stable U.S. monetary policy imposed through the dollar-exchange standard, has, for the time being, been lost. And with U.S. influence diminished, effective international cooperation in the petroleum market and in other aspects of relations between industrialized and developing countries has been beyond our reach.

In these circumstances, it is just as difficult to maintain a vision of an unbroken 3 percent trend rate of private-sector productivity growth as it is to discard a vision of a trend rate which continues to be significantly positive. It should, therefore, be no surprise that official and other responsible projections foresee productivity growth rates that lie above zero, but significantly below the average postwar rate.[17]

The uncertainty surrounding any such forecasts can hardly be overstated. The progress of science and the enlargement of the knowledge bases of technology go on apace. Our problem is to overcome or mitigate the forces that are checking our ability to give our growing knowledge practical application and to exploit its benefits fully. There are both physical and monetary sides to our present condition which make our prospects particularly perplexing. On the physical side is the new energy question. Quite apart from the policies we pursue – which may themselves be of crucial importance – we do not now know on what terms supplies will be available, even so far as they depend only on physical and technological considerations. We are uncertain about the elasticity of substitution between energy and other resources, and we do not know how much technological progress will itself be impeded as we try to move along a less energy-intensive path than we have followed in the past. The spread of industrialization from Europe and North America to Asia and Latin America also raises questions about the supplies of other primary materials. As for money, so long as we prove incapable of overcoming our present disposition to inflation, we shall not be able to reach and exploit what would otherwise be the growth potentials of our economy. But if we ever do regain a substantial degree of price stability, we may be happily surprised, even as the Stagnationists of the 1930's were astonished by our growth performance in the postwar period.

VII

In spite of these uncertainties and whatever pleasant or gloomy surprises they may hold, we can hardly avoid the present presumption that our policy choices in the calculable future will need to be made in a less favorable growth environment than that of the generation just past. Our problem of choice will be all the more aggravated if, as now seems likely, the burden of defense expenditures must increase.

That means, first, that our further pursuit of social welfare goals will have to be paid for out of smaller increments of output and income. So, there will be a more difficult problem of choice even if our growth rate itself were not affected by what we choose. It means, second, that the impact of our choices on the measured growth rate itself becomes a more pressing concern and may go far to determine whether the projections now entertained are, indeed, ratified by history or belied. The new, more confined growth environment means, third, that the role of government as a contributor to measured productivity will also be more vitally important, not merely insofar as the government may act to minimize its regulatory or fiscal impact on private performance, but also in the support it gives to research, education, information, labor mobility, and to human capital formation generally.

As we think about these questions, we should not be trapped in the grooves of popular debate. As already said, the alternative paths to economic progress do not present us with clear-cut choices between welfare through government production guidance and income redistribution on the one side, and welfare through private productivity growth on the other. Even if we cared for little except the private use of private earnings, we could not ignore the costs and conflicts arising from the economic and social displacements which accompany growth. We could not, for example, disregard problems which the changing structure and role of the family bring in their train. The state of our cities with all their problems of poverty, crime and deteriorating education, and all their exposure to the pressures of racial concentration and frustration, should be a sufficient reminder. All are bound up with the productivity growth process itself. They are sources of antagonism, conflict, and decline of personal quality which will work to constrain growth unless moderated.[18]

VIII

In the new, less-favorable growth environment, the tensions between productivity and other welfare goals are screwed several notches tighter. The success of our mixed economy and pluralistic society in the next generation will depend heavily on how those tensions are managed. In present circumstance, therefore, economic progress turns very largely on the policies we pursue, on what we do through government, and how we do it. As things now stand, however, we can hardly be said to be adopting policies so much as floundering among them, recoiling from growth and backlashing against the recoil, for lack of knowledge and for lack of proper political institutions to use such knowledge as we have.

The gaps in our knowledge define the job for economics. Virtually every facet of the way productivity depends on policy involves matters of fact still to be established. What is the elasticity of substitution between energy and other resources, and how much will it cost us in future output if we forego the cheapest mode of increasing energy supplies in order to provide a greater degree of protection for environment and people? What are the full benefits and what are the full costs of other environmental or safety measures as now legislated and applied? And how much could we save if we sought similar levels of protection more efficiently by making larger use of market incentives as regulatory devices? What are the effects of different levels and – just as important – different types of taxes and transfers on the supplies of saving, investment, and risky enterprise, and on the supply of labor and the quality of people? What is the full range of our government expenditure which has the character of capital formation – and what are the returns to investment in education and in research and development? What would our progress in productivity look like if we tracked it by a system of national accounts more relevant to long-term change in economic welfare than our conventional national product? The questions go on and on. These are matters to which, for the most part, economists have only recently turned. They are now being attacked with vigor, which is testimony to the fact that the aggravated tension between measured productivity growth and other welfare goals is eliciting a constructive response. There are promising beginnings of useful analytical and empirical work, and these will benefit from future experience and experiment. At the same time, our knowledge about this entire range of questions continues to be uncertain.

The weakness of our knowledge, moreover, is matched, probably exceeded, by the weakness of the political institutions and procedures through which that knowledge must be brought to bear. The structure of government and politics, which served us well enough during a more individualistic era and before the population movements of the last fifty years, has not been successfully adapted to the new scale and complexity of public functions. Let me just allude to three political problems.

One concerns federal budget procedure. In principle, the budget is the place where the conflicting claims of special interests should confront, not only one another, but also, the general interest in economy and in maintaining a balance between private and public uses of income. It is also the place where our concern for increasing welfare by raising measured productivity should be brought into balance with our interest in other welfare goals. But our budgetary process, in spite of improvements in recent years, remains weak. Tolerance for deficits is the overt, inflation is the covert, mode by which competing claims are reconciled. For lack of a systematic way of facing the future costs of present acts, three-quarters of the budget consists of "uncontrollable" items. Capital investment is not distinguished from current consumption. We have just begun to recognize that regulatory acts impose private costs of compliance, analogous to excise taxes, which must somehow be brought within the budgetary ambit of the public household.

A second matter is what, by pleasant euphemism, is called our system of local government. Fractionated geographically and functionally and poorly coordinated, operating in a confused relation to the federal government, plagued by financial crisis reflecting in part the disjunction between the populations they serve and the tax bases on which they rest, our towns, cities, and districts are fertile generators of external costs, duplicative and costly regulation, and chronic neglect. If, as historians generally agree, Britain could not have carried through its Industrial Revolution without the great Victorian reforms of local government, we ought to be asking whether we can meet the emerging problems of growth and welfare in the second half century of our mixed economy without also facing up to the need for systematic local government reform.

The third matter is both basic and diffuse, and that is the weakness of our party system. It is a commonplace that our national parties are no more than fluid, transitory, and undisciplined coalitions of regional and economic interest groupings. Their lack of central organization and authority, reflecting the size and diversity of the country and people, and our lack of ideological commitment, lays us wide open to the distorting influence of special-interest lobbies and single issue politics. In our political life, we are all too vulnerable to particularistic pressures and all too resistant to the needs of general interest legislation.

IX

The rationale supporting the development of our mixed economy sees it as a pragmatic compromise between the competing virtues and defects of decentralized market capitalism and encompassing socialism. Its goal is to obtain a measure of distributive justice, security, and social guidance of economic life without losing too much of the allocative efficiency and dynamism of private enterprise and market organization. And it is a pragmatic compromise in another sense. It seeks to retain for most people that measure of personal protection *from* the state which private property and a private job market confer, while obtaining for the disadvantaged minority of people *through* the state that measure of support without which their lack of property or personal endowment would amount to a denial of individual freedom and capacity to function as full members of the community.

The viability, to say nothing of the success, of this compromise demands a rough, three-cornered balance between the degree to which we look for economic progress through the development of our powers of production by private action, the degree to which we try through government to protect and promote those aspects of production which markets do not reach, and the degree to which we use governments to alter and cushion the market's income verdicts and to resolve the social conflicts which are inherent in growth and change. Until recently, we have paid inadequate attention to the requirements of achieving that balance wisely. We were able to neglect the problem because we enjoyed the amplitude of a run of fortunate years, when rapid and steady growth was the unseen moderator of the tensions of balance. In the new and less favorable environment of growth, however, the tensions between productivity and the alternative dimensions of welfare are aggravated and the problems of balance – of how much to do and how to do it – are more severe.

In the last analysis, values – feelings, tastes, and sympathies – control choices. But those feelings and sympathies should not have to be deployed with the sad deficiencies of knowledge which, in so many spheres, is the case today. Nor should we have to bring feelings and knowledge to bear through political institutions and procedures which are as imperfect as those through which we now act.

When Keynes spoke of the potential efficiency of a "wisely managed" capitalism, he was assuming that the knowledge necessary for wise management was either in hand or would be forthcoming. But he did not seem to be thinking about the limitations of the political process in bringing knowledge to bear. Now that economists and other social scientists have begun to work at it, we can be cautiously hopeful that our knowledge about both the tradeoffs and the complementarities between productivity growth and the other dimensions of economic welfare will gradually improve. For the calculable future, however, our limited political capabilities may well prove to be the most binding constraint on our ability to work out a social organization which, as Keynes said, "shall be as efficient as possible without offending our notions of a satisfactory way of life."

Contemplating these obdurate realities, what can one say to conclude this talk on an upbeat note? The best I can do is a somewhat inspirational passage from a lecture by Jacob Viner, who, as we all know, was no flaming New Dealer, no Great Society man, and no Keynesian. I am fond of this passage, not only because of its sturdy determination, but also because it displays so well Viner's precise but involuted mind, and his amiable weakness for the nonstop sentence. At the close of a long critique of the American welfare state, which is the mixed economy I have been talking about, Viner says:

For all these reasons, . . . there is in the abstract no reason for making an idol of the welfare state in its American form or for dedicating ourselves unreservedly to its continuance as it is today without qualification or amendment. Given the . . . imperfection of the procedures whereby it deals with problems which it cannot evade or defer or with problems which special interests may press upon it for premature resolution, it would be only by the dispensation of a benevolent Providence that it would ever make precisely the right decisions or always avoid major mistakes. It does not have theoretical superiority over all conceivable alternative systems. . . . If . . . I nevertheless conclude that I believe that the welfare state, like old Siwash, is really worth fighting for and even dying for as compared to any rival system, it is because, despite its imperfections in theory and in practice, in the aggregate it provides more promise of preserving and enlarging human freedoms, temporal prosperity, the extinction of mass misery, and the dignity of man and his moral improvement than any other social system which has previously prevailed, which prevails elsewhere today or which, outside Utopia, the mind of man has been able to provide a blueprint for. [pp. 166–67]

Table 13.1. *Growth rates of productivity (output per hour) in the private sector: measures across phases of depression or stagnation, and phases of prosperous development, 1892–1979*

	Growth rates of productivity:[a]		Deviations of cross-stagnation rates from neighboring phases of development		
	Across depression or stagnation phases[b]	Across phases of prosperous development[b]		Absolute differences[c]	Percentage differences
1892–99	1.47		1892/99 –1899/1907	−0.55	−27.2
1899–1907		2.02			
1907–13	1.26		1907/13 –1899/1907	−0.76	−37.6
1920–29		2.76	1929/37 –1920/29	−1.11	−40.2
1929–37	1.65				
1929–41	2.51		1929/41 –1920/29	−0.25	−9.1
1948–65		3.2	1965/79 –1948/65	−1.6	−50.0
1948–73		2.9			
1965–79	1.6		1973/79 –1948/65	−2.6	−81.2
1973–79	0.6		1973/79 –1948/73	−2.3	−79.3

[a]Shown in percent per year
[b]Terminal years of phases are NBER business cycle peaks, except 1965.
[c]Shown in percentage points.

Sources: 1899–1941, Kendrick (1961, Table A-XXII); 1948–79, see note 7, p. 373.

Table 13.2. *Indicators of change in material welfare*

	(Compound growth rates, (percent per year)			
	1948–65	1965–73	1973–79	
Productivity and per capita GNP				
(1) *GNP* per employed worker	2.57	1.60	0.25	
(2) Workers per capita	−0.42	1.02	1.43	
(3) *GNP* per capita	2.14	2.64	1.69	
Real disposable income per capita				
(4) All income (*PCE* deflator)	1.90	3.22	1.75	
(5) _____ (*CPI* deflator)	2.21	2.85	0.84	
(6) All income less transfers (*PCE*)	1.74	2.55	1.29	
(7) _____ (*CPI*)	2.05	2.18	0.38	
(8) All income less transfers and other labor income[e] (*PCE*)	1.58	2.27	0.79	
(9) _____ (*CPI*)	1.89	1.90	−0.11	
Workers earnings				
(10) Real compensation per full-time equivalent employee (*PCE*)	2.66	2.69	0.84[a]	
(11) _____ (*CPI*)	2.96	2.32	0.19[a]	
(12) Real wages and salaries per full-time equivalent employee (*PCE*)	2.35	2.20	0.10[a]	
(13) _____ (*CPI*)	2.66	1.83	−0.54[a]	
(14) Real wage and salary income, full-time white males (*PCE*)		3.01	−0.41[b]	
(15) _____ (*CPI*)		2.61	−1.03[b]	
Median real total income, persons 14 years old and over				
(16) All males (*PCE*)	2.44[c]	2.00	−1.09[a]	
(17) _____ (*CPI*)	2.65[c]	1.64	−1.73[a]	
(18) Year-round full-time male workers (*PCE*)	2.61[d]	3.03	−0.32[a]	
(19) _____ (*CPI*)	2.81[d]	2.66	−0.95[a]	
Median real total family income				
(20) *PCE* deflator	2.74	2.99	0.48[a]	
(21) *CPI* deflator	3.05	2.62	−0.16[a]	
Pretransfer				
(22) Official measure	21.3	18.2	19.2	21.0
(23) Adjusted official measure	–	18.0	18.2	21.1
(24) Relative measure	21.3	19.7	22.2	24.1
Posttransfer				
(25) Official measure	15.6	12.8	11.9	11.8
(26) Adjusted official measure	–	10.1	6.2	6.5
(27) Relative measure	15.6	14.5	15.7	15.4

Notes: PCE=implicit *GNP* deflator for personal consumption expenditure; *CPI*=Bureau of Labor Statistics Consumer Price Index, all items.

[a]1973–78

[b]1973–77

[c]Average 1947 and 1950 to 1965

[d]1955–65

[e]"Other labor income" includes "employers' contributions to private pension, health, unemployment, and welfare funds; compensation for injuries; director's fees, pay of the military reserve; and a few other minor items."

Sources: Lines (1) *Economic Report of the President (Report),* January 1980, Table B-2, col. (1) (1979, rev.) and Table B-27, col. (2)+col. (4); (2) *Report,* Tables B-27, col. (2)+col. (4) and Table B-26; (3) *Report,* Tables B-2 and B-26; (4) *Report,* Table B-22, col. (4); (5) *Report,* Table B-22, col. (3) deflated by *CPI,* Table B-49, col. (1); (6) *Report,* Table B-22, col. (1) less Table B-20, col. (14), divided by population, Table B-26 and *PCE* deflator, Table B-3, col. (2); (7) See line (6), except *CPI* deflator, Table 49, col. (1); (8) Disposable personal income less transfers current $, as in line (6) less "other labor income," *Report,* Table 20, col. (8) and deflated for population and prices as in line (6); (9) See line (8), except *CPI* deflator as in line (7); (10) and (11) *Survey of Current Business: A Supplement, The National Income and Product Accounts of the United States, 1929–1965,* Tables 6.1 and 6.4 and corresponding Tables for *SCB,* July 1977 and 1979, deflated by *PCE* and *CPI,* respectively; (12) and (13) *Survey of Current Business, 1929–65,* Table 6.5 and corresponding tables in *SCB,* July 1977 and 1979; (14) U.S. Bureau of the Census, *Current Population Reports,* Series P-60, with *PCE* deflator, as in line (6); (15) Same, with *CPI* deflator, as in line (5), above; (16)–(19) Same, Series P-60, No. 120, Table 14, with *PCE* or *CPI* deflators, as indicated; (20) and (21) *Current Population Reports,* Series P-60, No. 120, Table 3, deflated as in lines (16) to (19), except 1948 from *Report* January 1980, Table B-25, converted to 1972 dollars; and (22)–(27) Robert Plotnick and Timothy Smeeding, "Poverty and Income Transfers: Past Trends and Future Prospects," *Public Policy,* 27, No. 3 (Summer, 1979), Table 1. The official measures count the number of persons living below constant real (that is, inflation-adjusted) poverty lines defined for households with different characteristics. The adjusted figures correct the official figures for underreporting of income and, in the posttransfer estimates, for direct taxes and for receipts of transfers in kind. To obtain the relative measures, the authors "set the relative poverty lines equal to the federal ones [in 1965]. In succeeding years, the relative lines are increased at the same rate as the median income" (p. 258).

Notes

1. In 1976, government gross capital formation, including investment in human capital, was estimated to be just a trifle *larger*, 2 percent, than conventional gross private domestic investment (see Robert Eisner).

2. Compare Simon Kuznets.

3. See the articles by Michael Harrington and John Kenneth Galbraith reprinted in Burton Weisbrod (pp. 29–42 and 49–56, respectively).

4. Compare ch. 2 *passim*, *Economic Report of the President* (1964).

5. See U.S. Social Security Administration. Social welfare expenditures cover social insurance, public assistance, health and medical care, veterans' programs, education, housing and "other." At present, exhaustive expenditures account for nearly half and transfer programs for somewhat more than half of total welfare expenditures. (See Sheldon Danziger, Robert Haveman, and Robert Plotnick, pp. 6–8). The major reasons for the accelerated growth since 1965 appear to lie in the initiation and expansion of new programs, such as Medicare, and in the generous increase of benefit schedules in old programs like Social Security (see Plotnick, pp. 277–78).

6. *The Federal Register*, which records new regulations, contained 10,000 pages in 1953, but 65,000 pages in 1977. The federal budget to administer regulatory activities was $5 billion in 1978, having doubled since 1974. Compare Arthur Burns, p. 4.

7. I depend for these comparisons on the easily accessible Bureau of Labor Statistics figures for "output per hour of all persons" in the private business sector. See *Economic Report of the President* (1980, Table B-37).

8. Manifestly, some of the faster increase of households than of population was the result of changing tastes, rising incomes, and better provision for old people through Social Security. It was, therefore, the way in which people chose to spend income to best advantage. But part of the fast increase of households was due to the appearance of large cohorts of young adults who were reaching an age when the establishment of independent households was normal, and, in that sense, the extra expense of separate households was imposed on them.

9. Some representative references which illustrate the variety and uncertainty of the results obtained by different investigators are: Edward Denison, especially ch. 9; J. R. Norsworthy, Michael Harper, and Kent Kunze, pp. 387–421, and the accompanying discussion and reports by Peter Clark, Martin Baily, Denison, and Michael Wachter; G.B. Christainsen and Haveman; Robert Coen and Bert Hickman; Kendrick (1980); M. Ishaq Nadiri.

10. See *Economic Report of the President* (1980, Table B-72).

11. See James Tobin, Lecture III.

12. The large effect shown in Feldstein's original, much-noticed time-series analysis (1974) has been thrown into doubt by the discovery of a flaw in his computer program. In a forthcoming NBER working paper, he now finds a smaller but still significant effect. Such time-series estimates remain uncertain because it is hard to measure expected Social Security benefits and hard to separate the effects of Social Security wealth on saving from those of other variables during periods of relative stability, as in samples covering the postwar years alone. The conclusion that Social Security benefits work to reduce saving, however, is supported by other studies, based on samples of individual households and on cross-country evidence, to which Feldstein refers in his new working paper (published 1982).

13. See Feldstein and Lawrence Summers. This study measures the extra taxes imposed by inflation on corporate income both at the level of the corporations themselves

and at those of the households and institutions which receive dividends and interest payments or have an equity interest in the corporations. They find that the combined excess tax due to inflation averaged only 16.4 percent of corporate income tax from 1954 through 1968, but rose to an average of 52 percent from 1969 through 1977. As a result, the reduction in the effective combined tax on corporate income, which had been accomplished by the tax acts of the early 1960's, was reversed. The combined tax, which had fallen as low as 55 percent of real corporate income from 1962 through 1967, rose to an average of 68 percent from 1968 through 1977. This somewhat exceeded the rate of the latter 1950's, when the combined tax averaged 65 percent of corporate income from 1954 through 1961.

There is a presumption, though no direct proof, that the increase in the effective tax rate reduces the real after-tax rate of return on capital and, therefore, the rate of business capital formation. Feldstein and Summers also argue that, since the impact of inflation on taxes works unevenly, it makes for capital misallocation among industries, encourages more investment in inventories and less in equipment and structures, and tends to shift investment away from the corporate sector and towards residential construction and consumer durables (pp. 47–48). See also Patric Hendershott. Inflation, in conjunction with the tax system also works to increase real tax rates on forms of income other than capital, but this effect is relatively small. See Stanley Fischer and Franco Modigliani (pp. 10–11) which provides a general discussion of the costs of inflation.

14. In particular, it is possible to propose calculations of the effect of cyclical or other transient changes in the intensity of resource use which suggest that no underlying slowdown occurred before 1973. (See Denison, chs. 7–9). On such a view, there is a strong suggestion that our troubles do not lie in any generalized impact of the welfare and regulatory programs of government, but are mainly confined to the effects of two developments which either occurred or intensified after 1973, namely, the great increase in the price of energy and the rapid, accelerating, and erratic inflation. Our mixed economy is then implicated to the extent that it works to sustain, if not generate, inflation, and to the extent that our welfare concerns impede the formulation and execution of an energy policy consistent with the maintenance and rapid rise of measured productivity. Continuing work may well clear up these questions about the responsibility of public policy for the current retardation, but, for the time being, we have to live with uncertainty.

The puzzle is still further confused by the experience of the continental European countries. Their fiscal burdens are on the whole heavier than those of the United States, yet their productivity retardation does not generally begin before the oil shock of 1973–74 and the aggravated inflationary disorders that followed. One must, therefore, ask whether the longer persistence of high European productivty growth rates did not reflect a difference in "cyclical" experience. Unlike the United States, they did not generally enjoy a cyclically induced intensification of resource use in the early 1960's and, therefore, a cyclical acceleration of productivity growth. They had no occasion, therefore, to suffer a cyclical retardation in the latter 1960's, as the United States may have done as our economy approached capacity utilization. We may also ask whether the Europeans were more resistant to the incentive effects of heavy taxes and large transfers because of the special factors supporting their great postwar growth booms; or perhaps because their tax and transfer systems are designed differently than ours; or perhaps because of still other matters that differentiate their economies and societies from our own. Or is it the case that what I have referred to as the "suspect factors" – other than inflation and monetary disorder itself – have little to do with the observed retardations of productivity growth? Clearly, the theoretical and empirical issues embodied in these questions call for our very urgent attention.

15. The following figures support these statements. All are compound growth rates per year.

	1856–73	1873–1913
(1) Gross domestic product	2.2	1.8
(2) Man-hours	0.0	0.9
(3) Labor input adjusted for quality	1.4	1.7
(4) Output per man-hour	2.2	0.9
(5) Output per unit of quality-adjusted labor input	0.8	0.1
(6) Total factor productivity	0.6	0.0

Source: R. C. O. Matthews, C. Feinstein and J. Odling-Smee. Line (1), Table 16.1; lines (2) and (3), Table 16.4 (quality adjusted for age, sex, length of schooling, and intensity of work associated with number of hours); line (4)=line (1)−line (2); line (5)=line (1)−(3); line (6), Table 16.2 based on total factor input with labor input adjusted for quality.

16. The British experience, of course, presents a prior question. Which came first, the successful competition of the younger industrial countries in Britain's basic industries, or her own loss of dynamism? Britain in those years was suffering from more than foreign competition in world markets, but my argument makes that competition partly responsible for Britain's national economic retardation (compare Matthews, Feinstein, and Odling-Smee, ch. 17).

17. For example, in its 1979 *Economic Report of the President*, the Council of Economic Advisors estimated the current trend rate of advance of labor productivity in the national economy at 1.5 percent a year, corresponding to 1.75 percent in the private sector, which is little more than half the postwar pace. In its 1980 *Report*, moreover, the Council writes: "Since the average rate of increase during the past 6 years has been below that figure [of 1.5 percent], the trend rate of increase [in the national economy] may very well be still lower, perhaps 1 percent" (p. 88). For further discussion and other projections, see Fabricant (pp. 63 ff.).

18. This, however, does not mean that our present welfare and training programs are uniformly effective emollients and remedies for the dislocations and maladjustments of growth. Nor does it mean that our present income-support programs may not, in some instances, have little-understood, deleterious side effects on family life and individual quality. Nor does it mean that we now know how to do better.

References

A. F. Burns, "The Condition of the American Economy," *The Francis Boyer Lectures on Public Policy*. Washington 1979.

G. B. Christainsen and R. H. Haveman, "The Determinants of the Decline in Measured Productivity: An Evaluation," paper presented at a joint session of the Society of Government Economists and the American Economic Association, Atlanta, Dec. 1979.

R. M. Coen and B. G. Hickman, "Investment and Growth in an Econometric Model of the United States," *Amer. Econ. Rev. Proc.*, May 1980, 70, 214–19.

S. Danziger, R. Haveman, and R. Plotnick, "Income Transfer Programs in the United States: An Analysis of their Structure and Impacts," prepared for the Joint Economic Comm., mimeo., 96th Cong., 1st sess. 1979.

Edward F. Denison, *Accounting for Slower Economic Growth*. Washington 1979.

R. Eisner, "Total Income, Total Investment, and Growth," *Amer. Econ. Rev. Proc.*, May 1980, 70, 225–31.

Solomon Fabricant, *The Economic Growth of the United States*. Montreal; Washington 1979.

M. Feldstein, "Social Security, Induced Retirement and Aggregate Capital Accumulation," *J. Polit. Econ.*, Sept./Oct. 1974, 82, 905–26.

"Social Security and Private Saving: Reply," *Jour. of Political Economy*, June 1982, 90, 630–42.

and L. Summers, "Inflation and the Taxation of Capital Income in the Corporate Sector," Nat. Bur. Econ. Res. work. paper no. 312, Cambridge, Mass., Jan. 1979.

W. Fellner, "The Declining Growth of American Productivity: An Introductory Note," in his *Contemporary Economic Problems*. Washington 1979, 3–12.

S. Fischer and F. Modigliani, "Towards an Understanding of the Real Effects and Costs of Inflation." Nat. Bur. Econ. Res. work. paper no. 303. Cambridge, Mass., Nov. 1978.

P. H. Hendershott, "The Decline in Aggregate Share Values: Inflation and Taxation of the Returns from Equities and Owner-occupied Housing," Nat. Bur. Econ. Res. work. paper no. 370. Cambridge, Mass., July 1979.

John W. Kendrick, *Productivity Trends in the United States*. Princeton 1961.

"Discussion [on Denison]," *Amer. Econ. Rev. Proc.*, May 1980, 70, 232–33.

John Maynard Keynes, *The End of Laissez-Faire*. London 1926.

S. S. Kuznets, "Driving Forces in Economic Growth: What Can We Learn from History," in Herbert Giersch, ed., *Towards an Explanation of Economic Growth*, Tubingen 1981, 37–58.

R. C. O. Matthews, C. Feinstein, and J. Odling-Smee, *British Economic Growth*. Stanford 1981.

M. I. Nadiri, "Sectoral Productivity Slowdown," *Amer. Econ. Rev. Proc.*, May 1980, 70, 349–52.

J. R. Norsworthy, M. J. Harper, and K. Kunze, "The Slowdown in Productivity Growth: Analysis of Some Contributing Factors," *Brookings Papers*. Washington 1979, 2, 387–421.

R. Plotnick, "Social Welfare Expenditures: How Much Help for the Poor?" *Policy Analysis*, Summer 1979, 5, 271–89.

T. Scitovsky, "Can Capitalism Survive? – An Old Question in a New Setting," *Amer. Econ. Rev. Proc.*, May 1980, 70, 1–9.

James Tobin, *Asset Accumulation and Economic Activity*, Chicago: Oxford 1980.

U.S. Council of Economic Advisers, *Economic Report of the President*, Washington 1964; 1979; 1980.

U.S. Social Security Administration, Office of Research and Statistics, "Research and Statistics Note No. 15," Washington, Dec. 29, 1978.

J. Viner, "The United States as a 'Welfare State,' " in Edgar O. Edwards, ed., *The Nation's Economic Objectives*, Chicago; London 1964, 151–67.

Burton A. Weisbrod, *The Economics of Poverty, An American Paradox*, Englewood Cliffs 1965.